797,885 Books

are available to read at

Forgotten Books

www.ForgottenBooks.com

Forgotten Books' App
Available for mobile, tablet & eReader

ISBN 978-1-331-38961-3
PIBN 10183421

This book is a reproduction of an important historical work. Forgotten Books uses state-of-the-art technology to digitally reconstruct the work, preserving the original format whilst repairing imperfections present in the aged copy. In rare cases, an imperfection in the original, such as a blemish or missing page, may be replicated in our edition. We do, however, repair the vast majority of imperfections successfully; any imperfections that remain are intentionally left to preserve the state of such historical works.

Forgotten Books is a registered trademark of FB &c Ltd.
Copyright © 2015 FB &c Ltd.
FB &c Ltd, Dalton House, 60 Windsor Avenue, London, SW19 2RR.
Company number 08720141. Registered in England and Wales.

For support please visit www.forgottenbooks.com

1 MONTH OF FREE READING

at
www.ForgottenBooks.com

By purchasing this book you are eligible for one month membership to ForgottenBooks.com, giving you unlimited access to our entire collection of over 700,000 titles via our web site and mobile apps.

To claim your free month visit:
www.forgottenbooks.com/free183421

* Offer is valid for 45 days from date of purchase. Terms and conditions apply.

English
Français
Deutsche
Italiano
Español
Português

www.forgottenbooks.com

Mythology Photography **Fiction**
Fishing Christianity **Art** Cooking
Essays Buddhism Freemasonry
Medicine **Biology** Music **Ancient Egypt** Evolution Carpentry Physics
Dance Geology **Mathematics** Fitness
Shakespeare **Folklore** Yoga Marketing
Confidence Immortality Biographies
Poetry **Psychology** Witchcraft
Electronics Chemistry History **Law**
Accounting **Philosophy** Anthropology
Alchemy Drama Quantum Mechanics
Atheism Sexual Health **Ancient History**
Entrepreneurship Languages Sport
Paleontology Needlework Islam
Metaphysics Investment Archaeology
Parenting Statistics Criminology
Motivational

LIFE OF ALI PASHA

LATE

VIZIER OF JANNINA;

SURNAMED

𝔄slan, or the 𝔏ion.

BY

R. A. DAVENPORT, ESQ.

AUTHOR OF "THE LIVES OF EMINENT MEN,"
"THE HISTORY OF THE BASTILE," &c.

LONDON:
WILLIAM TEGG & CO.
PANCRAS LANE, CHEAPSIDE.

1878.

PREFACE.

For more than two centuries, the Ottoman empire, once so formidable, was gradually sinking into a state of decrepitude. Unsuccessful wars, and, in a still greater degree, misgovernment and internal commotions, were the causes of its decline. While, on its frontier, it was repeatedly attacked by its encroaching and unprincipled neighbour, the Muscovite, its efforts were palsied by a vicious system of administration, corrupt ministers, turbulent and undisciplined janissaries, and rebellious and extortionate pashas.

The present Sultan, Abd-ul Hamid II, a man of resolution, has made strenuous, and not wholly fruitless exertions to remedy these crying evils. It is much to be wished that his labours may be crowned with full success—for it is manifest, that the regeneration of Turkey, so as to render her an efficient power, would eminently contribute to preserve the peace of Europe.

Such being the case, the Proprietor of the Family Library imagines that a faithful picture of the character and actions of one of the most celebrated of the Ottoman pashas—one of the numerous dilapidators of Turkish resources, and scourges of the Turkish people—will be favourably received by the public. The reader will here see with what vampyre effect subaltern tyrants can exhaust the vital principle of an extensive empire.

A Life of Ali Pasha was published, in French, by M. Beauchamp, shortly after the fall of the Albanian chief. It was translated into English, something was added, and it went through two editions. To reprint this translation, corrected and enlarged, was at first the intention of the Proprietor of the Family Library. On examining it, however, I found it so inaccurate and incomplete in its statements, and so defective in its arrangement and composition, that I resolved to substitute a new work in its stead. It must be owned that some of its faults were unavoidable—at the time when it was written the materials were so scanty, that it was impossible to form from them any thing but an imperfect narrative. Many documents on the subject have since been given to the world; and these I have carefully consulted. I hope that the reader will derive such a portion of amusement and information from my labours as will induce him to consider them as not wholly thrown away.

PANCRAS LANE.
1878.

CONTENTS.

CHAPTER I.

Interesting Nature of Ali Pasha's History—History of Epirus—The Molossians—Actions of Pyrrhus—Cruel Treatment of the Epirots by the Romans—Nicopolis—Epirus repeatedly ravaged—First Appearance of the Name of Albania—Exploits of Scanderbeg—Death of Scanderbeg—Albania reduced under the Sway of the Turks—Progress of the Mahometan Religion in Albania—Description of Albania—The Natives call themselves Skipetars—Albanian Tribes—Manners and Customs of the Albanians—Character of Albanian Soldiers—Occupations of the Albanians

CHAPTER II.

Ancestors of Ali—State of Albanian Society—Grandfather and Father of Ali—Ali's early years—Precepts of Khamco his Mother—Her Projects—Atrocious Injury done to her and her daughter Shainitza—Early Struggles of Ali—Singular Event which enabled him to retrieve his Losses—He is taken Prisoner—Acquires the Friendship of Kurd Pasha—He marries Emina—His Treachery to Capelan—Marriage of Shainitza—His Stratagem to obtain possession of Tepeleni—Murder of Shainitza's Husband—Ali's perfidious Conduct to Selim—He is made Pasha of Trikala, and Inspector of Roads and Passes—He serves against the Russians—Enters into a Correspondence with Prince Potemkin—Death of his Mother—Machinations by which he obtained the Pashalik of Ioannina

CONTENTS.

CHAPTER III.

PAG

Valley of Ioannina—Lake of Ioannina—Description of the City—The Castron—Public and private Buildings—Seraglio of Litharitza—Palaces of Ali's Sons—Pavilion of Ali—Institutions for Education—Commerce—Climate—Diseases—Population—The Founder of Ioannina not known—Battle fought near it in 1082—History of Ioannina under the Great Despotate of Epirus—Tyranny of Thomas—Letter of Sultan Amurath to the People of Ioannina—The Inhabitants submit to Amurath—Revolt of Dionysius the Skelosophist—Subsequent History of Ioannina . 5

CHAPTER IV.

System of Ali—His treacherous and sanguinary Conduct to the Chormovites—Terror inspired by him—His Designs upon the Pasha of Berat—Marries his Son to the Pasha's Daughter—Employs an Emissary to poison Sepbir Bey—The Suliots—Description of the Territory inhabited by them—Origin of the Suliots—Their Character, Manners, Religion, Customs, and Appearance—Ali is defeated by them—Their Imprudence—Operations of Ali in Northern Albania—He endeavours to circumvent the Suliots, but without effect—He attacks them with a large Force—Heroism of Tzavella—Ali is defeated—He makes Peace—He is in Danger from the Porte—Stratagem by which he escaped . . . .

CHAPTER V.

Destruction of the Bossigradians—Operations of Ali in Central Albania—Kara Mustapha—Designs of Bonaparte on Greece—Report of M. Arnault on Albania—Objects of Ali—He writes to Bonaparte—His connexion with the French—Massacre at Aghio Vassili, &c.—Revolt of Passwan Oglou—Bonaparte writes to Ali—Ali turns against the French—Butrinto evacuated by the French—Ali defeats the French at Nicopolis—He takes Prevesa—Barbarous Treatment of the Prisoners—The Russians excite the Hatred of Ali—Honours lavished upon Ali . . 10

CHAPTER VI.

Ali is deprived of the Ex-Venetian Towns—His Rapacity as Rumili-valisee—He builds a Palace at Tepeleni—Measures adopted by him as a Preliminary to attacking the Suliots—Treason of George Botzari—Character of Foto Tzavella, and of the Monk Samuel—Ali puts his Army in motion against the Suliots—It is defeated—Infamy and Death of G. Botzari—Contemptuous Conduct of the Suliots—Ali's Army twice defeated—Suli blockaded—Ali's Troops again routed—Letters of the Suliots to Ali—The Suliots pressed by Famine—Spirit of the Suliots—League formed against Ali—It is broken up—Melancholy Fate of Phrosini—Successful Intrigues of Ali among the Suliot Chiefs—Exile of Tzavella—Noble Conduct of Tzavella—Gallant Exploit of the Monk Samuel—Treason of Gusi—Patriotism of Tzavella—Ali is defeated—Death of Emina—The Suliots capitulate—They are treacherously attacked on their March—Their valiant Defence—Heroism of Despo   13

CHAPTER VII.

Influence acquired by Ali—He is appointed Rumili-valisee—His Campaign—He foils a Scheme of the Divan to entrap him—Advantages gained by him as Rumili-valisee—His Persecution of the Etolians and Acarnanians—Tragical Fate of Sousman—Treachery and Barbarity of Veli Pasha—Flight of the Archbishop of Arta—Ali removed from the Government of Thessaly—Elmas, his Nephew, appointed to it—Ali causes the death of Elmas—He is re-appointed to the Pashalik of Thessaly—He saves Vasiliki—Russian Intrigues—Ali negotiates with England—He seeks to recover the Good Graces of France—Napoleon appoints M. Pouqueville Consul at Ioannina—Interviews of M. Pouqueville with Ali   .   1

CHAPTER VIII.

Plans of Ali—He obtains the Pashaliks of the Morea and Lepanto for his sons Veli and Mouctar—His Conduct at Prevesa—He visits a Part of his Territories—His sarcastic Treatment of his Kiaya—Singular Mode of administering Justice—Dialogue between Ali and a Papas—System of Government in Turkey described—Barbarism of the Prior of a Convent—English shipwrecked Sailors—Strange manner of clothing the Naked—Ali obtains Officers and Artillerymen from Napoleon—He besieges Santa Maura—Motives of Ali investigated—Ali becomes disgusted with the French Alliance—He courts the Friendship of Great Britain—His Letter to Lord Collingwood—A British Agent is sent to confer with him   1

CHAPTER IX.

Revolt in Thessaly—Characters of the Planners of the Revolt—Proceedings and Death of Blacavas—Ali in Danger from Mustapha Bairactar—Artful Letter of Ali to Lord Collingwood—He exerts himself to bring about a Peace between Great Britain and Turkey—Ali attacks the Pasha of Berat—Conquest of Berat—Double-dealing of Ali—He subdues the Kimariots—He evades an Order to join the Turkish Army—Characters of his Sons, Mouctar and Veli—Ali threatened with an Attack by the French—He makes Ibrahim Pasha Prisoner, and defeats a Confederacy against himself—He takes Argyro Castro—Hypocritical Speech of Ali—His horrible Revenge on the Gardikiots—Mustapha Pasha starved to Death—Yusuf the Dervise—Art of Ali—Demetrius Paleopoulo   21

CHAPTER X.

Designs of Ali upon Parga—Description of Parga—Customs, Character, &c. of the Parghiotes—History of Parga—First Attempt of Ali to obtain Possession of Parga—Shameful Conduct of Russia to the Parghiotes—Parga ceded to Napoleon by Russia—The Parghiotes make the French Garrison Prisoners, and put themselves under the Protection of Great Britain—Speech of one of the Citizens—Rage of Ali on not obtaining the Place—His Cruelty to the Kimariots—His extortions on the Marriage of Sali—Gustavus Adolphus of Sweden visits him—Ibrahim Menzour Effendi—His Anecdotes of Ali—The Palace of Ali at Tepelen consumed—Ali renews his Attempts for the Cession of Parga—The British Cabinet consents to give up Parga—The Inhabitants resolve to quit their Country—Their Departure   24

CHAPTER XI.

Extent of Ali's Dominions—Population of them—Difficulty of ascertaining the Population—Estimate and Sources of Ali's Revenue—Modes of raising Money which were employed by Ali—His Conduct to Nicoio Bretto—Chiflicks—Exactions under the Name of Restitutions—Threat used by Ali—Military Force of the Vizier—Vigilance of his Police and Spies—Composition of Ali's Divan—His State Officers—His Palaces—Mixture of Magnificence and Meanness in his Dwellings   27

CHAPTER XII.

Characters and Anecdotes of Ali Pasha—Character of Ali drawn by two French Agents—Character by M. de Vaudoncourt—Extraordinary Memory of Ali—His Manner of administering Justice—Character by M. Fouqueville—Dread excited by Ali's Visits—Abjectness of some of the Greeks—Terrors occasionally felt by Ali—His Tolerance—His Affection for his favourite Wife Vasiliki   29

CHAPTER XIII.

Characters and Anecdotes of Ali Pasha continued—Visit of Lord Byron and Mr. Hobhouse to the Court of Ali—Lord Byron's Poetical Description of Ali and his Court—His Interview with the Vizier—Interviews of Mr. Hobhouse with Ali—Mr. Hobhouse's Estimate of Ali's Character—Interviews of Dr. Holland with the Vizier—Description of Ali's Conversation, Manners, &c.—His Belief in Alchemy and the universal Panacea—Extent of his political Knowledge—His general Character—Interview of Mr. Richards with Ali—Character of Ali by an Albanian—Mr. Hughes's Description of the Person and Character of Ali—Ali's Government beneficial, on the whole, to the Albanians—Self-command of Ali   .   31

CHAPTER XIV.

Flattery lavished on Ali—His Forebodings—Ambition and Revenge two of his predominant Passions—Story of Ismael Pasho Bey—Incestuous Intercourse of Ali with his Daughter-in-Law—Pasho persecuted by the Vizier—Stratagem of Pasho—Letter of his Wife to him—Pasho takes Refuge at Constantinople—Is received into the Service of the Sultan—Decline of Ali's Influence in the Divan—Ali sends Assassins against Pasho—The Sultan deposes Ali—Situation of Ali—His Avarice prejudicial to him—Is deficient in military Skill—Measures adopted by him to resist the Sultan's Army—He appeals to the Greeks—Ismael Pasho appointed to the Pashalik of Ioannina—Ali promises his Subjects a Constitution—Failure of Moustai—Impolitic Measure of Suleyman—First Movements of the Turkish Armies—Barbarities of Pehlevan Baba—Ismael Pasho commences his Operations—Progress of the Turks—Treachery of Ali's Generals—The Turkish Armies approach Ioannina   35

CHAPTER XV.

Apprehensions of Ali—He destroys Ioannina—His Resources—The Turkish Army arrives—Stratagem of Ali—The Sons of Ali surrender—Daring Conduct of Shainitza—The Turks routed in a Sally—Ali conceals his Treasures—State of his Mind—Impolicy of Ismael Pasho—Ali gains over the Suliots—Victories obtained by the Suliots—Ismael is removed from the Command of the Army—Ismael defeats Ali—Kurschid Pasha takes the Command of the besieging Army—Ali opens a Correspondence with him—Ali's Proposals—They are rejected—The Greek Revolution breaks out—The Turks foiled in an Assault—Death of Shainitza—Fruitless Negotiations—Intrigues of Kurschid—Success of them—Ali surrenders—Death of Ali, and of his Family   38

THE
LIFE OF ALI PASHA.

CHAPTER I.

Interesting Nature of Ali Pasha's History—History of Epirus—The Molossians—Actions of Pyrrhus—Cruel Treatment of the Epirots by the Romans—Nicopolis—Epirus repeatedly ravaged—First Appearance of the Name of Albania—Exploits of Scanderbeg—Death of Scanderbeg—Albania reduced under the Sway of the Turks—Progress of the Mahometan Religion in Albania—Description of Albania—The Natives call themselves Skipebars—Albanian Tribes—Manners and Customs of the Albanians—Character of Albanian Soldiers—Occupations of the Albanians.

THE rugged and imperfectly known territory of Epirus has, at various periods, given birth to many remarkable personages. Among those personages there are three, who, born in ages far remote from each other, occupy a prominent station in historical record; the martial and conquering but magnanimous Pyrrhus, the patriotic and invincible Scanderbeg, and the subtle, treacherous, and sanguinary Ali of Tepeleni. It must be owned, indeed, that in the character and exploits of Ali we vainly seek for those virtues and heroic deeds which redeemed the defects of Pyrrhus and Scanderbeg; but, on the other hand, from its infinite variety, and its being connected with our own times and political interests, his story rivets more firmly our attention, and it is far better calculated than theirs to give beneficial lessons to mankind.

His life and death are eminently qualified " to point a moral and adorn a tale." From the rise of Ali to the summit of power, we learn how much may be achieved by stubborn perseverance and "courage never to submit or yield ;" his utter contempt of truth and honour, and his reckless shedding of blood, afford a melancholy proof of the evils which result from the possession of unlimited authority, and the absence of moral and religious restraints ; and his fall, mainly, if not wholly caused by his own ambition, avarice, and quenchless thirst of revenge, bears incontrovertible testimony to the danger which, sooner or later, springs from the passions being permitted to triumph over reason.

Before we enter upon the narrative of Ali's actions, it may not be improper to pause a moment, for the purpose of casting a glance upon the history of Epirus, the nature of the country, and the manners of its inhabitants. And first as to its history.

Epirus appears originally to have been divided into fourteen states ; if, indeed, the term states may be applied to such diminutive portions of territory. Molossis, which was the most important of them, eventually absorbed all the others. It was blessed with a fertile soil, and within its limits stood the venerable oracle of Dodona, which was considered to be the most ancient in Greece. The Molossian constitution is deservedly praised by Aristotle. The government was a monarchy, hereditary but not despotic. It was the custom of the Molossians to meet at Passaron, the capital, where, after sacrifices had been offered to Jupiter the warrior, mutual oaths were taken by the prince and the people. The former swore to rule according to the laws ; the latter as solemnly bound themselves to defend the royal succession. Fabulous history traces back the origin of the Molossian kingdom to the time of Deucalion's flood ; but the reigning family were content with deriving their descent from Neoptolemus. Pyrrhus, the son of Achilles, who migrated from Thessaly, overthrew Echetus, and became monarch of Molossis. As Epirus took no prominent part in Grecian affairs, few circumstances of its history have been recorded. It was at the court of Admetus, its ruler, that an asylum was sought by the banished Themistocles; and, though the Lacedæmonians and Athenians demanded that the noble exile should be delivered up to them, Admetus braved their anger by giving him a safe-conduct from his dominions. During the Peloponnesian war, while Tharyps, a minor, was on the throne, a body of Molossian troops, commanded by the regent, joined the Lacedæmonian forces in Acarnania. Tharyps appears to have been a wise and virtuous prince. He is declared to have visited Athens, for the purpose of acquiring knowledge, and to have been both a learned man and an enlightened monarch, who introduced many improvements among his subjects. The next striking event in the annals of this country is the marriage of Philip of Macedon with Olympias, the daughter of Neoptolemus. Alexander I., the son and successor to Neoptolemus, who was killed in Italy, is said to have been a prince of great ability and valour.

But the glory of all the other sovereigns of Epirus is dimmed by that of the celebrated Pyrrhus. Taking Alexander the Great for his model, he longed to rival him in renown. His life was a series of strange and rapid vicissitudes. Twice he lost his kingdom, and as often recovered it. He won the crown of Macedonia, and held it for some time, but was at length compelled to relinquish it. Being called into Italy, to the assistance of the Tarentines, he twice defeated the Romans, and advanced to within a short distance of Rome. Finding, however, that the republicans, though vanquished, were not to be subdued, he turned his arms against Sicily, in which island he signalised his valour on various occasions. Returning again to Italy, he renewed the war with Rome, but he was defeated by Manlius, and found it necessary to lead his forces back to Epirus. For this defeat fortune indemnified him, by restoring to him the kingdom of Macedon, which he regained in a single battle. His restless career was closed at the assault of Argos. A woman's hand brought him to the ground, by throwing a tile on him from the roof of a house, and he was despatched by the soldiers of Antigonus. Pyrrhus was one of the greatest captains of antiquity; by the high authority of Annibal he was pronounced to be second only to Alexander the Great. His merit was not confined to war alone. "Fierce as he was in battle," says an intelligent writer, "he was mild and gentle to his subjects and adherents; not allowing himself to be easily provoked, and more eager to requite a kindness than resent a wrong. 'A pecuniary debt,' he observed, 'may be repaid to the heirs of the creditor; but as a return of kindness can only be made while our friends are living, a good and upright man will severely regret his having lost the opportunity of requiting them.' The whole of his history shows, that he was misled by passions not sufficiently controlled, but that his understanding was powerful, quick, and acute."

Alexander, the son of Pyrrhus, was not unworthy of his father. He recovered his throne, which had been wrested from him by Demetrius, and he defeated the Illyrians; but with him departed the glory of Epirus. After three inglorious reigns, with the last of which terminated the race of Achilles, the country adopted a republican form of government. Epirus preserved its independence till the downfal of Perseus, king of Macedon; when, having made common cause with him against the Romans, it was involved in his ruin. The Roman senate determined to take a terrible vengeance upon the Epirots, and the task of exacting it was committed to Paulus Æmilius. As the valour and despair of the Epirots, had they been aware of what was intended, might have been productive of fatal consequences, the high-souled Romans stooped to mask their design under a fraud. Pretending that it was meant to withdraw all the garrisons, that the Epirots might be free as well as the Macedonians, Paulus sent small bodies of troops into the cities, and distributed the remainder of his army in such a manner that it might be able to act simultaneously. At the same hour, the work of pillage and destruction was commenced throughout the country, and the people, thus taken by surprise, were unable to offer any resistance. A hundred and fifty thousand persons were made captive, and sold into slavery; the principal persons were sent to Rome, where most of them were condemned to death, and the walls of no less than seventy cities were levelled with the ground. This event was a death-blow to the greatness of Epirus.

After these disastrous events, the government of Epirus was in the hands of Roman prefects. Twice was the empire of the world contended for within the limits of the ancient dominions of Pyrrhus; by land, at Pharsalia; by sea, at Actium. On the coast of Actium, Octavius, the conqueror of Antony, founded Nicopolis, or the city of victory, to immortalise the battle which had rendered him the master of the wide dominions of Rome. After having peopled it from the neighbouring towns, he erected superb edifices within its walls, organised a senate, instituted games, and conferred on it immunities and privileges, which in a short time made it one of the most flourishing cities of Epirus. At Nicopolis, St. Paul sowed the seeds of the Christian faith, which he had previously been disseminating in Macedonia.

Under Constantine the Great, Epirus formed a part of the province of Pannonia. Like the rest of Greece, it was favoured by the emperor Julian, who repaired several of its cities. For several centuries all that history records of this province is, that it was successively ravaged by merciless invaders. Alaric, Attila, the Huns, the Vandals, and the Bulgarians, swept over it like a tempest. Towards the latter end of the ninth century, the Bulgarians succeeded in establishing themselves in Epirus, and forming a kingdom; and though they sustained a severe defeat from Basil II., who was surnamed the Bulgarian-killer, they maintained their ground. In the eleventh century, Robert Guiscard and his son Bohemond led their Normans hither, and it is immediately after the battle of Durazzo that we find the first mention of Albanians as inhabitants of Epirus.

The conquest of Constantinople by the Franks, in 1204, gave rise to the despotate of Epirus, of which Ioannina was the capital. The narrative of what occurred during the existence of the despotate, we shall postpone to the third chapter, which contains the description of Ioannina, and the vicissitudes of that city, and shall pass over to the next great event in the annals of Epirus, or, as we must begin to call it, of Albania. We have now arrived at the glorious struggle which was maintained by Scanderbeg against the Turkish power, when that power was yet in all its youthful vigour.

Among the petty princes, or despots, of Albania, who submitted to Amurath, was John Castriot. He ruled over a small territory, in the north of Albania, which was then called Emathia, and now forms the district of Moghlena. Its capital was Croïa, about midway between Berat and Scutari, situated upon a hill, and strongly fortified: Ak-hissar is its modern appellation. The country round is covered with woody mountains, and intersected by difficult passes.

When John Castriot yielded to the arms of Amurath, he was compelled to pay an annual tribute, and send his four sons as hostages to the sultan's court. Three of the children died in their infancy; the fourth, George Castriot, gained the favour of Amurath, who had him brought up in the Mussulman faith, and intrusted him with high command. The youth, however, remained attached in secret to the religion of his fathers. His valour and bodily strength acquired for him the surname of Iskenderbeg, or prince Alexander, whence is derived his popular appellation of Scanderbeg. On the death of his father, Scanderbeg, who had then nearly reached his thirtieth year, expected that he should be allowed to take possession of his inheritance; but the sultan perfidiously seized it, sent a governor to Croïa, and employed Scanderbeg to combat against the Hungarian army.

Great as was the peril of the attempt, Scanderbeg resolved to hazard everything for the recovery of his birth-right. All being prepared for his flight from the Turkish camp, he paved the way for his success by a deed, the commission of one part of which it is impossible not to regret that he should have thought necessary to his safety. With his cimeter suspended over the head of Amurath's secretary of state, he compelled him to sign and seal an order to the governor of Croïa to deliver up the fortress, and all the country dependent on it, to the bearer, who was deputed by the sultan. As soon as the signature was affixed to the instrument, Scanderbeg stretched the unfortunate secretary lifeless on the ground.

Scanderbeg reached the neighbourhood of Croïa in

seven days, left in a forest six hundred men whom he had hastily collected, and then proceeded to the city, the keys of which were delivered to him by the unsuspecting governor. In the course of the night he introduced his followers, and the Turkish garrison was put to the sword. This took place towards the close of November, 1443. The massacre of the Turks at Croïa was succeeded by that of the Ottomans in the surrounding towns. In less than a month, all the strong places of the country, with the exception of Sfetigrad, were in the hands of Scanderbeg. His next step was to convoke a meeting of the numerous Christian tributary princes of this part of Albania. He was unanimously recognised as their leader, and an army of seven thousand foot and three thousand horse was brought into the field by the confederates.

The Turkish army of forty thousand men, commanded by a leader named Ali Pasha, advanced rapidly to suppress the revolt. Scanderbeg, who by this time was at the head of fifteen thousand men, took post in the Lower Dibra, and allowed the enemy to move through the passes. But, as soon as they were enclosed within a circle of mountains, he began his attack upon them. Hotly cannonaded from the heights, harassed by the Christians in the plain, and unable, from the confined space, to bring their strength into efficient action, the Turks were utterly routed. Barletius, doubtless with much exaggeration, states that twenty-two thousand of them lay dead on the field. It is certain the victory was complete.

The Hungarian war, and the abdication of Amurath, afforded a short breathing-time to Scanderbeg. On the renewal of the war, he successively defeated two Turkish generals, and drove them from Epirus. He was next engaged in a contest with the Venetians, who had seized upon the fortress of Dayna; but he made peace, in order to oppose the Ottomans, who were again advancing into his territory. A sanguinary battle ensued, and Mustafa, the Turkish general, was overthrown, with the loss of ten thousand men.

To wipe off the disgrace of these defeats, Amurath himself took the field, in 1449, with an army of a hundred thousand men. He began the campaign by the sieges of Sfetigrad and Dibra. Unable to meet the enormous force of the sultan in battle, Scanderbeg wore it down by perpetual alarms and attacks. He displayed the most daring bravery on all occasions, and slew in single combat Firons Pasha, one of the Ottoman generals. Amurath gained the two fortresses, but it was at the cost of twenty thousand of his best troops. As he could make no further progress, he led back his diminished army to Adrianople. In the following year, however, he returned and laid siege to Croïa. From the latter end of April till the middle of autumn, all the resources of war were employed to reduce the stubborn fortress. Repeated mines were sprung, and an incessant cannonade was kept up from artillery of immense magnitude. Ponderous stone bullets, such as were fired at the British squadron on its passage of the Dardanelles in 1807, appear to have been first used against the walls of Croïa. The count d'Uracontes, the governor, baffled all the efforts of the besiegers; nor was he to be moved by the twice-repeated offer of a splendid bribe to seduce him from his duty. Scanderbeg, meanwhile, allowed not a moment's repose to the Ottomans; he cut off their convoys, penetrated nightly into their camp, threw succours into the place, and reduced them to the necessity of covering their camp by entrenchments. In a single encounter eight thousand of them fell. Hopeless of success in the siege, Amurath offered to leave Scanderbeg in peaceable possession of the country, on condition of his paying a small annual tribute. The offer was disdainfully rejected. Foiled in all his attempts, the sultan decamped; but, in its retrograde march through the mountains, his army suffered severely from his indefatigable enemy.

During the next eleven years, the life of Scanderbeg was a series of astonishing exertions and almost uniform successes. Though Mohammed, after his accession to the throne, was too much occupied in giving the last mortal blows to the Greek empire to allow of his concentrating his efforts against the hero of Albania, he continued the war on a less extensive scale. At length, Scanderbeg sustained a defeat, and was compelled to raise the siege of Albanian Belgrade, by an overpowering Turkish force, under the command of Sewali. This reverse was embittered by the desertion of Moses of Dibra, one of his old companions in arms, which was followed by that of his nephew Hamza, to both of whom Mohammed confided armies, to act against the Albanian prince. Moses was so completely routed by Scanderbeg, that, despairing of pardon from the sultan, he threw himself at the feet of the victor, and was forgiven. Hamza, at the head of forty thousand men, next encountered his uncle, who had only eleven thousand. The battle was fought on the plain of Alessio, and it terminated in the destruction of the Turkish army, three-fourths of which lay stretched on the field. This event brought about a truce with the sultan, during the continuance of which Scanderbeg visited the court of Ferdinand, king of Naples, and aided him in the war against the king of France. In 1461, the truce was converted into a peace, by which Scanderbeg was left in full and free possession of Albania.

The treaty continued unbroken for three years; nor must the violation of it be attributed to Mohammed.

The war was recommenced by Scanderbeg. Pope Pius II. had preached a crusade against the Turks; and, at the solicitation of the Venetian ambassador, the papal legate, and his friend and counsellor, the archbishop of Durazzo, the Albanian prince resumed his arms. Paolo Angelo, the archbishop, was the main actor in this affair, and he is said to have quieted the scruples of his friend by the detestable doctrine, that faith is not to be kept with an unbeliever. A cardinal's hat was the reward of his convenient logic.

The first general whom the sultan despatched into Albania was Scherametbeg. With only ten thousand men, Scanderbeg defeated him near Ochrida, and slew as many Turks as there were combatants in his own army. To repair this check, Mohammed sent eighteen thousand men, headed by Balaban Badera, who had distinguished himself at the storming of Constantinople, where he was the first to mount the breach. Balaban began by obtaining a considerable advantage over his adversary. But he did not long enjoy his triumph; he was completely overthrown, and with difficulty effected his escape. In this action Scanderbeg was severely wounded. Undismayed by his disaster, Balaban returned with a fresh army, and was again put to the rout. From the field of victory Scanderbeg was hastily summoned, to stop the progress of Yacub, who, with sixteen thousand men, had penetrated on the side of Berat, and was wasting the country with fire and sword. The Albanian prince came up with him near the river Argilata, slew him in single combat, and nearly annihilated the Turkish host; four thousand fell, six thousand were taken prisoners. Scanderbeg returned to Croïa amidst the plaudits of his subjects.

Resolved to overwhelm his enemy, Mohammed in person, with a hundred thousand men, entered the dominions of Scanderbeg in June 1465. After having reduced Sfetigrade, Belgrade, and some other places, but not without a heavy loss of men, he sat down before Croïa. Day and night he was harassed by Scanderbeg, who was posted in the neighbouring mountains. At last, tired of a siege in which he made no progress, Mohammed departed, leaving Balaban with eighty thousand troops, to blockade the city. Learning that Yunis was advancing with a reinforcement to join his brother Balaban, Scanderbeg fell upon him, scattered his division, and took him captive, together with his son Khizr. He then loaded his two captives with chains, and exposed them to the view of the blockading troops. The Ottomans were struck with consternation at the sight, and before they could recover from it they were attacked by their enemy. Balaban was mortally wounded, the blockade of Croïa was abandoned, and, before it could effect its retreat through the defiles, a fearful havoc was made in the imperial army.

This was the last battle of Scanderbeg. He died shortly after at Alessio, on the 14th of January, 1467, at the age of sixty-three. His son, John Castriot, then a minor, succeeded him, under the guardianship of the Venetians. John did not long enjoy his sovereignty; he was expelled from it by Mohammed, in 1477, and took refuge in the kingdom of Naples, with many of his subjects, who would not submit to the Mussulman yoke. The surrender of Scutari, and its subsequent cession to the sultan by the Venetians, may be considered as putting the finishing stroke to the conquest of Albania.

The doctrines of Mahomet made but a slow progress among the Albanians for a considerable time after the country had submitted to the Turks. It was not till towards the close of the sixteenth century that they began to make numerous proselytes; at that period the Porte promulgated a law, which assured the possession of their property to those Albanian families who would bring up one of their children in the Mussulman faith. This law was productive of two results: the one, that a far less number of Turks settled in Epirus than in the rest of Turkey; the other, that it caused a vast proportion of property to be transferred into the hands of the Mussulmans. So great was its ulterior effect, that, at various periods, villages, towns, and even whole districts, were seen voluntarily renouncing the religion of their fathers, in order to obtain a few political advantages. On the other hand, the Christians, by ranging themselves among the warriors of the Crescent, were exonerated from the odious tribute of the Karatch, and acquired many franchises and immunities. Thus both mosques and churches are to be found among the Albanians, but the frequenters of the former are as little acknowledged by the Turks for true Mussulmans, as those of the latter are allowed by the Greeks to be orthodox Christians.

The Albanians, once so hostile to the Turkish sway, have long been devoted to the sultans, and are become not only their bravest warriors, but the most faithful and incorruptible of subjects. Ever since the time of Bajazet and Amurath, they have held rank in the corps of Janissaries, and distinguished themselves in innumerable battles; and for centuries they have been to be met with in all the pashaliks of the Ottoman empire, and in the Barbary provinces, as subsidised volunteers, known by the name of Arnauts.

Albania is bounded on the west, for more than two hundred miles, by the Adriatic and Ionian seas. Its north and north-west limits are Bosnia, Servia, and Turkish Dalmatia; its east and south-east frontier is

Rumeli or Rumelia; and its southern, the gulf of Arta. It is an exceedingly mountainous country, full of defiles and deep ravines, some of the mountains rising to the height of between four and five thousand feet. The principal rivers are the Boyana, the Drin, and the Voiussa; of which the first has a course of more than a hundred miles, the second, between a hundred and fifty and a hundred and sixty, and the third, of a hundred and thirty. In the lower regions of Albania the climate is nearly of the Italian temperature, but is subject to droughts and violent north winds; south of forty degrees latitude, it is colder than in Greece. Of its commerce we shall speak when we come to describe the capital of Ali Pasha. The population is supposed to consist of about a million and a quarter of souls.

Though the name of Albanians is that by which they are generally known throughout Europe, the appellation is not recognised by the natives; they call themselves Skipetars, and their country Skiperi. Their language is peculiar to themselves, and bears no resemblance to any of the idioms of the neighbouring nations. They are divided into tribes, of which the principal are the Guegues; the Mirdites, who are of the Latin church; the Toske, Toskides, or Toxides; the Tzami; and the Liape, which is the poorest, and the most dirty and predatory of them all.

The Albanians are of middle stature, muscular, erect, agile, stately in their walk and carriage, fond of ornaments, dancing, and music, frugal in their mode of living, and eager to acquire money, but not for the purpose of hoarding. "An Albanian Turk was asked in our hearing," says Mr. Hobhouse, "what he liked best.—'Wine?' 'No.'—'Pistols?' 'No.'—'Women?' 'No, no.'—'What then?' 'Why,' replied the young man with great frankness, 'I like money best; because with that I can get all those things you mention, whenever, and as much of them, as I want.' "—" Their women, who are almost all of them without education, and speak no other than their native tongue, are considered," adds Mr. Hobhouse, "as their cattle, and are used as such, being, except the very superior sort, obliged to labour, and often punished with blows." In other countries the estimation in which a thing is held increases with the scarcity of it; as far as regards women, it is not so in Albania. Females are less numerous than males, and a man there does not get a portion with his wife, but must give one; and, consequently, he is obliged to get together about a thousand piastres before he can expect to be married. As he buys his wife, he probably thinks that he has "a right to do what he will with his own."

"The Albanians have, in general," says M. de Vaudoncourt, "preserved the military dress of the Romans. They wear a tunic, held together by a sash or girdle, which at the same time bears their pistol, poniard, and two small cartridge-boxes filled with ammunition; a coat of mail without sleeves, on which galoons and embroidery have taken the place of iron network; a species of doliman or hussar's jacket, which is pendent, and not fastened before; a large cloak without sleeves, which they wear at all times; a pair of narrow pantaloons, something similar to the caracallæ introduced during the middle ages among the Roman military, and which are partly covered by the tunic; buskins similar to those seen in ancient monuments representing Roman soldiers, tied to the pantaloons by a leather strap, to which hang three ornaments formed into bunches out of gilt silver. Their head-dress consists of a red skull-cap, generally enveloped with a shawl, more or less rich, in the form of a turban, and which at the same time serves for the purposes of a knapsack, a handkerchief, and a nightcap.

"The Albanian soldiers, accustomed to the cold temperature of their mountains, and dressed in a cloak of some considerable thickness, dread neither cold nor heat, which they equally withstand without changing their clothes. In the winter, wrapped up in their cloaks, and in the summer, extended on them, they sleep on the hard ground; they seldom take pains to construct barracks for themselves, and still more rarely make use of tents. They are extremely sober; and their military ration, consisting of two pounds of flour of maize, wheat, or buckwheat, and this frequently reduced to one half, is sufficient for them, with a few black olives or pilchards, which they purchase out of their pay, of which they are extremely economical. They rarely receive meat, and still more so wine. With the exception of some rich beys, who dress with a certain degree of elegance, the Albanian soldiers are in general meanly clad. They wear their clothes till they fall to pieces in rags, and a dirty tunic is among them a sign of bravery. They are more active than the Osmanlis, or original Turks, among whom they enjoy such renown, that there is not a pasha of any consequence who is not desirous of having some of these Arnauts in his pay. They are in general brave, and ready to run into danger, and the fear of death makes no impression upon them. Amidst a number of examples tending to corroborate this assertion, the author will only quote one fact which happened in his own presence. An individual of the Liapis clan, being condemned to death, was brought out to be conveyed to the place of execution, which was situated without the walls of Prevesa. Being arrived about midway, he passed by a large fig-tree. 'Why,' said he to those who conducted him, 'do you wish me to travel half a league further in the hottest part of the day? Can't you hang me here?' This favour was granted him, and he himself put the rope about his own neck. A few hours afterwards, another Liapis passed by the same place, and seeing that the clothes of the deceased were better than his own, with the greatest indifference he began to undress him, and exchanged them for his own rags.

" The Albanian soldiers, however, have the defect of being vain and presumptuous, of exaggerating the recital of their own feats, and even frequently of boasting of imaginary victories. The title of honour, in which they take the greatest delight, is that of *palekari*, which signifies brave. With regard to the tributary and disarmed Greeks, they take pleasure in calling them by the appellation of *moré*, which is synonymous with *moros*, foolish. In their expeditions they have no idea of regular discipline, and even do not know what it is to be placed in rank and file. Each troop collects around its respective chief, and fights separately from its neighbouring one. They usually enter the battle with shrieks and reproaches, in which they delight, something like the heroes of Homer, and then the fire commences entirely at the will of the soldiers. After the battle has lasted for some time, a suspension of arms usually takes place, when the invectives and reproaches again commence; successively afterwards the engagement is resumed, and if at the expiration of some time neither party has been compelled to retreat, they come to close quarters, and make use of their atagans and sabres. Their marches are equally as disorderly as their order of battle, and frequently a column of six thousand men occupies a space of ground equal to five or six leagues. The usual arms of the Albanians are two pistols, which they carry in their sash or girdle; an atagan, or a species of cutlass slightly bent forwards, the cutting part of which is in the concavity, and something resembling the harpion of the ancient Greeks; a sabre, bent backwards, hung to a belt, and placed horizontally; and also a long musket, of the calibre of from five-eighths to seven-eighths of an ounce.

"The exclusive professions of the Albanians are those of shepherd, agriculturist, and warrior. There is still a fourth which might be added, since they follow it as much as the other three, and this is that of robber*. This trade is to them a kind of schooling in the art of war, whence the name of klephtes or robber, is by no means a reproach among them, and the most celebrated

---

* The reader must not affix to the term klephte, or robber, quite the same stigma that belongs to it in more civilised countries. "The Armatoli, or Greek militia," says Lieutenant-colonel Leake, "was an establishment of the Byzantine empire; their most important employment was to keep the roads free from danger, and to guard the mountain passes, which are so frequent in Greece, and of so much military importance. The Ottomans found it necessary to maintain the same kind of police; in some instances the inhabitants of the district adjacent to the passes were made responsible for the safety of the roads, were authorised to maintain armatoli, for this purpose, and, in consideration of the trust and expense, were allowed certain privileges; such as that of being exempted from the customary burthen of entertaining persons travelling in the service or under the protection of the government."
"As some of the most secluded districts of Northern Greece held out against Ali till the last, and as his armatoli were often provoked by his avarice and treachery to join the armed insurgents, his habitual opponents, the klephtes, were never entirely suppressed. And hence it will be easily understood that the armatoli and klephtes of Greece differed only in the circumstances in which they were placed; and that, although the latter were often obliged by necessity to resort to plunder, and to imitate the cruelty of their opponents, they were less to be considered as robbers, than as rebels against the government. Like the pirates of the Ægean, in the early ages of Greece, their name carried no disgrace with it. On the contrary, their cause being connected with the assertion of national and christian freedom against infidel oppression, and their life being passed in continual dangers, amidst the most romantic scenery, were calculated to call forth the poetical and enthusiastic spirit inherent in the people, and to keep alive among them the love of liberty and the hope of independence."

chiefs of banditti are sure to make their fortunes and arrive at honours, in testimony of which, we have Ali Pasha. This idea is so deeply imprinted among them, and the examples are so frequent, that an Albanian of this class, when asked what occupation he follows, will gravely answer ἰμαί ἐγο κλεφτές, I am a robber. This custom is not, however, general in all the cantons of Southern Albania. The Liapis, indeed, scarcely follow any other calling, but the Philates have very few banditti among them. The Zagoriats, successors of the Pelagonians, and who have voluntarily submitted to the pashas of Ioannina, know nothing of brigandage. Mild and hospitable, they have preserved the rigorous manners and character of the ancient Greeks; but, although the fierce and unfeeling qualities noticed among the other Albanians have disappeared from among them, they are not the less brave."

CHAPTER II.

Ancestors of Ali—State of Albanian Society—Grandfather and Father of Ali—Ali's early years—Precepts of Khamco his Mother—Her Projects—Atrocious Injury done to her and her daughter Shainitza—Early Struggles of Ali—Singular Event which enabled him to retrieve his Losses—He is taken Prisoner —Acquires the Friendship of Kurd Pasha—He marries Emina— His Treachery to Capelan—Marriage of Shainitza—His Stratagem to obtain possession of Tepeleni—Murder of Shainitza's Husband—His perfidious Conduct to Selim—He is made Pasha of Trikala, and Inspector of Roads and Passes—He serves against the Russians—Enters into a Correspondence with Prince Potemkin—Death of his Mother—Machinations by which he obtained the Pashalik of Ioannina.

THE precise period at which Ali Pasha first saw the light it is now impossible to ascertain; but it appears to be certain that he was born between the years 1740 and 1750, and probably nearer to the earliest than the latest of these dates. It was, no doubt, policy that made him always affect to appear younger than he really was. To have owned to extreme age might have afforded encouragement to his numerous enemies, who would have calculated upon his exertions being relaxed, and his course being speedily terminated.

The birthplace of Ali was Tepeleni or Tebelen*, about thirty miles to the south-east of Avlona, and seventy miles to the north-west of Ioannina. It is seated on the left bank of the Voïussa, the ancient Aöus, in a gloomy and treeless valley, surrounded by bleak and desert mountains, and subject to violent hurricanes. It fell under the sway of the Turks in 1401, and for centuries continued obscure and of little importance, till it was at length raised into importance by being the natal place of Ali, and was enlarged and embellished by the partiality of the triumphant pasha.

Some uncertainty hangs also over the origin of his family. The surname borne by the family is Hissas; and he affirmed that he was descended from Issa, or Jesus, the head of an ancient Natolian race, who passed from Asia Minor into Epirus, with the hordes of that Bajazet whose rapid movements and destructive progress gained for him the appellation Ilderim or lightning. Of this, however, he could give no proof. It would, on the contrary, seem to be indubitable, that Ali was of an Albanian stock. His ancestors, who were of the race of the Toxides, are believed to have held, from time immemorial, the rank of beys, or lords, at Tepeleni, and to have distinguished themselves as leaders of their countrymen in predatory and private warfare. Their pedigree, however, can be

---

* M. Von Hammer, whose authority is of great weight, declares the proper name of this place to be Depedelen.

traced back no further than towards the close of the fifteenth century.

The first of Ali's progenitors, whose name history has preserved, lived at a much later period, and won a more honourable fame than that of a chief of robbers. This was Mouctar, grandfather of Ali. He rose to the dignity of a pasha of two tails, and commanded a Turkish division at the siege of Corfu, in 1716, where he signalised himself by his courage, but was finally slain, in one of the desperate contests between the besiegers and the garrison under the gallant count Schulemberg. He had scaled the ramparts of the fortress, and fell while encouraging his troops to follow him. He left three sons, Salek, Mehemet, and Veli.

At the period when Mouctar fell, Albania was not yet under the rule of an absolute vizier. The Albanians consequently enjoyed a considerable portion of rude freedom. Each district, and frequently each town, was a species of self-governed republic, divided into pharas, or parties; and the authority of the pashas, appointed by the Porte, was likewise counterpoised by great feudatories. Such being the state of things, the Ottoman government did not place entire reliance on even its Mahometan subjects in this province. It strove to balance and restrain them, by forming bands of Christian Armatoles, to act as a sort of police; which bands, however, were under the orders of Osmanli pashas. But this measure of precaution was only partially successful. Hating and suspecting the Turkish pashas, both the Mahometan and Christian Albanians perpetually combined to thwart their proceedings, circumscribe their authority, and prevent them from extending the term of their sway beyond the lunar year, to which it was limited by the commission of the sultan. The efforts of the coalesced parties generally succeeded; so far so, indeed, that, in consequence of them, the deposition of the pashas themselves was not unfrequently procured from the Porte. "But scarcely were they relieved," says M. Pouqueville, "from the fears which the pashas had inspired, than the fickle Schipetars turned their arms against each other, tribe against tribe, Armatoles against Armatoles, so that no tranquillity was ever known. Notwithstanding the collision which it occasioned, this state of anarchy, in the wars arising from which little blood was shed, had the advantage of keeping up a warlike spirit among the Epirots, and especially of rendering them attentive to the maintenance of their liberties, of which they were exceedingly jealous. Slaves everywhere else, the Christians, by being ranked among the Armatoles and the warriors in the pay of the nobles, were freed from the servile tribute of the karatch, knew nothing of the sultan but his name, and enjoyed particular respect among the Turks, whom they sometimes made tremble. They had, by their courage, preserved the patrimony of their ancestors, and they had obtained free districts, the privilege of nominating the officers by whom they would be commanded, and franchises founded on special grants from the sultan. Such was in those days the political situation of Epirus."

This anomalous condition of society, though it might be favourable to the liberties of the Albanians, was fatally calculated to stimulate the passions, corrupt the morals, and harden the heart. Its maleficent influence was powerfully seconded by the Mussulman practice of polygamy, which is destructive of all the domestic affections. It is justly observed, by Pouqueville, that the fraternal spirit which animates brethren sprung from the same blood is never felt by the offspring of polygamy; that every child of the latter class has as many stepdames as his father has wives; that, from infancy, each takes part in the quarrels of the harem, espouses the quarrels and interests of his mother, and looks upon the progeny of another woman as strangers or as enemies; and that thence, in the very dawn of life, vindictive feelings are engendered, which, in process of time, never fail to break out in sanguinary deeds, especially when the decease of the father allows them to be manifested without control. So it was with the three sons of the slain Mouctar.

The patrimony which Mouctar left to his heirs produced an annual income of six thousand piastres, between seven and eight hundred pounds. In a country where the necessaries of existence were purchasable at a trifling price, this sum was sufficient for every purpose of comfort. But it was far from adequate to keep up the rank of beys, whose expenditure for the support of armed followers, domestic retainers, and horses, was necessarily large. The scantiness of their pecuniary means speedily introduced discord among the brothers. Salek and Mehemet, the two eldest, looked with an evil eye upon Veli, whom they considered as robbing them of a portion of the means of greatness. He was likewise the son of a slave; and though, by the Turkish law, he was equally entitled with his brothers to a share of the inheritance, their pride, and still more their thirst of gold, made them regard him as an inferior, and an enemy. Arms were resorted to by them, and Veli was at length driven from his home.

Thus cast naked upon the world, Veli proceeded to act on the system which " mine ancient Pistol " determined to adopt—" this world's mine oyster, which I with sword will open:" he commenced klephte or robber, a trade with which we may believe that he was already not wholly unacquainted. Whatever were his defects, want of daring and activity was not among them. He carried on his depredations with such spirit and good fortune, that, in the course of a few years, he not only enriched himself, but gathered round him a band of hardy, unscrupulous, and attached partisans, ready to undertake any enterprise which their leader might command.

The long-desired moment was now come when he could take vengeance for the wrongs which he had suffered. He had met with but little mercy from Salek and Mehemet, and he resolved to show them still less. Conducting his followers to Tepeleni, he easily forced his way into the town, and compelled his brothers to seek for shelter in their castle, which they barricaded, and essayed to defend. But their resistance was unavailing ; and, the doors of their abode being broken open, they fled to a pavilion. Thither they were pursued by the furious Veli, who consummated his revenge by setting fire to the pavilion, and seeing them perish in the flames.

After this fratricidal triumph, Veli fixed his residence at Tepeleni, of which he became the principal Aga. He relinquished, at least for a while, the hazardous occupation of a robber. He had already offspring by a slave ; but policy prompted him to strengthen his interest by an alliance with some powerful house. Khamco, daughter of a bey of Konitza, was the object of his choice, and her congenial nature rendered her a partner worthy of him. By this marriage he acquired a connexion with several of the chief Toscarian families, and especially with Kurd Pasha, vizier of Berat, who was said to be descended from the race of Scanderbeg.

Veli now obtained the dignity of sandjiak of Delvino, a considerable town, several leagues to the southward of Tepeleni. But his prosperity was not of long continuance. Either his own conduct, or the intrigues of his enemies, drew on him the displeasure of the Porte, and he was superseded in his office by Selim Bey. At the same time, he was engaged in virulent quarrels with his neighbours; quarrels which probably arose from his having resumed his habits of making free with the property of others. Flocks of sheep and goats are said to have been occasionally swept off by his armed bands. The beys of Kaminitza, Klissura, Premiti, and Argyro Castro, confederated against him; and, though he made an obstinate resistance, he at last succumbed, and the greatest part of his inheritance was wrested from him. He died soon after, at the age of forty-five. His death is attributed by some to excessive fatigue and a broken heart, and by others, to bacchanalian excesses. By Khamco he left two children, Ali, who became so celebrated, and a daughter, named Shainitza; by his favourite slave, three children remained.

The boyhood of Ali gave evident indications that it would be succeeded by a dark and tumultuous manhood. By one who knew him in his early years his character is thus described. " His turbulent disposition was manifest from the very moment of his quitting the harem; for there was remarked in him a petulance and activity which are not usual in young Turks, who are naturally haughty and of sedate manners. Whenever he could steal out of the paternal mansion, it was for the purpose of traversing the mountains, over which he wandered in the midst of forests and tracts of snow. It was in vain that his father endeavoured to fix the attention of Ali. Equally obstinate and indocile, he escaped from the hands of his tutor, whom he even maltreated, whenever he thought he could do so with impunity. It was not till he grew up to be a youth, and had lost his father, that he would learn to read, and appeared to be somewhat tamed. He then turned his affections towards his mother; he complied with her slightest wishes, and had no other rule than her advice. Above all things, she taught him to hate his half-brothers; sedulously fomenting in his heart the jealous passions which were boiling within it."

The enthusiastic admiration and attachment with which, at his outset in life, Khamco inspired her son, remained undiminished to the close of his existence. To sound her praises was his delight. " I owe," said he, to the French consul, " every thing to my mother, for, when he died, my father left me only a mere doghole and a few fields. Fired by the counsels of her who twice gave me life,—since it was she who made me a *man* and a *vizier*,—my imagination revealed to me the secret of my destiny. From that moment Tepeleni was nothing more in my eyes than the natal eyry, from which I was to swoop down upon the prey which in idea I already devoured. I dreamt of nought but power, treasures, palaces,—in short, of that which time has realised, and that which it still promises; for the point at which I have arrived is not the summit of my hopes."

The purport of the precepts delivered by Khamco to her son may almost be summed up in a few emphatic words, which Shakspeare puts into the mouth of the weird sisters in Macbeth—" Be bloody, bold, and resolute." We have seen with what demoniacal malignity she laboured to excite him against his half-brothers; and, too impatient to wait for his tardy aid, she is even suspected to have put an end to the eldest of them by poison, and to have reduced the second to imbecility by similar means. Devoid of all principle, practised in simulating and dissimulating, unforgivingly vindictive, and regarding power and wealth, by whatever means attained, as the supreme good, Khamco was an instructress whose lessons could not fail to render her pupil one of the scourges of mankind. Success, she incessantly told him, sanctified every thing. " My son," exclaimed she, " he who does not defend his patrimony deserves to lose it. Remember, that the property of others belongs to them only by the right of the strongest, and if you can wrest it from them, it belongs to you." By inculcating doctrines of a similar kind, she is affirmed to have likewise enconraged him to indulge freely in the most licentious excesses. Like the Roman empress, Julia Domna *, (who, however, was most probably, in this instance, calumniated), she boldly taught that, to men in high station, all that was pleasing was lawful.

Khamco was not a mere theorist; she had courage enough to execute any plan which her interest or her feelings could suggest. During the life-time of her husband, she gave, indeed, no signs of being qualified to act the part of a heroine; but no sooner were his eyes closed in death than her latent spirit blazed forth. Far from being intimidated by the calamitous circumstances in which she was placed, she not only resolved to stem the torrent of ill fortune which threatened to overwhelm her, but also, hopeless as the design might seem, to restore her family to its pristine splendour. Abandoning at once the habits of her sex, she threw aside the distaff and the veil, and appeared in arms. With an Amazonian spirit, she put herself at the head of her late husband's remaining followers, and she is said not even to have spared personal blandishments

---

* Quæ quum esset pulcherrima, et quasi per negligentiam se maxima corporis parte nudasset, dixissetque Antoninus, " Vellem, si liceret : " respondisse fertur, " Si libet, licet. An nescis te imperatorem esse, et leges dare, non accipere ? "—*Spartianus in Caracalla.*

and favours, to increase the number of her partisans. By her arts she succeeded in gathering round her a formidable band, to which she fervently recommended the cause of her favourite son; nor did she delay to try, in various skirmishes, her strength against the enemies of her race. In her excursions she was accompanied by Ali, whose wrath and eagerness for plunder she never failed to rouse, by pointing out to him the lands of which he had been despoiled, and the territories of the despoilers.

The growing resources and influence of this daring female, and her evidently ambitious schemes, at length excited alarm in the tribes which dwelt in the neighbourhood of Chormovo and Gardiki. As any longer delay in putting a stop to her career might endanger their independence, they began to make preparations for combating the haughty widow of Tepeleni. But, awake to their intentions, Khamco anticipated these new enemies by an instant declaration of war. Leading her clans against them, she set every danger at defiance, sometimes fought, and perpetually intrigued, and for a considerable time severely harassed them by her hostilities and her equally prejudicial arts. Finally, however, her good fortune deserted her, and absolute ruin appeared to be inevitable. Having fallen into an ambush, she was made prisoner, along with Ali and Shainitza her daughter, and they were thrown into a dungeon at Gardiki.

Disastrous as was the situation of the captives, the misery of the females was soon wofully aggravated by their being subjected to the last and worst insult which can be inflicted on their sex. Both Khamco and her daughter were exposed to the horror of violation, and compelled to suffer the brutal embraces of the principal inhabitants. The vengeance which this act called forth was long delayed, but it was terrible.

The prisoners would perhaps have spent the rest of their days in slavery, brooding over their misfortunes, and writhing under the tyranny of their captors, had they not been restored to liberty by the benevolence of Malicovo, a Greek merchant of Argyro Castro, who advanced for their ransom a sum amounting to nearly four thousand pounds sterling. They were thus enabled to return once more to their native place*.

After her return to Tepeleni, Khamco ceased personally to take part in the civil broils of Epirus. Her time was spent in re-establishing her fallen fortunes, and training up the youthful Ali as the avenger of her wrongs. Her exertions were not fruitless. Distinguished as much for his courage and address as for his apparent sweetness of disposition, Ali won the affections of the soldiery and of the principal vassals of his house. Eager to enter on the career of arms, he studied the warlike deeds of his ancestors and of his fellow-countrymen, and, that he might acquire a stock of useful knowledge for his future operations, he made himself informed, in the minutest detail, of the strength, character, and connexions of his enemies. The whole of what he learned he committed carefully to memory, and by this means he strengthened that faculty to such a wonderful degree that nothing ever escaped it; circumstances apparently the most trivial, a name, a date, were recalled to mind with the utmost facility and correctness after the lapse of many years.

Gifted with a strong constitution, and a vigorous intellect, it is not astonishing that Ali should acquire a distinguished pre-eminence in all the martial exer-

---

* M. Pouqueville asserts that the merchant, to whom Khamco and her children were indebted for their liberty, was poisoned in 1807, at Eleuthero Chori, by order of Ali Pasha.

cises of his country, and, embued as he was with the principles inculcated by his mother, it is as little surprising that he should be anxious to shake off the trammels of dependence, and aggrandise himself at the expense of his neighbours. He had already tried, on a small scale, his predatory talents. At the age of only fourteen, aided by some companions, he had begun to make inroads upon the flocks of sheep and goats in the surrounding districts, and with such success that he soon acquired a considerable booty. Weary, however, of this obscure system of pillage, he now longed to expatiate in a wider field, and he communicated to Khamco his wishes and his plans. But the schemes of Ali, for dividing his enemies, and separately defeating and destroying them, appear to have been too vast for even her to embrace them under the present circumstances. Her means were much reduced, and a single reverse might leave her wholly destitute. Besides, there seemed at that time to be insuperable obstacles to his success. 'Epirus," says M. Pouqueville, "was then governed by three pashas: those of Ioannina, Delvino, and Paramithia. Under their patronage, Kimara, Gardiki, Zulati, Argyro Castro, and Suli, were regarded as free cities and cantons. Kurd Pasha, a powerful and dreaded vizier, ruled over central and lower Albania, and all the Schipetars were subject to his orders. There was, therefore, no likelihood of innovating; time seemed even to have cemented the anarchical liberty of Epirus; for, when any one of the cantons was menaced by an ambitious neighbour, the others came to its aid, and re-established the equilibrium. Thus, in the midst of barbarism, there was a sort of political balance, composed of leagues knit together by chance, regulated by custom, and guided by a political instinct."

At length, however, impatient of inactivity, he

resolved to brave all hazards, to commence the execution of his projects. He had amassed some money from the produce of his rapine, and he is said to have been assisted by his mother; but others maintain that she refused to supply him on this occasion. Be that as it may, it is certain that he somehow procured funds for hiring followers enough to enable him to commence his career, though as yet on a humble footing. His earliest expedition seems to have been prompted by the spirit of revenge. It was directed against Chormovo, which, as we have seen, was one of the towns whose inhabitants captured Khamco and her children. In this opening enterprise he was scarcely less unfortunate than his mother had formerly been. He met with an unexpected and vigorous resistance; he was suddenly seized with one of those fits of trepidation which many warriors have felt on their first encountering the terrors of a battle; and, regardless of his fame, he fled from the field, and took refuge in Tepeleni. Stung to the heart by the disappointment of her hopes, and by the shame which he had brought upon himself, his mother met him with the bitterest reproaches and invectives. Holding out her distaff to him, she furiously exclaimed, " Go, coward! go and spin with the women of the harem; it is a trade which suits thee far better than that of arms."

In spite of this mishap, and spurred on perhaps by the sarcasms of his mother, Ali did not long delay seeking an opportunity to retrieve his character in the field. This time he went forth not in the character of a conqueror, but of a robber. To attempt to trace him with precision through all his early adventures would be a fruitless task, and, if it were not so, would be an unprofitable one. He seems to have experienced that alternation of good luck and reverses, but with a rather scanty proportion of the former, which is common to chiefs of his class. After having obtained some advantages in the vicinity of Tepeleni, he is said to have directed his course to the mountain chain of the Pindus, and to have been there defeated and taken prisoner by the vizier of Ioannina. He was, nevertheless, saved from death by the policy of the vizier. " The beys of Ioannina, of Argyro Castro, and Premiti, as well as Selim, pasha of Delvino," says General de Vaudoncourt, "insisted that capital punishment should be inflicted upon him. The vizier of Ioannina, however, dreaded the beys of the very district over which he presided, at all times ripe for a revolt: and he could not confide in those of Argyro Castro and Premiti, much less in Selim, pasha of Delvino, whose connexions with the Venetians rendered him extremely liable to suspicion. He was not sorry to have it in his power to afford him fresh occupation, and he released Ali, who gave him no further cause for uneasiness during the remainder of his days."

Again Ali returned to the charge, but fortune still continued to frown upon him. Near the sources of the Chelydnus, he received such a decisive defeat that the whole of his followers were either killed or dispersed, and he himself was compelled to take refuge alone on mount Mertzika. His cimeter and his horse were all that he saved, and such was the state of extreme want to which he was reduced, that he was obliged to pledge his weapon to obtain barley for his starving and wearied steed.

The wrath of his mother was again roused by his discomfitures, but he succeeded in appeasing it. She gave him a sum of money to raise another band of followers; warning him at the same time to expect no further aid, and enjoining him either to vanquish or die, and never again to appear as a fugitive amidst the tombs of his forefathers and his countrymen. Once more Ali departed, and once more his hopes were frustrated. He directed his course a second time through the valley of the Chelydnus towards Mount Mertzika and Premiti. A combat took place, and he was overthrown with heavy loss.

Stripped of the means of retrieving his losses, and dreading to face his angry parent, Ali resolved to try his fortune in another quarter. He passed over to Negropont, at the head of thirty picked men, and entered into the service of the vizier of that island. Either he was ill-paid or ill-treated, or the life which he led there was not sufficiently adventurous and stimulant, for he soon quitted Negropont, and entered Thessaly, where he resumed his occupation of a robber. By his daringness and activity, he reaped a rich harvest of plunder. He then penetrated into the chain of Pindus, and pillaged several villages in the district of Zagori. In that country he also acquired friends, by whom his pecuniary resources were greatly increased. He likewise began to enter into correspondence with the Armatoles of Thessaly, Etolia, and Acarnania.

It was probably at a period subsequent to the departure of Ali from Negropont, and while he was yet struggling with his adverse fate, that an event occurred, which is related by General de Vaudoncourt; but which he, erroneously it would seem, dates immediately after the second combat on the Chelydnus. The fact itself is, indeed, denied by M. Pouqueville, who, somewhat unceremoniously, denominates the general an adventurer, and asserts that Ali himself told him the story was a falsehood, invented by a lying Greek schoolmaster. But the authority of M. de Vaudoncourt, a man of honour and talent, who declares that he, too, obtained his information from Ali, is at least equal to that of M. Pouqueville; and, in speaking to the French consul, Ali, never remarkable for a strict adherence to truth, might choose that his success should be ascribed wholly to his own talents, instead of being considered as partly the work of blind chance.

Ali, after a defeat, had encamped the remnant of his troops near a ruined chapel, not far from Valera. To rest himself, as well as to meditate on the means of repairing his losses, he entered the desolate building. " There," said he, " I stood for a long while, pondering on my disasters, and on what could be done to ameliorate my situation, and comparing the weakness of my resources with the magnitude of those which were opposed to me by my enemies. While I was thus engaged, the violence of my feelings made me mechanically rake up the ground with the point of a stick which I held in my hand. Suddenly, my attention was recalled from my thoughts by some solid body resisting the stick, and giving forth a sound. I examined the hole, continued to remove the soil, and was so fortunate as to discover a coffer full of gold, which had no doubt been hidden there during one of the revolutions by which the country had so often been desolated. With this gold I took into pay two thousand men, and at their head I returned in triumph to Tepeleni."

Whatever were the means by which he accomplished his object, it is beyond doubt that Ali revisited Tepeleni with his finances recruited. To enjoy his gains in peace was, however, repugnant to his nature, and he accordingly recommenced his predatory operations with greater daring and in a wider circle than before. He spread his banditti among all the defiles which lead through the mountain chain of Pindus into Thessaly, Epirus, and Macedonia, pillaged and ransomed travellers and caravans, levied contributions on the villages, and sacked several small defenceless towns. It is probable that, in these exploits, he was seconded by the Armatoles of Thessaly and other provinces, with whom he had entered into correspondence after his leaving Negropont.

So extensive did the ravages of Ali become, that they at last came to the knowledge of the divan. Orders to put an immediate stop to them were in consequence sent to Kurd Pasha, who then held the office of dervendji pasha, or inspector general of highroads and passes. Having been worsted by the troops which Kurd despatched against him, Ali fell into their hands, and was led in bonds to Berat. His fate seemed now certain. His companions, who had been captured in the skirmish, were hanged, and he was threatened with the same punishment. But his better fortune prevailed. His youth, his personal beauty, his eloquence, his courage and activity, his relationship to the vizier, and perhaps the prospect of converting him into a useful ally, induced Kurd Pasha to be merciful to the captive robber.

The pasha retained Ali at his court for some years, loaded him with favours, and endeavoured, it is said, to reclaim him from his vicious pursuits. The low standard of Albanian morality may justify a supposition, that the efforts of the vizier to reclaim his pupil did not go much further than to convert him from a robber on the high road to a robber of cities and provinces. In his contests with the neighbouring chiefs he did not scruple to avail himself of Ali's assistance in the field; and to him he is affirmed to have been indebted for victories, which enabled him to make an advantageous peace with the vizier of Scutari. At length, moved by the entreaties of Khamco, who never ceased to importune him, he restored her son to liberty. A strict friendship was thenceforth maintained between Ali and the vizier of Berat.

From this period, through more than half a century the course of Ali was marked by uninterrupted prosperity, and he rose to an eminence, the possibility of reaching which he could hardly at his outset have ventured to contemplate. His first step, after again becoming his own master, was to offer his aid to such of the neighbouring chiefs as were engaged in feuds. His courage and address being well known, his services were eagerly accepted, and liberally rewarded; and he thus acquired many powerful friends, and a distinguished station among the beys of the country. When he was about twenty-four years of age, he much increased his influence, by gaining the hand of the beautiful and virtuous Emina, daughter of Capelan, pasha of Delvino, who resided at Argyro Castro, and whose ferocity and turbulence had earned for him the repulsive appellation of the tiger.* Emina, unlike

---

* Such ferocity, and such appellations, were not uncommon among the Turkish governors. Several instances of them are given, in his History of Modern Greece, by Jacovaky Rizo Neroulos, who had been prime minister to the hospodars of Wallachia and Moldavia. "The Europeans," says he, "having had no connection except with two of the Ottoman pashas, have been struck by the ferocity of those monsters; I allude to Djezzar and Ali. It is believed that those two pashas were the most remarkable for their tyrannical proceedings and their crimes; but if Europe had known the other Turkish governors, it would not have considered those two tyrants as exceptions. What would it have said of the vizier who was surnamed Kih Pasha, or the Stifler, from the pleasure which he took in strangling his victims? Or of another, called Bekir, who, when he condemned an unfortunate being, used to say to his sanguinary satellites, "Take away that dog, and give him a good lesson." The lesson was always death. A third pasha was called Cujudzy, because he ordered to be thrown into a well the victims who incurred his resentment. Haki Pasha, a governor of European Turkey, under the reign of Selim, always breakfasted in a turret of his palace, and this was the time that he chose for

her father, was universally beloved; and, when she had ceased to exist, her memory was long held in veneration by the natives of Epirus.

Capelan Pasha, of whose family Ali was now become a member, was one of those rebels and oppressors so common in Turkey, who, because they are at a great distance from the seat of government, believe that they may with impunity despoil and dishonour those who have the misfortune to be subjected to their authority. He, like many pashas, was also desirous to render himself wholly, or at least nearly, independent; and he had hoped that, by means of his son-in-law, he should obtain the support of other chiefs to realise his favourite scheme. Circumstances seemed to be propitious; for the Russians were now preparing to assist the Greeks to throw off the yoke, or, rather, they were cheating the latter with the shadow of assistance, in order to accomplish their own selfish purposes. Ali feigned to enter warmly into the views of his relative, but he was solely anxious to involve him in inexpiable guilt, that he might profit by his fall.

The arrival of the Russian expedition, under Orloff, was preluded by the breaking out of insurrections in various parts of Albania, and its vicinity: the Mon-

---

having brought before him, to be executed, the persons whom he had doomed to death. The pasha of Widdin, Afiz Ali, having defeated some Mahometan rebels, ordered their heads to be put into a sack, to be sent, with a letter, to the reigning sultan. By mistake the secretary stated in the letter a larger number of heads than the sack contained. He prepared to correct his error by recopying the letter; the pasha, however, simplified the operation. He ordered his officers to go through the streets, and kill men enough to make up the number which was mentioned in the letter. He was punctually obeyed; his officers murdered forty Christians, the first who came in their way, and thus the sack was filled and sent off to the Porte. Such is the conduct of the provincial governors."

tenegrins, the Kimariots, the Suliots, and the inhabitants of some districts of upper Albania, displayed the banner of the cross. Alarmed by this outbreak, the divan issued orders that all the Mussulmans should take arms. The Cadilisker of Rumelia hastened to Philippopolis, and the Rumili-Valisee summoned all the great vassals of his government to march against the insurgents. To Capelan Pasha was assigned the task of joining Kurd Pasha, for the purpose of reducing the Kimariots and Suliots to obedience. Fatally misled by the treacherous counsels of Ali, Capelan disobeyed the order to form a junction with the vizier of Berat, and, though he did not openly aid the revolters, he acted in such a manner as to throw serious obstacles in the way of the Ottoman troops who were opposing them. The consequence of his disobedience was, that the Ottomans could obtain but partial success. The Montenegrins were, indeed, beaten, and the Kimariots were compelled to retire to their mountains, but no impression whatever could be made on the Suliots, covered as they were by their almost impregnable fastnesses.

The event, which Ali had so basely laboured to bring about, was not slow in coming to pass. The failure of the campaign was attributed to the criminal negligence, or the treason, of Capelan, and he was called upon to vindicate himself before the Rumili-Valisee. The evidence, in support of the charge, had been supplied by Ali, who, in his secret correspondence with the officers of the Porte, had represented the conduct of his father-in-law in the most unfavourable point of view. Eager to seize on the treasures and power of his relative, which he flattered himself would fall into his hands, he now carried his perfidy to a higher pitch. That the victim might not escape, he advised him to obey the summons of his judge, and finding that Capelan hesitated to face the danger, he is said to have been guilty of an act of horrible atrocity—that of inducing the unconscious Emina to urge, with entreaties and tears, her father's departure. Capelan finally yielded; and on his arrival at Monastir, where sentence had already been passed, he was instantly beheaded. His punishment was, for many reasons, well deserved; but the promoter of it was not the less a monster.

" 'Tis the sport," says Shakspeare, " to have the engineer hoist with his own petar." Unfortunately, Ali did not suffer in his person, but he missed those objects for which he had perilled his soul, and he reaped nothing from his crime but disgrace and shame. Instead of appointing Ali to the vacant pashalik, the Porte bestowed it on Ali, bey of Argyro Castro. Entirely devoted to the Sultan, the new pasha would not allow the homicidal son-in-law to touch the property of the deceased Capelan, the whole of which he secured for his sovereign.

As soon as Ali recovered from the severe shock which was given to him by this unexpected blow, his active mind sought on all sides for the means of repairing his defeat, and it was efficiently assisted in the search by Khameo. The recently appointed successor of Capelan was yet unmarried, and she proposed that a union should be brought about between the two families, by his taking to wife her daughter Shainitza, who was young, handsome, and attractive. By dint of perseverance and intrigue she accomplished her object, and the nuptials were solemnised under apparently happy auspices, since they promised to unite families which would otherwise have been deadly rivals. The husband of Shainitza manifested a sincere regard for her brother; but the feeling was not reciprocal on the part of Ali; resentment still rankled in his heart, and, though he cautiously and effectually dissembled his feelings, he was ever on the watch for an opportunity of ruining the man by whom his hopes had been frustrated.

The pleasure which the son of Khamco derived from the success of his mother's plan was soon poisoned by the failure of a similar project, which he had himself formed, and which, if he could have carried it into execution, would have materially forwarded his ambitious views. He had long flattered himself that it would be possible to gain the hand of Kurd Pasha's daughter, on whom his person, bravery, and talents, are said to have made a powerful impression. But he had now the mortification of receiving intelligence, that Kurd Pasha was dead, and that, on his deathbed, he had betrothed his daughter to Ibrahim, bey of Avlona; intelligence which was rendered still more galling by the circumstance of Ibrahim being at the same moment raised to the viziership of central Albania. The rage of Ali on this occasion is said to have been unbounded; he vowed a deadly hatred to Ibrahim, and, though years elapsed before it was fully accomplished, the vow was never forgotten.

For some time after these events, Ali seems to have remained in comparative quiet. His mind, meanwhile, brooded over his situation, and the result of his reflections was not consolatory. Though he had increased his property, and acquired the fame of a brave and intelligent leader, yet these advantages were not sufficient to satisfy his desires, for he was still nudistinguished by title and place. Every thing short of rank and despotic authority appeared to be unworthy of his notice. To obtain a fulcrum for his future operations, he at length determined to make himself absolute master of Tepeleni. The mode in which he effected his purpose, he himself, with a shameless candour, related to the French consul. "I felt," said he, "the necessity of firmly establishing myself in my native place. I had in it partisans who were willing to serve me, and I had likewise formidable enemies, whom it was necessary for me to push into some crime, that I might have a pretext for exterminating the whole of them. I therefore conceived a scheme, with which I ought to have begun my career in life. I was accustomed, after my hunting parties, to take a *siesta* under the shade of a wood near the Bencha, and by means of a trusty adherent, I caused it to be proposed to my enemies to lay in wait for and assassinate me there. I myself sketched out the plan of the conspiracy; and, having arrived at the chosen spot before my intended assassins, I muzzled a goat, tied it down on the ground, and covered it with my riding-cloak. Then, disguising myself, and taking a by-road, I returned to the seraglio, while my enemies imagined they were murdering me by a volley of musquetry. They were not allowed time to ascertain their success; for a piquet of my soldiers appeared at the very instant that the discharge was heard. My supposed murderers entered Tepeleni, vociferating 'Ali Bey is no more! we are rid of him!' These exclamations were heard even in the interior of the harem, and I immediately distinguished the screams of my mother and her women, mingled with the exulting shouts of my foes. I allowed them to enjoy their fancied triumph, and give the most decisive evidence of their guilt; I waited till they were drunk with wine and joy; and then, after having undeceived my mother, I rallied my partisans around me, and fell sword in hand upon my adversaries. Justice was on my side; they were all annihilated before dawn of day; I distributed their property, their riches, and their habitations, among my creatures; and from that moment I could say that Tepeleni was mine."

By this Machiavelian enterprise, Ali gained a firm footing. The resources and influence which he now possessed gave him the means of acquiring more; they were like the ball of snow which finally swells into the terrific avalanche. He had the ability to recompense service, and his policy taught him to win the affections of his followers, by his affable manners, and his attention to their complaints and wants.

It has already been mentioned, that Ali cherished a deeply rooted hatred against the pasha his brother-in-law; nor could he always conceal it, in spite of his talent for dissimulation. In vain, by benefits and sympathetic kindness did his relative endeavour to awaken the feelings of gratitude and fraternal affection. The implacable soul of Ali was proof against tenderness, and he meditated a crime almost unexampled in the history of human guilt. Anxious for the destruction of the man whom he detested, he scrupled not to propose to his sister to destroy her husband by poison. Shainitza shrunk from the commission of such an atrocious act, but sisterly love prevented her from disclosing his criminal suggestions. Thus disappointed, he had recourse to duplicity; he feigned repentance, always spoke of his relative with respect, and succeeded in making Shainitza believe that he had relinquished his murderous designs. But this was only a perfidious calm which preceded the direst of treasons. In the person of Soliman, brother of the pasha, Ali had found a fit accomplice, to whom, as the reward of fratricide, he promised the hand and fortune of Shainitza, reserving to himself only his pretensions to the pashalik. The secrecy of the compact was secured by the most horrible oaths, and measures were quickly taken for the consummation of the deed. A brother prepared to steep his hands in a brother's blood, while another brother was to reward the fratricide by the incestuous marriage of his sister with her husband's murderer.

The near relationship of the conspirators to their intended victim, and their being the sole depositories of their secret, gave them every facility to accomplish their sanguinary purpose. They were in the daily habit of visiting the palace, and they had no accomplice whose indiscretion or treachery might betray them. An opportunity soon occurred for the work of iniquity. In a private interview, which the pasha granted to Ali and Soliman, the latter shot his brother to the heart. The report of the pistol reached the harem, whence Shainitza rushed into the chamber, and beheld her husband stretched lifeless between his assassins. She was about to shriek for assistance, but Ali enjoined silence under pain of death, and gave Soliman the signal to cover her with his pelisse, by which ceremony the latter declared her to be his wife; and, that nothing might be wanting to complete the horror of the deed, this unhallowed marriage is said to have been completed in the chamber of death, and by the side of the yet warm remains of the slaughtered husband. A report was then spread by the criminals, that a fit of apoplexy had put an end to the pasha. It was not long, however, ere the truth became known, and as Shainitza quickly forgot her grief in the arms of Soliman, and one of her sons by the late pasha died, it was generally believed that she was participant of the black catastrophe.

Ali, it has been seen, had hoped to secure for himself the succession to the vacant pashalik. This object, pursued at the expense of so much guilt, he failed to attain. The Porte conferred the dignity of pasha of Delvino upon Selim Bey Coka, a member of one of the principal families of Yapuria. That in a semi-barbarous country great crimes, being considered as indicative of great talents, should win for the criminal popularity among the crowd, is not astonishing; but that men of the same rank as the victims, and who may naturally expect to become victims in their turn, should blindly confide in a betrayer and assassin, may well excite our wonder. Yet such was the error committed by Selim. He treated Ali as his son, lodged him in his palace, and relied upon him with implicit confidence. This conduct is the more surprising, as Selim himself was a benevolent man; and though all the dark deeds of Ali might not have reached the ear of the pasha, the wily and desperate character of the man could scarcely be quite unknown to him. It seems to have been the striking personal appearance, and especially the bland insinuating manners, of Ali by which Selim was misled. Ali might truly say, with the Comus of Milton,

"I under fair pretence of friendly ends,
And well-placed words of glozing courtesy,
Baited with reasons not unplausible,
Wind me into the easy-hearted man,
And hug him into snares."

The very virtues of Selim were wrested into the means of his destruction by the traitor whom he had taken to his bosom. Various circumstances, all of which were honourable to him, contributed to bring about his ruin. Irritated by the insurrectionary movements of the Greeks, the Porte, at this period, persecuted implacably its Christian subjects. Selim, on the contrary, strained every nerve to protect such of them as were under his jurisdiction, and his administration was daily marked by wise and beneficent actions. It was not difficult for his enemies to pervert this really prudent mode of proceeding into evidence that he was secretly in league with the rebellious. Suspicion appeared to be converted into certainty by the policy of Selim with respect to the Venetians. The district which he governed adjoined, on one side, the Venetian territory of Butrinto, the occupation of which had always been matter of dispute between the Porte and Venice; but, far from manifesting the same hostile spirit as his predecessors, he was studious to keep up a good understanding with the commissioners at Corfu. This laudable anxiety to avoid adding another enemy to those with which the Porte was contending, was misconstrued into a violation of his duty. He was, however, unconscious of his critical situation, and, to complete his misfortune he took another step which afforded the treacherous Ali an opportunity of striking the long-meditated blow. Selim had recently sold to the Venetians a forest situated near lake Peloda. The sale was confined to the timber, but Ali suppressed this fact, and denounced the pasha to the government, as having alienated a portion of the dominions of his highness; adding that, if he were not prevented, he would soon deliver up to the infidels the whole of the province of Delvino. It cost him, he hypocritically said, the severest pain to make known the plots of his benefactor, and it was solely a regard for the interests of the sultan, his master, which had determined him to disclose a transaction which so materially affected both religion and the state.

The Venetians were suspected by the Ottoman government, though the suspicion was groundless, of acting underhand in concert with the Russians, and fostering the revolts in Greece: and it was thence inferred that the pasha of Delvino was undoubtedly guilty of treason. As accusation in Turkey, especially of a correspondence with Christians, is equivalent to condemnation, unless the accused party be powerful enough to inspire fear, the calumnious charge brought against the pasha was sufficient to destroy him.

Without instituting any judicial inquiry, without demanding further proof, the divan despatched a firman of death against Selim, and charged Ali with its execution.

Ali, who, for the better management of his plot, had retired for a while to Tepeleni, now hastened back to Delvino, where he was received with more kindness than ever by his devoted victim, who lodged him, as he was wont, in his palace. There, trampling upon the sacred laws of hospitality, and assisted by some hired ruffians, he prepared for the consummation of the crime which was to raise him from obscurity. It was his custom to wait every morning upon his host, to pay him the customary compliments; but one day, feigning indisposition, he sent to request that Selim would visit him in his apartment. In the meanwhile, he concealed the assassins in a closet, ordering them to rush out when he should give the signal by letting his coffee-cup fall. As soon as the unconscious pasha entered the room, the assassins issued forth, and he fell, pierced with many wounds, exclaiming, almost in the same words as Cæsar, "Is it thou, my son, who deprivest me of life?"

Hearing the tumult, the guards of Selim hastened to the chamber. There, in the midst of the assassins, they found Ali standing, with the firman in his hand, exclaiming in threatening accents, "I have killed the traitor, by order of our glorious sultan. Behold his imperial mandate." At sight of the fatal scroll which he displayed, the guards bent low in sign of obedience, and while the head of Selim was separated from his body, they stood motionless in silent terror. Ali then summoned the cadi, the beys, and the primates, to repair to the palace to attest that the sentence had been executed. As soon as seals were placed on the property of the pasha, his murderer quitted the scene of blood, taking with him, as a hostage, Mustapha, the son of Selim. That son eventually, though not till many years had passed away, shared the fate of his father, and by the same hand.

The service which Ali professed to have rendered, of unmasking and punishing a traitor, who was selling the dominions of his master, did not receive a commensurate reward*. A native of Constantinople, a weak and narrow-minded man, had just been placed in the important office of dervendji pasha, or general inspector of roads and passes, in Rumelia. Ali proposed himself as lieutenant to this officer, and was accepted; probably, on a speculation that so active and accomplished a robber would best be able to foil and hunt down his brother robbers. But Ali had no present intention to ruin the trade which he had followed so long. His design in taking the lieutenantcy was to fill his own purse, not to prevent the purses of others from being emptied. He accordingly began to traffic in granting licences to the klephtes; and, by the sums which he was paid for them, and the share which he exacted of the plunder, he is said, in the short space of six months, to have amassed more than twelve thousand pounds sterling. His eagerness to enrich himself spoiled this lucrative business. The klephtes became so daring, that not a road was free from their marauding parties. The attention of the divan was at last awakened, the dervendji pasha was recalled, and his incapacity or connivance was punished by the forfeiture of his head. Ali escaped unhurt; shielded, no doubt, by a prudent distribution, at court, of some of the gold which he had accumulated.

---

* M. Pouqueville asserts, indeed, that Ali was appointed pasha of Trikala; but this appointment seems undoubtedly to have taken place at a later period.

At length, aided again, perhaps by the seduction of bribes, Ali attained the rank and power which he had so long coveted. About the year 1783, he was nominated to the pashalik of Trikala, in Thessaly, and the general inspectorship of roads and passes. At the period when he assumed the government, Trikala, and almost all the towns and villages in the plain of Thessaly, had been burned or plundered by the Albanian Mahometans and the Janissaries of Larissa. He has himself given a lively picture of the state of the people, and of the course of policy which he adopted. " I left behind me in lower Albania," says he, " a phantom of a pasha, who was the sport of the beys of Ioannina, and I took care not to pass through that town on my way to my post. I passed through the Zagori, where the trusty Noutza, my old friend,—God be with his soul, for he was a noble fellow!—replenished my purse. Without asking leave of Soliman, who was then Sanjeac bey of Epirus, we raised with the help of God and my brave Skipetars, a trifling contribution, which stood me in good stead ; for, when I reached Trikala, I found nothing but an exhausted country. They had been hanging a crowd of poor peasants, whose labours enrich such folks as we are. The agas of Larissa had invented projects of revolt, in order to have a pretext for seizing their sheep, and their wives and children. They ate the one, and they sold the other. I saw instantly that there were scarcely any other rebels and thieves than the Turks. I was soon, therefore, in a state of hostility with the beys of Larissa. However, my preliminary step was to pounce upon the Armatoles, who infested the plains, and I drove them back to their mountains, where I kept them penned up, as corps de reserve, till I should find a fit occasion for using them. At the same time,

I sent some heads to Constantinople, to amuse the sultan and the populace, and some money to his ministers, *for water sleeps, but envy never sleeps.*"

The conduct of Ali Pasha as dervendji was diametrically opposite to what it had been when he was only the lieutenant of a dervendji. The motive, however, was the same in both cases; it was interest. Keeping a body of troops in his pay, which he gradually augmented to the number of four thousand men, all well armed, he soon showed what might be expected from his vigilance and activity. He scoured the country in all directions; and routed, dispersed, and drove into their mountain fastnesses, the hordes which overran the plains; and he often pursued them even to their remotest haunts. His severity made the inhabitants of Larissa tremble; and such was the terror of his name, that order and security, to a degree never before known, reappeared, from the chain of Pindus to the passes of Thermopylæ. By thus clearing the country of the banditti, he not only acquired the character of a skilful governor, but also the means of ultimately becoming formidable to the Porte. Those means were also augmented by the manner in which he administered the law. Affecting a strict regard to justice, he never seemed to punish for the pleasure of punishing; but, at the same time, he took good care to select as victims the wealthy beys, and other opulent persons, by the confiscation of whose property he might increase the treasure which was to consolidate his power.

The war which broke out, in 1787, between Austria, Russia, and Turkey, afforded Ali Pasha an opportunity of acquiring honourable reputation in arms. During the campaign of that year, he served, at the head of his Albanian corps, in the army of Yussuf Pasha, the grand vizier. It is said that his conduct was brilliant, and that his military talents and the valour of his soldiers obtained for him general esteem. But, though he exerted his valour and abilities in the cause of his sovereign, he did not scruple, we are told, to enter into a treasonable intrigue with the enemies of his country, in the hope of forwarding his own ambitious schemes. "Knowing," says M. de Vaudoncourt, "the projects of Russia on Greece, and fully aware of the secret measures of the Russian government in Albania, Epirus, and the Morea, he resolved to turn himself on that side, in order to secure to himself a point of support in case the war proved disadvantageous to the sultan. Under the pretext of obtaining the release of Mahomed Pasha, one of his nephews, who had been made prisoner, he entered into a correspondence with prince Potemkin. This correspondence soon became active, and took a direction favourable to the interests of Russia, which at that time could rely on Ali in case of a fresh expedition in the Mediterranean. The author himself saw at Ioannina, a watch set in diamonds, which prince Potemkin caused to be presented to Ali, after peace was signed, in testimony, as it was then said, of esteem for his bravery and talents. The correspondence of Ali with Russia lasted till he himself became master of Ioannina, as well as nearly of all Albania, when he had no longer any direct interest in aiding that power to establish itself in his vicinity."

About this time, Khamco, who had long been afflicted with hydrothorax and uterine cancer, terminated her restless career. If the narrative of M. Pouqueville may be credited, she maintained her desperate and sanguinary character to the close of her existence. We may, however, suspect that, according to his illaudable custom, he has coloured highly, as well to produce a dramatic effect as to gratify his hatred of all who were connected with Ali. He tells us that, after having poisoned the sole remaining half-brother of Ali, she spent her last moments in hearing her will read to her. This document, which rather resembled the composition of an incarnate fiend than of a human being, enjoined Ali and Shainitza, under pain of her curse in case of their neglect, to exterminate as speedily as possible the hated inhabitants of Chormovo and Gardiki, pointed out various individuals who were to be murdered, and villages which were to be consumed, recommended to Ali to enrich the soldiery and to trample on the people, and directed that a pilgrim should be sent to Mecca, in her name, to present an offering on the tomb of the Prophet for the repose of her soul!

Anxious to embrace her son in her dying hour, Khamco had despatched courier after courier to hasten his coming, but Heaven denied her that consolation, and she breathed out her impious spirit in the arms of Shainitza. It is said, that she expired in the most dreadful paroxysms of rage,

"Dicens in superos aspera verba Deos."

Ali did not arrive till an hour after she was no more. He shed a flood of tears over her remains, and, clasping his sister's hand within his own, they swore, over the body of Khamco, to pursue and destroy, without pause and without mercy, all those whom she had devoted to spoliation and death.

Grief did not long detain Ali from following up his projects of aggrandisement. In truth, the vow which he had taken over the corpse of his mother, gave him an additional motive for pressing their execution. The acquiring of additional power would enable him to gratify not only his love of riches and domination, but also of revenge. He had, for a considerable time, been eager to bring under his sway the pachalik of Ioannina, nominally at the head of which, as we have seen, was a pasha who possessed scarcely the shadow of authority.

Circumstances were favourable to the designs of Ali. Since the conquest, the inhabitants of Ioannina had preserved a semblance, which was now become but a mockery, of liberty. It was not till 1716 that they were subjected to pay the karatch, or tribute, and to be governed by a pasha. Even this change was little more than in name; nor had their situation been since deteriorated by the Porte, except in as far as its neglect had operated. While, however, because they could indulge in occasional licence, the people imagined they were free, they were, in reality, the slaves and tools of the beys and agas, who, perpetually warring against each other, compelled them to take part in the quarrels of their superiors, and thus exposed them to be plundered and ransomed by the contending factions. In only one thing did the rival beys agree, which was, in confining the pashas to the old castle in the lake, harassing them incessantly, and obtaining their deposition from the Porte, whenever the despised governors seemed inclined to rouse themselves and assert the dignity of their office. In Ioannina there was, of course, the most complete anarchy. It was often unsafe to venture into the streets, and such atrocious murders were committed in the face of day, that at last the very bazar was deserted.

The machinations of Ali, to secure his prey, were skilfully and perseveringly carried on for a great length of time. His local position was favourable to them; for Trikala being situated on the principal communication with Constantinople, and also with Thessaly, on which province western Greece often depends for subsistence, he had in his hands effectua' means of cramping the commerce, and diminishing the supplies of Ioannina. Sedulously fomenting, by his agents, the dissentions of the people, he succeeded in establishing a party of his own, which, though it was but a small minority of the inhabitants, was of essential service to him. Lastly—and this was his master-stroke—he availed himself of the aid of the Armatoles and klephtes of Thessaly and Acarnania to harass the territory of Ioannina, by perpetual incursions and depredations. This system of annoyance was resolved upon, in 1786, in an interview between Ali Pasha and Demetrius Paleopoulo, the vaiwode of Etolia. Paleopoulo was led to believe that Ali might ultimately be induced to contribute to the liberation of Greece, and he therefore resolved to second the plans of the pasha, for obtaining an augmentation of power. In this resolution he was joined by Canavos, his father-in-law, and by Boucovallas, both of whom, like himself, were among the principal leaders of the Thessalian, Acarnanian, and Etolian Armatoles. While the bands of these three chiefs tormented and ruined the unfortunate people of the pashalik of Ioannina, who in vain sought for succour from their pasha and the beys, there were not wanting emissaries to point out to the sufferers how much happier was the lot of the Thessalians, living in peace and prosperity under the vigilant care of Ali. Nor did other emissaries fail to insinuate, to the Ottoman Government, how much the imperial treasury would be benefited, by placing the disturbed district under the control of one, who, like the pasha of Trikala, was capable of putting down resistance, and increasing the revenue.

It is probable that the divan would have listened to these suggestions, and displaced the puppet pasha who vegetated at Ioannina, had not some prevailing arguments been employed to avert a change. The beys, always unanimous when their interest was concerned, could not contemplate without dread the appointment of such a man as Ali to be their pasha. They well knew that he would never be satisfied with less than implicit obedience, and that he would not hesitate to walk through blood in order to enforce it. Accordingly, there can be no doubt that they exerted all their influence, the influence of bribes, to maintain in his office their nominal ruler. At length, however, the pasha died, and an opening was thus made for the elevation of Ali. Still, the beys persisted in their abhorrence of him, and, when they began to suspect that he would be nominated, they swore to perish rather than submit to "the son of the prostitute." He, meanwhile, was silently laughing in scorn at their idle fury, and preparing for their irretrievable ruin.

"When Ali thought affairs were ripe enough for his presence," says Mr. Hughes*, "he collected a considerable number of troops, passed the chain of mount Pindus, and made his appearance on the plains to the north of Ioannina. This manoeuvre caused great consternation in the city: the beys, in imminent danger, stifled their enmity towards each other, joined their forces together, and advanced to meet the invader. In a great battle, which was fought at the head of the lake, they were beaten and driven back into the city by Ali, who encamped before it with his victorious troops. Not being strong enough to attempt it by storm, he employed a surer method for success. He had already gained a considerable number of adherents amongst the Greeks in the city, and especially in the district of Zagori: these, by bribery and

---

* The narrative of Mr. Hughes agrees, in the main points, with that of General de Vaudoncourt, and bears more internal evidence of correctness than is to be found in the story told by M. Pouqueville.

large promises, he engaged to enter into his views, and send a deputation to Constantinople, to solicit for him the pashalik. They acted as he required; but the opposite interest proved too strong for them at the Porte, and they were made the bearers of an order to their principal to retire immediately to his own government and disband his troops. One of the deputies, most attached to his interest, rode forward night and day, to give him early information of the failure of their mission; and on this occasion Ali executed one of those strokes of policy which had given him such advantage over the imbecility of the Ottoman Porte. After a short consultation with his friend, he dismissed him to return and meet the deputies, who waited a few days on the road, and then proceeded straight to Ioannina. The beys, to whom its contents had been already intimated, advanced as far as the suburbs to meet the firman. It was produced, and drawn out of its crimson case; when each reverently applied it to his forehead, in token of submission to its decrees. It was then opened, and, to the utter consternation of the assembly, it announced Ali, pasha of Ioannina, and ordered instant submission to his authority.

"The forgery was suspected by many, but some credited it; whilst others, by timely submission, sought to gain favour with the man who they foresaw would be their ruler: in short, his partisans exerted themselves on all sides, the beys were dispirited, and, whilst they were irresolute and undetermined, Ali entered the city amidst the acclamations of the populace. His chief enemies in the mean time sought their safety by flight, passing over the lake, and taking refuge in the districts of Arta, Etolia, and Acarnania.

"Ali's first care was to calm the fears of all ranks;

to the people, he promised protection ; to the beys who remained, rich offices and plunder ; his friends were amply recompensed, and his enemies reconciled by his frankness and engaging affability. In the mean time, he put a strong garrison into the castron or fortress, and thus acquired firm possession of the pashalik before the imposture of the firman was discovered. It was now too late to dispossess him of his acquisition: his adherents increased daily ; a numerous and respectable deputation, led by Signore Alessio's father, carried a petition to Constantinople, and, seconding it with bribes to a large amount, ultimately prevailed in establishing his usurped dominion. Thus, according to custom, despotism succeeded to the turbulence of faction, and the people not unwillingly admitted the change."

The firman, which legalised the seizure of the pashalik, was granted by Abdul Hamid towards the close of 1788, but a few months before his decease. It was confirmed by his successor, Selim, in the following year, and thus Ali found himself securely fixed in his new dignity ; which dignity, however, he did not regard as the boundary of his career, but merely as a stepping-stone in his ascent towards a loftier elevation.

CHAPTER III.

Valley of Ioannina—Lake of Ioannina—Description of the City—The Castron—Public and private Buildings—Seraglio of Litharitza—Palaces of Ali's Sons—Pavilion of Ali—Institutions for Education—Commerce—Climate—Diseases—Population—The Founder of Ioannina not known—Battle fought near it in 1082—History of Ioannina under the Great Despotate of Epirus—Tyranny of Thomas—Letter of Sultan Amurath to the People of Ioannina—The Inhabitants submit to Amurath—Revolt of Dionysius the Skelosophist—Subsequent History of Ioannina.

SITUATED in the centre of Epirus, the valley of

Ioannina, which was denominated Hellopia by the ancients, forms an elevated plain, or table-land, extending from north to south about eight leagues, and having an average breadth of about two leagues. This fertile and extensive vale, covered with groves, gardens, and plantations, and bearing the richest productions of the country, is bounded by lofty mountains on every side. To the east rises the triple chain of Pindus, a diverging ridge of which, named Mitzikeli, stretches along the shores of the lake of Ioannina to the lake of Labchistas, and then bends to the north, as far as the defile of Protopapas. From this point a range of undulating hills runs from north to south, till it reaches the defile of Velchistas, whence it turns in an easterly direction for about a league, and then follows a southward course, till, beyond the khan of St. Dimitri, a ramification of the Five Wells mountain links it with the chain of Mitzikeli. Behind the undulating hills, on the west, is the lofty range of Olitzika.

The central part of the table-land is occupied by two lakes; of which the upper bears the name of Ioannina, and the lower that of Labchistas. These lakes are not mentioned by ancient writers, and it seems doubtful whether they have not been produced in later days, either by an earthquake, or by the bursting out of latent springs. On the other hand, M. Pouqueville is of opinion, that the greatest portion of the vale was once overspread with water, and that the lakes were reduced to their present compass by the opening of the Katavothra, at the western extremity of the Labchistas.

The upper lake, which in form resembles a truncated isosceles triangle, is about fourteen miles in circumference. Its base, along which passes the road from Mezzovo, is three-quarters of a league in extent.

On quitting the defile of Mezzovo, the traveller enters the valley of Barcomoudi, which extends four or five miles to the southward. In this are the villages of Barcamoudi, Catzana, and Choria, inhabited by Greek and Walachian christians, the cultivators of this fertile soil. Nearly in the middle of the base of the lake, on a rocky mountain of moderate height, are the ruins of an ancient Epirotic city, now called Gastritza; the masonry of which, in the pseudo Cyclopean style, is extremely fine. The walls of this city are in several places surprisingly perfect, and with many of the towers remain to the height of eighteen or twenty feet. From the summit of these towers is a beautiful view of all the eastern part of the basin of Ioannina; but the prospect on the west is interrupted by a chain of hills, which commences at Catchika.

At the south-western angle of the lake, near the village of Catchika, the road from Mezzovo joins that from Arta; and, after passing the khan of Pogoniani, the traveller enters Ioànnina by the gate of Calo Techesmé, near which are two pavilions, erected by Ali Pasha.

On the north, the lake of Ioannina terminates at the village of Perama. Two channels, flowing for six miles through a large tract of marshy land overgrown with reeds, connect it with the lake of Labchistas, or lower lake. Westward of these channels, on a circular hill, near the village of Gardikaki, stand some ruins, which have been supposed to be the remains of the celebrated Dodona. The summit of the hill, a truncated cone, is, says Mr. Hughes, " entirely surrounded by very fine pseudo Cyclopean walls, dilapidated in many places: in that circuit, which appears to be about a mile and a half, are observed several towers and gateways; but in the interior we could not discern, after the most patient investigation, any vestiges of buildings, except a few subterranean vaults or reservoirs."

In winter and spring, when the mountain torrents and the melting snows swell the volume of water, lake Labchistas covers a space of a league square. But in summer it shrinks to half that extent, and the land which it has deserted is sown with maize. The only outlet of its waters is by subterraneous channels, called Katavothra, of which Mr. Hughes counted between twenty and thirty. They disappear under a mountainous ridge, and again come to light at a distance of five miles, where they pour their streams into the river Velchis, near the village of Velchistas. "In about one hour and a half," says Mr. Hughes, "we arrived at the opposite side of the ridge, and looked down upon the picturesque glen, at the head of which the waters of the lake (as they are conjectured to be) ooze out of the ground in an infinite number of small streams, till they form a large body of water; this foams impetuously down the glen, from rock to rock, in a vast variety of cascades, and sets in motion a number of water-mills, which, together with groups of Albanian girls, washing linen in the stream, give an air of indescribable life and beauty to the scene. As the valley widens, the plains of the river Kalamas, or Thyamis of antiquity (those plains where Atticus, the friend of Cicero, had his delightful country-house, to which he retired during the most disastrous times of the republic), come finely into the prospect, bounded by the blue mountains of Thesprotia."

From whatever quarter it is approached, the city of Ioannina presents a beautiful aspect. European travellers have usually journeyed to it by the road of Arta, and, as seen in that direction, they have uniformly described it in enthusiastic language. "Knowing our vicinity to Ioannina," says Dr. Holland, "we were now impatient to obtain the first view of that city, which is long concealed from the eye by the low eminences traversing the plain. At length, when little more than two miles distant, the whole view opened suddenly before us; a magnificent scene, and one that is still almost single in my recollection. A large lake spreads its waters along the base of a lofty and precipitous mountain, which forms the first ridge of Pindus on this side, and which, as I had afterwards reason to believe, attains an elevation of more than 2,500 feet above the level of the plain. Opposed to the highest summit of this mountain, and to a small island which lies at its base, a peninsula stretches forwards into the lake from its western shore terminated by a perpendicular face of rock. This peninsula forms the fortress of Ioannina; a lofty wall is its barrier on the land side; the waters which lie around its outer cliffs, reflect from their surface the irregular yet splendid outline of a Turkish seraglio, and the domes and minarets of two Turkish mosques, environed by ancient cypresses. The eye, receding backwards from the fortress of the peninsula, reposes upon the whole extent of the city, as it stretches along the eastern borders of the lake. Repose, indeed, it may not unfitly be called, since both the reality and the fancy combine in giving to the scenery the character of a vast and beautiful picture spread out before the sight. No volumes of smoke, nor even the sounds of carriages and men, break into this description of the distant view; the tranquillity of the Turkish character is conveyed to the Turkish city also, and even to the capital of the chief who governs the warlike and half-civilised Albanian tribes. You are not here looking upon a lengthened and uniform mass of buildings, so often the only characteristic of a European town; but there is before the eye a variety and a richness in the grouping of the objects, which is peculiarly in the cities of the East. The lofty palaces of the vizier and his sons, the minarets of numerous mosques, each surrounded by its grove of cypresses, which give something of appropriate sanctity to the place; the singular intermixture of houses and trees through every part of the city, a circumstance more striking from the want of wood in the general landscape: these, together with the noble situation on the lake, and the magnificence of the surrounding mountains, are the features which will most impress the stranger in approaching the capital of Ali Pasha."

More brief in his description of the scene, Mr. Hughes is no less alive than Dr. Holland to its attractions. "About two miles before we arrived at Ioannina," says he, "we ascended a gentle eminence which brought the city full into our view, with its glittering palaces and mosques, stretched along the shore of its magnificent lake. The air was frosty, the atmosphere transparent, and the snowy mountains were beautifully reflected in the smooth surface of the water, over which a number of canoes glided lightly, carrying sportsmen after the myriads of wild-fowl, which rose at times like dark clouds into the air. Nothing was wanting but classical authority to make us believe these really to have been the famed Elysian fields of antiquity surrounding the Acherusian lake."

That part of the city of Ioannina which is in the immediate vicinity of the lake stands on a flat, but the north and north-western quarters of it are built on slopes of rising and uneven ground. The whole length of the city is rather more than two miles; its breadth is various, but never more than a mile, not including the castron or fortress. The castron, which is near the middle of the city, and in which reside only Turks and Jews, forms a large promontory, jutting out into the lake, and separated from the other part of the town by fortifications and a moat. This was "the site of the primitive town, and its figure is not unaptly compared to the double head of a spread eagle, whose wings are represented by the outstretched habitations of the city." The peninsula, which widens as it advances into the lake, is terminated, at the angles, by two distinct rocky promontories. One of these is crowned by a large mosque, the lofty minaret and extended piazzas of which are shaded by cypresses; the other is occupied by the old seraglio of the pashas of Ioannina, a vast, irregular, but wildly magnificent edifice, over the projecting roofs and painted walls of which rise the minarets and cypresses of a second mosque. One of these mosques, that of Calo Pasha, is ornamented with granite columns, brought from the temple of Pluto in Thesprotia.

Opposite the castrou, and more than midway to the eastern shore of the lake, is a small rocky island, belonging chiefly to Mouctar Pasha, which is exceedingly picturesque. Near the north-eastern corner is a village, almost hidden by the luxuriant foliage of chestnut and palm trees. It consists of about two hundred houses of almost unparalleled neatness. The vizier has a small palace on this island, and here are also seven convents, which have frequently been used as state prisons. From the highest point of the isle is an exquisite view of the castrou and the city.

The principal street of Ioannina extends the whole length of the town; that which is next in importance crosses it at right angles, from the fortress to the hills. " The interior aspect of Ioannina," says Dr. Holland, " except where there is some opening to the landscape that surrounds it, is gloomy and without splendour. Few of the streets preserve a uniform line; a circumstance which makes the topography of the place very difficult to the stranger. Those inhabited by the lowest classes consist, in great part, of wretched mud-built cottages, and are chiefly in the outskirts of the city; the middle ranks dwell in a better description of buildings, the upper part of which is constructed of wood, with a small open gallery under the projecting roof: the higher classes, both of Greeks and Turks, have, in general, very large houses, often forming two or three sides of the areas attached to them, and with wide galleries which go along the whole front of the building, taken as it were from the first floor, and sheltered under the roofs. In this style of building, which is common throughout the Turkish towns, there is something picturesque in the distant effect, which is lost in the nearer approach. In the best streets of Ioannina there is an air of heaviness; and the most respectable houses have the appearance of prisons; presenting, externally, little more than lofty walls with massive double gates, and the windows, if seen at all, at the top of the building."

Ioannina, which is the seat of a Greek archbishop, contains seven or eight churches, which offer nothing remarkable, either in the exterior or interior, except an abundance of tawdry gilding, and rude paintings of saints and martyrs. There are eighteen mosques, each standing on an open space of ground, from the summits of which the crescent is seen rising out of their groves of cypress-trees.

Near the castron is the bazaar, which consists of ten or twelve very narrow streets, intersecting each other at all kinds of angles. This place, dark from its construction, is rendered still darker by the low projecting roofs, which overhang the shops. Each trade has a separate district to itself. At night the whole is shut up by lofty wooden gates, and is guarded by a swarm of fierce dogs, which no one wearing the Frank dress can approach, without running the risk of being torn to pieces.

To the south of the castron, stands the new seraglio of the vizier, which is called the Serai, and sometimes the castle of Litharitza. "It is an immense pile of building, lofty in itself, and situated on an eminence which gives it a command over every part of the city. It may not unfitly be termed a palace upon and within a fortress. High and massive stone walls, on different parts of which cannon are mounted, support a superstructure of wood, of great extent, but apparently without any regularity of plan; the several portions of the edifice seem to have been successively added, as a necessity was found for enlargement. Yet, notwithstanding this irregularity, the magnitude and character of the building give it an air of magnificence, which is not always obtained by a more rigid adherence to architectural rules. The style of construction is entirely Turkish; the roofs projecting far beyond the face of the buildings, the windows disposed in long rows underneath, the walls richly decorated with painting, occasionally landscape, but more generally what is merely ornamental, and without uniform design. The access to the Seraglio is exceedingly mean. It is surrounded by narrow and gloomy streets, without any circumstance to mark the approach to the palace of the Albanian ruler." Mr. Hughes pithily characterises this fortress seraglio as "the picture of a tyrant entrenched among his slaves."

At a short distance from the seraglio of Ali are the palaces of Mouctar and Veli, the sons of the Pasha. These edifices are built after the Turkish fashion, and the palace of Veli, which is nearly square in form, and stands on a considerable elevation, is handsomer in external appearance than his father's. Both are chiefly remarkable for being ornamented with fresco paintings, executed by some Armenian daubers. The subjects of these paintings display the bad taste and the ferocious spirit of the selectors. Over the principal entrance of Mouctar's abode, he is delineated, surrounded by his troops, and witnessing the execution of two Greeks, whom the hangman is tying to a gibbet with the same rope. In another place are exhibited decapitated trunks, with the blood spouting from them. These are much admired, though considered by the connoisseurs as inferior to another, in which the prince appears seated, surrounded by oxen, horses, mules, and asses. The paintings in Veli's palace represent camps, piles of heads, standards, and sieges. In the latter productions of Armenian genius, the bomb-shells are considerably larger than the houses.

The only remaining building which deserves notice, is the kiosk or pavilion of Ali, in the suburb, at the north-west end of the city. It is situated in the midst of extensive gardens, abounding in fruit and forest trees, and displaying more of the wild graces of nature than the laboured efforts of art. This was the vizier's favourite place of retirement. The kiosk, which is of elegant construction, is profusely ornamented with carving and gilding, in the best Turkish style. " Its interior is divided into eight compartments, or deep recesses, diverging out of the great area, in the middle of which stands a curious *jet-d'eau*. This consists of a small castle, surmounted by cannon, and surrounded by regular lines, which play upon each other, in imitation of a bombardment: between the cannon, on the parapet, stand figures of parrots, lions, and other birds and beasts, who spout water out of their mouths, as if in mockery of what is going forward: the motion of the water gives voice to a small organ attached to a pillar in the apartment."

There are two institutions at Ioannina in which the ancient languages are taught. The first of these, the Gymnasium, which was long presided over by Signor Psalida, a Greek of considerable talent, was founded, nearly forty years ago, by a rich merchant named Picrozoe, and afforded instruction to about one hundred boys. The second was established a century and a half since, by Ghioni, a merchant. The funds for its support were placed in the bank of Venice, and, after the confiscation of them by the French, in 1797, the school was entirely indebted for its continuance to the noble munificence of the family of Zosimas. This seminary numbered about three hundred scholars.

The commerce of Ioannina is not insignificant. It is chiefly carried on with Constantinople, Russia, Venice, and Malta, and the merchants are travelled men, well acquainted with European habits, and speaking several languages. Constantinople sends to Ioannina shawls, turbans, amber, and various toys; Russia furnishes oxen, horses, skins, and ermine; Venice sends rich velvets, red skull-caps, arms, and many articles of hardware; and from Malta come a variety of English manufactures and colonial produce. An *ad valorem* duty of four per cent. is paid on each article at the Dogana. In exchange for these, the exports are cotton, raw silk, Valonean bark, prepared goat and sheep skins, and sometimes grain, though not often. The distribution of the imports among the towns of Epirus, is a source of much profit to the merchants. "Their domestic manufactures," says Mr. Hughes, " are not numerous: indeed, here, as in other countries, the state of manufactures is a fair criterion of the state of civilisation: whilst the workmanship of all articles that may conduce to general comfort, convenience, and utility, or to the interests of philosophy and science, is quite contemptible, great industry and considerable skill are exhibited in the embroidery of cloth, in filagree, in working silver handles for pistols, muskets, and ataghans, and in ornamenting pipe-heads." An idea of the low state of the mechanic arts may be formed from one circumstance. When Lord Byron visited Ioannina, there was no one in the whole city who could mend an umbrella, and only one man, a poor Italian, who was capable of making a bedstead.

The climate of Ioannina varies more than is usual in Greece. Its situation on a table-land, elevated from a thousand to twelve hundred feet above the sea, and encircled by lofty mountains, may account for some of the peculiarities of its temperature. The heat in summer is extremely oppressive. In winter it is equally cold, and is at times very rainy. Even as late as the beginning of April, snow has fallen at Ioannina. Fuel is scarce, and of course dear, so that the richer classes are obliged to be economical in the use of it, and the poor can with difficulty obtain sufficient to cook their provisions. The rich, therefore, wrap themselves up in robes lined with furs, and the common people shelter their limbs under cloaks of thick homespun cloth. " Earthquakes are common, and most frequent in the autumn; they sometimes throw down the houses, and the fish have been known to be cast out of the lake upon dry ground."

Fevers of every kind, especially nervous ones, are common at Ioannina; and are principally caused by unhealthy dwellings, dirty habits, filth accumulated in the streets, and scanty nutriment; but, above all, by the great number of Albanian troops, often as many as from ten to forty of whom are quartered upon each inhabitant. The city has been more than once devastated by the plague. In 1814, it was daily expected once more to make its appearance, it having for some time been raging in the environs. This would inevitably have been the case had not prompt measures been adopted by Ali, who immediately drew a strong cordon of troops round the infected districts. Immediate death was the punishment for attempting to pass it. At the same time he ordered, that upon the decease of any person in Ioannina, the house was to be closed till the nature of the disease had been ascertained; and he added, that should it be found to be the plague, every soldier stationed on the road through which it had been introduced should be put to death, as well as all the relations of the deceased.

The extent of the city would imply a larger population than it really contains. This discrepancy is occasioned by the vacant spaces of the mosques and Turkish burying-grounds, and by all the better houses having a space attached to them, in which there are commonly a few trees. Estimates of the population vary from thirty-five to fifty thousand persons. Forty thousand is, perhaps, about the real number. It forms a heterogeneous mass of Greeks, Turks, Albanians, Franks, Jews, Arabs, Moors, and Negroes; among whom the Greeks are the most numerous, respectable, and long established, many of the families having been settled at Ioannina for centuries.

Such is, or rather such was, the capital of the ruler of Albania. In speaking of that which the labour of man contributed to the erection of Ioannina, the past tense must be used. Its magnificent site, its beautiful lake, its encircling mountains, remain unchanged, but the palaces, the mosques, the churches, and all, or nearly all, the city, have ceased to exist: they were, as we shall soon have occasion to describe, consigned to ruin by the desperation and rage of Ali himself, at the moment when he was closely tracked by his enemies, the fabric of his power was at length tottering to its fall, and life was about to terminate in disaster and disgrace.

By whom, or at what time, Ioannina was founded, is not recorded in history. The many military and other advantages which belong to its site render it probable that some establishment was formed there at an early period of the Eastern empire. The style of building of some ancient ruins in the castrou, induces Mr. Hughes to refer the construction of the original edifice to the reign of Justinian. His supposition acquires likelihood from the circumstance of the monarch having erected innumerable castles in Epirus and Macedonia. That at least a castron, or citadel, existed there long before the end of the eleventh century, is certain from the Norman Bohemond having found one which was dilapidated, no doubt from age, and which was repaired by him.

The first event which gave Ioannina a place in the annals of the East was the battle which, in 1082, was fought under its walls, between Bohemond and the emperor Alexis. The combat lasted from sunrise till sunset, and Alexis, after having displayed prodigies of valour, was defeated by the Norman. The city is stated to have been subsequently either restored or refounded, but writers differ as to the person who accomplished it, and even the century in which this occurrence took place. The work is ascribed, and in each instance apparently without reason, to John Cantacuzenus, to Michael Ducas, and to Thomas and John, Epirot despots, of whom nothing is known. In some part of the twelfth century, the rising town is said to have been destroyed by the combined Normans and Neapolitans, whom the historians of that day denominate Catalans and Latins. It appears, however, to have speedily recovered from this disaster.

We again lose sight of Ioannina till after the disruption of the empire, which was the consequence of the conquest by the Latins. When the great despotate of Epirus, or of the West, as it is sometimes denominated, was established by Michael Angelus, Ioannina was one of the cities which he reduced under his sway. After the death of Andronicus the Third, Epirus was conquered by Stephen Duscian, cral or prince of Servia. This barbarian monarch, who assumed the title of emperor of the Romans, bestowed Ætolia and Acarnania upon his brother Simon, or Sinissa, and Ioannina, Triccala, and Larissa, with the dignity of Cæsar, upon Prelupus, one of his satraps. Subsequently to the death of Prelupus, Ioannina acknowledged the authority of Simon, who, however, in consequence of his being involved in a war with the Albanians, seems to have left its inhabitants to govern and defend themselves. The city was soon attacked by the Albanians, but the citizens resisted the besiegers with much courage. At length, being driven almost to extremity, they sent an embassy to Simon, to entreat that he would assist them. Simon listened to their prayer, and sent them a body of forces; but, unfortunately, he sent, as their governor, his son-in-law Thomas, whom a manuscript history of the place stigmatises as " an imp of darkness and a son of Satan," and who seems, indeed, to have been deserving of those discourteous appellations.

The new governor entered the city, with the princess Angelina his wife, amidst the acclamations of the populace; and for a while he appeared disposed to govern uprightly. The mask, however, was soon dropped, and the people had reason to lament that they had resorted to Simon for aid. To pillage the church, in order to enrich his Servian followers, to drive into exile the excellent bishop Sebastian, and to strip the cathedral of its ornaments, and convert it into granaries and storehouses, were among the first acts of the profligate Thomas. The leading and wealthy citizens were next driven into exile by him, and their property was confiscated. " Amidst the tyrannical acts of this monster, which became so great that even his own Servians deserted the city, none excited greater horror than that which he committed against Elias Clauses, one of the best and richest of the citizens; whom he compelled to reveal his treasures by unheard-of cruelties, making him drink water mingled with ashes, and burning his naked body with torches and brimstone, till he expired under the torment."

Twice in ten years, in 1368 and 1378, Ioannina was desolated by pestilence, which destroyed great numbers of the inhabitants. When the disease was gone, the despot compelled the rich widows to marry his abandoned companions, and seized on the property of the orphans. Four times within the same period Ioannina was exposed to invasion from the Albanians. In the first instance, Leoses, their leader, was prevailed on to retire by means of great bribes and his receiving the hand of Irene, the daughter of Thomas. In the second, Spartas, who had usurped the sovereignty on the decease of Leoses, was bought off by the sacrifice to him of Helen, the tyrant's sister, with a regal dowry. In the third, the Albanians were defeated, and lost a great number in killed and prisoners. The fourth time, the city was in the utmost peril. A tower in the castron was betrayed to two hundred Albanians; they were joined by a large body of their countrymen, with Valachians and Bulgarians mixed; and they made themselves master of the whole of the castron, and its principal gula or citadel. An insurrection seems to have now broken out, and for three days the city was in the most terrible commotion.

The Albanians in the castron and in the island on the lake were, meanwhile, preparing for a general assault. The expedition from the island was, however, met and defeated. " From this danger," says the veracions chronicler, " the citizens were delivered by the interposition of Michael the archangel, who appeared at the head of their armament with his flaming sword." For this service Michael still continues to be regarded as the patron of the city. Cut off from all succour, the Albanians in the castrou surrendered at diseretion; they were all put to death, except a few who, deprived of eyes, ears, and noses, were sent back as a warning to their countrymen. The surname of the Albanian-slayer was now assumed by the victorious Thomas. Spartas avenged this slaughter by ravaging the vicinity of the city; and Thomas, in return, hung up before the walls all the Albanians whom he took, or sent them mutilated into the camp of their sovereign.

In the course of the next seven years, the despot,—for that title was conferred upon him in 1380, by the emperor Manuel,—continued to inflict on his subjects the most barbarous cruelty, fortified various strong castles in his own territory, twice called in the aid of the Turks, to help him to devastate Albania, and, by the aid of these allies, conquered the cities of Velas, Drynopolis, Bagenetia, and Catuna. At length his crimes rose to such a pitch as to be no longer endurable. Four of the officers of his bodyguard conspired against him, and they effected their design, on the night of December the 20th, 1385, by stabbing him in his bed. With him expired the Servian government in Epirus.

The tyrant had long been alienated from his virtuons and benevolent consort, Angelina. Shortly after the death of Thomas, she gave her hand to

Izans, count of Cephalonia, an excellent prince, whom the citizens of Ioannina joyfully recognised as their lord. The Byzantine court sanctioned his election, and gave him the regal title. At home, he exerted himself to repair the mischief which had been done by his predecessor; and, on the frontiers, he efficiently protected the country from its enemies. The only calamity which Ioannina suffered under his reign was not the work of man. In 1387, the tower of the convent called Archimandreion was thrown down by lightning, and fourteen persons were crushed to atoms under the ruins.

In 1395, Izans lost his wife, Angelina, who died universally lamented; and, in 1397, he married Irene, the daughter of the Albanian prince, Spartas. Shortly after his nuptials, he and his father-in-law routed the Turks, in a bloody battle near Drisco. He was not so fortunate in the following year; for he was defeated and made captive by Ghioni Zenevisi, a potent Albanian chieftain. He was ransomed, however, for ten thousand florins. He died at Ioannina, on the 29th of April, 1401.

Izaus was succeeded by his brother Sghurus, who also obtained the government of Arta, on the death of Spartas. Though possessed of more resources than his predecessor, he was unable to retain the throne. He was driven from his dominions by an immense army of Servians, Albanians, Bulgarians, and Valachians, headed by a celebrated leader named Bonghoes, which devastated the country, burned towns and villages, and slaughtered thousands of the inhabitants. What became of Sghurus, is not known; there is reason to believe that his fall did not take place till after the year 1413.

A despot Charles is mentioned as having subsequently reigned at Ioannina, and died in 1430; but his existence is doubtful, and the city is believed to have been governed by an aristocracy after the ruin of Sghurus. In 1432 the conquests of Amurath II., in Greece and Macedonia, alarmed the citizens, and they sent a detachment of their best troops to guard the passes of Mount Pindus. By this detachment all the Turkish troops opposed to it were cut to pieces. This act of hostility roused the anger of Amurath, who addressed to the citizens the following letter:

"Sultan Amurath, Sovereign of the East and the West, to the people of Ioannina, greeting:

"I counsel you to deliver up to me with good-will your fortress, and to receive me as your sovereign, lest you should move me to great wrath, and I should come up against you with my army and take your city with the sword: then you will suffer all the calamities that other places have suffered, which refusing to acknowledge my power have been conquered by my arms; whose inhabitants have been sold into slavery through the East and through the West. Come then, let us make a treaty and ratify it with an oath, I on my part that I will respect your rights, and you on yours that you will obey me faithfully."

The citizens of Ioannina met to deliberate upon this brief, but peremptory and alarming missive. Dread of the sultan's power prevailed, and they sent an embassy to Thessalonica, the residence of Amurath, to deliver to him the keys of their fortress. A Turkish garrison accompanied the envoy back, to take possession of the castron, or rather that part of it which was called the gula or citadel. Having built houses in that quarter of the city which is named the Turcopaleo, the Mahometans were desirous to complete their domestic establishments by the addition of female partners, and, to accomplish this, the sultan permitted them to take wives among the daughters of the Greeks. It would appear, however, that the Greek ladies, or their parents, were averse from forming unions with the professors of Islamism; and the consequence was, that the latter adopted the primitive Roman mode of procuring wives. " Watching the opportunity of a great festival, at which the Greek families attended divine service in the cathedral, they armed themselves secretly, and waited at the doors of the church till the congregation came out; then, each person seizing upon the damsel that pleased him best, carried her off in defiance of her relations and friends. The parents, after a short time, seeing no remedy for the evil, consented to the nuptials, and gave the customary dowry to the husbands."

This imitation of the rape of the Sabines, and the destruction of the ancient church of St. Michael, seem to have been the only serious injuries which the citizens sustained from the Mussulmans during a period of more than a century and three quarters. They paid a moderate tribute, enjoyed a considerable degree of freedom, and remained in possession of the castron, with the exception of the citadel. But, in 1611, an event occurred by which their condition was woefully altered. The cause of the mischief was a man of the name of Dionysius, who had been ejected from the bishopric of Triccala for dabbling in astrology and magic, and who had somehow acquired the ludicrous appellation of the Skelosophist, or dog-sophist. Having dreamt that the sultan rose to receive him, he considered this dream as prefiguring that he was destined to deliver his country from the Ottoman yoke. He began the work of deliverance by wandering about in quest of proselytes, with a wallet at his back, and a flagon of wine by his side. In the course of his peregrinations, he approached Ioannina, and hearing that the Turkish garrison was not numerous, and dwelt out of the fortress, he determined to strike the first blow in that city. He had by this time collected a large troop of followers. In the night he led them to Ioannina, which place they entered, singing the Kyrie Eleison. They were joined by a multitude of the people, and immediately proceeded to their task; they killed about a hundred Mahometans, and burned several houses, and it was not without much difficulty that the governor escaped into the citadel. The next step was to plunder, after which, by a natural progression, they got drunk. This last imprudence was fatal to them. The Turks rallied, fell upon them while they were in a helpless state, slew great numbers of them, and took many prisoners, who were soon consigned to the severest tortures.

Dionysius escaped, for a while, and found shelter in a cave, under the north-east precipice of the castron, which is still called the Cave of the Skelosophist. He was supplied with bread by a baker, one of his partisans; but was at length discovered by some Jews, and given up to the Turks. He was flayed alive, and his stuffed skin was sent to Constantinople, that the sultan might see it. On its being carried into the seraglio, the monarch is said to have risen to view the spectacle, and thus to have literally fulfilled the dream by which the skelosophist had been so lamentably deluded.

"After this rebellion", says Mr. Hughes, "Ioannina was treated by the Turks like all other conquered cities. The principal conspirators, together with many innocent persons, were subjected to extreme punishments, some being impaled, others sawn asunder, and many burned alive: every Greek church within the castron was then razed to the ground, from which place all christians were banished for ever by a special firman of the sultan; but the Jews were allowed to retain their habitations, and received various immunities in consequence of the assistance they had rendered to the Mahometans. This expulsion of the Greeks from the castron, tended greatly to increase the city, which soon began to extend its arms along the banks of the lake. It seems to have enjoyed a considerable degree of tranquillity amidst the convulsions that agitated this part of the world, during the last efforts made by the Christian powers to preserve some portion of European Turkey from the overwhelming force of its Ottoman invaders. It was governed by beys and pashas of two tails, sent by the Porte, but never became the head or capital of a sandjiac till the time of Ali. His experienced eye soon saw the advantages of its strong central situation, and from the first he determined to make it the focus of his extended dominion. Under him it has risen to that degree of splendour, importance, and population, which it now possesses."

CHAPTER IV.

System of Ali—His treacherous and sanguinary Conduct to the Chormovites—Terror inspired by him—His Designs upon the Pasha of Berat—Marries his Son to the Pasha's Daughter—Employs an Emissary to poison Sephir Bey—The Suliots—Description of the Territory inhabited by them—Origin of the Suliots—Their Character, Manners, Religion, Customs, and Appearance—Ali is defeated by them—Their Imprudence—Operations of Ali in Northern Albania—He endeavours to circumvent the Suliots, but without effect—He attacks them with a large Force—Heroism of Tzavella—Ali is defeated—He makes Peace—He is in Danger from the Porte—Stratagem by which he escaped.

"HAVING," as an eminent traveller well observes, "established his interest on a firm footing as well in Constantinople as Albania, and wielding the resources of an extensive dominion, Ali Pasha began to act upon a larger scale, and to pursue his grand plan of consolidating an independent power in Epirus, a country which Nature itself seems to have marked out for independence by the mountain barriers with which she has surrounded and protected it. The means which he resolved to take for the completion of this plan, were to amass treasures, to keep agents in pay at the Ottoman court, to infuse suspicion of other powers into the minds of the divan, to render himself useful to whatever European state was able to return his services, and, finally, to seize upon the property of his neighbours whenever and by whatever methods he could. In the execution of these measures, his rapacity was boundless, his penetration deep, his aggressions innumerable, his perfidy more than Punic, and his success for a time complete."

The first care of Ali, on his attaining the high situation to which he had so long aspired, was to humble the beys of Ioannina, by stripping them of their wealth; he being convinced that he should thus most effectually prevent their forming intrigues against him in the divan. At the same time he gained over the Albanians, upon whom he bestowed all employments of consequence. By a singular innovation upon established customs, he also admitted Greeks into his confidence, whose information and abilities he well knew how to appreciate. To further his interests still more, Ali, who had no respect for any set of religious opinions whatever, conciliated the different sects by avowing, when a suitable opportunity occurred, a pretended conviction of the truth of their tenets. With the Turks he was a zealous Mussulman; a Pantheist with the Bektadgis*, he pro-

---

* It is the belief of the Dervises Bektadgis that God is all, and all is God; and that matter, being eternal, never had a commence-

fessed materialism; and a Christian when in the company of Greeks, he pledged repeated bumpers to the health of the blessed Virgin. Obsequious to the Ottoman court, so long as it did not interfere with his individual authority, he was punctual in the payment of his tribute to the Sultan; nor did he omit to bribe, by munificent presents, those of the ministry who possessed the greatest interest. To this system he constantly adhered, persuaded that, in absolute governments, gold is more potent than the despot himself.

Having thus humbled the beys, and cajoled the people by flattering promises (for no man ever was gifted in a greater degree with a bland and insinuating eloquence), Ali thought the time was now arrived to begin fulfilling the last wishes of his mother, and gratifying the appetite for vengeance which was so strong in himself and his sister Shainitza. He therefore resolved to attack the strong town of Chormovo, the inhabitants of which, as we have seen, had been confederates of the Gardikiotes in that contest which was productive of captivity to him, and of the foulest injury and insult to his mother and sister.

His conduct on this occasion marks his implacable nature, and his predilection for treachery. While he was preparing for his expedition, alarm began to be felt by the Chormovites, who had probably obtained some intimation of his purpose. They in consequence despatched two of their leading men, to Ali, to learn the cause of his meditated hostilities, and the means of averting them. The deputies were received with much civility by the pasha. He had, he said, no reason to be hostile to the people of Chormovo in general; there were, indeed, certain families, which he

---

ment, nor will ever have an end. This was also Pliny's opinion. "Idemque rerum naturæ opus, et rerum ipsa natura."—Hist. lib. ii. c. I. Spinoza's system is similar.

specified, against whom he had cause of complaint; but if they were expelled, and their habitations burned, he would not molest them. When the deputies returned home, a meeting was convened, the message of Ali was delivered, and the obnoxious families consented to become exiles for the good of their fellow-citizens. The price of their property was paid to them, and they retired to Argyro Castro. The deputies were again despatched to Ali, with intelligence of this peace-offering. He expressed his satisfaction, told them that he would visit their town in a few days, and, to avoid putting them to expense, would bring only two hundred men; but, added he, " in the mean time take back with you some of my people, for as yet I can scarcely trust those who have so often deceived me." With this escort, or rather detachment of spies, the envoys retraced their steps to their native place.

Ali shortly after paid his promised visit to Chormovo. Though he brought twelve hundred men instead of two hundred—a circumstance which was not a little alarming—the Chormovites put on the semblance of extreme pleasure, treated him magnificently, and assigned the most comfortable quarters to his troops. The Albanians, however, soon began to quarrel with their hosts. Faithful to his system of deception, the pasha sternly reprimanded some of them, and even punished others, asking them how they dared to insult his excellent friends, the good people of Chormovo, who had so kindly invited him into their city? Having thus apparently given proof of his friendly feeling towards them, he called together the principal inhabitants, whom he thus addressed:—" I feel much for you, my good friends, because my residing amongst you must be a heavy burthen on your finances. I will therefore alleviate the weight by retiring, with the major part of my retinue, to the monastery of Tribuchi, where you shall come to me, that we may sign articles of friendship and alliance."

The convent to which Ali declared his intention of going is situated in the mountains near Chormovo, and is dedicated to the Panaghia. Thither he went and, on the following day, he summoned to a conference about a hundred of the principal citizens. So well had he played his deluding part that the victims fell into the snare, without a suspicion of the danger. To give more solemnity to the treaty, it was to be drawn up and signed in the church. For the purpose of executing this agreement, the hegumenos, or prior, was already standing in full dress at the high altar. As no Greek ever enters armed into a place of worship, the citizens left their weapons at the church door. The arms were immediately seized by order of Ali. The shameless mockery was still acting in the sacred edifice, when one of the Chormovites had occasion to quit the church. Perceiving that the weapons were gone, he rushed back into the church, exclaiming that "the priest might stop proceedings, for they were betrayed by the infidel!" This tardy warning was fruitless. The Albanian troops burst into the church, bound the astonished citizens with ropes, and sent them prisoners to Tepeleni. Ali then led them against Chormovo. A multitude of the inhabitants were slaughtered, the women and children were sold into slavery, and the town was levelled with the ground. One man, the head of a family named Prifti, was especially obnoxious to Ali, for having participated in the outrage upon Khamco and Shainitza, and he was punished with commensurate barbarity. A spit was run through his body, and he was roasted alive between two fires. The horrible task of performing this act of cruelty was committed by Ali to a foster-brother, who bore the appropriate surname of the Blooddrinker. Frightful as the tragedy of Chormovo was, a yet more frightful tragedy remained to be acted, though after a long interval, before the vengeance of Ali and Shainitza could be satisfied to the full extent*.

The consternation inspired by this massacre was such, that many of the neighbouring tribes could see no hope of safety but in instant submission. The town of Liboovo, the valley of Caramoutadez, the district of Konitza, and a part of that of Premiti, were in consequence added to the dominions of Ali, without his having the trouble to strike a single blow.

These districts belonged to central Albania, which was subject to the pasha of Berat. From its richness and fertility this pashalik was the most desirable and necessary conquest for the pasha of Lower Epirus. As far as regarded mere military operations, it was also likely to become an easy one; for as leader of the Klephts, and as Bey of Tepeleni, Ali had formed numerous connexions in the country, the localities of which were perfectly known to him. In addition to the proximity and the riches of central Albania, the noble race of horses, which is peculiar to it, rendered its possession a most valuable object. But, above all, the attainment of it was of importance to him, in order to deprive the inferior beys of the independent cantons of Epirus of the support which they were accustomed to find in the ruler of Berat. To take possession of this pashalik by force, and that, too, in defiance of the Porte, would, however, have been a difficult and hazardous enterprise. Ali, therefore,

---

* Mr. Hughes states the destruction of Chormovo to have occurred before Ali's accession to the pashalik of Ioannina. M. Pouqueville places it subsequently to that event, and he seems to be in the right. But it is difficult to ascertain the chronology of some of Ali's exploits.

resorted to indirect means, and we shall see that, at length, thanks to favouring circumstances, and to his ability and perseverance, he effected his purpose.

The ruler of Berat was Ibrahim Pasha, a descendant of one of the greatest Arnaut families, who, as we have seen, had married the reluctant daughter of Kurd Pasha, and thus deprived Ali of a mistress, or a wife, as well as of the prospect of advancement. Ali, then only a bey, had even been subjected, on that occasion, to humiliating and ill-founded taunts, with respect to his extraction. In this instance, therefore, it so happened that revenge and ambition were combined to stimulate him, and that the policy of the new pasha was in perfect accordance with the passions of the man.

Though Ali had undoubtedly been the first to provoke hostilities, he was so fortunate as to avoid the onus of being the first to commence them. Indignant at the encroachments made upon his territory, Ibrahim demanded redress. An abortive negotiation ensued, which ended in Ibrahim sending into the field a body of Masakian Toxides, under the command of his brother Sepher, Bey of Avlona. To meet this force, Ali, whose policy it was always to oppose Mahometans to Christian foes, and Christians to Mahometan, called upon the Armatoles for their assistance. His summons was not unavailing; glad of an opportunity to plunder and destroy the enemies of their faith, Paleopoulo, Canavos, Boucovalles, his son-in-law Stathas, and other enterprising chiefs, descended with their bands from the mountains of Agrapha, Pindus, and Olympus. A desultory but harassing and destructive warfare ensued, in which carrying off flocks and herds, pillaging and hanging peasants, and burning villages, were the principal exploits.

Ibrahim was soon tired of a contest in which he was

the greatest sufferer, and he sought a reconciliation. Ali, who knew that he could safely and surely accomplish more by secret perfidy than by open violence, readily consented to a peace. The treaty was negotiated by Emina, the wife of Ali. It was agreed that Mouctar, the eldest son of the pasha of Ioannina, should marry the eldest daughter of Ibrahim; and that, as the dowry of the bride, Ali should retain the whole of his encroachments and conquests. Having thus far effected his purpose, Ali dismissed his allies, the Armatoles, to whom he gave so rich a reward, in slaves and money, as to bind them thenceforth devotedly to his service.

Scarcely were the nuptials of Mouctar celebrated, which seemed to guarantee the tranquillity of Albania, before a fresh cause of discord arose between the families of Berat and Ioannina. Anonymous letters were sent to Ibrahim, asserting that his wife intended to poison him, for the purpose of being married to Ali, who had prompted her to the deed. The pretended plot was dressed up in the most specious colours. Any other Turk but Ibrahim, taking suspicion for proof, would have immediately inflicted death upon the accused; but Ibrahim saw through the design of his concealed enemy, and was convinced of the innocence of her whose destruction had been determined upon, for no other reason than that her talents and firmness were dreaded.

This intrigue, defeated by prudence, remained a secret between the two families. It was, however, soon followed by another, which was but too successful. Ali no longer dreaded Ibrahim, for he had acquired a knowledge of the weakness of that pasha. But he was extremely jealous of the influence and abilities of Sepher Bey, the brother of Ibrahim; and accordingly he determined to rid himself of one who was so obnoxious; an enterprise the more difficult as the destined victim was on his guard.

The district of Zagori, the ancient Perrhæbia, has, from time immemorial, supplied a considerable part of Turkey with medical practitioners, who are known by the denomination of Caloiatri, or good physicians. The knowledge of these men is merely traditional; they are, in fact, only empirics, ignorant of the principles of medicine and anatomy, though in some surgical operations they display much manual dexterity. It was one of these quacks that Ali selected as the instrument of his crime, and he promised him forty purses as a reward for the destruction of his enemy. No sooner had the doctor taken the road to Berat, than, more effectually to cover his plans, Ali caused his wife and children to be arrested, as being privy to his flight, and detained them, ostensibly as hostages, but in reality as pledges for the emissary's secrecy and fidelity. At the same time he wrote to Ibrahim, desiring him to send back the fugitive. Thinking that a man so persecuted must be deserving of his confidence, Sepher Bey took him into his service, and the cunning Perrhæbian so ingratiated himself with his new protector, that he became his physician and confidential friend. A slight illness of Sepher soon furnished the treacherous attendant with an opportunity of consummating his villany. The fatal potion was administered. As soon as he had perpetrated the crime, the assassin, aided by the emissaries of Ali, took flight, and hastened to Ioannina to receive the price of blood. Ali complimented him on his address, and gave an order upon the treasury for the stipulated sum; but when the homicide was about to quit the seraglio, he was seized and hanged by command of Ali, who was anxious to rid himself of the sole witness of his guilt. He even took advantage of this act of perfidy, by proclaiming that he had caused the assassin of Sepher Bey to be punished; at the same time publishing the particulars of the poisoning, the suspicion of which he artfully contrived should fall on the wife of Ibrahim Pasha, whom he represented as being jealous of her brother-in-law's influence. This base insinuation he was sedulous in propagating, not only at Constantinople, but wherever he possessed any interest; and, although he doubted its being generally credited, yet he well knew that, notwithstanding the wounds inflicted by calumny may be healed, their scars will last for ever. The pertinacity with which he slandered the wife of Ibrahim, who had once loved, and was even believed to have too far yielded to him, may perhaps be accounted for by her having become sincerely attached to her husband, as well as by Ali's supposed dread of her talents and resolute character.

Pushing still further his mingled hypocrisy and effrontery, he converted his own calumnies into a pretext for invasive projects. He began to arm, and, as a reason for arming, he assigned his wish to avenge the death of Sepher Bey. As it was obvious that his hostilities were intended to be directed against Ibrahim, that pasha prudently determined to save Berat from invasion, by finding sufficient occupation for Ali in an opposite quarter. He accordingly contrived to incite against him the beys of Thesprotia, and they drew into their league the hardy mountaineers of Suli, who were already preparing to make war upon the Turks at the instigation of Russia. It was thus that originated, in the spring of 1790, the first war between the Suliots and Ali Pasha.

Before we proceed to the narrative of the Suliot contest, it may be proper to give a brief account of the singular people by whom it was so bravely and perseveringly maintained, and of the wild and almost impenetrable district which was their abode. Whence was derived the name of Suli is doubtful; some trace it to the Sollion mentioned by Thucydides; but the natives themselves traditionally deduced it from an Albanian Mahometan, called Sulis, slain by their ancestors, the first settlers, whose name they gave to their principal town, in order to commemorate their victory. The Selli of Homer, are supposed to have inhabited this district.

The territory which was occupied by the Suliotes is situated in one of the ruggedest parts of the rugged and lofty Cassiopæan chain of mountains, near the source of the ancient Acheron, which now bears the name of Glykys. From Suli to Ioannina and Arta is fourteen hours' journey, to Prevesa thirteen, to Parga and Paramithia eight, and to Margariti six. The beauty, or rather the sublimity, of the country, and the almost insuperable difficulties which such a country opposes to an invader, may be understood from the descriptions which travellers have given of their first approach to it. "After riding half an hour, and turning to the left," says Mr. Hughes, "we were astonished by a view of the dark rocks of Suli, and the defile of the Acheron; but no pen can do justice to the scenery! It seemed as if we were about to penetrate into Tartarus itself and the awful recesses of the Plutonian realms!—the scenery increased in grandeur as we proceeded, and the pass was bordered on each side by perpendicular rocks, broken into every form of wild magnificence: through these some terrible convulsion of nature had opened a passage for the torrent, whose waters, thundering along their deep and rocky bed, formed, as they fell from crag to crag, a tumultuous kind of melody, that finely harmonised with the scene." After having ascended "a winding path cut on the side of precipices, so narrow as not to admit two persons to ride abreast," he reached the central point of the Suliot republic; and here, says he, " the singular and striking features of this wild mountain scenery kept us for a time almost breathless with astonishment; its huge broken masses, rocks, precipices, and chasms, appeared like the ruins of a disjointed world, or like that picture of poetic confusion where Pelion, Ossa, and Olympus, are heaped upon each other by the arms of Titanic monsters." The feelings of Dr. Holland were no less excited than those of Mr. Hughes by this miraculous scene.

" On the second day," says he, " I reached a pass, where the river Suli (the Acheron), making a remarkable bend to the north, enters the magnificent region of the same name. The landscape here is singularly fine; and from the place where I reached its banks to the castle of Suli, and the plains of Paramithia, the scenery along its course is more singular than any other I have seen in Greece, striking as this country is in all its natural features. Crossing the river by a deep ford, where it makes this sudden turn to the north, I ascended the mountain on the eastern side of the pass or chasm which it now enters, and which is so much contracted by opposing cliffs, to the height of some hundred feet above the stream, that no access is possible, except along the higher ledges of its mountain boundary. The ascent was one of extreme difficulty, and some danger. Skirting under the summit of the mountain, upon narrow and broken ledges of rock, I came to a spot where the interior of this profound chasm opened suddenly before me; vast, and almost perpendicular precipices, conducting the eye downwards to the dark line which the river forms in flowing beneath. The view from this place, I have never seen surpassed in grandeur,— if grandeur, indeed, be a word which expresses the peculiarity of the scenery: not only its magnitude, but also the boldness and abruptness of all its forms, and a sort of sombre depth and obscurity in all its features, to which it could not be easy to find a parallel. In one view you may trace the progress of the river for six or seven miles, between mountains, some of which are upwards of 3,000 feet in height; their precipitous sides beginning to rise even from the edge of the water; their projecting cliffs and ledges covered with small oaks and brushwood; and higher up, where they recede further from the perpendicular line, retaining the same sombre character from the dark thickets and rows of pines which appear at intervals among the rocks.—I continued my route along the valley I have described, on a rugged path, which winds through the rocks at the height of about 600 or 700 feet above the river. When advanced about four miles within the pass, we suddenly turned to the right, through a deep recess among the mountains. From this there seemed no egress; vast precipices, covered with pine, meet the eye on all sides; and no point seems accessible beyond that on which you stand at the moment."

The traditions of the Suliots, with respect to the origin of their community, did not extend further back than towards the middle of the seventeenth century. The manner in which it was formed is variously related. Some persons (and their opinion is not unplausible) imagine that the nucleus of the Suliote population consisted of Albanians, who, after the death of Scanderbeg, sought refuge in this inaccessible district from the despotism of the Turks. By some it is said that, about a century and a half ago, some goat and swine herds, who had led their animals to feed on the heights of Kiaffa, were struck with the eligibility of the site, and occupied it with their families; while others affirm, that the primitive settlers were shepherds from the neighbourhood of Gardiki, who fled hither, with their flocks, to escape from the tyranny of their Ottoman masters. It is obvious, that the last two stories are by no means incompatible with each other. But, however the republic may have begun, there seems to be no doubt that, about the year 1660, it consisted of four large villages, Kako Suli, Kiaffa, Avaricos, and Samoniva. These were collectively called the Tetrachorion. They stood upon a fine plain, two thousand feet above the bed of the Acheron; the rock, forming a natural breastwork, descended precipitously to the river, and behind rose a lofty chain of mountains. A single serpentine defile, three miles in length, passing through a labyrinth of steeps, forests, and rocks, and fortified at every mile with towers, supplied the sole means of access to these aërial haunts.

Forty years subsequent to this period, the population had so much increased, that the Suliots founded seven new villages towards the foot of the mountain, in the country which they had subjugated. These villages, Tzicuri, Pericati, Vilia, Alsochori, Kondati, Gionala, and Tzephleki, bore the collective appellation of the Heptachorion. They constituted a part of the general league called the Warrior Confederacy, and were considered as advanced posts. On the first rumour of war, they sent their families up the mountain to the four parent villages, and took arms to defend the entrance of their defiles.

In process of time, the Suliots extended their conquests into the adjacent plains. They had to sustain several wars against the agas of Margariti, Paramithia, and Ioannina, in the course of which they made themselves masters of sixty-six villages, peopled by more than seven thousand inhabitants. Their policy, however, was not equal to their valour. It has often been remarked, that those who possess the greatest share of freedom are the harshest masters; the Suliots certainly did not form an exception to the rule. Instead of attaching to them their fellow Christians, and converting them into an accession of strength — for the majority of the vanquished were Christians—they contrived to make the Mahometan sway regretted. In peace, they disarmed and in various ways oppressed them; in war, they carried off the provisions of their tributaries, when they were not strong enough to defend them, and this injustice they aggravated by refusing to grant them an asylum in the fastnesses of the hills.

The Suliots, in truth, though possessed of heroic qualities, had but a scanty portion of those qualities which conciliate affection. In their eyes bravery and love of country were the cardinal virtues; and war and plunder the chief business of life. As they held traffic of any kind to be a degradation, and their circumscribed territory did not always produce enough for their subsistence, they supplied the deficiency by pillaging their Mussulman neighbours, and also such of the Christians as were unable to shake off the yoke. Their creed upon this head was contained in a few pithy words. "The lands which the Turks occupy," said they, " are not theirs; they belonged to our forefathers. Our forefathers were deprived of them by force; and we, their children and heirs, have a right to obtain the means of existing, by wresting from the Turks all that we are able to seize upon. As to the Greeks and the other Christians, who labour for the Turks, let them take up arms with us, to reconquer our country, or let them submit to be treated like those who have robbed us of it."

Of the Suliot population, fifteen hundred men were usually in readiness to take the field, of whom the Tetrachorion furnished a thousand, and the Heptachorion five hundred. In the desperate struggles with Ali, the Suliots appear to have increased their force by an additional thousand men. As soon as hostilities were begun, the villages in the plain were abandoned, after having been stripped of their moveables and provisions, and all the community hastened to the defence of the passes, each man knowing beforehand the post which he was to occupy. In the day of action, the women brought food and ammunition to their relatives, encouraged them to fight manfully, covered them with reproaches when they gave way, and even, on urgent occasions, fought with unflinching courage. Never to fly, never to be dismayed by any number of enemies, were maxims which were early instilled into the minds of the mountaineers of Suli; weapons were put into the hands of boys at the age of ten years, and the use of them, and a deadly hatred of the Turks, were the first, and almost the only, lessons which they were taught. A Suliot was never separated from his arms; not even when he went to church, drove his flocks to pasture, ate, or slept. Their tactics were simple and desultory; depending rather on individual intelligence and activity than on combined and simultaneous efforts. One peculiarity of their military system, if system it can be called, deserves notice. To a large force they opposed a small one; to a small force, a large one. In the one case, the lesser number sufficed to hold their ground, and more was not to be hoped from any increase which they could make; in the other their aim was to render success as complete as possible, and to swell the amount of prisoners, that they might enrich themselves by plunder, sale, or ransom.

One mode which was employed to stimulate the courage of the Suliots displays a considerable knowledge of human nature. If a Suliot manifested any signs of cowardice, the ignominy was visited upon his wife in a manner which could not fail to wound her feelings deeply. When she went to the spring to draw water, or to take her cattle to drink, her more fortunate companions, though there might be a hundred of them, were entitled to keep her aloof from the spring, till they were first served. A Suliot female, who wished to avoid this insult, or its repetition, had no other resource than to separate from her husband, or to rouse him to the retrieving of his character by some signal act of intrepidity.

Of the religion of the people of Suli, M. Fouqueville speaks in very unfavourable terms. "To fast under pain of death during the four Lents, to keep the long series of holidays in the Greek calendar, to give some alms to the churches, and to cross themselves frequently, constituted," says he, " all the religion of the Suliots." After darkly hinting at their being tainted with oriental depravity, he adds, "the prayer of a Suliot to God was, to ask him for rich booty in his expeditions, and the opportunity of sacrificing some Mahometans. The Turks, on their part, believed that they were doing an acceptable service to Heaven, by putting such men to death whenever they could lay hands on them. Thus barbarism being opposed to barbarism, and fanaticism to fanaticism, produced on both sides an atrocious warfare."

There were no courts of justice, no written or unwritten laws, no judicial precedents, in the republic of Suli. Whatever differences arose between individuals were settled by the heads of tribes to which the parties belonged, and their sentence was final. The tribes were called Pharas, and were forty-seven in number. Each Phara was presided over by its oldest and most respected member; and the whole forty-seven leaders of tribes formed a council, which decided upon all public affairs.

Of their customs some were curious. Men were forbidden to interfere in any quarrel, whether between men or women, even though their object was to reconcile the quarrellers. Women alone were allowed to act the part of peace-makers. It was doubtless, and wisely, apprehended, that the intervention of a male mediator, especially as that mediator always bore arms, would tend only to envenom a dispute, and increase the number of combatants. Those who begin by being reconcilers, often end by being inveterate participators in a feud. The lives of women were protected by a singular custom, which, however, is said to have been effectual. "The Suliot who murdered a woman," says M. Fauriel, " was condemned to maintain at his own cost as many citizens as it was to be presumed the deceased female would have borne children had she not been killed. To a Suliot such a punishment was worse than death; and, accordingly, each avoided, with a sort of terror, every occasion of being in a passion with and striking a woman." There were, nevertheless, if M. Fouqueville may be credited, certain cases in which little mercy was shown to the softer sex. He tells us that, even on the slightest suspicion of gallantry, a husband, or the head of a tribe, could order a wife to be sewn up in a sack, and thrown from the summit of the rocks into the waters of the Acheron.

The appearance of the Suliots was in unison with their character and pursuits. Among them were to be found models of form. Exposed constantly to the elements—for they had no tents in their expeditions, and slept on the bare ground wrapt in their shaggy capotes—their skin assumed almost the hue of bronze.

The sabre, not the ataghan, was their favourite weapon. "By his middle stature, his voice as piercing as an eagle's, his gestures, his abrupt and agile movements," says M. Pouqueville, "he shows to you at the first glance, the mountain warrior. His irascibility, and his bursts of passion, betray his antique origin. You recognise in him the descendant of the victors of the Granicus; he has their fire, their daring, their splendid qualities, and their defects."

With such a people, situated so perilously as they were for him on his southern frontier, it is not likely that, under any circumstances, Ali would long have remained at peace. They were too sharp a thorn in his side for him not to make an attempt to pluck it out. But the contest seems to have been hastened by the intrigues of the Russians and of the pasha of Berat.

It was in the spring of 1790 that hostilities commenced between Ali and the Suliots. He had not yet learned to appreciate justly their courage and resources. Three thousand men, whom he sent against them, found the Suliots entrenched in the mountains, and, not daring to attack such a formidable position, they seized all the peasants, provisions, and cattle belonging to the villages on the plain, which the Suliots had not had time to remove. Enraged at this, the mountaineers despatched from their rocks a body of troops, which, falling furiously on the pasha's soldiers, routed them with great slaughter, rescued the captives, secured the spoil, and pursued the fugitives into the valley of Ioannina, burning all the country-houses and mosques which lay in their route.

Ali would probably have endeavoured to take immediate vengeance for this defeat, had he not been summoned to join the Turkish army on the Danube. He did not return till autumn. We have no record of his exploits in this campaign. M. Pouqueville asserts, that they were confined to seeing the smoke of the German bivouacs, and to bringing back with him several hundred Servians and Bulgarians, of whom he formed two small colonies in his pashalik. There is, however, no ground for believing that he would shrink from the perils of war; a want of courage was not among his faults.

In the spring of 1791, the Suliots emerged from their rocky recesses, and began their operations by plundering and wasting Amphilochia. They pushed their incursions to such an extent that commerce with Lower Albania was entirely interrupted, and it was impossible to pass the defiles into the south of the valley of Ioannina without numerous escorts, which they often defeated. They were even daring enough to extend their ravages as far as the defiles of Pindus; nor did they withdraw to their own district till winter compelled them. In these inroads they were guilty of more than one act of gross impolicy; they pillaged friends as well as foes, and involved themselves in a quarrel with the leaders of the Armatoles, and with various Turkish districts which had hitherto been friendly to them, or at least neutral. Ali availed himself of their imprudence to bind closer to his interest the chiefs of the Armatoles.

Finding that their reduction could not easily be accomplished without first depriving them of the support of the pasha of Berat, Ali represented to him that it was their mutual interest to destroy a Christian confederation, which only served to slay the followers of Mahomet, and diminish the power of the Porte. He at length succeeded in gaining over Ibrahim, who, giving way to his religious prejudices, conceived that he performed a meritorious deed in abandoning the Suliots to their fate. The marriage of his youngest daughter with Veli Bey, Ali's second son, already affianced to her, confirmed their reconciliation.

Previously to renewing the war against Suli, Ali seems to have thought it prudent to secure his northern frontier. His movements in that quarter had a double purpose; to establish, in the first place, a safe communication between Ioannina and his native territory of Tepelen, and, in the next, to hold more completely the pasha of Berat in check. For these ends he seized upon, and fortified, the strong post of Klissura, on the road to Berat, where the Aous or Voïussa, enters the deep defile which was occupied by Philip in the first Macedonian war, and where, till the key of his position was betrayed, that monarch held at bay the legions of Flaminius. Ali also made himself master of the districts along the Desnitza, from its source to its confluence with the Voïussa, and of various others in this part of Albania.

Ali, meanwhile, was not negligent of his principal object, the subjugation of Suli. Irritated by the Suliots, many of the Armatoles had, as we have already stated, enrolled themselves under his banner; those who did not join him, consented to remain neutral. From the beys of Thesprotia, who were roused by having been plundered, he obtained reinforcements, and he was joined by a corps of auxiliaries, supplied by Ibrahim Pasha. These, with his own troops, formed an army of fifteen thousand strong, the Mahometan portion of which had sworn on the Koran to conquer or die. The confederates moved from Ioannina on the 1st of July, 1792.

Large as his force was, it was chiefly on a plan for surprising the Suliots that Ali built his hopes of success. At the outset, therefore, he did not make public his real object, but gave out that he intended to attack the Mussulman town of Argyro Castro, the beys of which had early been his enemies, and who had now rejected a governor whom he had nominated. Such being his pretended purpose, he strove to lull the Suliots into security, and deprive them of a part of their strength, by complimenting their valour, and inviting them to co-operate in his expedition. The letter, which he wrote to two of their most celebrated captains, was conceived in the following terms:—

"My friends Botzari and Tzavella,

"I, Ali Pasha, salute you, and kiss your eyes. Being well acquainted with your courage and spirit, and thinking that I stand in the utmost need of your assistance, I most earnestly entreat that, on the receipt of this letter, you will, without delay, assemble all your palikars, and come to meet me, that I may march against my enemies. The moment is now arrived, in which you can essentially serve me, and give proofs of your friendship and affection. Your pay shall be double that of my Albanians, for I know your valour is superior to theirs. As I shall not go to war before you arrive, I entreat you to come quickly. This is all I have to communicate at present, and so farewell."

A council was called, by Botzari and Tzavella, to which this letter was read. The artifice of the pasha was seen through by the sharp-sighted Suliots; being, however, unwilling to enrage him by showing that they had penetrated his secret, they replied, that their warriors were wanted at home to defend their country, but that being desirous to oblige his Highness, and acquire his good will, they had given permission to Captain Tzavella to join him at the head of seventy palikars. "This reinforcement," said they, "will suffice to render you everywhere victorious."

Though inly stung by his disappointment, Ali concealed his anger, and as soon as the detachment arrived from Suli, he began his march in the direction of Argyro Castro. Scarcely had he proceeded twenty miles, before he halted and encamped. Either to repose, or to indulge in their accustomed manly sports, Tzavella and his companions incautiously laid aside their arms. This opportunity, which the halt had been made for the purpose of affording, was instantly seized to arrest them. Only three of the Suliots could snatch their weapons; two of them fell, covered with wounds, the third escaped, swam unhurt amidst a shower of bullets over the river Kalamas, and reached Suli in time to warn his countrymen of their danger.

Ali then turned his march towards Suli, and reached the mountain on the following day; but finding the Suliots on the alert, he deferred his attack, and resorted again to artful negociation. Ordering Tzavella to be brought before him, he alternately tried promises and menaces, the hope of ample riches, and the dread of being flayed alive, to induce him to betray his country. " Release me from my fetters then," said Tzavella, " for while you retain me in them my countrymen will never submit." At the same time the Suliot held forth an expectation that, if liberated, he would use his influence to lead them to submission. On Ali demanding what security his captive would give to return, should he not succeed, Tzavella replied, " My only son, Foto, who is a thousand times dearer to me, and more valuable to his country, than my own life." The terms were accepted, and the Suliot chief was set at liberty.

On reaching Suli, the chief assembled the council, expatiated in the strongest terms upon the treachery and sanguinary disposition of Ali, recommended hasty preparations for a strenuous resistance, and nobly declared, that no concern for him and his relatives ought to have the slightest weight with them, as every member of his family would glory in sacrificing his existence for his country. As soon as all was ready to meet the vizier's attack, Tzavella despatched to him the following letter:—

"Ali Pasha, I rejoice that I have deceived a deceiver: it is to defend my country against a robber that I am here. My son will die, but I will fearfully avenge him before my death. Some Turks, like yourself, will say that I am a pitiless father to make my son a victim for my own liberation. I answer that if you had taken our mountain, you would have massacred my son, with all my family and my countrymen, without my having the power to revenge their murder. If we are victorious, I shall have other children, for my wife is young. As to my son, young as he is, he will be happy to sacrifice himself for his country, or he is not worthy to live, nor to be acknowledged as a child of mine, He will die with courage; if he do not, he does not deserve to be called a worthy son of Greece, our country. Advance then, thou traitor! I am impatient for revenge; I, thy sworn enemy, Captain Lambro Tzavella."

Exasperated as he was at the failure of his scheme, Ali did not deem it expedient to put young Tzavella to death, but sent him to be imprisoned at Ioannina. When the youth was brought before Veli Pasha and Ali's minister, Mahomet Effendi, they put his courage to the test, by telling him that they had received orders to roast him alive. "Have you?" said the intrepid stripling, "then if my father conquers, he will serve you the same." Veli then directed him to be confined in one of the monasteries of the island.

Ali seemed at first inclined to try the efficacy of a blockade in reducing the Suliots. But intelligence which he received of a plan formed by them to carry him off even from the midst of his camp, irritated him so much, that he determined to come immediately to action. As was their wont, the Suliots abandoned the villages in the plain, and posted themselves in their towers, and among the rocks, for the defence of the passes. The Albanians advanced, but at the pass of Klissura they were met by such a heavy fire from the tower of Tichos and from the Suliots on the eminences, while fragments of rock were rolled down on them by the women and children, that they fell by hundreds, the entrance of the strait was nearly choked up by the dead, and the survivors began to show signs of hesitation. Ali, who was watching their movements from a neighbouring mountain, restored their ardour by the promise of large rewards, and particularly one of five hundred purses to the man who should first penetrate into Kako Suli. Again the combat was renewed, with redoubled fury, and, at length, after several hours' fighting, the Suliots, exhansted, and short of ammunition, fell back towards Kiaffa. The Turks followed, leaving behind them unreduced the tower of Tichos. Another struggle, long, desperate, and deadly, ensued, which was only suspended by a farther retreat of the Suliots towards their capital, the position of Kiaffa being no longer tenable. Even the great fort upon Khungi, which commanded the profound chasm of the Tripa between Kiaffa and Kako Suli, was so weakly garrisoned as to be unable to intercept the pursuers. The retiring Suliots were closely tracked by their exulting foes. Never before had the feet of infidels advanced so far into the mountains of Suli. At this moment, and when the fate of the republic hung as it were by a thread, the tide of war was turned by female heroism. Roused by the cries of danger, which echoed through the hills,

Mosco, the wife of Tzavella, armed the women of Kako Suli, and rushed forward with them to join in the general defence. They stopped their receding countrymen, and headed them in a vigorous attack upon the assailants, who, breathless with climbing the steeps, were ill able to repel this furious charge. All animated by the same generous passion, the love of their country, the Suliots, both men and women, seemed now to have but one soul, and, as it were, one body. While some, re-supplied with ammunition, kept up a hot fire, others united their strength to roll down immense masses of rocks on their invaders. The Albanians fled; and at this moment their confusion was increased by assaults upon their flanks. The Turkish column was broken to its very centre. The scattered fugitives endeavoured to escape down the pass, but their number was every moment thinned by their pursuers, and when they reached the tower of Tichos, their flight was effectually intercepted by a sally of the garrison. Of those who had entered the defile scarcely a man escaped, and the bed of the Acheron was encumbered with the bodies of the slain.

Foremost among the victorious republicans was the heroine Mosco. On her reaching the tower of Tichos, she found her nephew lying dead there, with nine other young Suliots, who had died in defending it. Throwing herself on the bleeding corpse, she kissed his lips, covered him with her apron, and exclaimed, " My beloved nephew, I am come too late to save thy life, but I can at least avenge thy death upon thy murderers." Having uttered these few words, she rushed onward with her countrymen to complete the victory, by crushing the remaining force of the pasha. No farther stand was attempted to be made by the panic-smitten Albanians. They were hunted and cut down in all directions, and happy were those who could find a temporary refuge in the woods and mountains. About six thousand were slain or taken prisoners, and it was some weeks before all the dispirited remnants of the Turkish army could be collected together. Baggage, ammunition, and arms, all fell into the hands of the conquerors. Ali himself was so hotly pursued, that he killed two horses before he could reach his capital. He could only rally a thousand men, and with these he entered Ioannina during the night. To conceal his defeat, he preceded his arrival by a proclamation, forbidding the inhabitants to appear at the windows, or even in the streets; and so much were his spirits depressed by his reverse of fortune, that he shut himself up in his harem for several days, and admitted only a few of his confidential friends.

By a juction with the Kimariots, the Suliots soon became sufficiently strong to commence offensive operations. Unable to make head against them, Ali was compelled to consent to a disadvantageous peace. He ceded all the territory which they had won, as far as Dervitziana, restored the seventy prisoners and the son of Tzavella, and paid a hundred thousand piastres for the ransom of his captive soldiers. The beys of Paramithia and Margariti, whom he had seduced or intimidated to join him in warring upon the Suliots, were also under the necessity of signing a separate treaty, by which they bound themselves to be thenceforth in alliance with the republic.

Scarcely were these treaties signed before Ali found himself implicated in an affair that threatened his very existence, and to clear himself from which required the utmost efforts of the crafty Albanian. His enemies had discovered his secret correspondence with Russia, and had obtained proof against him, bearing his seal, which appeared sufficient to decide his fate. A capidgi bashi was immediately despatched from Constantinople to Ioannina, to institute a judicial inquiry.

Upon the arrival of the officer, he immediately proceeded to open before Ali the evidence of the pasha's intelligence with the enemies of the Porte; and for this once truth appeared likely to prevail. But, though the satrap was alarmed, he did not lose his presence of mind. " In the opinion of his highness," said he, " I must be culpable, for this is my seal, and I cannot deny it; but the body of the letter is not in the writing of my secretaries; some one must have surreptitiously used my seal, for the purpose of ruining me. I entreat you to grant me a few days, that I may fathom this mystery of iniquity, which compromises me in the sight of my master and of all good Mussulmans. May God enable me to establish my innocence, which, though appearances are against me, is as pure as the light of the sun."

After the lapse of a few days, during which Ali affected to be engaged in a secret investigation of the plot formed against him, but which were really passed in forming plans to extricate himself, he hit upon a scheme which promised to answer his purpose. He sent for a Greek, on whom he thought he could rely, to whom, without betraying its real tenor, he communicated his design. "Thou knowest," said he, "that I have always esteemed thee, and the moment is now come when I will make thy fortune. From this day thou art my son, thy children are mine, and my palace shall be ever open to thee. In return for my benefits, I ask from thee but a trifling service, a mere matter of form. Thou art aware that the rascally capidgi bashi, who arrived here within these few days, has brought with him certain papers, bearing my seal, which are to be made use of to extort money from me. I have given too much already; and this time, without opening my purse, unless to a good servant like thee, I wish to silence my enemy. Therefore, my son, when I give thee notice, thou must be before the tribunal, and there, in the presence of the capidgi bashi and the cadi, thou must declare that thou art the writer of the letters attributed to me, and that, without my knowledge, thou didst make use of my seal, in order to give them an official value."

At these words the Greek turned pale, and was about to reply. " What dost fear, my beloved friend? Am I not thy kind master? Thou gainest my affection for ever. What canst thou apprehend while I protect thee? Would the capidgi bashi dare to act here without my leave? No; I have thrown twenty men of his sort into the lake. Ali Pasha is not fallen so low as to suffer any one to interfere with his rights. With a subject I would not condescend to resort to entreaty —but I am not on such terms with thee, I know thy attachment, and, if thou hast still any doubts, I swear to thee, in the name of my prophet, and by my own and my children's heads, that *no harm shall befall thee from the capidgi bashi.* But, that our affair may succeed as we wish, mind that thou dost not talk about what I have confided to thee."

The Greek, who knew that the sword of Ali impended over his head, was fain to comply: he promised to give the required testimony, and he was immediately dismissed. Ali then ordered the capidgi bashi to be introduced, and said, with much apparent emotion, " I have at length got to the bottom of the infernal plot which has been hatched against me. It is the work of a man paid by the implacable enemies of the empire, an agent of Russia. I have him in my power, but have given him hopes of a pardon, provided he will make ample confession. Repair, therefore, to the tribunal, and let the cadi, the judges, and the primates of the city, be assembled to hear the deposition of the delinquent."

The court was speedily convened, and the trembling Greek was asked, in presence of the capidgi bashi, whether he knew the hand-writing of the letters. " It is mine."—" Whose is this seal ? "—" It is that of my master, Ali Pasha."—" How came it at the bottom of these letters?"—" I myself affixed it, abusing the confidence of my master, who sometimes entrusted me with it, for the purpose of signing his orders."—" That is enough, withdraw !"

Anxious for the success of his scheme, Ali was entering the cadi's court-yard, when a signal from one of his officers informed him of its prosperous issue. According to previous order, the deluded Greek, upon quitting the Court, was instantly seized and hanged, without being allowed to utter a single syllable. Ali then entered the justice-chamber, and demanded the result of the inquiry. His innocence was declared by acclamation. " It is well," said the satrap, " the guilty author of the crime which was imputed to me is no more ; he has just been hanged by my command. Thus perish all the enemies of our glorious Sultan." Copies of the examination were then taken, for the purpose of being sent to Constantinople, and the good word of the capidgi bashi was ensured by a present of fifty purses. Ali, at the same time, forwarded rich presents to many members of the divan, by whose influence he was again restored to the confidence of the Grand Signior.

CHAPTER V.

Destruction of the Bossigradians—Operations of Ali in Central Albania—Kara Mustapha—Designs of Bonaparte on Greece—Report of M. Arnault on Albania—Objects of Ali—He writes to Bonaparte—His connexion with the French—Massacre at Aghio Vassili, &c.—Revolt of Passwan Oglou—Bonaparte writes to Ali—Ali turns against the French—Butrinto evacuated by the French—Ali defeats the French at Nicopolis—He takes Prevesa—Barbarous Treatment of the Prisoners—The Russians excite the Hatred of Ali—Honours lavished upon Ali.

HAVING thus escaped from the danger which threatened him, Ali, the more effectually to hoodwink the government as to his designs, now determined to gratify the wish of the divan, by exerting himself in his capacity of dervendji bashi, to suppress the numerous banditti by which Rumelia was infested. The performance of this task would also afford him an opportunify of extending his encroachments. Among the most obnoxious of the robbers were the inhabitants of Bossigrad, a small town between the lakes of Kastoria and Ochrida, the fame of whose depredations extended as far as Constantinople. The task of chastising them he committed to Paleopoulo and Canavos, two of the leaders of Greek Armatoles. The enterprise failed, in consequence of the disgust excited in the Albanian Mahometans, by their being placed under the command of Christians. Force having proved ineffectual against the freebooters, Ali resorted to artifice. He sent them a letter, in which he told them, that, being a sincere admirer of their courage, he wished to have them for his most faithful servants, and therefore would give them honourable and lucrative employments, if they would enter into his service. The love of flattery, and the love of gain, by which so many have been ruined, were destructive to the Bossigradians. Seduced by his compliments and his offers, numbers of them hastened to Ioannina, and his perfidious kindness soon thinned Bossigrad of its bravest defenders. When this was accomplished, Ali despatched some chosen troops, under Yussuf, who traversed the ridge of Pindus by unfrequented roads, fell suddenly upon the town, and put to the sword or to the torture all who dared to resist. At the same time the Bossigradians whom he had lured to Ioannina perished by the hand of the executioner. This treacherous conquest opened to the pasha the road to the canton of Caulonias; an important position, as it laid open to him a passage into Central and Upper Albania.

Ali's expedition against the Bossigradians was scarcely terminated, when Albania experienced one of those political storms so common in Turkey. Mustapha Busakli, the pasha of Scutari, either guilty or suspected of treasonable designs, was declared *fermanli* by the Porte, or, in other words, was excommunicated and put to the ban of the empire. The pashas, beys, and other great feudatories, in consequence received orders to march against Kara Mustapha, or Black Mustapha, as he was opprobriously called after the passing of the sentence against him. As in this instance his interest was in unison with his duty, Ali was one of the first to take the field; the service of his sovereign was his pretence, his own aggrandisement was the real motive. Accordingly, instead of joining the Rumili-valisee, who had proceeded towards Dibres, he marched in the direction of Caulonias. On this occasion, he rallied round his standard many of the chiefs of the Armatoles, among the most conspicuous of whom were Paleopoulo and his brother-in-law Canavos. The valour displayed by these chiefs in various skirmishes and assaults is said to have excited his envy, and of course his hatred. Having seized the strong post of Gheortcha, he took Ochrida by storm, and put the vanquished to the sword. By becoming master of Ochrida, he gained over to his party the neighbouring beys of western Macedonia, who were naturally jealous of the authority of the Porte. Nor was this the sole advantage arising from the conquest. The province of Ochrida, situated in the mountains between Macedonia and central Albania, includes within itself all the defiles which lead from Constantinople into the pashalik of Berat. Thus, Ali not only very nearly cut off the communication between the Ottoman capital and Upper Albania, but, likewise, flanked the possessions of Ibrahim Pasha on the east and north, as he already did on the south, and could in future harass him on every side except that of the sea. The post of Gheortcha also gave him an excellent military position, which covered a considerable part of his northern frontier, and formed, on the east, the key to the whole range of Pindus, that divides Epirus from Thessaly.

The real purpose being answered for which he had put his troops in motion, Ali seems to have slackened in his exertions, if even he did not discontinue them. It is certain that he accomplished nothing more against Kara Mustapha; it is not unlikely, that he had a secret understanding with him. Though he was sorely pressed by the Ottoman general, the proscribed Mustapha at length came triumphant out of the contest. With only seventy-two men he gallantly defended the castle of Scutari against twenty thousand besiegers, till a general insurrection of the Albanians of his pashalik, which was provoked by the excesses of the Turks, compelled the Rumili-valisee to raise the siege, and fly with his shattered army. Finding that it could not put down Mustapha, the Porte retracted its anathema, confirmed him in his office, and even appointed him Rumili-valisee in the place of his recent opponent. Either, however, because he had so agreed with Ali, or that the league of Macedonian beys which the astute pasha had formed was too powerful for him to encounter, Mustapha remained at Scutari, and made no attempt to take up his residence at Monastir, which was the official abode of a Rumili-valisee.

Hitherto, the shock of the French revolution, which had convulsed so many European states, had not been felt in the Ottoman dominions. Its influence now began to be extended to them. By their shameful subversion of the Venetian government, the French republic acquired the possessions of that government in the Adriatic, and consequently became a neighbour of Turkey in that quarter. It appears, too, that projects which as yet perhaps had hardly assumed a definite shape, but which certainly were not favourable to the Porte, were being brooded over both by the directory and by Bonaparte. It is indubitable, that a correspondence was opened by the latter with the Greeks of the Morea, and with the pashas of Scutari, Ioannina, and other Albanian districts; and that he ordered his officers in the Ionian Islands, to encourage the Greeks in a wish for independence, and " to talk of Greece, of Athens, and of Sparta." In one of his letters to the directory, at a later period, he says, " I have already some intercourse with the principal chiefs of the country, and Greece may yet arise from its ashes." To conciliate these expected allies, but ostensibly as a " mark of his esteem and friendship for the Porte," he also issued a proclamation, directing that, in all Italian ports occupied by the French.

Ottoman subjects should enjoy perfect liberty, and that a special protection should be granted to the Greeks, and particularly to the Albanians.

Along with the squadron which was despatched to take possession of the Ionian Isles, Bonaparte sent M. Arnault, an eminent literary character, who has since acquired fame as a dramatist. Arnault was entrusted with the mission of examining the situation of the islands, and, which was perhaps the main point, of personally obtaining information with respect to Albania. He seems to have had but little liking for his task, especially the latter part of it, and to have cast only a hasty glance upon the coast of Epirus. The report which he made to Bonaparte was evidently not designed to induce the general to look upon the Greeks and Albanians as likely to be efficient auxiliaries. The poetical missionary appears, indeed, to have been strongly and equally prejudiced against both parties. It will be seen, too, that of the information which he gleaned, some is trivial, and some erroneous.

"As to the questions," says he, "which you put to me respecting Albania, there are several to which I can give no answer, but I will communicate to you all that I have been able to learn relative to the manners of its inhabitants, who are more barbarous than those whom we call savages in America.

"It would be an act of self-deception to suppose that there can be any other connexion between the French colony and the Albanians than what may result from a very limited commerce; they have uniformly destroyed every establishment which an attempt has been made to form amongst them. Lasalle, a French shipwright, was the victim, not many years since, of an essay of this kind. Ship-timber and cattle are the principal riches of Albania, which is peopled by hordes of robbers and shepherds.

"These shepherds, unlike the companions of Apollo, those who abode on the banks of the Alpheus and Amphrisas, have exchanged the crook and scrip of their ancestors for the musket and cartridge-box; the wild fig-tree, round which they assemble, is a real guard-house, where a sentinel is always upon duty.

"The spirit of robbery is carried to such a pitch among the Albanians, that the right of escheat, the right of seizing the fragments of a wreck, extends to the shipwrecked person. A bit of gold lace, a silver button, an object of the most trifling value, excites their cupidity, and causes the death of a human being.

"The appearance of an Albanian is strange and terrible; his costume is the ancient Greek costume, to which he adds an enormous mantle of coarse woollen cloth with a hairy surface, which, when he wraps himself up in it, gives him the look of a goat. His shirt, of coarse linen, with large sleeves, and descending to the knees, above the pantaloons, bears a perfect resemblance to the ancient tunic.

"His shoes, like the buskin of old, are fastened to his legs with straps; two monstrous mustachios intersect his sunburnt face; two pistols and a dagger fastened to his girdle; a long sabre, with the handle hanging downward, suspended to his side; a musket slung obliquely behind his back; a case with a pipe; and boxes for tobacco, shot, and powder; such is the complete equipment of an Albanian: he is a walking arsenal. Husbandmen, shepherds, robbers, all carry fire-arms, and make use of them with a skill which realises the prodigy of the man who could split balls into two equal halves by firing at the edge of a knife.

"Some Albanian villages are dependencies on the Venetian possessions, and at this moment are subject to the provisional government of Corfu. The rest of Lower and Upper Albania belongs to the Turks, and s ruled by two pashas hostile to each other; the Albanians follow the fortunes of these chiefs, one of whom, Ali, pasha of Ioannina, is in open rebellion against the Porte, while the other, Mustapha, pasha of Delvino, adheres to his sovereign. Frequent and furious combats take place, and frequent conflagrations hasten the depopulation of these deserts, which are stained with blood by a warfare no less obscure than calamitous.

"The two parties equally seek to gain the support of the French; Ali Pasha, especially, has made great advances. I believe even that he has asked and obtained an interview, of the object and issue of which only General Gentili (the governor of Corfu) can inform you.

"Besides the war between pasha and pasha, there also exists in Albania wars between pashas and individuals. In my short excursion to the coast of Epirus, I saw a papas (priest) who enjoyed such credit among his flock, that, at his mere summons, every man in the district would fly to arms. Ali, who has never been able to subdue him, offers an enormous price for his head. This soldier-priest, attended by his clergy, his staff officers, came to visit me, and solicit the friendship of the French.

"The Albanians speak neither Greek, nor Turkish, nor Italian; they have a peculiar idiom, which is interpreted to us by the Corfiotes, who farm the continental domains of the Venetian government. It would be difficult to keep up the least intercourse with them by means of printing; the knowledge of reading and writing being still more rare among them than it is in the islands, where we correspond with the villages only through the medium of the priests.

"This is what I have gathered as to Albania. I have likewise procured some particulars, which may be relied on, as to the present state of the Morea. With these I will close my letter, which perhaps is already too long.

"The glory of the French army, and the fame of your exploits, have resounded amidst the ruins of Sparta and Athens; but do not believe that the Greeks are our sincerest admirers; the Greeks (except the Mainotes) degraded and perverted by the subjection in which the Turks hold them, devote themselves wholly to husbandry and commerce, which are despised by the Mussulmans.

"Thieves, perfidious, inhospitable, they see in a stranger only an enemy or a prey; the Turks alone expect you, and repeat your name with enthusiasm, and, to the shame of an enlightened people, liberty has no partisans but among a people of tyrants."

Unfavourable as Arnault's report was to the Albanians, there was something in it which, in the judgment of the person to whom it was addressed, could not fail to neutralise all that was said against them. In the eyes of Bonaparte, one of the "moving arsenals," as the poet sarcastically called them, was of more value than a host of shepherds. Such men would be fit instruments, in case it became necessary, as he anticipated it would, to secure a share of the spoil in a partition of Turkey. Besides, it was necessary at present to be on good terms with the pashas of Albania, more especially with Ali, in order to procure the needful supplies for the Ionian Islands. The French general, therefore, still continued to carry on a correspondence with the satrap of Ioannina, the pasha of Scutari, and others, in spite of M. Arnault's invective.

Ali, on his part, had more than one reason for being desirous of French support. Backed by so powerful an ally as France, he might hope to establish his power on a firm basis; opposed by France, his situation would be unsafe and precarious. By lending his aid to his new neighbours, he might also hope to obtain the cession of one or more of the Venetian towns on the continent, an object which he had much at heart. It was, indeed, of the utmost importance to Ali that the French should not adopt towards Epirus the policy of the Venetian republic. The governors of the Ionian Islands, availing themselves of the anarchy which prevailed among the higher class of Albanians, had organised a league, composed of the beys along the coast, and of all the independent tribes, who, although divided when their individual interests were concerned, never failed to unite against the encroachments of the pashas. Thus, the Venetians covered their *terra firma* possessions, from Butrinto to Prevesa, by various confederations, which held in check the pasha of Delvino. On the other side, by means of the beys of Margariti and Paramithia, they, without striking a blow, arrested the enterprises of the pasha of Ioannina; while, to keep down the Mahometan beys, they made use of the Christian tribes of Suli and Acroceraunia. By these means, they had acquired a great preponderance in the affairs of Albania. Nor was this all. The politic Venetians had procured a clause to be inserted in their treaty with the Porte, that no subject of that state should build a fort or erect a battery within a mile of the Ionian coast, nor sail with any armed vessel through the channel of Corfu. Ali, therefore, could neither form a marine, nor fortify the single harbour which he possessed, the small port of Salagora, on the gulf of Arta.

It appears to have been early in the summer of 1797 that Ali first wrote to Bonaparte. His lan-

guage was highly flattering to the conqueror of Italy.
"The esteem and veneration which I cherish for
you, general," said the pasha, "and for a great and
powerful nation, have induced me to wish for its
friendship, which I cultivate with its ministers and
ambassadors: in following the example of my sovereign, I satisfy an inclination which is innate in me.
At all times I have given essential proofs of this
sincere feeling to all your countrymen whom I have
had the pleasure of knowing within my government,
and especially to M. Tozoni, your vice-consul here,
and to M. Dupré, your agent at Arta. They have
witnessed my joy on learning your victories, which
bring my friends nearer to me, and my unfeigned
wishes for the prosperity of your republic.

"Your heroic actions, general, which I admire in
common with all the world, make me desire to gain
your personal friendship; and the sympathy of our
military tastes is a sure pledge to me that I shall
obtain it.

"It will be agreeable to me to receive a testimony
of it, and to draw closer with the hero of France the
ties of friendship, which my heart has always deeply
felt for your nation; it is a real pleasure to me to
give the most distinguished reception and the most
decisive support to every Frenchman who comes
within the limits of my government.

"These feelings, general, embolden me to request
of you the favour to lend me, for a year or two, two
brave master artillerymen, and two bombardiers, who,
however, shall always be at your orders. I beg of
you to send them through the medium of M. Dupré,
your agent at Arta, who will be answerable to you
for them, and for the reward of their good services.
I shall be exceedingly grateful to you for this favour.

"I wish ardently, general, that time and circumstances may offer me the means of giving you proofs of my esteem and devotedness."

The intercourse thus opened with Bonaparte was kept up between Ali and General Gentili, who commanded the French troops in the Ionian Islands. As a proof of his amity, Ali not only exerted himself to afford supplies to the islands, but also furnished more than six hundred oxen, and offered, in case of need, to furnish corn and wine, for the squadron of Admiral Brueys. For these supplies he was never paid by his new friends. If, however, Ali failed to obtain the money which was justly due to him, he did not fail to derive considerable advantage from his connexion with the French. At an early period he began to manifest to Gentili his anxiety to be master of one of the coast towns, which had lately belonged to the Venetians; Butrinto, immediately opposite to Corfu, was the place which he was then desirous to obtain. Gentili, though he believed him to be a sincere friend of the republic, would not comply with the wishes of the pasha, and his conduct was approved of by his superior. Bonaparte, nevertheless, was not averse from seeing Ali aggrandised, provided it were not at the expense of France. "You have done very right, citizen general," said he, "to refuse granting what Ali Pasha claimed. Yet, while you prevent him from encroaching upon what is ours, you must favour him as much as you can. It is for the interest of the republic that the pasha should obtain a great accession of territory, that he should beat all his rivals, in order that he may become a sufficiently powerful prince to render services to the republic. Our establishments are so close to him, that it is impossible he should ever cease to have an interest in being our friend. Send engineer and staff officers to him, to procure for you accounts of the situation, population, and customs of the whole of Albania. Have drawn up geographical and topographical descriptions of all the country, which is now so interesting to us, from Albania to the Morea; and contrive to obtain a thorough knowledge of all the intrigues by which it is divided. It is necessary, too, citizen general, that you should treat in a flattering manner all the tribes in the vicinity of Prevesa, and, generally, those which border on our possessions, and, which appear to be so well disposed in our favour."

Though he was disappointed in the hope of obtaining a share in the spoil made by his French allies, Ali soon profited by their disposition to favour him at the cost of others. He complained bitterly, that the Venetians had never ceased to give indirect assistance to his enemies, or rather those of the Porte; and, as a striking proof of their hostile feelings, he instanced the clause in the treaty which forbade him to navigate the channel of Corfu. This clause he described as being intended, among other purposes, to prevent him from reducing to obedience certain towns on the coast, which had revolted from his authority. His remonstrances had the desired effect. The French governor at Corfu was instructed to further the schemes of Ali whenever they were not at variance with those of France, and, accordingly, he gave permission to the pasha to sail with his flotilla through the strait of Corfu.

Ali was not tardy in availing himself of this permission. By the first blow that he struck he destroyed two independent tribes, and gained a position from which he could annoy his enemy, the pasha of Delvino. These tribes, who were under the protection of the ruler of Berat, inhabited the small towns of Aghio Vasili, Nivitza, and Udessovo, situated in the maritime chain of the Kimara mountains, to the north-east of Corfu.

Having secretly fitted out an expedition in the gulf of Arta, Ali's general, Yusuf, arrived with it, after sun-set, on Easter eve, in the bay of Loucovo, a few miles from the devoted towns. He landed undiscovered, and commenced his march. The resurrection of our Saviour is celebrated by the Greek Christians with peculiar solemnities. The different families meet together to eat the Paschal Lamb; all discords cease; and in the countries under Turkish government, Christian prisoners are set at liberty, that they may participate in the family banquet. At midnight they assemble in their churches, where, absorbed in prayer, they wait till the joyful tidings "Christ is arisen" are announced by the priest from the interior of the sanctuary; then, rising, they give each other the kiss of peace, and indulge the transports of religious joy. This, too, is the moment when marriages are principally celebrated. The sacramental words had just been uttered, the youths and maidens were advancing towards the priest to be united, when the Turks, who had advanced unseen under cover of the night, forced open the doors of the churches, and with hideous shouts rushed upon their defenceless victims. The ministers of heaven, while invoking the name of the Deity, were butchered by their ferocious murderers; the altars of Him who came to bring peace upon earth streamed with the blood of his worshippers; men, women, children, fell in indiscriminate slaughter, while the flames from their burning habitations arose on all sides. The few who escaped the horrors of that dreadful night found only a short respite; they perished next morning by the hands of the executioner. In one instance, a family of fourteen individuals were seen all hanging upon the same tree, which, in consequence, was ever afterwards called "the Martyrs' Olive." Many were cut to pieces, others died by fire; to be only beheaded was considered as a mercy. The number sacrificed is said to have been not less than six thousand. The few survivors Ali transported into Thessaly.

Ali immediately fortified the monastery at Aghio Vasili, as a useful post against the pasha of Delvino. He then extended his conquests along the coast, and acquired the important fishery at Santa Quaranta, as well as the capacious and excellent harbour of Porto Palermo, where he afterwards built a large fort.

This catastrophe, in which Christians only had suffered, was generally agreeable to the Mahometans and the Divan; the more especially as Ali paid tribute to the sultan for every place he conquered, and held it under an acknowledged feudal tenure. It gained for him the surname of Aslan, or the Lion; by which appellation he was styled in the military firmans addressed to him by the Divan, when engaged in the expedition against the revolted vizier of Widdin.

Passwan Oglou, the vizier of Widdin, was of a character somewhat resembling that of Ali, but he was of a higher order of mind than his notorious contemporary; equally gifted with talent and firmness, he was far less base and barbarous. He had so long harassed and alarmed the Turkish government, that it determined to make a desperate effort to crush him. By great exertions, the Porte collected a hundred thousand men, at the head of whom it placed the capitan pasha and grand vizier, Kutchuk Hussein, with orders to annihilate the rebellious chief. On the approach of this army, Passwan dismissed the greatest part of his forces, and shut himself up with twelve thousand selected soldiers, and two years' ammunition and provisions, in the almost inaccessible fortress of Widdin. When he was summoned by Hussein, he received the envoy on a terrace of his palace, whence he was observing through a telescope the movements of his enemies. His reply to the summons was brief and spirited. "Go, tell your master," said he, "that having had it in my power to meet him with a hundred thousand men, I have preferred vanquishing him with ten thousand." The result did not belie the vizier's prophetic confidence of success.

Such was the man against whom, at the call of the Porte, Ali led his contingent of sixteen thousand Arnants and Rumeliots; leaving the government of his territory in the hands of his son Mouctar. It is more than doubtful, whether his heart was in the cause for which he took the field. In his History of Napoleon, M. Thibadeau asserts, that, under pretence of settling a boundary which was in dispute, General Chabot, who had succeeded Gentili, "sent Captain Scheffer, his aide-de-camp, to Ali, to prevent him from declaring against Passwan. Ali complained, that Gentili and Brueys had deluded him with vain promises; that, far from aiding his schemes of independence, they had not even paid him for the supplies which he had furnished to the French fleet; and that he could not disobey the Divan, unless he received a succour of ten thousand men and a hundred thousand sequins." That he was conscious of being suspected by his commander-in-chief, and perhaps by his sovereign, appears from an anecdote which is related of him. Pretending to wish to bestow public approbation on his services, the grand vizier requested Ali's attendance in full divan. To decline appearing would have looked like a tacit confession of guilt, and he therefore obeyed the summons; but he took good security for his own safety, by surrounding the vizier's tent with six thousand of his faithful Arnauts. The baffled vizier of course received him graciously, and dismissed him speedily.

That Bonaparte counted much on the active co-operation of Ali, and was exceedingly anxious that the resistance of Passwan should be successful, there is abundant evidence to prove, though whether he had any communication with the latter chief is uncertain. In many of his letters, written while he was in Egypt, he presses his correspondents to send news of him; and he places considerable reliance upon the effect of the diversion made by the pasha of Widdin, in preventing the Turks from despatching an army against his own. With respect to Ali, however, Bonaparte had opened a direct correspondence with him, independent of that which was carried on by the governor of Corfu. From Malta, as soon as he had seized upon that island, he sent his aide-de-camp, Lavalette, to bear to the pasha a flattering letter, and to make proposals, the exact nature of which still remains a mystery. After much compliment and profession, the letter darkly says, " I have instructed the bearer to make certain overtures to you on my part; and, as he is not acquainted with your language, have the goodness to employ a sure and faithful interpreter in the conversations which he may have with you. I request you to put faith in all that he may say on my behalf, and to send him back speedily with a reply, in the Turkish language, and in your own hand-writing." In his instructions, Lavalette was charged to give the letter himself into the hands of Ali, that he might be sure of the pasha having read it. " After which," said Bonaparte, " you will tell him, that, having made myself master of Malta, and being in these seas with thirty ships and fifty thousand men, I shall have connexions with him, and that I wish to know whether

I may reckon upon him; that I wish, too, he would send back to me, in the frigate, some person of note, who enjoys his confidence; and that, in consideration of the services which he has done the French, and his bravery and courage, if he places a reliance on me, and will second me, I may greatly increase his glory and his elevation." The service required of Ali is supposed to have been his seizing upon Macedon, and supporting the insurrection of Greece. His reward would probably have been the precarious princedom of Epirus, or rather, of such part of it as the French might think proper to spare to him.

When Lavalette arrived at Corfu, he learned that Ali had marched to the Danube; and as his mission was personal, it was, of course, at an end. But as General Chabot had previously received orders to send one of his principal officers to bear a letter of thanks from the French government to the pasha, for the supplies which he had furnished to the fleet, he now resolved to execute those orders. The person whom he selected was Adjutant-general Rose, who had already been thrice employed as an envoy to the satrap, had received a handsome Greek wife from his hands, and been loaded by him with protestations of friendship. The choice was a judicious one, not only on this account, but also because Rose was acquainted with the language, and, therefore, did not need the dangerous assistance of an interpreter. On his reaching Ioannina, he neglected none of those ceremonies and forms of etiquette which he thought, and in this case not unwisely, would give an air of dignity and importance to his mission. He met with the warmest reception from Mouctar and Veli, who seemed to be rejoiced at his assurances that they and their father might depend upon the protection and amity of the republic. A courier was instantly despatched by them to Ali, to give him an account of this interview. From what he witnessed on this occasion, Rose ventured to assure Bonaparte that, if ever he should undertake any expedition, he might confidently reckon upon Ali Pasha and his sons Mouctar and Veli. He also informed him, that he had received a letter from the chief of the Maniotes, declaring that he was entirely devoted to the French republic. Chabot bore testimony, no less strong than that of Rose, to the partiality of Ali for France; and it is somewhat curious that he expressed a belief that, as soon as Ali learned the reduction of Malta, and the approach of the French troops, he would do everything in his power to quit the army, and return to Ioannina.

Ali did in reality return, as the French general had foretold. But his return was influenced by other motives than those by which Chabot had expected it to be caused. It was produced by the pasha having acquired the certainty that, irritated by the invasion of Egypt, and pressed by the solicitations of England and Russia, the Porte was on the point of declaring war against France. In this situation of affairs it behoved him to act with caution. Though, backed by France, he might have ventured to brave the vengeance of the sultan, the chances of failure were alarmingly increased, now that two powerful states were taking the field in support of Turkey. Besides, Ali was, perhaps, not wholly without misgivings as to the result of his connexion with the French, even supposing them to succeed to the full. He was desirous of just as much aid from them as would suffice to establish his sway, but the presence of a large army, and their schemes for rendering Greece independent, or rather for making it a tool of France, were by no means to his taste. Still, on the whole, there is reason to believe, that he would have adhered to the

French, had he found that they would be able to retain their footing in the Ionian Islands. In the meanwhile, whichever side he might ultimately take, policy dictated to him not to alarm his Gallic neighbours. He therefore appeared more favourable than ever to them, and wrote to the governor of Corfu, lavishing professions of attachment, and adding that General Chabot must not be surprised if he recalled his troops from Widdin, and raised fresh ones, his only intention being to preserve an armed neutrality. At a later period, he is said to have offered, though with a treacherous intention, his alliance to the French general, on condition that Santa Maura and the continental Venetian towns were given up to him, and a body of his troops admitted into Corfu, to participate in its defence. This offer was, however, declined.

It would, perhaps, have been wise in General Chabot to embrace Ali's proposal. The pasha might have been sincere, in which case his aid would have turned the scale in favour of France; if his perfidy were suspected, precautions might have been adopted to foil his design upon Corfu; while, on the other hand, it was obvious, that Chabot had not the means of successfully defending the numerous posts which were entrusted to him. He had in vain solicited his government for troops, ammunition, provisions, and money; he had been able to throw up only a few imperfect entrenchments on the most exposed points, and all the force which he could muster did not exceed three thousand five hundred men. He had been directed by Bonaparte to keep on his guard, but vigilance was of little avail without soldiers, ammunition, and money.

Affecting the utmost zeal for the interests of the Crescent, Ali despatched repeated couriers to Constantinople, to represent to the Divan, that the late Venetian towns commanded a most important line of coast, cut off Epirus from all communication with the sea, and deprived it of every means of exterior military defence. Till this line of coast was in his power he should not, he declared, either have freedom of commerce, or security from attack. His representations having inspired the Divan with the resolution of seizing the towns, he offered to act in concert with the allies, by undertaking himself the reduction of the places in question. His offers were accepted, and he received full discretionary powers.

Ali had now an additional reason for wishing to master without delay the towns on the coast. It was the dislike which he felt of having the Russians for his neighbours. When the alliance was first formed between England, Turkey, and Russia, it was arranged, that England should act in the Adriatic, and Russia and Turkey in Egypt; and, in consequence, instructions were sent out to Lord Nelson, to despatch to the Albanian shore a division of his fleet, under Sir Sydney Smith. "The expedition," says an eminent traveller, " was on the point of sailing, when the scheme was disconcerted by the cunning policy of one of the confederates. The Russians, ever on the alert to seize any opportunity of distinguishing themselves on this theatre, and of amalgamating themselves with the cause of Greece, waited only till they had obtained a passage through the straits of the Dardanelles, before they declared their intention of sailing immediately for the Ionian Islands instead of Egypt; and this they did under the pretext of many strong invitations sent to them by the inhabitants, who desired liberation and protection at the hands of a nation which professed the same religious faith as themselves: but that it was only a pretext, appeared evident from the circumstance, that the greatest part of their crews and land forces in the expedition, both officers and men, were composed of Greeks. It was, however, now too late for the other allies to raise objections and hazard a rupture. The English squadron was cheerfully despatched to the shores of Egypt, since our interests were much more concerned in that quarter; and the Porte, though duped, determined to yield with a good grace, and to accompany the Russian fleet with a portion of its own, though they sent the greatest part to co-operate with the British admiral." Such has always been the insidious and fraudulent policy of the Russian cabinet.

It was, therefore, urgent for Ali to commence operations before the arrival of the allies. His troops were ready towards the end of September, and only waited for orders to march. Ostensibly to communicate some information which was of importance to the governor of Corfu, but really to ascertain correctly what were the resources of the French, he now invited Adjutant-general Rose to hold a conference with him at the town of Philates. Confiding in the friendship of the pasha, and incautious in his disposition, the unsuspecting officer exposed the nakedness of the land to his crafty interrogator. From what Ali heard, he concluded, that Corfu was not in a situation to make a long resistance, and that little or no hope was entertained of receiving succour. This was sufficient to decide his conduct. He immediately arrested and imprisoned Rose, and, subsequently, though not till after the Divan had several times demanded the prisoner, he sent him to Constantinople, where he died in the autumn of 1799. He next made an attempt to get into his hands the governor of Butrinto, but in this he failed.

He began hostilities, in the middle of October, by investing Butrinto. General Chabot hastened to its relief with three hundred men and some field-pieces.

Whilst engaged in reconnoitring, he was suddenly surrounded by Ali's cavalry, and, rather than fall into the hands of such enemies, he was on the point of committing suicide, when he was fortunately delivered by a platoon of grenadiers. The French had just time to re-enter the fort, after having lost fifty men and two officers. The general having returned to Corfu, a council of war was held, by which it was resolved to evacuate and destroy the fort of Butrinto.

Though the possession of this town was doubtless gratifying to Ali, and, as the reader has seen, had been recently coveted by him, it was now but a secondary object. At the entrance of the gulf of Arta, and commanding that entrance, stands the once Venetian city of Prevesa. Not far from its site was fought the naval battle of Actium, which rendered Augustus sole and undisputed owner of the Roman empire. At the time of which we are writing, Prevesa was a handsome and flourishing city, with a population of sixteen thousand souls. " Blessed with a delicious climate and an incomparable fertility of soil, it possessed also the finest fisheries in the Ionian seas; olive grounds and vineyards which were the envy of its neighbours; sheltered harbours and timber for the whole navy of Greece in woods spreading round the Ambracian gulf; in short, it combined every advantage both of agriculture and commerce." This was the prize which Ali was eager to gain, and his eagerness was probably increased by the vicinity of Prevesa to Santa Maura, of which island he had firmly resolved to become master.

Prevesa is situated in a peninsula, on the narrow isthmus of which are the ruins of the ancient city of Nicopolis. The defence of it was committed to General La Salcette, the governor of the two minor divisions of the Ionian isles. Between seven and eight hundred men, of whom only four hundred were French, was all the force which he could spare for the protection of the place. Availing himself of the local advantages, he resolved to cover the isthmus by a line of intrenchments and redoubts. But scarcely was the work begun before it was suspended, in consequence of the intrigues of Ali, who had gained over to his side a considerable number of the Prevesans. It was artfully suggested by his partisans, that the most effectual mode of defending the peninsula would be to insulate it, by cutting a deep and wide canal across the neck of land. This suggestion, which was bad only because there was not time to carry it into effect, was readily adopted by the Prevesans, and the construction of the entrenchments was abandoned. La Salcette was then at Santa Maura, and, when he returned from thence, though he immediately ordered the works to be resumed, it was too late to complete more than a single redoubt and a small portion of the lines. The general had negotiated with the Suliots to make a diversion in his favour, and had sent them a supply of ammunition, and they had promised to co-operate with him; but here again he was disappointed, the watchful Ali having bribed some of their chiefs to thwart the purposed junction with the French.

Such was the situation of La Salcette when, at midnight, on the 22nd of October, he was attacked by several thousand Albanians, under the command of Ali, and his son Mouctar. This first onset, led by Mouctar, was repulsed, with considerable loss to the assailants. At day-break the contest was renewed. Watched by Ali from the tower of Michalitchi, his whole army, brandishing their weapons, and shouting their savage war-cries, descended the heights, traversed the valley, and rushed impetuously upon the French. They were received with a heavy fire of musketry and artillery, and suffered severely. Twice they were driven back, and a third time they were impelled to the charge by the threats and exertions of Mouctar and the dread of Ali, whose eyes they knew to be upon them. At this moment, either from treachery or cowardice, several Prevesan captains, in the centre of the French line, took flight with their soldiers. La Salcette endeavoured to fill up the void by closing his wings upon the centre; but it was too late; the Albanians broke through, and soon completely enveloped their antagonists. After an honourable resistance, La Salcette and the remnant of his troops were compelled to surrender.

Those Prevesans who had traitorously lent themselves to the designs of Ali had soon reason to repent of their conduct. While the main body of the Albanians was completing the destruction of the French, a division penetrated to Prevesa, and began the work of ruin and slaughter. For two days the city was exposed to all the horrors which can be inflicted by an infuriated and licentious soldiery. A few of the inhabitants were fortunate enough to escape in boats to Santa Maura; nearly four hundred others sought a momentary shelter among the bushes, on the opposite side of the bay. That the latter might not escape him, Ali commissioned the archbishop of Arta to cross the bay, and induce them to return, on a promise of being kindly treated. Placing a fatal reliance on the pledged faith of their pastor, they consented to submit, and Ali put the seal to his wickedness by sending them, with two hundred other Greeks, to Salagora, where, under his own eyes, they were all executed.

Connected with this infamous massacre, M. Pouqueville records a noble instance of presence of mind and humanity. An Ithacan, Gerasimo Sanguinazzo by name, who was residing at Santa Maura, learned that his brother and cousin were among the destined victims. He hastened to Ali to ransom them, and received an order for their being delivered to him. On his arrival at the spot, he found that he was too late; the pallid and bleeding heads of his relatives met his view. Only ten Prevesans remained alive. Suppressing every indication of his agonised feelings, Sanguinazzo pointed out two of the survivors as the persons of whom he was in quest; they were given up to him, and he had the satisfaction of snatching these two unfortunate beings from impending death.

The fate of the French prisoners, about a hundred in number, was scarcely less severe than that of the Greeks. Being led towards a loathsome mass of what appeared to be a mixture of blood and hair, they with difficulty recognised in it the heads of their late unfortunate countrymen. Clubs and sabres were then employed to force them to the revolting task of stripping off the skin, which they were afterwards compelled to salt, and convey to Ioannina. In their journey through Albania, to Constantinople, all that brutality could suggest was inflicted on them, and many perished from the excessive rigour of the winter, as well as from famine and fatigue. No sooner did one of these unfortunate beings show symptoms of weariness than one of his savage conductors struck him to the earth, severed his head from his body, and gave it to his companions to carry. On their arrival at Constantinople, both officers and men were immured in the prison which was appropriated to the slaves.

The Russians at length arrived on the coast of Albania, and their very first proceedings gave Ali abundant cause for abhorring them. While they were occupied at Cerigo and Zante, he led his army to the strand of

Playa, opposite Santa Maura, and demanded the surrender of the island, threatening, in case of resistance, to treat it like Prevesa. As he had a considerable party among the inhabitants, and the French garrison was weak and hopeless of succour, he was on the point of gaining his object, a negotiation having been already entered into, when his design was frustrated by Russian intervention. After having stopped the flotilla of Ali, and compelled the commander to release several captured boats full of Prevesan citizens and property, a Greek officer, the captain of a small vessel in the service of Russia, proceeded to Santa Maura, and put an end to all treating with the pasha. Ali was equally unfortunate in subsequent attempts upon Parga, which, backed by Russia, and an alliance with the Suliots, set his threats at defiance. These circumstances, especially his disappointment at Santa Maura, excited in him a deadly hatred of the Muscovites.

It was probably while his feelings were rankling under this insult, that Ali resumed his correspondence with the French officers in the Ionian Islands. To the governor of Santa Maura he stated, that he had been obliged to take up arms, because the French had passed the boundary line, and he feared that he should be accused of selling the Sultan's territory, had he not endeavoured to drive them back. To general Chabot he was more explicit. His motive for seizing Rose was, he said, that he might have with him, apparently as a hostage, but really as the depository of his secret thoughts, an unacknowledged agent of France. This assertion derives some support from the fact of his having so reluctantly obeyed the commands of the Divan, to send Rose a prisoner to the Ottoman capital. Ali concluded his letter with arguments which were at least specious. " There are," said he, " cases of necessity in which we are obliged to submit. Consider my situation, and let your wisdom judge impartially of it. The Porte has declared war against your republic. I am besides informed that the sultan has concluded an offensive and defensive treaty of alliance with Russia and England, powers which are the irreconcilable enemies of your country and ours. Their fleets are advancing towards the Ionian Isles; ought I to have waited till the Russians were established in Epirus, by the occupying of the four districts which belonged to Venice? I was, therefore, reduced to the hard extremity of making myself master of Butrinto and Prevesa; Vonitza is about to open its gates to me; and I venture to hope that you will evacuate Parga. Our common interest requires this condescension on your part. By being thus beforehand with our enemies, we shall involve them in a quarrel with the sultan, and you will ensure in me an ally, rendered the more sincere by my local situation making me independent. I shall then be enabled to asssist you, in the event of your being blockaded, while the besiegers will be entirely dependent on me for subsistence, which I shall not fail to refuse them, without compromising myself with the Porte."

A circumstance soon afterwards occurred, which seems to prove that the sentiments expressed in the letter of Ali were not merely simulated. A Turkish privateer, which had captured some French officers in the way to Malta or Italy, put into the port of Butrinto, near which the army of Ali was encamped. Two of the prisoners had been delivered up to the Turkish admiral, but the privateer captain had secreted three; M. Poitevin, colonel of engineers, M. Charbonnel, colonel of artillery, and M. Bessières, one of the learned men who had accompanied Bonaparte to Egypt. These he offered to transfer to Ali, and the offer was accepted. Ali treated them with great humanity, and even released their servants from the clutches of their captor. Through the medium of the pasha's secretary, Tosoni, they learned that his master complained bitterly of the want of confidence manifested by the French generals commanding in Corfu, with whom he had wished to become allied, in order to make common cause together. When Ali returned to Epirus, he took with him the French officers; two of them accompanied him to Ioannina, and the third, which was Colonel Charbonnel, he employed in establishing a military school at Bonila, and gave him the command of his cannoneers. At the colonel's request he also liberated all his French prisoners from their close confinement.

The celebrity of Ali was raised to a high pitch by the recent events, and honours began to pour in upon him. Lord Nelson, who was cruising in the Ionian sea, sent an officer to compliment him on the victory of Nicopolis and the fall of Prevesa, and to express the regret of his lordship that he could not personally pay a visit to the hero of Epirus. From the sultan he received public thanks for his eminent services, a superb pelisse of ermine, a sword decorated with brilliants, the dignity of pasha of three tails, which confers the title of vizier, and lastly the important office of Rumili-valisee, or viceroy of Rumelia.

CHAPTER VI.

Ali is deprived of the Ex-Venetian Towns—His Rapacity as Rumilivalisee—He builds a Palace at Tepeleni—Measures adopted by him as a preliminary to attacking the Suliots—Treason of George Botzari—Character of Foto Tzavella, and of the Monk Samuel—Ali puts his Army in motion against the Suliots—It is defeated—Infamy and Death of G. Botzari—Contemptuous Conduct of the Suliots—Ali's Army twice defeated—Suli blockaded—Ali's Troops again routed—Letters of the Suliots to Ali—The Suliots pressed by Famine—Spirit of the Suliots—League formed against Ali—It is broken up—Melancholy Fate of Phrosini—Successful Intrigues of Ali among the Suliot Chiefs—Exile of Tzavella—Noble Conduct of Tzavella—Gallant Exploit of the Monk Samuel—Treason of Gusi—Patriotism of Tzavella—Ali is defeated—Death of Emina—The Suliots capitulate—They are treacherously attacked on their March—Their valiant Defence—Heroism of Despo.

ALI did not long retain the possessions on the coast of the Adriatic which he had so vigorously exerted himself to conquer. By the treaty of 1800, between the Turks and the Russians, which called the Septinsular republic into existence, the Porte did, indeed, become the sovereign of Prevesa, Vonitza, and Butrinto, and nominally of Parga; but under restrictions which left to the inhabitants all their ancient privileges. The Mahometan voiwode, who was to govern them, was the only Turk allowed to settle within their boundaries, and his office was rather honorary than active. Yet, though the welfare of the people was thus in some measure provided for, the cession of the towns excited much disapprobation throughout Europe, and was believed, apparently with good reason, to have been procured by bribery. Count Capo d'Istria, chief deputy from the islands to Constantinople, was so strongly suspected of having had a principal hand in the cession, that during the rebellion of 1803 in Corfu, his house would have been burned, and he would have fallen a victim to popular indignation, had not the British resident interceded in his favour. Ali became furious on learning the treaty, and tried every means to destroy or evade the stipulations of it. His efforts, however, were fruitless, and he was obliged to resign his prey to Abdoulla Bey, a member of the Ulema, whom the Porte had appointed voiwode of the ceded towns. Ali was already incensed against the Russians, and from this period he cherished an inveterate hatred of them.

For the disappointment which he had thus sustained, Ali resolved to indemnify himself in another quarter, by the destruction of the Suliots. His abhorrence of that people was now increased by the vicinity of the Russians, who could furnish them with supplies, which might render them still more annoying to him than they already were. But he forebore from attacking them, till, by extortion and intrigue, he should have ensured the means of success.

In the mean while, he fixed, for a time, his residence at Monastir, the seat of his government, as Rumili valisee. There he carried to a scandalous pitch his system of levying heavy contributions, and seizing upon every article which he could turn to any use, all of which he sent off to his magazines at Tepeleni and Ioannina. Twelve beautiful bronze busts were among the pillage which he obtained on this occasion; of these eleven were melted down, the twelfth escaped, and was carried to England.

After having visited Tepeleni, and erected there a palace, with a vast tower, in which he deposited his wealth, he returned to Ioannina. His first care, on arriving in his capital, was to ascertain what progress was made in his new military school at Bonila. He was accompanied by the two pashas, his sons, and his whole court, together with the garrison of Ioannina. Ali was so satisfied with the manner in which bombs were thrown by colonel Charbonnel, that he bestowed various marks of favour on him, among which were a pelisse and a complete Turkish dress.

All that depended upon his own exertions being now ready for the execution of his designs against the Suliots, Ali resorted to a singular and rather hazardous measure, to rouse, by the influence of superstition, the courage of the Albanians. He addressed to the beys a circular letter, in which he announced, that the Ottoman empire, being surrounded by enemies, which enemies he declared to be the French and the Russians, was on the decline; but that, even after the destruction of the empire, Albania would, for a certain period, be preserved from the enemies of the faith, provided it was firmly united. Such, he affirmed, was the promise made by the Koran. The impious race of the Suliots must, therefore, be exterminated, and he consequently called upon his co-religionists to join him, and to swear, in the name of Allah and the prophet, that they would conquer Suli or die. The result of this circular was the convocation of an assembly of the agas and beys, in the presence of the vizier. To these persons he produced a venerable sheik, who expounded to them several obscure passages of the Koran, to which he of course gave the same interpretation as had been given by Ali. Nor did he forget to dwell on the earthly rewards which would be lavished on those combatants who survived, and the still more splendid prize which was reserved by Heaven for those who fell. Some were doubtless convinced by the arguments or heated by the enthusiasm of the speaker; while others were induced to comply by the fear of exciting Ali's formidable anger: all signed the agreement to subdue Suli, at whatever cost; and this agreement was kept so profound a secret, that those who were marked as its victims remained utterly ignorant of its existence.

In pursuance of this pact, the beys and agas exerted themselves to raise their contingents, and, in the course of three months, twelve thousand of their troops were prepared to take the field. To keep the Suliots in the dark as to the real destination of this force, various rumours were spread: Corfu, Egypt, and Santa Maura, were successively mentioned as the purposed objects of attack. Though they were not without suspicions and fears, the Suliots were so far deceived by these reports that they neglected to lay in the stores which were necessary for a protracted contest.

But neither the want of information nor the deficiency of supplies was so prejudicial to the Suliots as another circumstance, which could not be guarded against, because there was scarcely a possibility of its being foreseen. There was a traitor among them; and this traitor was George Botzari, who, in the former struggle, had distinguished himself by his courage and patriotism. Disappointed ambition is said to have been the cause of his crime. He had for a time held the chief command; but his countrymen, who wisely thought that it was dangerous to trust one person too long with unlimited authority, had refused to renew his lease of power, and had substituted another leader in his stead. This disgrace, as he deemed it, rankled at his heart. A fitting agent was at hand to excite him to revenge. There had for a considerable period been living at Suli a man named Palasca, who had been the head of a gang of robbers in the mountains of Zagori, and had been so hotly pursued by Ali's troops as to be obliged to seek an asylum among the Suliots. There he, on many occasions, did good service against the Albanians, and married Botzari's daughter. Ali, who rightly judged that the fugitive was devoid of principle, opened a communication with him through his selictar aga, with whom the robber was acquainted, and he was soon prevailed upon to betray his unsuspecting hosts. The double traitor then tried his influence upon his father-in-law, and found him ready to turn his parricidal hand against his country. The lure which was held out to Botzari is said to have been ten thousand piastres, and a promise that, when the Suliot territory was subdued, he should be raised to the government of it. He began the execution of his treacherous contract by suppressing all intelligence of the vizier's designs, appropriating to himself and his friends the public money, and preventing the purchase of ammunition and stores. Still, no doubt of his fidelity appears to have arisen in the minds of his countrymen.

The purpose of Ali at length became too obvious to be any longer mistaken by the Suliots. A hasty muster was, therefore, made of their resources, in men, ammunition, and subsistence. The troops, which could immediately be called into action, amounted to fifteen hundred men; nor do they appear at any time to have been more than twice that number, if even they were so many. There were thirty-one leaders, of whom the principal were Foto Tzavella, the monk Samuel, Dimo Diamante, and Giovanni Zerva, Dimo Draco, Cazzonica, Georgio Calespera, Kitzo Pandasi, Giannachi Sefo, and Anastasia Cascari. Inferior to none in courage and love of country, we must add to them the heroine Mosco, the widow of that captain Lambro Tzavella who had borne so conspicuous a part in the last war against Ali, and had now been dead some years.

Of these chiefs the most remarkable were Foto

Tzavella, and the monk Samuel, the former of whom, in his boyhood, we have seen setting at defiance the torments with which he was threatened by the sons of Ali. His manhood did not belie the promise of his youth; for he had been carefully trained up in the path of honour by Mosco, his mother. To the qualities of courage, successful daring, bodily strength, fleetness of foot, acuteness, and sagacity, he added the virtues of honour, good faith, and a generous disposition.

But of all the leaders of the Suliots the most singular character was undoubtedly the monk Samuel, who is said by M. Pouqueville to have been of the monastic order of St. Basil. No one knew his country or his origin, or whence he came; and the mystery which this threw round him increased the effect which was produced by his bravery, his activity, and his enthusiastic language. From his frequent recurrence to those words, and the subject of them, he was usually known by the name of The Last Judgment. By turns a consoler, an orator, a preacher, and a soldier, he exercised a boundless influence over the Suliots. Sometimes, laden with chaplets, relics, and images, he made sudden visits to the neighbouring towns, to exchange his consecrated burden for provisions; at others, disguised as a beggar, he ventured into the camps of the Turks to ascertain their numbers, and procure a knowledge of their designs. The palikars, and even the women, followed him to battle with that implicit confidence which a belief in his doctrine was calculated to inspire. "Loss of life was," he told them, "nothing more than the road leading to a future, where astonished death and nature should see the creature reborn in imperishable glory."

The vizier now put in motion his army, which consisted of nearly twenty thousand men. It advanced along the Ionian shore, from Louro, near the gulf of Arta, and, skirmishing as it proceeded, it compelled the Suliot outposts to fall back before its superior numbers. It was summer, and the rivers and torrents were in consequence either dried up or easily fordable. This circumstance, and the seemingly overwhelming force which he had brought into the field, encouraged Ali to hope that he might end the war at a blow. Yelling forth their barbarous war-cries, the main body of the Albanians made a desperate attempt to penetrate by the pass of Glyky, while a division of three thousand men, under the selictar of the vizier, which had been lying in ambush, endeavoured to descend upon the rear of the Suliots from the Bogoritza mountain. The main army of the assailants no sooner approached the chasm, than it was received with a storm of bullets from behind the sheltering rocks, and of ponderous stones rolled from the impending crags; the troops led by the selictar fared no better; they were fallen upon by Foto Tzavella at the head of two hundred palikars, and were routed with great slaughter. After a desperate contest, which cost the satrap five hundred men, while only twenty of his antagonists were slain, he was compelled to sound a retreat.

The traitor Botzari, who, with all the men of his phara, had deserted to Ali at the commencement of the attack, had assured him that Suli would certainly be subdued by the first effort of his numerous army. Irritated by the recent repulse, Ali bitterly reproached him as a deceiver, and insisted that he should prove his sincerity by leading his own men against their gallant countrymen. Though honour was dead in his bosom, shame would have withheld Botzari from taking an active part, had not the more powerful fear of death induced him to comply. With a heavy heart, therefore, he led his band over the summit of Raithovùni, intending to fall by surprise upon Kako Suli and Kiaffa, while the forces of the vizier called the attention of the Suliots to another quarter. The scheme failed. The Suliots, aware of it, held the vizier in check with the bulk of their forces, while with the remainder they assailed Botzari and his renegade band. The most of the traitors fell beneath the sword of their indignant countrymen; the rest were driven to disgraceful flight. Their unworthy leader escaped the vengeance of those whom he had betrayed, but he died despised and hated by all, about five months after his defeat. Weary of a dishonoured existence, he is said to have hastened his end by poison.

Ali was now under the mortifying necessity of desiring a short truce, that he might ransom the dead, the wounded, and the prisoners. On this occasion the Suliots manifested their scorn of the enemy, by the value which they set upon them in exchange. The wounded were bartered for sheep and goats, and the soldiers for an equal number of horned cattle. In the same derisive spirit they acted at a somewhat later period. An ass belonging to them having strayed into the Turkish camp, they sent a flag of truce to request that it might be returned. The captors complied with the request, upon condition of receiving an equivalent. The Suliots sent back an aga, and a message, stating that, if he were not deemed an adequate compensation, they were willing to give something to boot. In another instance, the vizier having issued a proclamation, offering a reward of fifty piastres for every Suliot head, they retorted by another, in which the utmost worth of a Turk's head was estimated at ten cartridges.

To swell his army still further, Ali obtained from the Porte a firman, by which Hassan Bey of Margariti, Pronio Aga of Paramithia, Mahmoud Daliani of

Konispoli, and other independent chiefs, were commanded to assist him in his conquests. Pronio and Mahmoud accordingly brought fifteen hundred men into the field ; but this nominal accession of force was in reality an incumbrance, its leaders being secretly hostile to the pasha. Ali now resumed his operations. Encamping at Lippa, he sent forward half of his army, under Mustafa Ziguri, one of his favourite generals. With a small but chosen band, Tzavella marched to encounter this new antagonist. Having placed an ambush, he sent forward a few of his swiftest palikars, to insult and irritate the enemy, whose vanguard was by this time at hand. The stratagem was successful. The fiery Albanians pursued their taunting foes, fell into the ambuscade, and were slaughtered without being able to resist. Ziguri, hastening forward to succour his men, fell by a shot from Tzavella, and his fall spread a panic through the whole of his division. A volley from the Suliots completed the terror of the Albanians, who fled in all directions, with a heavy loss in slain and prisoners.

Raging at this defeat, Ali branded his troops with cowardice, and ordered that they should make a general attack on the morrow. The order was secretly communicated to the Suliots, by Pronio Aga of Paramithia, who advised them to concentrate all their forces, and give battle to their dispirited adversaries. In pursuance of his advice, the choicest troops of the republic were placed under Foto Tzavélla and Dimo Draco, two of the most able officers. Leading their forces undiscovered through the defiles, Foto and Dimo managed so well that they broke in upon the Albanian line of march. At this critical moment a furious hail-storm descended, which was driven by the wind into the faces of the invaders. Unexpectedly assailed by the Suliots, who rushed on with appalling shouts, and buffeted and blinded by the storm, the Albanians scarcely made a semblance of resistance; they threw down their arms, and fled over the mountains, not so swiftly, however, but that great numbers of them became captives to their pursuers.

Finding that, harassed and discouraged as his troops were, offensive operations could at present only lead to fresh defeats, Ali determined to try what might be done by the slow but safer and surer effect of a close blockade. Dividing his army into five divisions, he stationed a division at the entrance of each principal pass. To bar all egress from the passes, sixty-four small towers were thrown up in one night. For these towers a lesser number of redoubts, each capable of containing from two hundred to four hundred men, were afterwards substituted. The Suliots, on their side, formed their force into five battalions, to each of which was adjoined a troop of females, who supplied the soldiers with food and ammunition, and not unfrequently took a part with them in active warfare.

Impatient of the tardy system which he had been reluctantly compelled to adopt, Ali once more resorted to open force. He had, however, reason to repent that he had not adhered to his new plan. In a general assault which he ordered, the Albanians suffered a defeat, and only escaped utter destruction by taking shelter in their works.

As his army had been considerably thinned by these encounters, Ali obtained from the Porte another firman, directing the Albanian chiefs to furnish him with their contingents. Among those who were thus called upon was Ibrahim Pasha of Berat, who was obliged to send two thousand of his troops. It is not improbable, that one of the motives of Ali in obtaining these firmans was, to wear down the resources of the pashas and beys against whom he was meditating hostile designs.

Proud of their warlike renown, the soldiers of Berat desired that a separate station might be assigned them, where the praise won by their superior valour might not be claimed by colleagues who had no share in earning it. Their request was granted. To prove their deserts, they resolved to dislodge an advanced post of Suliots from an opposite hill. They attacked with great spirit, and maintained the combat for three hours, but at length they were driven down the heights by Tzavella. That gallant leader, however, having outstripped his followers in the pursuit, was severely wounded by a shot from a concealed enemy. As soon as he fell, the Beratians rallied, and a sanguinary conflict with sabres ensued over his body. At length the Suliots succeeded in carrying him off, and he eventually recovered.

While Foto was incapable of taking the field, a stratagem, which is worthy of record, was played off by a Suliot. Having heard that a body of the new levies was on its march to the vizier's camp, he communicated his plan to his countrymen, and then throwing himself, as though by chance, in the way of the enemy, he surrendered to them. A sharp firing presently arose on a neighbouring mountain, and he was asked the cause of it. A party of the vizier's troops were, he said, engaged with his countrymen, and, if they wished to save them, they must hurry to their assistance. The deluded Albanians believed this Suliot Sinon, and ascended the hill, but they were suddenly placed between two fires, one half of their band was killed or wounded, and few of the survivors were able to escape. He, meanwhile, had succeeded in reaching a place of safety.

Ali was again compelled to rely solely upon the system of blockade. His soldiers suffered severely from epidemic diseases, which swept off hundreds of them; and they had contracted such a dread of their republican enemies, that they positively refused to advance into the mountains. The Suliots, they said, were not human beings, but incarnate fiends, created for the express purpose of killing men. But even the blockade did not prove as efficient as the vizier had expected. The Suliots were so well acquainted with all the passes, some of which were not known to his troops, that availing themselves of dark nights, they made their way through the investing circle, carried off corn and cattle from the neighbouring villages, and occasionally pillaged and spread terror through the camps of their enemies.

Force and patience failing to achieve his purpose, Ali tried deceit and treachery. He proposed to put an end to hostilities, on condition that the Suliots should give him twenty-four hostages, as a security for their not making incursions into his territory. As, notwithstanding their exertions, they were much in want of supplies, they acceded to his proposal. But no sooner were the hostages in the power of the vizier than he imprisoned and threatened them with death by torture, unless their countrymen would consent to an unconditional surrender. When the notification of his purpose was made to them, the inflexible mountaineers replied by the following letter:—

"Vizier Ali Pasha, we greet you.

"By such treacherous conduct you only sully your own reputation, and increase our determined resistance. Know this, that we have already lost seventeen victims sacrificed in their country's cause; let these twenty-four then be added to their number: their memory will live in the breasts of their fellow-citizens:

but the republic will not on that account surrender itself. Henceforward we neither desire nor will we entertain any friendship with you; since in all transactions, and on every occasion, you are a violator of good faith."

The Suliots were so irritated by the perfidy of Ali, that all correspondence with him was strictly forbidden, and his letters were thrown unread into the fire. He succeeded, nevertheless, in opening a communication with them during a cessation of hostilities. His selictar, accompanied by Kitzo Botzari, a brother of the deceased traitor George, was despatched to Suli, to make an offer of two thousand purses, and permission to settle, free of taxes and contributions, in any part of his dominions, provided they would evacuate their territory. The mission of the selictar was a fruitless one. All that he bore back to his master was the following patriotic reply:

"Vizier Ali Pasha, we greet you.

"Our country is infinitely more dear to us than your money, and the fine territory which you promise to bestow on us. You are, therefore, giving yourself useless trouble. Our liberty is not to be bought by gold; all that the world contains would not purchase it. It cannot be had but with the blood and life of the last Suliot."

Foiled in his attempts upon the mass, Ali essayed the effect of corruption upon individuals. To Dimo Zerva, one of the most eminent of the Suliot captains, he held out the lure of eight hundred purses, with any honours that he might desire, if he would only consent to withdraw with his tribe from the community of Suli. Dimo was incorruptible; after having read to the other chiefs the vizier's letter, he thus answered it.

"I thank you, vizier, for the friendship you profess:

but as to the eight hundred purses which you offer, I beg that you will not send them. I should not be able to count them; and even if I were able, I would not give you in return even a single pebble of my country, much less that country itself. As to the honours you promise me, I have nothing to do with them. My honours and riches consist in my arms, with which I immortalise my name, and defend my beloved country."

Ali next endeavoured to prevail upon them to give up some districts to him, for a pecuniary equivalent; but they refused, saying, "We are not merchants; it is by force only that we acquire, and it is to force alone that we will yield." He threatened to march against them with twenty thousand men. "We wish that thou mayst live and come," they replied. He was equally unsuccessful in an attempt to obtain their submission by corrupting their spiritual pastor. The bishop of Paramithia, who was the diocesan of Suli, refused to lend his influence to destroy the love of freedom among the Suliots; and his refusal so exasperated Ali, that the bishop was under the necessity of taking refuge at Parga to save his life.

Though in the nine months which the war had lasted Ali had lost nearly four thousand men, his army was kept up to its original magnitude by the pouring in of fresh reinforcements, and the blockade was closely maintained. The Suliots began to suffer greatly from the rigorous investing of their territory: for their provisions were nearly consumed, and the surrounding country was so much exhausted that they could gather little from it even in their most fortunate excursions. A small supply of arms and stores, which was landed about this time from a French brig, did not last long, and was rather an injury than a benefit, as it excited a prejudice against their cause in the minds of the British and Russians, who might otherwise have interposed in their favour.

When twelve months had passed by, famine began to press hard upon the Suliots. Roots, acorns, and herbs, and the bark of trees boiled with a scanty proportion of meal, constituted the whole of their subsistence. To relieve themselves in some degree, they contrived to send all the useless mouths to Parga and the Ionian Islands, where the exiles met with a hospitable reception. As their distress grew daily more pinching, it became necessary for them to resort to some desperate means of obtaining supplies. A sally was in consequence resolved upon. Accordingly, four hundred and thirteen of the bravest palikars, and a hundred and seventy-four females, the latter of whom were headed by Mosco. marched silently, under cover of night, through the pass of Glyky, were fortunate enough to avoid the blockading parties, and reached Parga in safety. The Parghiotes joyfully greeted their free brothers, feasted them for four days, and then set them on their way with as much provisions as they could carry. The Albanians, to the number of twelve hundred, were waiting to intercept them; but, from some unexplained reason, they made no attack on the weary and burthened republicans. When the latter reached their homes, they were struck with astonishment at the withering effect which want had produced during the last five days, in the countenances of their compatriots.

In some instances, the Suliots added to their scanty means by stratagems which may excite a smile. A contrivance of one Gianni Strivinioti will serve as a specimen. Learning that the Turks had received a supply of cattle, he dressed himself in his white capote and camise, and concealed himself till nightfall. Then, quitting on all-fours his hiding place, he mingled with the herds, remained unseen, and was stalled with them. When all around appeared to be buried in sleep, he opened the door and drove forth the herds towards a party of his friends. The Albanians heard the noise; but fearing that an ambuscade was planted for them, they kept within their tents.

In the midst of all their toils and privations, the lofty spirit of the Suliots remained unbroken. Only two among them were weak enough to parley with the enemy, and breathe a wish for peace. Cuzzonica and Diamante Zerva were the leaders who consented to have interviews with the vizier, and to lay his proposals before the council of the republic. Foremost in moving to reject those proposals were Foto Tzavella, Dimo Draco, and the monk Samuel. They took a solemn oath, in which they invited their fellow-citizens to join them, that they would continue the contest till they triumphed over the tyrant, or ceased to exist. Peace, at the price of concession, was universally disclaimed. Repentant of his error, Diamante broke off his correspondence with the enemy, and pleaded that he had been induced to enter into it only by a desire of procuring the release of the hostages, and a sum of money for the public service; but his excuse was listened to with an incredulous ear, and he found that the confidence of his fellow countrymen was lost for ever.

Firm as the Suliots were, it seemed impossible that they could hold out much longer against the privations which they were enduring. But at this critical moment of their fate, a plan was brought to bear, which afforded them at least a respite, and which, if others had possessed as much courage and activity as the republicans, might have involved their inveterate enemy in destruction. Confederacies are almost proverbially liable to fall to pieces; and in the confederacy which was formed against Suli there was a more than common portion of discordant elements. Many of the chiefs who had been congregated under the standard of Ali hated him; all dreaded him. They could not but be aware, that the annihilation of the Suliots would lay themselves more open to his encroachments than they already were. We have seen, that Pronio Aga of Paramithia was secretly their friend. His weakness, however, compelled him to act apparently in subservience to the vizier. But, before the period to which our present narrative relates, a more powerful chief, Ibrahim Pasha of Berat, had openly seceded, and had covertly supplied the Suliots with ammunition and stores. Many other of the Albanian chiefs had been recently exasperated by the vizier, who had hanged several officers, and refused pay to the troops, as a punishment for not having cut off the gallant band of Suliots which conveyed the succour from Parga.

To Foto Tzavella and Dimo Draco is ascribed the merit of having induced some of the auxiliaries of Ali to turn their arms against him. An offensive and defensive treaty, for the due performance of which hostages were given by the contracting parties, was concluded between the Suliots and Ibrahim, pasha of Berat, Mustafa, pasha of Delvino, Pronio, aga of Paramithia, Daliana, aga of Konispoli, and some of the chiefs of the Kimariots. A subsidy of forty purses was advanced by the Albanian chiefs, to enable the republicans to purchase ammunition and provisions. While, from Berat to the mountains of Suli, Ali was thus menaced on the north, the west, and the south-west, another danger arose in the south. To avenge the death of Canavos, whom the vizier had caused to be assassinated, Paleopoulo called into the field the Etolian Armatoles, and he was seconded by the beys of Salona. Thus, from almost the northern extremity of Albania to as far as the gulf of Lepanto, a host of foes started up against Ali. Had they acted in concert and with only a common degree of ability, he must have fallen under their blows; but their ill-assorted league was as incoherent as a rope of sand.

The Suliots were, doubtless, too acute to expect that the new alliance would long hold together. But, however short might be its duration, incalculable benefit would be derived from it, by its necessary effect of breaking up the blockade, and enabling them to procure supplies. They were not slack in turning it to account. No sooner was the treaty signed, than they recommenced active operations against the vizier's army. They fell upon the weakened outposts of the enemy, spread slaughter and dismay among them, and took many prisoners, whom they disarmed and dismissed, telling them contemptuously to go home, provide fresh weapons, and then return, for that the Suliots were still short of arms. They were next called upon to extricate from danger their firmest ally. Desirous of speedily putting down Pronio Aga, whose territory adjoined that of the Suliots, and who could therefore lend them more ready assistance, Ali marched a large force against Paramithia. The republicans, however, were on the alert, and, with Tzavella and Dimo Draco at their head, they rushed from their mountains, routed the invaders, and saved, for the present, their friend from destruction.

Though foiled on this side, and enraged by his defeat, Ali had taken such measures as he was convinced would ultimately bring about the dissolution of the confederacy. One of its members he had already detached from it. By dint of bribery he had made himself master of the fortress of Delvino; an event which had terrified the feeble Mustafa into the signing of a separate peace. At Delvino the vizier found the six hostages who had been given by the Suliots as a pledge to their allies. Of these, in revenge for the defeat at Paramithia, he hanged four: two, a younger brother of Tzavella, and a son of Dimo Draco, he craftily spared, either to excite a suspicion that those chiefs were in his interest, or to damp their zeal by the dread of losing such near relatives. Whatever was his purpose in this spurious clemency, it was frustrated. As soon as the two leaders were apprised of the massacre, they convoked their countrymen, declared that they looked upon their beloved relatives as inevitable victims, and desired that they might be prayed for as such. This being done, they led the Suliots to battle, routed the Turks, and took a terrible vengeance upon them for the murder of the hostages.

Ali, meanwhile, perseveringly followed up his scheme of annihilating the confederacy. Gold, not steel, was the weapon which he principally employed. In a country where rivalry and hatred are universal, it was not difficult to stir up enemies against the chiefs who were leagued with the Suliots. Money was not spared to bring these willing auxiliaries into play. The beys of Musakia, in consequence, revolted against Ibrahim Pasha, and, headed by Omar Bey Vriones, at length compelled him to make peace with the satrap of Ioannina. The same system was pursued, and with the same success, against Pronio Aga and the beys of Kimara. Pronio was driven from Paramithia, and such effectual means were employed to spread discord among the Kimariot leaders that they were abundantly occupied by their own disputes.

The Armatoles and the beys of Salona had not yet arranged their plans, and were therefore unable to resist. Paleopoulo was glad to find shelter in the mountains of Agrapha; and Etolia remained at the mercy of Ali, who did not fail to swell his coffers with the confiscated property of wealthy delinquents.

Though Ali had succeeded in breaking up the hostile alliance, he was not immediately able to avail himself of this advantage. A circumstance occurred, which compelled him to direct his troops to another quarter, and the Suliots thus obtained a welcome respite. The Porte had occasion for all its forces to quell a new revolt, and it summoned him to furnish his contingent. The danger to the Ottoman government was considerable; for Georgim Osman, the pasha of Adrianople, had thrown off his obedience, and there was reason to fear that the still more formidable Passwan Oglou would recommence hostilities, and effect a junction with Georgim. Ali was therefore under the necessity of sending a considerable part of his army to assist in suppressing the rebellion. Mouctar Pasha was invested with the command of it.

It is not improbable that Mouctar was appointed to the command in order to afford Ali an opportunity to break off an illicit connexion which his son had formed. The vizier accomplished his purpose with his wonted cruelty. The victim, Phrosini, the daughter of Greek parents, was celebrated at Ioannina for the beauty of her person, and no less so for the graces and accomplishments of her mind. Though only seventeen years of age, she had long been married. While her husband was absent at Venice, on commercial pursuits, Mouctar became enamoured of her, and, in an evil hour, the frail fair one yielded to his passion. The influence which she acquired over him was so great that it roused the jealousy of his wife, the daughter of Ibrahim Pasha. For some time the slighted wife was unable to obtain any proof against Phrosini; but at length a brilliant ring, which had been committed to him for sale by the mistress of Mouctar, was brought to her by a jeweller. It was instantly recognised by her as a nuptial present, which she had given to her husband. Complaint was made to Ali, and he promised to avenge her. It is said, however, that it was his own wounded pride that prompted his vengeance; he having himself sought Phrosini's love, and been refused. In the dead of night, attended by his body guard, he obtained admission into her abode, proceeded to her chamber, roused her from sleep, and holding out the fatal ring inquired if she knew it. In vain she appealed in the most pathetic manner to his mercy; in vain she attempted to bribe him with all her jewels; he readily took the bribe, but refused to pardon. He ordered her to put on her clothes, and follow him, and he gave her into custody of an officer, permitting only one favourite maid to attend her. They were conducted to a Greek church, near the lake, and, soon afterwards, fifteen women of Ioannina, suspected of incontinency, were conveyed thither. "There they passed the night in prayer," says Mr. Hughes, "expecting every moment to be their last. The next day however came to a close without the fatal order being given. The despot himself seemed struck with remorse, and hesitated before he could sign the sentence of death: he even declared afterwards, that he waited only for proper intercession to spare their lives. One man, indeed, a poor Greek, did present himself before him to beg the life of his guilty spouse, who was amongst the unfortunates locked up with Phrosini: the vizier, laughing aloud, asked him if he were content to live in wedlock with a prostitute? and on the man replying in the affirmative, he gave an order for her release. The execution of the rest took place at night: they were taken in a barge from the church to some distance on the lake, tied up in sacks, and precipitated into the deep. Phrosini and her faithful maid, watching an opportunity, when the guards were inattentive, clasped each other in their arms, and plunged into the water to rise no more."

Georgim Osman having submitted to the Porte, and all fears with respect to Passwan Oglou being also removed, Mouctar was on his march homeward, when a letter from Veli disclosed to him the fate of Phrosini. In the first transports of his rage, he shot the courier who brought the news. He then hurried in disguise to Ioannina, where he shut himself up in his palace. Ali was speedily informed of the return and the rage of his son, and he sent him an imperative order to come without delay to his father. He was obeyed. "Approach, Mouctar," said the vizier, holding out his hand to him to be kissed, " I will overlook your bursts of passion; but, in future, never forget that he who, like me, braves public opinion, fears nothing on earth. As soon as your troops have returned to Ioannina, and recovered from their fatigue, you must prepare to march against the Suliots. I will then make known to you my intentions. You may withdraw."

The Suliots, meanwhile, had not wholly neglected to prepare for the contest which was about to be renewed. Samuel the monk had been appointed their polemarch, or principal leader; and, under his active superintendence, provisions, arms, and ammunition, had been procured, and additional strength had been given to the fort of Agia Paraskevi, on the hill of Kunghi. During the temporary inaction of the vizier's forces, Foto Tzavella, at the head of forty palikars, accompanied by his no less courageous sister Caidos, had nightly distinguished himself, by surprising the cantonments of their enemies, and carrying off a rich booty in herds and flocks. So brilliantly was his valour displayed in these encounters, that to swear by his sword became a custom among his countrymen.

The successful inroads made by Tzavella induced Ali to hasten into the field the army of Mouctar. The son of the vizier was, however, directed to avoid general actions, and only to harass the Suliots by skirmishes, and gradually shut them up again within their own narrow boundaries. In the course of a few weeks this was accomplished, and Suli was once more in a state of close blockade.

This system was, probably, adopted as much from a wish to leave room for intrigues and gold, as from dread of the enemy's desperate valour. Ali did not miscalculate the effect of those potent auxiliaries. There was no longer among the Suliot leaders that unanimous determination, which had formerly inspired them, to make no concession whatever. Some were, doubtless, seduced by bribes; others, perhaps, had fallen into that state of languor and inaptitude for exertion, which often succeeds to strong excitement and overstrained energy; a third class might honestly, if not wisely, believe that, by gaining time, they would be enabled to renew the contest with advantage at a future period. The proposal which Ali now made was intended to operate on the last two of these classes. He offered to make peace, on condition that he should be allowed to build and garrison in their territory a tower for forty men, to prevent incursions from being made into his pashalik; and that Foto Tzavella should be obliged to retire from Suli. These propositions were laid before the council by Kitzo Botzari and Cuzzonica, to the former of whom was to be committed the guard of the tower.

The proposal to expatriate their bravest leader might well have excited suspicion, and would once have done so; but such a change had come over the spirit of the republicans, that they were willing to accede to it. Even some whose patriotism was unimpeachable were of opinion that it would be politic for him to retire for a while from Suli, and thus put to the test the sincerity of the vizier's desire to live at peace with them. Careless of his own interest, but alive to that of his country, Tzavella overlooked the injury to himself, and only insisted on the danger of placing confidence in a man whose treacherous character was notorious. Finding that his arguments were in vain, " I will go," he exclaimed; " I will obey you; but for Heaven's sake, watch over the welfare of our country, and do not suffer the name of our ancestors to be dishonoured." Then, proceeding to his dwelling he set it on fire, that " the house of a Tzavella might never be polluted by the footstep of an enemy." This being done, he withdrew, accompanied by twenty-five of his bravest men, to the village of Khortia, at some distance from his native mountains.

Easily provoked to revenge himself, and incapable of forgiving, Ali had calculated that similar feelings would render Tzavella an enemy to his country. In the most flattering terms he invited him to Ioannina, in order, as he said, to settle with him the affairs of Suli, and obtain to the treaty the signature of a man whom he honoured for his signal bravery. It was not, however, till his own countrymen had entreated him to do so, that Foto consented to accept the invitation. Caresses and compliments were lavished on him by the vizier, who next proceeded to solicit his aid in subjugating Suli, and to tempt him with the hope of punishing those who had paid his services with ingratitude. But on these points the chief was immovable. Ali then pressed him to withdraw from the republic his own tribe and all who were of his party. Anxious to visit Suli as soon as possible, that he might unveil to his countrymen the vizier's perfidious designs, Foto adroitly led him to believe that he would try his influence, and he promised to return to Ioannina with the result of his attempt.

When the Suliot leaders were assembled in council, Tzavella unfolded to them the projects of the vizier, and conjured them to be on their guard. He then denounced the traitors among them, of whose guilt he had obtained proof at the court of Ali, and demanded that they should suffer the penalty of their crime. Everything but this, his hearers were ready to grant; but this he failed to obtain, and, without it, he was convinced that all else was unavailing. In spite, therefore, of their entreaties that he would remain, and their offers to place him at their head, he persisted in redeeming his word by going back to Ioannina. On Foto's arrival there, he was immediately consigned to a dungeon by the vizier, who was already informed of what had passed at Suli.

The war was now recommenced. The operations, on the vizier's side, were, however, limited to strengthening the blockade. Of the works which he had caused to be erected, the strongest was situated at Vilia, between the mountains and the Acheron, and commanded the main pass. It was in fact a fortress, built of stone, with four towers on the angles, and a tower in the centre, and had a garrison of a hundred and eighty men with cannon. In a dark and windy night, on the 12th of May, 1803, the monk Samuel, with two hundred men, approached the fort undiscovered. Samuel and Mitococalis, one of his officers, then stole with a spade and pickaxe to the foot of a tower, excavated a large hole under it, deposited a quantity of gunpowder in the mine, laid the train, and rejoined the Suliot detachment. A loud shout was then uttered by them, which brought the Turks to the spot where they supposed that an attack was intended. The train was fired by the besiegers, the mine exploded, and nearly forty of the enemy perished. The Suliots rushed to the breach, entered the central tower, and began to carry off the stores, which they delivered to the women and children who had followed them. The remaining Albanians, who had barricaded themselves in the three towers, were now summoned to surrender. They threw down their arms, in token of submission, but resumed them, and poured in a murderous volley upon the Suliots, while the latter were advancing to secure their prisoners. Irritated by this act of treachery, the republicans heaped up piles of wood and barrels of pitch before the doors of the towers, and burned or suffocated the whole of their perfidious opponents.

Roused by this daring enterprise, Ali issued proclamations, calling in the most peremptory terms upon all true Mahometans to join his standard, and take vengeance on the Suliots. His call was obeyed, and in a short time his army was increased to twenty thousand men. The command was given to Veli Pasha, who stationed his troops in such a manner as to close up all the passes in the mountains of Suli.

From May till September the contest was continued, without any advantage being gained over the Suliots, who, on the contrary, so incessantly harassed their antagonists, that the vizier's troops again began to murmur at the protracted and profitless warfare in which they were engaged. But treason was busily at work to render valour unavailing. Among the Suliot traitors the pre eminence in infamy belongs to Cuzzonica and Pylio Gusi, especially to the latter. Having displayed signs of cowardice in an engagement, Gusi became the laughing-stock of his countrymen, and he resolved to punish their contempt by betraying them. In pursuance of his malignant purpose, he entered into a negotiation with Veli Pasha, and engaged to conceal two hundred Albanians in a large insulated house which he inhabited near one end of the town of Suli. In the night of the 22nd of September, the wretched patricide led the detachment through bye-paths, and reached his dwelling unperceived.

On the following morning, according to the plan which had been agreed upon with the renegadoes Gusi and Cuzzonica, Veli Pasha advanced, with his whole army, into the pass which leads to Suli. That town was at this moment guarded by not more than sixty men; the rest having been distributed in posts which were supposed to be more open to attack. As soon as the approach of Veli became known, the garrison of Suli, and as many of their companions as could be hastily collected, marched to arrest his progress. But, while they were contending against his superior numbers, they found themselves suddenly assailed in the rear by the two hundred hidden Albanians. Thus unexpectedly placed between two fires, they were compelled to give ground, and it was not without much difficulty and loss that they succeeded in reaching a position where they could check the career of their enemies. In the course of the day, Samonica and Avarikos were also evacuated by the Suliots.

Kiaffa and the fort of Kunghi were the only positions which the Suliots retained. The troops assigned for the defence of Kunghi were commanded by the bold and enthusiastic monk Samuel, who was determined not to survive the independence of his country. In order to enable his army to follow up its recent success, Ali despatched Mouctar with reinforcements, and directed that no respite should be allowed to the republicans. But the Suliots had recovered from their astonishment and alarm, and they now fought with all their wonted courage. During forty days, incessant assaults were made upon them, without producing any other effect than disgrace and loss to the assailants. Not an inch of ground was gained by the soldiers of Veli.

Ali had often acted on the system of dividing to conquer, and he now again had recourse to it. He knew that the men who composed the tribe of Foto Tzavella were among the most brave and devoted of the Suliots, and he doubted not that, if he could separate them from their compatriots, he should bring the contest to a speedy close. About the beginning of November, therefore, releasing Foto from his dungeon, he proposed to him to return to his native mountains, and lead from them his own tribe, which he might settle wherever he pleased. Foto gave a feigned assent to this proposal, and departed, leaving his wife and family as hostages in the hands of the vizier. His first step, on reaching the Turkish camp, was to communicate to Veli the arrangements into which he had entered with Ali, and to demand a passport to Parga for his followers. The passport was readily granted, and hostages were promised to be given for the safety of those whom it concerned.

On his arrival at Kiaffa, Foto disclosed to the council of the republic the real purpose of his visit. Famine, he reminded them, would, at no distant period, take from them the power of resistance. To avert, or at least to delay, this evil, he had been induced to delude the vizier into a belief that he would remove his tribe from among them. Instead, however, of withdrawing his warriors, it was his design to send to Parga, under the protection of Veli's passport, the aged, the females, and the children, who consumed subsistence without adding to the means of defence. This plan was highly approved of by the council, his patriotism was deservedly applauded, and it was resolved that he should go to Parga, to induce the citizens of that place to receive the non-combatant Suliots, and to supply them with vessels for their conveyance to Corfu.

The Parghiotes cheerfully consented to the request of Foto, but he was under the necessity of obtaining permission from the Russian governor of Corfu for the Suliots to pass into that island. The wind being adverse to the return of his messenger, he departed from Parga, desiring that the answer might be sent after him. When he reached Kiaffa, he found that his labour was lost, and that his country was on the verge of ruin. During his absence, the emissaries of the enemy had been but too successful in their exertions. The whole tribe of Zerva, with the exception of the brave Dimo and some of his nearest relations, had entered into a treaty with Veli Pasha to lay down their arms. Without hesitating a moment, Foto rallied round him his tribe and those who were willing to follow him, and threw himself into the fort of Kunghi, where Samuel had already collected together a part of those who remained faithful to their country.

Impatient at the length of the war, and exasperated by the stratagem of Foto, the vizier joined his army, and severely reproached Veli for his slow progress, and his having treated with the tribe of Zerva. In his rage he was unwilling that a single Suliot should be spared. Foto was summoned to lay down his arms instantly, under pain of being cut to pieces if he delayed. "Come and take them," was his laconic reply. To punish this audacity, the vizier put nine thousand of his best troops in motion against Kunghi, and lavished gold and promises of further reward to stimulate their courage. At the head of a small body of men, Foto, with his sister Caidos by his side, advanced to meet the enemy. The Albanians strained every nerve to toil up the steep and craggy hill; but such a deadly storm of bullets was poured upon them by their sheltered antagonists, that every attempt to reach the summit was unavailing. So incessant was the fire kept up by Tzavella's little band, that their muskets became too hot to be used, and they resorted to rolling down fragments of rock. They were now joined by the garrison of the fort, and the defence acquired additional vigour. Vast stones, logs of pine, and whole trees, were hurled from the cliffs upon the hostile masses below. After a contest of seven hours, finding that it was impossible to gain any ground, Ali suffered his exhausted and decimated army to retire to its camp. Seven hundred of his best troops were slain; and more than thrice that number were wounded. Humiliated by his overthrow, he would not protract his stay, but returned to Ioannina, leaving Veli with full powers to conclude the war in whatever manner he might deem most advisable.

This defeat envenomed still more Ali's hatred of the Suliots, and made him redouble his efforts to complete their ruin. Reinforcements, ammunition, and provisions, were daily despatched to his army, and the pay of the soldiers was largely increased. Every Suliot who was taken prisoner was put to death without mercy. So unbounded was his cruelty that, moved by pity, and perhaps also by a fear of the retaliation that might be exercised upon her sons, his favourite wife Emina, the mother of Mouctar and Veli, ventured to intercede with him in behalf of the Suliots. The very mention of the Suliots excited such frantic emotions in his breast, that he fired a pistol at her, and she fell. She was carried to her apartments, and was found not to be wounded. Recovering from his paroxysm of passion, Ali wept, and soon afterwards proceeded to her bed-room. He was refused admission, upon which he forced open the door. This second shock was too much for the unfortunate Emina, and she went into convulsions, in which she speedily expired. Ali was deeply affected by this catastrophe. For many years, at the festal board, the council chamber, and even in his sleep, her spectre seemed to haunt him. He dared not be in a room by himself; he feared to put his arms out of bed; and, in the dead of the night, he was often known to start up, exclaiming " My wife! my wife! it is she! save me from her wrath!"

For this domestic calamity the vizier was in some measure consoled by the final success of the plan which he had so greatly at heart. The moment at last arrived when it was impossible for the Suliots any longer to resist. To famine was added the still more insufferable evil of thirst. The enemy having cut them off from the springs, they had no water but the scanty supply which they obtained from occasional rains, or from letting down sponges into the Acheron. These resources now failed, and for seven days they were without a drop of water to moisten their parched lips. Not overcome by valour, but worn out by the severest privations, they finally consented to a treaty with Veli Pasha. Forlorn as their condition was, he did not deem it prudent to tempt their despair. He agreed that they should retire wheresoever they pleased, and should be furnished gratuitously with the means of conveying their sick and wounded, their women and children, and their property and ammunition. To those who might choose to remain in Albania, he promised not only "honour, safety, and protection," but also grants of lands and villages in full property; and, in the most solemn manner, he invoked on his head the worst earthly disgrace, and the vengeance of Heaven, should he ever violate the treaty. This compact was signed on the 12th of December, 1803.

There was one Suliot who had taken no part in the negotiation, he having resolved not to survive his country; this was Samuel the monk. He saw unmoved the Mahometans advance to take possession of the fort of Kunghi, and when they intimated that he nad much to fear from the anger of the vizier, he replied, "He who holds life as cheap as I do, has no fear of viziers." He then set fire to the powder, and blew into the air the fortress and all that it contained. It is said that Ali had sworn, if he took him, to flay him alive, and stuff his skin,

Whether Ali had really given orders to violate the treaty, or whether Veli was provoked by this act of the dauntless monk, is not known, but it is certain that the treaty was perfidiously broken. The Suliots had not proceeded far on their march before they were furiously attacked by the troops of the vizier. The largest column of the Suliots, about two thousand in number, under Foto Tzavella and Dimo Draco, took its way towards Parga, whence it was to pass over to Corfu. It was pursued by four thousand Albanians, who came up with it not far from Parga. Sending forward the main body, which formed a hollow square, containing the women and children, Foto Tzavella with a feeble rear-guard kept the enemy at bay, and succeeded in covering the retreat, with no other loss than a small portion of the baggage.

A second Suliot column, of about a thousand individuals, which designed to proceed to Arta to embark for Santa Maura, was less fortunate than the first column. It was overtaken at Zolongos, and threw itself into the monastery of that place, where it was soon invested by the enemy. About sixty women, with their children, were cut off from the rest, and fled towards a steep rock. There, seeing no hope of escape, the despairing mothers fondly kissed their babes, averted their faces from them, and threw them down the precipice. Then, joining in a frantic dance, they successively approached the edge of the cliff, and leaped after their mangled offspring. For two days the Suliots in the monastery repelled the attacks of their besiegers. On the second night they made a sally, to break through the Albanian lines, but they were discovered, and a fierce contest ensued, in which half their number fell. About a hundred and fifty, however, escaped into the woods, and ultimately, after having encountered numberless perils, succeeded in reaching Parga.

A similar calamitous fate attended a body of Suliots, who, under Kitzo and Notki Botzari, had settled at Vourgareli. Learning what had befallen their countrymen, they resolved to remove, and seek a refuge among the Armatoles in the mountains of Agrapha. They had defeated the parties sent in pursuit of them, and had reached the bridge of Coracos, on the Aspropotamos, when they found their progress stopped by a division of the vizier's troops, entrenched behind the bridge and on the surrounding heights. At the same time their pursuers, with increased force, closed in upon their rear. In this emergency, they took post in the monastery of Veterniza, where they defended themselves for several months against a formidable army. At last, pressed by famine, they endeavoured to force a passage, but, after having displayed the most undaunted courage, nearly the whole of them were destroyed. " Let us die!" exclaimed the females, when they saw that all was lost; and with one accord, two hundred of them, pressing their babes to their breasts, and followed by their daughters, plunged into the waves of the Aspropotamos. Of all this band of Suliots only fifty-five men and one woman escaped the slaughter, and found safety at Parga.

Equal heroism was manifested, in another instance, by a family of females. By permission of Veli Pasha, some widows and children of Suliots had taken up their abode at the village of Rhimassa, between Parga and Prevesa. These unfortunate beings were now sought out and cruelly slaughtered. One of them, named Despo, the widow of George Botzi, dwelt with her seven daughters and daughters-in-law, and three of their children, in a large tower, called the tower of Dimoula. They barricaded the door, and fired upon the Turks, who summoned them to surrender. Convinced that resistance must be unavailing, Despo placed a chest of cartridges in the middle of the chamber, called her family round her, and holding a lighted match in her hand, asked them whether they preferred death, or being captured and dishonoured by the Turks. " Death!" was the ready and unanimous reply. As soon as the word was pronounced, the matron applied the match to the powder, and the tower with all its noble-minded inhabitants was blown into the air.

To massacres on a great scale succeeded a series of executions and cruelties which made humanity shudder. When his thirst for blood was somewhat slaked, Ali turned his attention to the securing of his difficult and dearly-purchased conquest. He repaired the forts, and built a strong fortress and serai on a lofty insulated cliff in the vicinity of Kiaffa, in which he placed a large garrison of his trustiest Albanians. Partly exterminated, and partly driven into foreign lands, the Suliots he believed to be extinct as a people; and he would doubtless have laughed in scorn, had it been prophesied to him that a time was to come, though at a distant period, when he would be profuse of promises and bribes to gain support from their arms.

CHAPTER VII.

Influence acquired by Ali—He is appointed Rumili-valisee—His Campaign—He foils a Scheme of the Divan to entrap him—Advantages gained by him as Rumili-valisee—His persecution of the Etolians and Acarnanians—Tragical Fate of Sousman—Treachery and Barbarity of Veli Pasha—Flight of the Archbishop of Arta—Ali removed from the Government of Thessaly—Elmas, his Nephew, appointed to it—Ali causes the death of Elmas—He is re-appointed to the Pashalik of Thessaly—He saves Vasiliki—Russian Intrigues—Ali negotiates with England—He seeks to recover the good Graces of France—Napoleon appoints M. Pouqueville Consul at Ioannina—Interviews of M. Pouqueville with Ali.

THE destruction of the Suliots, who for nearly a century and a half had baffled all the efforts of the Mahometans, and who for the last thirteen years had maintained an almost incessant struggle against all the resources of the power, wealth, craft, and treachery of Ali, considerably increased the celebrity and influence of their destroyer. "His influence," says Lieutenant-Colonel Leake, "found its way into every part of northern Greece, and left very few retreats in which the Greeks could enjoy the fruits of their industry in safety." His exploits were sung throughout Albania, and were recounted from one extremity of Turkey to the other. The Turks carried their exaggeration to such a pitch as to give him the appellation of the

Saviour. His fame at length reached the ears of the Sultan Selim, who rewarded him, or rather laid a snare for him, by conferring upon Ali the title and authority of Rumili-valisee, which the pasha had once before enjoyed. At this moment, the office required to be filled by a man of a bold, active, and vigilant character. The whole of that part of Rumelia, which formed the ancient Macedonia and Thrace, was suffering severely from numerous predatory bands, composed of Bulgarians, Sclavonians, and other uncivilised tribes. These plunderers bore the name of Kersales or Chrysalides, and were commanded by daring leaders. They devastated the environs of Philippopolis, and the valleys of Mount Pangeus, and pushed their marauding parties even into the canton of Ghiustendil, on the north-eastern verge of Albania. The pashas of Smocovo and Uskiup were suspected of secretly favouring these robbers. The caravans could no longer travel in safety, commerce was interrupted, couriers were rifled, and all authority was set at defiance. To remedy these evils was the task which was imposed upon the conqueror of Suli. But, in choosing him for its agent, the Porte, which already began to feel a jealousy of him, was playing a double game, and expected to benefit whether he succeeded or not. It had found itself incompetent to put down the hordes of robbers, and, consequently, if he achieved that object, he would have performed an essential service; while, on the other hand, if he were baffled, his failure would furnish a pretext for his ruin, and he might be seized with greater ease when he was at a distance from his own government, where his resources and the nature of the country would enable him to make a protracted resistance.

It was, however, no easy undertaking to entrap the prudent Ali. Though he appears to have had no certain knowledge of the machinations against him, his suspicions were awake, and he omitted no precaution to ensure the success of his expedition and the safety of his person. As soon as he received the imperial diploma, he collected ten thousand Albanian soldiers; men in whom he knew that he might confide. At the head of these he passed Mount Pindus, in the spring of 1804, and encamped at Monastir, a considerable town, called also Bitolia, which is situated about a day's march to the eastward of the lake of Ocbrida, and is the capital of an extensive sandjiac. His first care was to extirpate a swarm of robbers, by which the neighbourhood was infested. Having accomplished this, he was joined by the ayans of Illyria and Macedonia, after which he proceeded on his march, and crossed the Vardar at Koprili.

The army which Ali had drawn together was formidable in point of numbers. Under his standard were ranged the contingents of the pasha of Delvino, the vizier of Berat, the beys of Musakia, the vaiwodes of Taulantia, the sandjiac of Scodra, the chiefs of the Dibres, of Ochrida, of Baxor, of Pristina, and of many other places, and all the spahis of Thessaly. As he moved onward, he was joined by the cavalry of the Serres, the agas of Thessalonica, the timariots of numerous districts, and the whole array of the populous city and sandjiac of Sophia. By the time that he reached Philippopolis, he was at the head of eighty thousand men. Two-thirds of the pashas of European Turkey were under his command.

Having established his camp in the plain near the city, he ordered that the rebel chiefs who had been taken should be brought up for judgment. Among them were the pashas of Smocovo and Uskiup, men of gigantic stature, to whom he bore a personal hatred. They were condemned to lose their heads. Some of the least important of the other criminals were also put to death; but those who possessed influence were retained as hostages, perhaps as future instruments, by the politic Ali.

His march, and probably the favour shown to some of the guilty, and his astonishing activity in collecting so vast an army, gave rise to an opinion that he meditated striking a fatal blow against the empire. He had likewise levied contributions on all the towns through which he passed, and extorted considerable sums from wealthy persons. The supposition that he wished to cast off his allegiance was, nevertheless, unfounded. His sole ambition, at the utmost, was to establish an immense feudal dominion, which he might transmit to his children. He was too acute not to be aware that, as far as regarded any scheme of independence on his part, no reliance whatever was to be placed upon the army which he had so rapidly assembled. Many of the leaders of it were his rivals, and even his inveterate enemies. Besides, how could he expect to preserve for any time the union of such a body of men, differing so widely in country, in language, and in interests, influenced by long-standing jealousies, and speaking a Babel compound of the Turkish, Sclavonian, Valachian and Bulgarian dialects? An army so composed contained in itself the seeds of dissolution, and could not fail to be broken up upon the least dissension or misunderstanding.

Obscure hints and dark rumours had already produced a considerable fermentation among this heterogeneous force. Seditious expressions began to be common throughout the camp, revolutionary songs are said to have been sung even by some of the officers, the name of Selim was mentioned with affected contempt, and the intention of raising a new standard was not obscurely avowed. At length an insurrectionary movement took place. Ali then suspected, and is asserted to have soon procured proofs, that this movement was organised by the Divan itself. His intentions were more strongly than ever suspected by the Divan, and it hoped to entrap him into a rebellion, which would have ensured his destruction. But the sharp-sighted pasha avoided the snare. The mutineers had already seized their arms, and were proceeding to his head-quarters, when, suddenly appearing before them, surrounded by his faithful Albanians, he exclaimed, "You are weary of inaction; I applaud your feelings. Strike your tents, and let every one follow me to the general rendezvous at Sophia."

Ali immediately began his march; being convinced that this would be the signal for the withdrawing of the most mutinous of the divisions. He was not mistaken, for they seized this opportunity of returning home, while, on his part, he retook the road to Monastir. The fears, however, of the Divan were not wholly allayed till he had repassed the Vardar. Ali himself did not feel secure till he approached Epirus, and was once more in a friendly country. Without, however, betraying either suspicion or alarm, he demanded from the Divan a *carte blanche*, in case he should be required to make another campaign. He immediately received the thanks of the ministers; but was informed that, satisfied with what the pasha had done, the sultan deemed it unnecessary to require the continuance of his services in Rumelia.

The appointment of Rumili-valisee is considered as a burthen to the person who receives it. But Ali was accustomed to turn every thing to advantage, and he did not swerve from his system on this occasion. He drained the provinces by heavy contributions; ransomed those whom he ought to have punished; carried off from the fortresses all the artillery which was transportable; and re-entered Ioannina laden with the spoils of Rumelia. From motives of policy, as well as from avarice, he left an exhausted country to his successor, whose embarrassments he soon afterwards increased by setting at liberty the klephtic chiefs whom he had detained as hostages.

As soon as Ali entered Epirus, he announced this event to the people; and all who were rich, or had cause to dread his anger, hastened to celebrate his return by giving him splendid entertainments. But he well knew that these seeming manifestations of pleasure were hollow, and, accordingly, far from remitting in the rigour of his sway, he continued and even increased it. While he was doubtful whether he should succeed in baffling the machinations of his enemies at the Porte, he had promised that the taxes imposed upon the Albanians should be diminished; he now postponed, till the Greek calends, the fulfilment of his promise; and statute labour, which was already too burthensome to the peasantry, he rendered still more so. Some consolation was, indeed, afforded to the lower classes by his impartial tyranny. The beys, their old oppressors, were not spared any more than themselves; the fortified towers and keeps of those petty despots were overthrown, and the masters of them were reduced, as to power, to the same level as those over whom they had, for centuries, been accustomed to lord it without control.

Ever greedy of gold, Ali now hit upon another means of gratifying his passion for it. A persecution was commenced against the rich landed proprietors of Etolia and Acarnania, on the pretext of their being in secret confederacy with his hated enemies, the Suliots. Many of them perished, victims of this false accusation. Among the Etolians whom the pasha sacrificed there was one whose fate was aecompanied by circumstances of more than common baseness and cruelty in his murderers. The name of this individual, who traced his descent from the ancient Servian monarchs, and was held in high estimation by his countrymen, was Sousman, or Shousman. Ali had already unjustly put to death the brother of Sousman; but, though he was eager to seize the wealth of Sousman himself, he was deterred, probably by the fear of encountering universal odium among the Etolians, from being seen as the destroyer of a man who was the object of general affection. The detestable task was therefore committed to Veli Pasha, and he executed it with consummate villany.

Veli began his operations in January 1805, by going to Missolonghi, under pretence of making a tour of military inspection in southern Greece. On his way the customary present was sent to him from Sousman, who, however, avoided paying him the complimentary visit which is usual on such occasions, but wrote to excuse his absence. In his answer, Veli affected to be entirely satisfied with the apology, regretted that false reports should have occasioned Sousman to be suspected by the formidable vizier, and desired him to dismiss all fear, for that the danger was gone by, and he would himself settle the business to the entire satisfaction of the terrified Etolian, and would write to him when it was arranged.

Sousman and his family had been on the point of taking refuge in the mountains among the Armatoles: a circumstance with which it is probable that the vizier's son was acquainted. But the letter of Veli calmed the apprehensions of the Greek, and induced him to wait the issue at home. The purpose of the delusive epistle was thus effected. In the course of a few months, Veli visited Arta, from which city he again wrote to Sousman. He assured him that Ali had restored his favour to him, and he invited him to come to Arta with his son, to receive personally the assurance of being pardoned by so great a prince as the vizier, in whose heart he held a place. The postscript of this insidious letter was in Veli's own handwriting; a condescension which, in the East, is regarded as a very high favour granted by a prince to an inferior. "I am your friend," said Veli, " and will be always your defender. If this assurance be not sufficient, I convert it into an oath to defend you, and, in the name of religion and by the heads of my children, I swear to you eternal friendship!"

The oath of eternal friendship Sousman probably estimated at its real value; but he believed that Veli was only anxious to obtain presents from him, and that, if his cupidity were gratified, he would secure him from future persecution. Though he might have found an asylum among the Armatoles, or at Santa Maura, to which island he had been invited by the Russians, he was reluctant to quit his native home, and was willing to purchase the privilege of remaining there, at the cost of a portion of his fortune. It was, in vain, therefore, that his family dissuaded him from trusting himself at Arta, and that, when he reached Prevesa, the caution was repeated by his friends, who strenuously advised him to discontinue his ominous journey.

The predoomed victims, the father and the son, landed at Salagora, the post-town of Arta. There they found waiting for them horses, a guard of honour, and a Greek named Dherman, who had been sent to compliment them on the part of Veli. On their arrival at the abode which the pasha had prepared for them at Arta, he sent his secretary to welcome and invite them to join in a banquet at his palace, on the morrow. His musicians also came to serenade them, his dancers to amuse them, and his gardener to present them with bouquets; they were crowned with flowers, and perfumes were poured on their heads, and they retired to rest, delighted by their reception, and longing for the dawn of that day the close of which they were destined never to behold.

In the morning they were summoned to the palace, to which they were conducted on splendidly caparisoned horses. Veli gave them his hand to kiss, seated them by his side, spoke in the kindest tones, and smiled at the fears which they had entertained. He kept them with him while he dined; and at the close of the meal, when the musicians and buffoons were introduced, he graciously dismissed them to partake, as he said, of a banquet which he had ordered to be prepared for them. " We are going to divert ourselves here," he added, " while you are being regaled in the room below: and, as soon as your business is despatched, you shall be of our party." The two deluded Etolians bowed respectfully, and retired.

Veli now seized a lyre and struck a few notes as a signal for the dancers and musicians to begin, and immediately a band of gipsies sang the songs of the country in praise of Ali's martial and marauding exploits. Heated with wine, Veli threw off his turban and pelisse to join the lascivious dance, and, at length, maddened by his passions, he disrobed himself of his remaining clothing, and plunged without restraint into the most revolting excesses that obscenity can inspire.

While this disgusting revel was at its height, a cry of " Here they are!" was heard in the banqueting-room. It was uttered by two executioners, who came forward with the blood-dropping heads of Sousman and his son. Veli burst into a fiendish laugh as he looked on the two bleeding evidences of his baseness and ferocity, spat on them, and ordered that they should be deposited in silver-gilt dishes. He then commanded the dance to be resumed; but not even the fear of him could prevent his slaves and accomplices from betraying the horror which the sanguinary scene had excited: Dherman fainted, the gipsies were struck dumb with consternation, and Veli was at last obliged, with a few of his stronger-nerved associates, to retire to his private apartment, where the whole of the night was spent in inebriety and licentious enjoyment.

The catastrophe of Sousman and his son took place in the palace of the archbishop of Arta, where Veli resided during his stay in the city. We have seen that the archbishop was induced to lend his influence to the vizier, to put an end to the gallant resistance of the Suliots. Seeing the fatal consequence which it had produced, he had, however, repented of that weak or treacherous act; and now, his disgust, and probably his fear, being excited by the foul slaughter which had been committed in his abode, he abandoned his diocese, and sought a refuge at Corfu. Ali endeavoured, but without success, to get him again into his power. At the same time, the pasha sent several detachments to attack the Armatoles, in the mountains of Agrapha, and desolate their territory. The chief purpose of these attacks was to compel them to banish the formidable chief Paleopoulo, whose courage and perseverance he dreaded. The brave Etolian was finally forced to quit his country. After having for nearly four years been a dweller in woods and caves, and suffered the severest hardships, Paleopoulo at last went to Constantinople, where he was fortunate enough to obtain protection from the French ambassador. Other leaders of the Armatoles concluded treaties with the pasha, and were admitted into his service.

The Porte, meanwhile, was far from viewing with indifference the conduct of the pasha of Ioannina. There was one universal cry against his depredations, and the public voice was seconded by the complaints of the Russians by whom the Ionian Isles were now occupied. They remonstrated against the daily outrages committed upon the islanders by their turbulent neighbour, and demanded that Butrinto should be given up to the vaiwode, appointed by the treaties to govern Vonitza, Prevesa, and Parga. Anxious to keep upon good terms with Russia, the Porte partly complied with the wishes of that power. At once to punish Ali, and to diminish his formidable influence, it deprived him of the government of Thessaly, but, desirous not to irritate him too far, it preserved an appearance of consideration for him, by conferring the pashalik on Elmas, his nephew, the son of Soliman and Shainitza.

The proud and ambitious Shainitza was enraptured with the elevation of her son. He was of a mild and pacific disposition, accustomed to passive obedience, and she, therefore, flattered herself that she would, in reality, exercise that authority of which he was the nominal possessor. In the intoxication of her triumph she did not hesitate either to represent her son as superior in rank to Mouctar and Veli, or to declare openly her hopes and intentions; all that she said was carefully reported to Ali. He, on his part, suppressed all signs of his inward perturbation, and appeared to be resigned to his deposition, and even to participate in her feelings. He wished, he said, that she should appear with a splendour worthy of her rank, and he accordingly supplied her with costly furniture and equipages, and a glittering train of attendants, and ordered that she should be escorted with all imaginable pomp to the Thessalian frontier. He did not forget to place on her establishment a confidential physician and sharp-sighted spies. As soon as he learned the period at which the firman of investment would arrive, he sent, as a present to his nephew, a fur pelisse of extraordinary value, such as might have been reckoned a magnificent gift from a sovereign; and with this he desired that Elmas might be robed when he received the imperial diploma.

On the appointed day, Shainitza put the pelisse upon Elmas; and, as is customary in the East, she was present at the ceremony of investiture which her ambition had so much longed for. "My son is a pasha!" exclaimed she to the females who waited on her; "My son is a pasha; and my nephews will die of vexation that he is so!" But in the course of a few days her son began to complain of a languor in his whole frame. An irresistible tendency to dozing, frequent sneezing, and an unnatural lustre in his eyes, indicated a serious disease; the fatal present of Ali had accomplished its purpose. The pelisse, not less deadly than the robe of Nessus, impregnated with the morbific miasms of a young girl who died of the small pox, and who had been purposely wrapped in it, had spread its poison through the frame of the unfortunate Elmas, who had not been inoculated. An eruption appeared, the nature of which was unknown to the women who attended him; the physician was called in, he bled the sick man, and his lancet, no less murderous than a dagger, precipitated Elmas into the tomb.

The rage and anguish of Shainitza were extreme. In the first transport of her furious sorrow she ordered that the physician should be put to death; but, anticipating what would be his fate if he ventured to encounter her anger, he had prudently taken flight. As soon as the funeral rites were performed, Shainitza returned to Ioannina, to seek for consolation from her brother. He, too, seemed overcome with grief; and so ably did the subtle deceiver play his part, that she never suspected by whose hand was dealt the blow which destroyed at once her favourite son and her schemes of ambition.

The field was again open to Ali, and he was not a man to lose an advantage by delay. He immediately despatched a deputy to manage for the present the affairs of Thessaly, and took steps to obtain from the Porte his own restoration to the government of the province. His intrigues, or his gold, were successful, and he was reinstated, without even being under the necessity of ceding Butrinto to the Russians. To crown his good fortune, a third son was born to him. This last and most cherished of his offspring was the child of a Georgian slave, and bore the name of Sali Bey.

From the re-accession of Ali to the pashalik of Thessaly, arose an event which was ultimately productive of much happiness to himself, and, probably, of no small benefit to many of his subjects. At the same time that the Porte forwarded to him his diploma of investiture, it also sent him orders to detect and exterminate a gang of coiners, which was established at the village of Plichivitza, near the frontier of his territory. These coiners not only counterfeited the Turkish coin, but also Venetian sequins, and that, too, with such skill that the public treasury, as well as individuals, was daily deceived by the spurious money. Ali took his measures so well that he surrounded the delinquent village before daylight, and pounced unawares on the whole group of coiners and distributors, in the midst of their moulds, melting-pots, and other apparatus of fraud. The tools he is said to have retained; those who had used them he had no interest in sparing. Accordingly, the chief of the gang was immediately condemned to the gibbet, and his house was ordered to be rased to its foundations. The whole population of the village was about to be doomed to death, when it was saved by a fortunate incident. Flying from the soldiers, a beautiful girl, twelve years of age, rushed up to the vizier, threw herself at his feet, clasped his knees, and implored him to intercede with the terrible Ali to spare her mother and her brothers. " My lord !" exclaimed she, " my father is no more, be our protector in his stead; we have done nothing to deserve the anger of the dreadful master who has killed him. We are poor children; my mother never offended him; I give myself to you, take me among your slaves; you have perhaps children of my age, or a mother." The youth, beauty, and tearful innocence of the suppliant prevailed, and nature for a moment resumed her rights in the breast of Ali. Pressing her to his bosom, he said, " Dismiss your fears, my dear child; I am that wicked vizier." —" Oh no! no !" replied she, " you are good, my good master !"—" Be comforted, my child," responded Ali, " my palace shall be henceforth your home. Show me your mother and your brothers; I will spare them, your prayers have saved their lives." Having said this he directed that her family should be placed in safety, and that she should be sent to Ioannina. This youthful pleader was Vasiliki, who afterwards became his wife.

While his footing was not yet firmly established in Albania, it had been the policy of Ali to cultivate as much as possible a good understanding with Russia. But his former friends were now become the objects of his jealousy and hatred, and he bent all his efforts to the thwarting of their designs. It must, indeed, be owned, that he was not without sufficient reasons for changing his conduct with regard to those perpetual encroachers, the Russians; with their usual insidious spirit, they were already looking forward to the moment when they might recommence their attacks on Turkey, and they foresaw that he would probably interpose serious obstacles to their progress. Hence they were constantly at work, though with more zeal than wisdom, to counteract his plans and impede his movements. It was impossible that he should not feel irritated by these machinations, of which he was no doubt punctually informed by the vigilant spies whom he employed at Constantinople, and in other quarters. Besides, at this moment, he received fresh cause of alarm, by a circumstance which occurred on the northern frontier of Albania, where a voluntary oath of allegiance was taken to the Russian government by the republican Montenegrins, who were able to bring twenty thousand muskets into the field.

To secure himself, at least on one side, from the Russians, Ali strenuously endeavoured to dispossess them of the Seven Islands. The treaty of the twentieth of March afforded him some hopes, as by one of its articles the Ionian republic was declared to be placed under the joint protection of Russia and Turkey. In consequence of this, the Russian forces soon afterwards retired. It was now that Ali conceived the idea of gaining possession of Corfu and Santa Maura. For the more secure attainment of his object, he is said, by means of secret agents, to have fomented disturbances in the islands, and then to have represented to the Porte that, in order to restore tranquillity, he must be allowed to re-occupy the ex-Venetian towns, and to garrison Corfu, Santa Maura, and Parga. Though the Ionian senate remonstrated strongly against this scheme, Ali was about to obtain the wished-for order, when his hopes were completely frustrated by the Russians, who adroitly prevailed on the senate to solicit their protection. The troops of the autocrat soon after arrived, and took possession of the islands. By this measure Ali's hatred of the Muscovites was not a little increased.

But the apprehensions of Ali were not excited by Russia alone. A still more formidable power was approaching towards his boundaries. The rapid progress of the French in Dalmatia would speedily bring them to his door, and he did not so far miscalculate his resources as to imagine that, even when backed by the forces of the Porte, he could offer an effective resistance. In this emergency he deemed it necessary to strengthen himself by some efficient alliance; and he, in consequence, turned his views towards the English government, with which he had carried on an active correspondence through the medium of Lord Collingwood. The immediate result of this overture was, that Major Leake, who had this year been sent on a commission to Ali, was instructed to remain in Albania, for the purpose of taking a military survey of the country, and pointing out the best means of defending it against an invading enemy. Ali, meanwhile, employed himself in building and improving fortresses, reforming the police, clearing his territory of robbers, and sowing dissension among his enemies.

The treaty which followed the victory of Austerlitz produced another change; and it must be confessed not an indefensible one, in the policy of Ali. By that treaty Dalmatia and Illyria were ceded to Napoleon, who thus became the neighbour of the pasha. The English alliance, however beneficial it might have been under other circumstances, could now prove only injurious. It was, therefore, abandoned, and Ali applied himself to recover the good graces of the French sovereign. Napoleon, on his part, was not averse from being on amicable terms with the wily Albanian. By accepting the proffered friendship of the pasha, he severed him from the English and Russians, and whatever course he himself might ultimately decide upon pursuing with respect to Turkey, whether he appeared as her protector or her destroyer, the assistance of Ali would be highly valuable.

Before, however, Napoleon commenced a negotiation, he took the preliminary step of causing an exact report to be made to him of the person and character of Ali, his political situation, and the means which he possessed of acting either on the offensive or defensive. The data were not difficult to be obtained, as two French officers had had a very near view of the pasha, his court, his capital, and his dominions.

This elaborate report gave a satisfactory account of the talents and resources of Ali; proving that he ought to be considered as no contemptible ally. The portion of it, however, which was most likely to conciliate Napoleon was that which described the pasha as having always been a great admirer of the exploits performed by the French armies, attributing them to a species of magical influence, by which victory was ever rendered propitious to the Gallic banners. The report was wound up by reflections upon the importance of the ancient commercial relations between France and Albania. Before the Revolution, France, it said, had imported timber from that country, which, far superior to that procured from the Baltic, had been employed in the dock-yard of Toulon with particular success, the finest French frigates having been constructed of it. But ten years' war had interrupted all this commercial intercourse. The French interest, being now more widely extended, required a more solid basis. During the reign of Louis XVI. that monarch had established at Ioannina a consul-general, for the purpose of promoting commercial relations with the Albanians. By reviving this establishment great advantages, both civil and political, might be expected; for Ioannina was not only one of the most active cities in all Greece, but was also the seat of the modern power of Ali Pasha. For these different reasons it was better calculated to be the residence of a French consul-general than either Arta or Prevesa. Everything showed that Ali considered this distinction as a particular mark of the esteem of the French emperor, for whom he had ever testified the highest regard; and that, if some trifling disputes still existed between Ali and France, they would soon be accommodated by regulating and settling the old outstanding accounts for stores, &c. furnished by Ali to the French army during its occupation of Corfu. Besides, by the establishment of an agent in his capital, France would be the better able to cope with her rivals, the English, who, being masters of some important positions in the Mediterranean, were now also directing their views towards Epirus, for the purpose of obtaining ship timber, and also of injuring as much as possible the French marine in the south. In short, by forming an intimate connexion with Ali Pasha, the French would become the better acquainted with the localities, and by that means be enabled to discover resources, which might be of infinite advantage to the government at home.

The arguments adduced by the report were deemed conclusive in favour of a connexion with Ali. Some valuable presents were, in the first instance, sent to the pasha, through the medium of General Massena.

M. Pouqueville, a learned and intelligent traveller, had already been nominated as consul-general at Ioannina. Ali himself declared that Napoleon also offered to make him independent king of Epirus; but this fact rests only on his own bare word. If the assertion of Ali be true, it is probable that the offer was made for the purpose of discovering to what lengths he was willing to go.

Near the close of the year 1805, the consul-general sailed from Ancona, accompanied by M. Julien Bessières, who was commissioned by the government to introduce him to the pasha, with whom M. Bessières had already had frequent personal communications. On his arrival at Ragusa, he despatched a mounted courier to the vizier, informing him of his arrival on the Turkish frontier. About the end of January, the two envoys arrived in Epirus with a Valachian, who had been sent by Ali to act as their interpreter. On their entering the port of Panormo, they were recognised by the Pasha's garrison, and saluted with volleys of musketry. An officer of the vizier was in waiting to compliment them, in the name of his master, on their arrival. They took the road to Delvino. War had broken out between the vizier and the beys of that town, which the two envoys found in possession of Ali's troops. The bazaar, or public market, was in flames: it had been set on fire by Ali's soldiers, in order to destroy the shops after they had been pillaged. The clamour and tumult resounded from afar, while the flames strongly illuminated that part of the town which remained untouched. The French were smuggled, not without danger, into the house of a bey, one of Ali's adherents, and had little cause to praise either their lodging or their fare. The next day they took the road to Ioannina, through the districts of Drynopolis and Pogoniani; and after a two days' march, they met the vizier at the Seraglio of Dzitza, who gave them their first audience. The narration it may be as well to continue in M. Pouqueville's own words:—

"My curiosity was strongly excited; I was at last about to behold a too famous man, a new Theseus, an old warrior covered with scars, a satrap who had grown grey in the trade of arms, the modern Pyrrhus of Epirus—for all this had I heard of him. We reached the gates of the seraglio, which turned groaning on their hinges; we passed through a silent court, we ascended a gloomy staircase, a trap-door was lifted up, a curtain was raised, and we found ourselves in the audience-hall of Ali Pasha, who stood waiting for us. He greeted us, embraced M. Bessières, and then, falling back with a staggering motion, he dropped into a corner of the sofa, without seeming to have perceived me. A white-bearded spectre, dressed in black, who was with him, honoured me by a slight movement of the head, by way of telling me that I was welcome. This scene, in which also figured a Greek secretary prostrated in the attitude of fear, was illuminated by the wavering light of a yellow wax candle, placed on the floor, which just allowed objects and persons to be distinguished.

"After the usual compliments, the private interpreter of the vizier was called, in order to open the conversation, which the pasha began by asking questions with a volubility very uncommon among the Turks. Through the half-dispelled gloom of the apartment I could distinguish the coruscations of his eyes, and observe the convulsive workings of his features. I listened to his conversation, apparently vague and unconnected, yet full of cunning. He swung himself about, he laughed, he talked, but, notwithstanding the rapid flow of his speech, no word escaped him that had not its import. At times he threw scrutinising glances on me, and at length the black spectre, and the Greek secretary, who were stealthily watching the proceedings, were ordered by him to withdraw. We remained with the interpreter, who continued to stammer out the questions and replies; and, after a conversation of two hours, we retired, leaving the vizier struggling between hopes and fears.

"This interview sufficed to destroy some of the illusions which I had been under. Ali Pasha was neither a Theseus, a Pyrrhus, nor an old soldier covered with scars. I quitted him with quite different ideas; his manners had disgusted me, and, though I was far from foreseeing all the vexations which he caused me, I could not but secretly lament that fate had destined me to live in the court of such a man as he was."

After this interview, the two envoys retired to the Monastery of the Prophet Elias, which had been assigned them as a residence. They were received by the Greek monks with the utmost hospitality and kindness. The next day the pasha invited them to a second conference: he had risen before daylight expecting them. The two envoys proceeded towards the seraglio. Two heads, recently severed from their bodies, were stuck upon stakes, in the middle of the court-yard, without appearing to excite the least attention. Wholly unaffected by this horrid spectacle, crowds of suppliants and courtiers were pressing towards the staircases, in order to arrive in the presence. "Cahouas, a species of ushers carrying long wands," adds M. Pouqueville, "made the crowd fall back to facilitate our approach; and for the second time I saw Ali Pasha. He was verging on his sixtieth year; and his figure, which was not above five feet nine inches high, was deformed by excessive corpuleney. His features, loaded with wrinkles, were, however, not wholly effaced; their flexibility, and the brilliancy of his small blue eyes, had the effect of a mask, in which cunning was joined with ferocity. Amidst the bursts of a guttural laugh, many things which he said were tinctured with a certain elegance. Eagerly receiving the presents brought by M. Bessières, he became quite joyous, and launched out into a number of common-place protestations of friendship. He called us his children, his brothers, his kind friends; and as though he had seen me for the first time, he condescended to promise me his protection in the exercise of my consular functions. It was at length decided that we should set off the next afternoon for Ioannina. After this interview, the vizier, who had ordered a grand hunt, mounted his steed, and the next moment numbers of Albanian horsemen were seen tracking the game on all sides, and driving them towards their master."

The chase being ended, the consul-general and his friend directed their course towards Ioannina. A boat awaited them at the head of the lake, from which they were landed at the castle called Chatirwan, where apartments had been prepared for them. A large fire, pages, servants, and all the display of Eastern tinsel, indemnified them in some measure for the privations which they had undergone. It was agreed that they should remain incognito, till a courier should return from Constantinople, with the customary *barat* or *exæquatur* for M. Pouqueville, without which he could not be legally accredited. Finding that day after day elapsed without the return of the courier, M. Bessières was under the necessity of setting off for France. "I separated from my friend with the greatest heaviness of heart," says M. Pouqueville. "I saw myself, as it were, abandoned amidst barbarians; for very few Europeans had as yet visited Ioannina. I found myself at the mercy of a man, of whom, in spite of his apparent kindness, we had already had cause to complain. Shall I own it?—the general aspect of the country and its inhabitants terrified me, and I was filled with the most melancholy forebodings. But the step was taken, and necessity commanded the most perfect resignation."

The courier having at length returned, the Greek and Turkish primates were convoked the next day at the Mekemé, to hear the *exæquatur* read, which was duly entered in the register of the cadi. After this ceremony had been performed, and the customary fees paid, M. Pouqueville was recognised as French consul-general at the court of the vizier of Ioannina. Scarcely had he entered upon his new office before he determined to take an accurate survey of Epirus, a country as yet but little known to Europeans. He wished at first to go to Ochrida, by traversing the chain of Pindus from south to north; but his plans were constantly thwarted by Ali, under specious pretexts. The French were at that time in possession of the Illyrian provinces, and he strongly suspected, nor was the suspicion absurd, that the object of their consul's journey into the north was to show them the road to Epirus. As the vizier was very uneasy, and as it was prudent to conciliate him, the consul did not insist upon carrying his plans into execution.

CHAPTER VIII.

Plans of Ali—He obtains the Pashaliks of the Morea and Lepanto for his sons Veli and Mouctar—His conduct at Prevesa—He visits a part of his Territories—His sarcastic Treatment of his Kiaya—Singular mode of administering Justice—Dialogue between Ali and a Papas—System of Government in Turkey described—Barbarism of the Prior of a Convent—English shipwrecked Sailors—Strange manner of clothing the naked—Ali obtains Officers and Artillerymen from Napoleon—He besieges Santa Maura—Motives of Ali investigated—Ali becomes disgusted with the French Alliance—He courts the Friendship of Great Britain—His Letter to Lord Collingwood—A British Agent is sent to confer with him.

THE ruin of the Suliots being completed, Ali next undertook to clear Cassiopeia of the bands of Armatoles, by which that provice was overrun. Under pretext of establishing order in the vaiwodolik of Arta, he also seized upon Acarnania, and Etolia. Having nearly accomplished the subjugation of these territories, he entrusted the finishing of the task to his relative and lieutenant Yusuf, upon whom he relied so implicitly as to make him his *alter ego*, the executer of his vengeance upon the tribes who yet strove to maintain their independence. Torrents of blood, therefore, again flowed, the principal towns of the districts which were in arms were consumed, multitudes were sold into slavery, aud a flourishing country was reduced to the most utter state of desolation.

Still pursuing his encroachments, Ali reduced to obedience Salona, a town near Amphissa, the inhabitants of which he insulted by giving them a papas, or priest, for a governor, threatening, if they refused him, to send them one of his scullions. By the end of 1806, he was, in fact, master of the whole of Greece, with the exception of Bœotia and Attica, and even in the latter he contrived to obtain an influence, by procuring one of his creatures to be sent to Athens as voiwode.

Whilst these enormities were being perpetrated in the name of a pitiless conqueror, Ali tore from the arms of her father the third and last daughter of Ibrahim Pasha, to bestow her in marriage upon his nephew Aden Bey, the second son of Shainitza. Had Ibrahim united his daughter to some powerful neighbour, he might have found a support against Ali's ambitious projects; but, by this union, no refuge was now left him. Some hopes were, however, indulged from Ibrahim's only son being affianced to a daughter of Veli Pasha; but Ali had proposed this union merely with a view of more effectually deluding the man upon whose ruin he had resolved.

At this period it was the plan of Ali to obtain the pashalik of Salonika for his nephew Aden Bey, to replace Ibrahim Pasha of Berat by his son Mouctar, and to establish Veli in the Morea. He had some reason to flatter himself that Santa Maura would fall into his hands; and, in that case, he designed, it is said, to make the gulf of Arta the centre of a piratical system not less famous than that of Algiers. As to his intention of turning pirate we may, however, be allowed to entertain doubts; not on the score of his morality being likely to stand in the way of his doing so, but because he was too cunning a politician to pursue a course which would inevitably have raised up many powerful enemies against him.

A part of his plan he had the good fortune to realise. General Sebastiani, the French ambassador, was then all-powerful in the Divan; the bribes which he distributed among its members, the high renown of Napoleon, and a very natural dread of Russia, secured in the Ottoman counsels the ascendancy of France.

Through the influence of Sebastiani, Ali procured the pashalik of the Morea for Veli, and that of Lepanto for Mouctar. Veli was delighted with his promotion, but Mouctar was stung with envy at being, as he deemed it, degraded to the less splendid government of Lepanto. Ali repaid the service which he had received from the French minister, by accelerating a rupture between Russia and Turkey. As soon as the rupture was decided upon, he obtained the permission which he had so long and ardently desired, to re-occupy the continental dependencies of the Ionian Islands. He lost not a moment in pouncing upon his prey. "Upon taking possession of Prevesa," says Mr. Hughes, " he reduced that unfortunate place by systematic oppression to the state of abject misery in which we saw it. Having, in defiance of the treaty of 1800, deprived most of the original proprietors of their lands and houses, which he distributed among his Mahometan followers, he demolished two-thirds of the city, overthrew the churches, laid the foundation of a splendid serai, and built a spacious mosque. All this was done not only to prevent European states from taking an interest in its restitution, but to furnish a plausible pretext to the Ottoman Porte for refusing ever after to restore a *Turkish* city to the protection of an infidel power. Vonizza and Butrinto were in like manner ruined, though these places were insignificant when compared with Prevesa. Parga luckily escaped the storm, by receiving a Russian garrison into its fortress." At the same time, M. Flory, the Russian consul at Ioannina, was arrested, and preparations for war were made on all sides.

While his agents were engaged in the political intrigues and negotiations, which we shall presently have occasion to narrate, Ali determined upon making a progress through various parts of his pashalik. In some of his excursions he was attended by the consul-general of France, whose experience and abilities he well knew how to appreciate. Some sulphur mines had recently been found in the mountains of Kimara, and Ali, who was much interested in this discovery, engaged the consul to accompany them in a journey which he purposed taking to view them. He at first directed his course towards Dgerovina, a village encircled on all sides by hills wooded with ancient oaks. At this place there is a lake, of which many marvels are related; such as that it has no bottom, and that it absorbs whatever is thrown into it. The vizier informed M. Pouqueville, that he had himself formerly passed over the same lake in a boat, a fact which completely falsified its pretended quality of absorption; " unless," said Ali, smiling upon his hearers, " we make an exception as to stones." He next stated, that, having caused the depth of the lake to be ascertained, the line had reported thirty fathoms at the borders, then forty, and in the middle from a hundred to a hundred and twenty. He could not help laughing when the French consul told him that one of the professors of the college of Ioannina maintained that the lake, like that of Labchistas, ran under ground and formed the Pistritza. " This sort of people," said he, " never see anything like other folks. Yet he has lived here; but, like his brethren, he prefers adhering to old traditions rather than give himself the trouble of investigating facts. I know some (said he, looking at his kiaya, or lieutenant-general), who have a knack of telling these old-women's stories, which would make you go to sleep standing — what is your opinion, wise one?" The kiaya, quite disconcerted, had not a word to say. " That man," continued Ali, " is one of those who can see with his eyes shut. Would you believe it?

he pretends that the plague consists of a vast number of animalcules, which might be seen through a magnifying-glass, if one could be procured of sufficient power." After having thus amused himself at the kiaya's expense, he said to him, " You shall dine with us to-day. Let us have some of the best wine. You have no objection to a glass, have you?" The kiaya excused himself.—" Why! you were not so scrupulous formerly; and, as you intend to reform your conduct, go and dine in the kitchen."—" But, my lord, the law of our Prophet—" " Silence! I am a prophet in my own country, and if I had a mind," added he in an ironical tone, " I could make you own it too." At these words the kiaya withdrew, to take his meal in another apartment.

His splendid retinue of servants and pages having arranged the repast upon a service of silver gilt, Ali and his guest ate their food from plates of Sèvres porcelain, ornamented with designs by French artists. According to the vizier's custom, there was placed before him a whole lamb, weighing twelve pounds, of which, without masticating it, he devoured more than half, besides cloves of garlic, hard eggs, an eel, and a great variety of other things; contenting himself afterwards with touching many dishes with his finger, to show that he liked them, and that they might be cleared away. Pilau, or boiled rice, the usual dessert of the Turks, over which they pour curdled cream, was now brought up. On dipping his spoon into it, the vizier discovered a tuft of feathers, which proved that the rice had been boiled in the same water that had been used to scald off the feathers. " At that instant," says M. Pouqueville, " I saw the satrap turn pale; and immediate symptoms of terror were manifested by his attendants."—" What is this? how!" His voice was completely altered, when his eyes accidentally meeting mine, he was unable (I know not why) to continue his invective, and he burst into a loud fit of laughter. " You see, my son, how I am treated? Some day or other I shall certainly hang them."—" That will not teach them better cookery."—" Oh, indeed, it will. If you knew how essential this is to good order."—" For this once, however, I hope you will forgive them?"—" Yes; but they must eat the pilau boiled in the dish-water, with all the feathers in it. Had it not been for you, their heads should have been exhibited in the court-yard." At this time there were about half a dozen heads of robbers exposed on stakes, previously to their being sent to Constantinople. The ludicrous sentence, passed by Ali on the cook, was strictly executed.

The sulphur mine, the object of the journey, upon which so many grand projects and speculations had been built, was found near the surface of the earth. The native sulphur was contained in a black earthy envelope. Trials having been made upon some specimens of it, orders were given to erect furnaces, and the peasants were about to be condemned to waste their lives in mining, when, fortunately for them, the stupidity of an Italian, who was appointed superintendant of the works, disgusted the vizier with a scheme which he renounced with as much indifference as he had displayed eagerness to undertake it. This lucky blunder of the Italian consisted in attempting to burn out the sulphur instead of subliming it.

On his return to Ioannina, the pasha stopped at an *ambari*, or granary, where he was joined by the French consul. As M. Pouqueville entered, the inhabitants of the neighbouring village of Coucoulios came to present his highness with a cup of milk and a few handfuls of meal, in token of the prosperity and abundance which spring up under the feet of a powerful man. "May you enjoy a long and happy life!" said they to him; "may you be full of years! but we pray that you will either hang or drown us, or diminish the taxes with which we are overwhelmed." The pasha, without seeming to understand these complaints, invited the consul to sit down by him on a pile of maize, covered with a carpet. He then made a sign to the peasants to retire, telling them to go in peace, and pray God for him; assuring them, that, if Providence spared his life, they should want for nothing. At length his harangue being concluded, the petitioners had already passed the door, when he ordered them to be called back, and upon his saying to them that "he held them near his heart," the consul began to hope that the vizier had relented towards these unfortunate villagers. But his hopes were soon blighted; for, after a moment's pause, Ali proceeded to finish his speech in these consoling words—" As a proof of which, you shall build me, at your own expense, a residence contiguous to this storehouse: let it be done in six months without fail, or woe be to your heads!"—" Write," said he to one of his secretaries, to whom he dictated the plan, the dimensions, and other particulars; and he added, amidst loud bursts of laughter, " It is a most charming spot; I shall often have hunting-parties here; I must have some place to alight at."

This decision was so strange, that, though it ruined a whole village, the French consul involuntarily joined in the laugh. "This is your way," said the vizier to him: " Now these rascals have been draining me dry; they owe me heaps of money, interest upon interest; besides, they were my father's enemies." As the poor wretches whom he thus accused were probably not born in the lifetime of Ali's father, the consul, recollecting the fable of the wolf and the lamb, was about to relate it to him, when one of the vizier's counsellors made him a sign not to plead the cause of the inhabitants of Coucoulios. In truth, their champion would probably have been as successful in their behalf as Don Quixote was in redressing the wrongs of the shepherd-boy.

In this, as in his other journeys, the vizier held his assizes wherever he happened to be, sometimes in a palace, at other times by the side of a ditch. The monks of the monastery of Losino, near Coucoulios, were now summoned before him, and required to give an account of the tithes belonging to the treasury, and of the rent due for commonage. As they were able to produce receipts sealed with his highness's seal, they were, as a special favour, under pretence of their not liking him, only condemned to cut and cart every year to Ioannina eight thousand logs of fire-wood for his palace. After this acquittal, they were leaving the granary, when they were stopped by Mouctar Pasha, who was come to meet his father, and, in his turn, ordered them not to fail to bring an equal quantity of wood for his own use.

The next who was brought before the judgment-seat was a *papas*, whom the inhabitants accused of having caused the burning of a tower, of which he had the care as dervendji. They cried out, too, that he was a drunkard, and an incapable fellow. The only answer made by the vizier was, that he wished to have his tower in the same state as when he appointed the balouk-bashi, or captain, to the command of it. To this the papas coolly replied, that he could not have it so, " even though you were to hang me for it, which, however, will not be the case." —" Well!" said the vizier, " this is extraordinary indeed!"—" In the first place, my lord," responded the accused, " all the property I have in the world is my wife, who is old, and fourteen goats, which she takes out to feed in the mountains. If they were all sold, they would not fetch enough to pay for the door of the tower; and this my enemies well know. But there is one thing of which your highness seems to be ignorant; namely, that these men, so zealous in your service, have owed you for ten years the tithes upon wine. They who tax me with drunkenness make the poor supply wine, and then they drink it themselves."—" This is always the way I am served," said the vizier, sighing, "and yet people wonder that I am poor—and how much does this come to in a year?"—" More than ten thousand okkes of wine, without reckoning the brandy they distil."—" Yes, wine and brandy! I have not a soul, positively not a single soul, who cares about my interests; this is the way I am ruined—and how much does this make?" —" More than four thousand piastres a year, my lord, at the very lowest."—" Let me see! fifty thousand piastres, and as much for interest; for they have, no doubt, robbed me in many other ways! My son, I appoint thee codja-bashi (primate), in the place of thy accusers, who shall remain in prison till they pay me what they owe me. The village must rebuild the tower at its own expense; and, for thy part, be a faithful servant to me."—" But, my lord, where shall I live? I am in rags; who is to find me clothes?"—" Oh! I give you the house of this man," said the vizier, pointing to one of the dismissed codja-bashis; then, turning to one of his secretaries, he added, " Write an order to the shopkeepers of Ioannina, to clothe the papas from head to foot, and in a handsome style, for the love of me."

Having seen enough of this mode of administering justice, M. Pouqueville quitted the room when another cause was called on. He was followed by the counsellor, who had made a sign to him when he was going to repeat the fable, and who, as soon as they were out of ear-shot of Ali and his officers, addressed him in the following words. " You have just seen a specimen of our government. It is uniformly the same, in great things and in small. I who am a Turk, and a favourite of the prince, cannot tell whether I shall sleep to-morrow in my bed. You wished to plead in behalf of the inhabitants of Coucoulios; set your heart at ease, the hunting-seat will not be built. Philip (this was a surname which he gave to Ali Pasha, in allusion to the wily father of Alexander) only wants to ruin the inhabitants, that he may force them to sell their landed property, and convert their village into a chifflick; this is the whole secret. The codja-bashis, who have just been turned out, will be plundered; and as soon as he has become rich enough, so will the papas who has taken their place. This is the way everything goes on! The primates rob the Greeks, the pashas squeeze the primates, the sultan inherits from the viziers, and he is pillaged by his wives and his courtiers; such is the habitual circulation of the public riches. Here you have a faithful picture of our empire; an empire which, in spite of its inconsistencies, and of rebellions, and the plague, holds together, and will continue to do so, as long as it shall please God to allow of its existence."

M. Pouqueville now took his way to the convent of Jacovo, where he was to lodge for the night. There he found the kiaya and his divan effendi, or chief secretary; and, at supper, they were joined by Dr. Louis Franck, who was then physician to Ali. During the repast, the kiaya, who was probably piqued into this display by the previous sarcasms of his master, made a great parade of his learning, which, however, was entirely confined to extravagant necromantic tales, and dissertations upon judicial astrology; two favourite themes with the Turks. The party then stretched themselves to rest on the floor. Soporific as the prosing of the kiaya was, it failed to produce its natural effect on the French consul, its influence being counteracted by the hard boards on which he was lying, and by the smokiness of the chamber. He consequently rose to look for some one to converse with. In one of the corridors he found the prior, who was carding wool. After a little preliminary conversation, the consul inquired if the holy man had any manuscripts. " Ah ! " exclaimed the prior, " old histories, God keep us from them ! we are orthodox, and all that was written by those Jews or Greeks, who produced nothing but what was heretical, has been burnt, and shall be again, if I can catch any more of their parchments*."—"But," said M. Pouqueville, " the monks were the preservers of those very parchments, and it is to their care that we are indebted for the finest works of antiquity."—" I know nothing about that," growled the barbarian ; " they would have done better to mind only carding their wool." Disgusted by such brute stupidity, the consul hurried back to his chamber; but there he found the pitiless kiaya awake, who inflicted upon him the monotonous and interminable narrative of his life.

The next morning, when it was scarcely daylight, they were informed by a courier that the vizier expected them at the khan of Mazaraki, to which place

---

* The caloyers, says M. Pouqueville, have destroyed more manuscripts and monuments of the arts than the barbarians who desolated Greece. If a statue or a basso-relievo with figures is found, " the sight of them will pollute the beams of the sun." It is lucky when they will content themselves with burying them again ; for they oftener make lime of them. It is the same with inscriptions, &c.

he had repaired before sun-rise. They immediately quitted Jacovo, and, keeping the right bank of the Thyamis, they perceived the ruins of Velas, the ancient Photicæ, where statues and architectural remains have been found, which prove it to have been a flourishing city in the time of the Hellenes. The vizier informed the French consul that he had himself seen dug up the head of a human figure, of colossal proportions, and, according to his own expression, as big as a buffalo's.

In proceeding to join the vizier, the party lost their way, and got entangled among the marshes, and the kiaya and his divan effendi were plunged with their horses into the quagmires. Their unseemly plight furnished Ali with a fresh opportunity of exerting his sarcastical powers on the unfortunate kiaya. After a short halt, at Mazaraki, to breakfast, the vizier gave the signal for departure: and for this once he took his leave without making any exactions—a circumstance which might be looked upon as marvellous, were it not satisfactorily accounted for by the fact of the inhabitants of the neighbouring town of Pagouna having all fled to the mountains, on being informed of his approach.

Having deviated from the direct road, to visit the picturesque cataract of Glizani, on the Thyamis, M. Pouqueville was returning to the party when he saw a horde of furious barbarians dragging two foreigners before the vizier. Hearing that they were Franks, he made his way on horseback through the crowd; and, as he neared them, the two prisoners, who were bound together and almost naked, cried out to him that they were Englishmen. The consul made a sign to them to remain quiet, and running to the pasha, was the first to inform him what was going on. They proved to be two sailors, who had been shipwrecked on the Acroceraunian coast, and had been plundered by the Kimariots. An attempt had been made to cut off the head of one of them, and the wound was still open on his neck. The consul, though his country was at war with England, was too humane a man not to interest himself warmly for the sufferers, and he pleaded their cause with effect. Ali, indeed, could hardly be averse from granting a request which was in accordance with his policy as respected England. The captives were accordingly placed at the disposal of M. Pouqueville. He next desired that they might be supplied with clothing, and Ali gave directions that it should be done. The business was speedily and economically accomplished. Accustomed as he was to similar scenes, it was not without surprise that M. Pouqueville witnessed the Albanian mode of clothing the naked. The officer, who was charged with this benevolent task, gave a box on the ear to a Greek, snatched off his cloak, and threw it over the shoulders of one of the sailors; another operation of this kind furnished the second sailor with a garment. " Dealing about his blows upon all who came nigh him," says M. Pouqueville, " he in a moment found shoes and caps for these two men, who were no less astonished than I was, at a scene which proves how difficult it is, when we have to do with a tyrant, to render a service without inflicting injury on some person or other."

Such is the picture of the progress of a Turkish viceroy through his territories. It is sufficiently repulsive. Yet those who call to mind how justice was often of old administered even in England, and what insufferable nuisances were royal progresses, will make allowance for the customs of semi-barbarous Albania. Bad as the situation of the Albanians was under Ali, it can scarcely be considered as much worse than that of our countrymen, in the times when every feudal lord was an irresponsible tyrant, when torture by fire or on the rack was in use, when the monarch could arbitrarily press into his service musicians, goldsmiths, embroiderers, and other artificers, and when, as Burke happily expresses it, " the royal purveyors, sallying forth from under the gothic portcullis, to purchase provision with power and prerogative, instead of money, brought home the plunder of a hundred markets, and all that could be seized from a flying and hiding country, and deposited their spoil in a hundred caverns, with each its keeper." The same causes, however, which operated to remove these evils in western Europe will, no doubt, ultimately remove them in Turkey, and the natives of that country will rise to a higher rank than is at present occupied by them among civilised nations. With much that is faulty in their character, there is blended much that is worthy of praise; and where virtue is not wholly extinct, there is always ground for hope.

In his efforts to aggrandise his dominions Ali was no less active than in swelling his hoards by every means in his power. To attain possession of the Seven Islands, or at least a part of them, was an object of which he never lost sight. In the most urgent manner, he pressed the French consul-general to prevail on his government to furnish him with officers, artillerymen, and more especially ordnance, and military stores, of which he stood in need. In case of his receiving these, he engaged to act against the Russians with such vigour, as not only to embarrass them in the islands, but also to prevent them from annoying the French in Dalmatia, and sending succours to Cattaro. Early in 1807 his wishes began to be gratified. A detachment of twenty-two artillerymen, under the command of colonel Nicole and captain Ponceton, commenced, on the 14th of February, their march from Ragusa across Bosnia to the north of Albania. These auxiliaries were followed by an entire company from the kingdom of Naples, with several officers, a corvette, a gun-boat, and a considerable quantity of military stores. These troops, which, on their arrival, were quartered at Porto Palermo, Santi Quaranti, Prevesa, Missolonghi, and Lepanto, were placed, by his government, under the direction of M. Pouqueville. Colonel de Vaudoncourt, an officer of engineers, whom marshal Marmont had entrusted with a mission to the beys and pashas of Albania, remained in Ali's dominions to superintend the defensive operations. Under his guidance, Ali first constructed entrenchments round his capital; he also fortified his seraglio of Litaritza, and raised lines and redoubts at Prevesa.

Ali did not suffer his French auxiliars to remain long inactive. Having made Prevesa his grand depôt, he resolved to commence his operations by the siege of Santa Maura. For this service he placed eight thousand Albanians under the command of his favourite general Yusuf. The French officers were willing to lend their aid to this enterprise, as, whatever was the result of it, one consequence of it would be to prevent the enemy from sending succours to Cattaro. When M. Pouqueville arrived on the coast, to inspect the artillerymen from Dalmatia, he found the army encamped on the beach of Playa, opposite Santa Maura, where the channel of the Dioryctos is narrowest. On the rising ground of Periata, a redoubt had been constructed by the French, facing the hostile forts Alexander and Constantine; and a bridge had been thrown across the neighbouring stream, to facilitate the communication with the battery of Teket, whence it was proposed to cannonade the citadel of Santa Maura. The labourers were also busy in erecting forges and constructing flat-bottomed boats. Colonel Nicole and captain Ponceton set the example of working to the soldiers and Grecian peasants placed under their orders, while the Albanian soldiers, secure in their entrenchments from the Russian fire, are alleged to have insulted their new confederates.

From what he now saw, M. Pouqueville was led to conclude, that any kind of military amalgamation with the Turks is impracticable: this conclusion he drew from the contempt and injustice with which they treated the French artillerymen, whose conduct and discipline he declares to have been irreproachable. But though it must be confessed that Turkish prejudices are strong, it is not improbable that, on this occasion, the Albanian soldiers were partly influenced by suspicions as to the good faith of their Christian companions. M. Pouqueville himself owns, that the sole object of the French was merely to effect a diversion, by drawing the attention of the Russians to this quarter, in order to hinder them from reinforcing Cattaro: and it is not unlikely that this may have produced a lukewarmness in their co-operation, which could not but be displeasing to Ali, who was eager to become master of the Ionian Islands, or at least of Santa Maura.

This desire of acquiring the Islands displayed the prudent politician. Pyrrhus, and every ruler of Epirus who had understood his own interests, had expressed the same wish. Not that, as many have imputed to him, it was the intention of Ali to render himself an independent sovereign; his only aim was to establish a large fief; an undertaking not altogether novel in the Ottoman empire. The pashas of Mosul, the great Turkish beys of Asia Minor, the Mamelukes of Egypt, and several agas of Macedonia, were already in hereditary possession either of whole provinces, or of numerous districts. The vizier of Ioannina cannot, therefore, be justly charged with being actuated by a rebellious spirit. So far from it, that, in all his relations with the French government, he was careful to preserve the interests of the Turkish empire. In fact, the successive acquisition of all the small maritime cantons of Epirus was a work of enlightened policy, and one which was highly advantageous to the interests of Turkey in general. We should be guilty of historical partiality, were we to view only the evils which these small Christian provinces have suffered. As a Mussulman, and as a vizier of the Ottoman Porte, Ali could not be expected to be either the protector of the Christian religion, or the promoter of European civilisation. Why, then, should not allowances be made in his favour, for the principles in which he was brought up, and the views with which he was naturally inspired by his relative duties to his country and his sovereign?

That the subject ought to be regarded in this light, we have the testimony of an able and disinterested witness, by no means partial to Ali, but who, having been the British envoy at Ioannina, had the best means of correctly estimating his conduct. "Ali Pasha," says Lieutenant-colonel Leake, "may have thwarted the execution of all the measures of the Porte which tended to reduce his authority, and in general those which did not originate with himself; he may have transmitted a larger sum to Constantinople in the shape of presents to persons in power, than in that of tribute to the imperial treasury; and, in the latter respect, he may never have sent as much as satisfied the wishes of government; nevertheless it is probable that the Porte, during his reign, was more truly master of Greece than it had ever been before, and that it derived, upon the whole, as much revenue from the country; while it is certain, that by leaving Ali to oppose the armed Greeks to one another, and to suppress the spirit of revolt by the military strength of Albania, she most effectually secured herself against the consequences of foreign intrigues among the Christian subjects of European Turkey; and that the concentration of power in Ali's hands was the best protection which the empire could possess on a frontier where it was endangered by the increase of the power of France, not less than the north-eastern side was menaced by the encroachments of Russia."

Animated by other passions, and actuated by far different motives, the officers and agents of the French government could not consider Ali in this point of view. It was easily to be seen, therefore, that no great length of time would elapse before the vizier would be regarded by them as a faithless tyrant, ready to sacrifice everything to gratify his own cupidity and ambition. Already M. de Vaudoncourt complained that all his plans were counteracted by the vizier's insatiable avarice. But as he had it in his instructions to do all that might contribute to keep the Russians in check, he submitted to the caprices of the pasha, not, however, without complaining of him very bitterly in his official correspondence, and describing him in the most unfavourable colours.

Ali, meanwhile, resolved to open a direct communication with Napoleon, in order to avoid the delay and probable misrepresentation which might be caused by his corresponding only with the French ministers. He accordingly appointed as his envoy a renegade Italian, named Mollach Mehemet Effendi, who had been interpreter to Bonaparte in Egypt, and was now the pasha's secretary. The envoy was instructed to obtain a promise that the Ionian Islands, or at least Santa Maura and Parga, should be delivered over to

P

Ali whenever a peace was made, and to urge, as a reason for the cession, that it would be conformable to the interests of France, by securing to her a powerful ally in the Mediterranean. The envoy was admitted to an interview, at Warsaw, by Napoleon, who appears to have put him off with that vague kind of language which keeps hope alive, and yet may eventually be construed as he pleases by the person who has used it. Mehemet followed the victorious monarch to Tilsit, where, at the conferences for a peace, he made another effort to accomplish his master's object. But that which Napoleon had avoided granting while the contest was undecided, he was not disposed to concede at the moment when his triumph was complete. He was, in truth, secretly hostile to the Turks, though his ambassador at Constantinople was lavishing upon them professions of friendship. His conduct with respect to an article of the treaty of Tilsit affords irrefragable proof of his double-dealing in regard to the Porte. By that article, it was stipulated that the Russians should evacuate Moldavia and Wallachia, which they had treacherously seized upon without a declaration of war; but, in conversations with Alexander of Russia at Tilsit, the French emperor encouraged him to delay withdrawing the Russian army, declared that it was no longer possible to tolerate the continuance of the Turks in Europe, and talked of driving them into Asia. At last, indeed, he changed his opinion so far as to say, that they might be allowed to retain Constantinople and some of the neighbouring provinces. It was, no doubt, partly with a view to eventual hostilities against Turkey, that, by a secret article of the treaty of Tilsit, the dominion of the Ionian Islands was transferred to France. Having secured them for himself, Napoleon, of course, was not disposed to relinquish any part of them to the satrap of Albania, the more especially as it was highly probable that the satrap would soon be enrolled among his enemies.

Ali was, in fact, not long before he became highly exasperated against his Gallic allies. As soon as the treaty of Tilsit was entered upon, the French officers and artillerymen refused to act against the Russians, and he was, in consequence, obliged to desist from the siege of Santa Maura. The paroxysm of rage, into which he was thrown by this event, had scarcely subsided before it was renewed by another circumstance. Disappointed in his expectations as to Santa Maura, he still hoped that he might succeed in obtaining Parga. When, therefore, Cæsar Berthier was sent by Napoleon as governor of Corfu, Ali despatched to him two agents, to claim the surrender of the town and territory of Corfu, in conformity with the treaty of the 25th of March, 1800. Berthier is said to have been on the point of complying, when he was prevented by the representations of the Ionian senate, and of deputies who arrived from Parga. "If," said the deputies, "it accords with the interests of the French empire, that the small surface of land on which our country is situated should be given up to the Turks, let, at least, a rock be granted to us, on which we may preserve our liberty and independence, far from the tyrant who has butchered our neighbours and our brethren." The pleading of the senate and the deputies prevailed, and the demand of Ali Pasha was refused.

It was manifest that he had now nothing to hope, and much to fear, from the French; who were likely to prove more formidable neighbours than the Russians could have been. In this emergency, it was natural that he should look towards England for support. He, therefore, sent an agent to Malta, to press the English to attack the Ionian Isles, and settle their differences with the Porte, and he prepared to send an envoy to London, to enter into a negociation with the British court. In taking these steps, he is said to have had the approbation of the Ottoman government. At the same time, to lull suspicion asleep, he despatched George Ianco to Venice, where Napoleon then was, to make overtures to the French emperor. Napoleon, however, refused to listen to the envoy. "Take back your despatches," said he, "and tell your master that I will hear no more about him. I know how to obtain his punishment from the grand signior, if he should dare in future to violate the treaties which exist between France and the Ottoman Porte." With this brief and bitter message, Ianco was dismissed.

The receipt of this defiance was the signal for Ali to expedite his envoy Seid Achmet to the British capital. He did not immediately engage in direct hostilities against the French garrisons in the islands, but his conduct towards them strongly marked his aversion. Having become exceedingly distressed for money, the authorities in Corfu sent a deputation to him, soliciting a loan. To this application he haughtily replied, that the pasha of Ioannina was neither a banker nor a merchant. To distress the French still more, he threw as many obstacles as possible in the way of their procuring supplies of corn, cattle, and firewood, from the Continent; he imposed enormous duties on those exports, and required that the money should be paid in advance. Cæsar Berthier was at length so irritated, that he determined to compel Ali to resign the three ex-Venetian towns on the mainland; but he delayed so long, that Ali had time to throw large garrisons into them, and render the conquest impracticable.

A correspendence, which soon became frequent, had been opened by Ali with Lord Collingwood, the British admiral in the Mediterranean, who was blockading Corfu and the other islands. In his letters, his lordship laboured to impress on Ali the danger which he had to apprehend from the vicinity of the French, and the necessity of stopping their supply of provisions from Albania. Ali, on his part, was profuse in protestations of good-will. " I am persuaded," says he, in one of his letters, " that it will be most agreeable to my government at Constantinople to renew the good old friendship that subsisted with the English, and I feel extremely happy in being placed in a situation where I may render any service to two nations who were once the strictest friends and allies. I hope that with your excellency's concurrence, I shall ere long effect the wish of my heart in the restoration of friendship with the illustrious British nation, and that the union of the two kingdoms will be confirmed for ever. If the machinations of the French be as bad as your excellency represents them to be, the event must still depend upon the divine will. In God's mercy are all our hopes, and frequent are the examples which we have of it; for he has many times left our enemies deluded with shame. I hope, however, that I shall soon have the pleasure to hear of the triumphs of the British arms, and that the enemy will be destroyed in the midst of his evil projects. As for myself, I shall ever be the same, at all times and in all circumstances. I spoke to Mr. Leake of what I thought most necessary at present, and I hope he has mentioned it to your excellency. I anxiously wish that it may be put in execution as soon as possible, until we can stop the supplies of troops and provisions from entering the islands. The French ambassador endeavours, by the most flattering words, to lessen the vigilance and attention of my government; but all this will have no effect on the attachment which we bear to the English nation. I beg of your excellency to favour me with any news you have; and I should be glad if you would write to me in future either in Italian, French, or Greek, as I have not a good interpreter for the English language. In the name of God I wish you health, happiness, and the accomplishment of all your desires. Your sincere and true friend, THE VIZIER, ALI PASHA."

In consequence of this correspondence, an English agent was sent to have a conference with Ali. The Pasha was then residing at Prevesa. The mode which he adopted to prevent the interview from being known to the French consul is characteristic of the man. Having invited M. Pouqueville to a rural festival near Vonitza, on the gulf of Arta, he suddenly left his guest in the midst of the amusements, crossed the gulf in a swift-sailing boat, mounted a horse which was in readiness, and galloped over the plain to the spot where our envoy was waiting for him. The meeting took place at midnight, among the ruins of Niçopolis, and it was in that desolate scene that the future plan of operations was concerted by the British representative and the satrap of Albania.

CHAPTER IX.

Revolt in Thessaly—Characters of the Planners of the Revolt—Proceedings and Death of Blacavas—Ali in danger from Mustapha Bairactar—Artful Letter of Ali to Lord Collingwood—He exerts himself to bring about a peace between Great Britain and Turkey—Ali attacks the Pasha of Berat—Conquest of Berat—Double-dealing of Ali—He subdues the Kimariots—He evades an Order to join the Turkish Army—Characters of his Sons, Mouctar and Veli—Ali threatened with an Attack by the French—He makes Ibrahim Pasha Prisoner, and defeats a Confederacy against himself—He takes Argyro Castro—Hypocritical Speech of Ali—His horrible Revenge on the Gardikiots—Mustapha Pasha starved to Death—Yusuf the Dervise—Art of Ali—Demetrius Paleopoulo.

ABOUT the period when Ali was carrying on an active correspondence with the British admiral in the Adriatic, a revolt broke out in Thessaly, which wore at first a formidable appearance. The plan of it seems to have been concerted long before by three remarkable individuals; though, ultimately, the attempt to carry it into execution devolved upon a single leader. One of these persons was Demetrio Paleopoulo, who, as we have already stated, was driven by Ali from the intended scene of action before the scheme was matured. The second was Niko-Tzaras, a Thessalian, born at Alassona. His ancestors had all been klephtes, and his father was a captain of Armatoles. He received a good education; but, with his father, was driven by the treachery of the Turks to seek an asylum in the mountains, and resume the klephtic profession. On the death of the elder Tzaras, who was killed in a skirmish, Niko took the command of the band, and distinguished himself by his activity and valour. At length he concluded a treaty with Ali, retired into private life, and married. It is probable that he would have continued to exist in privacy, had he not been provoked to take up arms by the perfidy of Ali, who employed assassins to way-lay him. In 1804 or 1805, in consequence, it is supposed, of his having entered into the Russian project of producing an insurrection in Greece, he undertook, with three hundred men, an expedition into Macedon, intending, it is said, to pass mount Rhodope, and join Prince Hypsilanti in Wallachia. The Turks were aware of his purpose, and, near the bridge of Pravi, on the Karasou, they surrounded him with three thousand men. Taking post on a height, he defended himself for three days against numerous attacks, though he had neither water nor provisions. On the third evening, his men having no longer any cartridges, he led them to the charge, broke through and dispersed the encircling enemy, forced the passage of the bridge, which was closed with iron chains, and took possession of Pravi, where they halted, and refreshed themselves. As the march towards Wallachia was now become impossible, Tzaras led his gallant band back to Thessaly, and reached his native mountains in safety. He then turned pirate, and soon became dreaded by the Turks; but, in 1806 or 1807, as he was going on board his vessel, he was mortally wounded by an Albanian, who fired at him from behind a tree. Tzaras was remarkable for manly beauty, and almost preternatural agility and strength; his men thought nothing impossible which he undertook; and the Albanians held him in such superstitious terror that they deemed him invulnerable. His death, and the absence of Paleopoulo, were circumstances which threw " ominous conjecture on the whole success" of the Thessalian insurrection.

The third leader, Euthemos Blacavas, or as he was usually called, Papas Euthemos, was brought up to the church; but, when his father died, he quitted the altar, and girded on the sword. His main object, however, was not plunder; it was the liberation of Greece. To him is attributed the first proposal for effecting a rising in Thessaly. There is no proof that he took any part in the Russian project; nor, indeed, does he appear to have been desirous of Russian aid in his own. As it was thought imprudent to attempt a general revolution at present, it was resolved, by the three chiefs, that their early efforts should be confined to overthrowing Ali, and establishing a Greek government in the provinces over which he ruled. For the destruction of the vizier, they knew that they might calculate upon the co-operation of a multitude of Turkish agas; and, if that were accomplished, they might hope to succeed in rousing to arms the remainder of Greece.

Notwithstanding the loss of Tzaras and Paleopoulo, Blacavas determined to persevere. A day was fixed for the chiefs to meet in the Thessalian part of Pindus, whence they were to descend with all their force into Lower Thessaly, rouse the natives to arms, and then direct their march on Ioannina. As a preliminary step, Blacavas resolved to seize upon Kastri, a post which is the key of the defiles leading into Macedon and Epirus. His brothers Theodore and Demetrius, with about three hundred men, were accordingly despatched to secure it. The town was taken; but, before the brothers could put it in a state of defence, they were surrounded by four thousand Albanians, at the head of whom was Mouctar Pasha. The plan of the insurrection had been betrayed to Ali, by a traitor named Deli Ghianni; and, ere the chiefs could draw together their followers, the vizier had made arrangements to frustrate their design. Demetrius and Theodore fought with the utmost valour, and were nobly seconded by their troops; but numbers prevailed, and the whole of the Greeks perished. Blacavas, with five hundred men, still kept the field, and was aided by a few other chiefs. He could, however, effect nothing, and his situation grew daily more desperate. The chiefs were detached from him by the gold of Ali, and the exhortations of Gabriel, the archbishop of Larissa, dissuaded the Thessalians from joining the standard of revolt. Blacavas was, therefore, compelled to fly. It is uncertain whether, as some say, he was delivered up by the Capudan Pasha, to whom he fled, or whether he voluntarily surrendered, on a promise that his life should be spared. His fate is not doubtful. He was fruitlessly tortured at Ioannina, in the hope of drawing confessions from him, and was then cut alive into pieces by the public executioner.

The danger which had threatened Ali from this insurrection was trifling compared with another peril to which he was soon after exposed. He was believed, and not without an appearance of reason, to have had a share in fomenting the insurrection of the janissaries relative to the Nizam Djedid, and in the subsequent intrigues which led to the deposition of Sultan Selim. Mustapha Bairactar, the pasha of Rudschuk, was now at the head of a powerful army, to restore his dethroned sovereign, and to punish the rebels. Ali was, of course, one of the objects of his hatred. In vain did the pasha of Ioannina endeavour to conciliate this formidable foe. " Go back to Ali Tepelen," said Mustapha to one of the pasha's messengers, "tell him that I have prolonged the truce with the Russians, and that you saw me setting off to Constantinople to restore order. Henceforth, I will have nothing more to do with that traitor than what is necessary to deprive him and his criminal race of their heads. Let him know that, should I fall in the enterprise which I have undertaken, I have bequeathed the care of taking vengeance for me to my lieutenant Kurschid Pasha. I give you your life, you may be gone."

Ali is said to have been alarmed beyond measure by these threats, to have meditated flight to his native place, and to have sought, but in vain, the intercession of the French consul at Ioannina, to procure for him the good offices of Napoleon's ambassador at the Ottoman capital. The entrance of Mustapha into Constantinople, and his appointment as grand vizier, must have added to the fears of the satrap. Ali, however, was not a man to sink without a struggle. He appears to have intrigued strenuously at the Turkish metropolis, and he sought support from the British admiral in the Adriatic. In one of his letters to Lord Collingwood he thus expresses himself: "Your great judgment and profound knowledge of our affairs make me hope that you will not imagine what has been done by Mustapha Pasha is agreeable to the will of the nation, or of its principal members. Among the rest, Ismael, bey of Serres, who thinks as I do, will set off in a few days, at the head of a strong force, to Adrianople, for the purpose of being present at what may take place. Many events will happen, and much blood be spilt, before the management of affairs will be left to Mustapha Pasha, who has been instigated to these acts by the insidious arts of our enemy. It is true that he at present holds the seals, but it is only by violence, and I make no doubt that affairs will soon assume a more pleasing aspect. For this reason it is necessary that there should be in my neighbourhood a sufficient naval force, of which the senior officer should receive full powers to concert and co operate with me in all that is necessary. Your excel lency is well aware that mankind at present seem unhappily urged on by the desire to subvert and desolate. I have proposed to your government to provide against such disposition and its necessary effects; but it is beyond my ability alone, and I cannot counteract them unless support be afforded me. Your government, which makes daily so many sacrifices, and sends, as we hear, ships and money to the Baltic, should not be disheartened. If it could do the same in this quarter, it would be better served than it may expect, and an opportunity would be afforded me of demonstrating with honour my anxious zeal and inclination towards it. Whatever may be the event of affairs in the capital, it is evident that I shall be the object of persecution; and as I have dedicated myself entirely to your nation, I hope that it will feel a pride in protecting me, and assisting me in such a manner as may enable me to defend my person and property, and accomplish those services which I feel the greatest inclination to render."

It is manifest, from this letter, that Ali had made up his mind to venture upon a contest with Mustapha Bairactar, and even, if it must be so, with the sultan, provided he could procure the support of Great Britain. His courage, however, was not put to the proof. The insurrection at Constantinople, in which Bairactar fell, relieved Ali from the danger which threatened him. The new sultan, Mahmoud, confirmed him and his family in all their charges and dignities, and revoked the commission of Rumili-valisee, which had been given to Kurschid, the friend of Bairactar. A present of two thousand purses, from the vizier of Ioannina, is said to have influenced the sultan. The gold had doubtless its weight; but, whatever might be the real opinion and intention of the monarch, with respect to Ali, he was at present surrounded by too many difficulties to think of engaging in hostilities against his powerful vassal.

Ali now renewed his exertions to bring about a peace between Turkey and Great Britain. Mr. Adair, the British minister, had been on the point of quitting Constantinople in despair of success, but had been earnestly dissuaded from it by the vizier of Ioannina. Early in 1809, the negociation was conducted to a prosperous close. As soon as it was completed, Ali despatched an envoy to England, to represent the services which he had rendered. For these services he had already tried to obtain payment, by procuring a promise from Mr. Adair, to aid him in getting possession of Parga; but the British ambassador had refused to consent to that city being delivered up to him. As, however, Ali had undoubtedly been useful, the British cabinet rewarded him, by a present of several hundred Congreve rockets and a fine train of artillery. Major Leake was sent over with the gift, to teach the Albanian troops the management of it, and to act as English resident. In return, the vizier opened his ports to our cruisers and merchants, and furnished supplies for the navy, and for the armies in Spain and Portugal.

Being once more firmly fixed in the seat of government, Ali resumed his projects of ambition. He had for many years cast a longing eye upon the territory occupied by Ibrahim, pasha of Berat, the father-in-law of Mouctar and Veli, and a favourable opportunity for gratifying his longing was now thrown in his way by the folly of Ibrahim. On the ground that the Divan had abandoned him to an enemy who was sold to the British ministry, the pasha of Berat wrote to the French government, desiring to be taken under its protection, and offering to it the exclusive commerce of the port of Avlona, and the admission of some French artillerymen into the fortress. This was indubitably an act of treason towards the sultan, as well as of decided hostility against the vizier of Ioannina, who had every reason to believe that if France obtained a footing at Avlona his dominions would not long be safe.

To have disclosed to the Divan the misconduct of Ibrahim, would have been the proper mode of proceeding for Ali to adopt; but that would not answer his purpose, as the Turkish government might perhaps merely replace the offending pasha by another person, and thus the vizier of Ioannina would derive no benefit from the downfall of Ibrahim. By making war on him himself he should become master of the pashalik of Berat, and he, therefore, resolved to attack him. The general to whom he committed the enterprise, was Omer Bey Vrioni. This individual was a personal enemy of Ibrahim, who had banished him from Berat and confiscated his property. Omer went to Egypt, where he distinguished himself against the English during the invasion in 1807, and he had recently returned from the country, with an enormous fortune, and a high reputation for valour.

The character which he had acquired was well sustained on this occasion by Omer. The citadel of Berat stands upon a lofty and partly precipitous eminence on the right bank of the Apsus, and overlooks the city. Its reduction, had it been well defended, must have been a work of time and difficulty. But Omer plied the siege so vigorously, and the bombardment and the Congreve rockets inspired the garrison with so much terror, that in a short time the fortress capitulated. Ibrahim Pasha was allowed to retire to Avlona, on condition of giving his only son as a hostage. The feeble defence made by the castle of Berat, M. Pouqueville, rather ludicrously, ascribes to the poverty of Ibrahim, which prevented him from raising a sufficient garrison. It is, however, not easy to believe the poverty of any pasha, much less of one who had for many years ruled a rich and extensive pashalik. The assertion of M. Pouqueville is rendered the more absurd, by his telling us, in the very next page, that Ali employed the treasures of Ibrahim to bribe the Divan, and by that means obtained pardon for his unauthorised attack upon Berat. The government of the conquered pashalik was conferred upon Mouctar, though, as a mark of respect for his age and past services, the title of Vizier was preserved to Ibrahim.

The conquest of Berat being accomplished, Ali passed rapidly to the southern part of his dominions. The British troops, under General Oswald, were besieging Santa Maura; and, trusting that he should find an occasion to interfere, the vizier encamped with a large force opposite to the island. He was ardently desirous of possessing Santa Maura, and, as the English gave him no hopes, be, with his wonted contempt of honour, began to make overtures to the French. During the siege, he secretly introduced Baudrand, a French colonel of engineers, into the fortress, while he himself was entertaining General Oswald, and Mr. Foresti, the English resident, at supper, and cajoling them with professions of inviolable fidelity, He also assisted M. Pouqueville in getting provisions and signals into the place, and is even said to have offered, if the governor would evacuate the citadel, to take possession of it himself, and then make common cause with the French against the besiegers. So secret, however, did he keep his intrigues, that, on the surrender of the citadel, he received the thanks of the British general, for having contributed to the successful result of the enterprise. He now repeated his solicitations to obtain the cession of the island. They were pressed in vain; and he then asked permission to build barracks on the coast for his soldiers, which was granted. Instead of barracks, he constructed two forts, which commanded not only the channel between the continent and the island, but even the citadel of Santa Maura.

Foiled in his expectations at Santa Maura, Ali found consolation in the triumph which he elsewhere obtained. The Kimariots had long struggled against him with courage and good fortune. So recently as the latter end of 1807, they had defeated a sudden attack which he made upon them, and caused him a loss of 1500 men. Since then he had been active in his efforts to disunite and weaken them, and he had succeeded. Believing them to be sufficiently enfeebled, he now marched his forces against them, and, by dint of bribery as well as arms, he at last crushed them. Their principal village, called Vouno, was betrayed to him by four brothers, of the name of Casnezzi. The bravest of the Kimariots still held out, and fought sword in hand, with scarcely any pause, for three days after they had expended their ammunition; the major part of them were slain, the remainder submitted, and gave hostages for their future obedience. Pronio Aga of Paramithia, and Hassan Zapari of Margariti, were the next victims; they capitulated, and, in violation of the treaty, were consigned to a dungeon at Ioannina.

Ali was now summoned to take the field with his forces, and join the grand vizier at Schumla. It has been surmised that, in giving these orders, the sultan was moved by a desire to draw him to a distance from his friends and resources, that he might safely destroy him. The pasha himself evidently suspected some such design, and determined not to throw himself in the way of danger. A positive refusal to obey would, however, have been nearly as dangerous; and, therefore, he had recourse to stratagem. He immediately retook the road to his capital, causing himself to be carried in a litter, as though dangerously ill; he wrote in the most submissive terms to the Divan, lavishing professions of attachment upon the Sultan, and lamenting that his heavy infirmities kept him from wielding the sword for his master; he wore green spectacles on account of the blindness with which he affected to be threatened; he never appeared in public without being surrounded by a throng of physicians; and he backed all this by what was of greater weight, by magnificent presents, and still more magnificent promises, to the Ottoman ministers. The trick succeeded, and he was allowed to send his sons Mouctar and Veli as his substitutes.

The brothers departed with a reluctance which seems to have excited the bile of their father. "Our coxcombs are set off," said he, shortly after, to the French consul; "unfortunate Ali! thou hast hatched nothing but hens!" It is to be regretted, for the sake of humanity, that his brood did not possess the innocence of the bird to which he sarcastically likened them.

The two eldest offspring of Ali have been variously described. M. de Vaudoncourt represents Mouctar as possessing personal courage, probity, and generosity, being a friend to the arts and sciences, plain in dress, temperate, unsuspecting, and punctually fulfilling his engagements. "The Greeks," says he, "love and esteem him, and the reverence of the Albanians for him knows no bounds." A far different picture of him is given by Mr. Hughes. "He had," says Mr. Hughes, "not one virtue to recommend him but his martial courage, nor had he made any progress during his residence in Albania to secure the affections of any class of his father's subjects, except perhaps a portion of the Albanian soldiery. Brutal ferocity, degrading sensuality, and monstrous perfidy, were the leading features of his character; he was considered to be forgetful of favours and a deserter of his friends, without any portion of that political talent which might have enabled him to retain dominion, if fortune had put it into his hands." When we call to mind the decorations of Mouctar's palace, and the violence of his passions*, we shall be tempted to believe, that the dark portrait drawn by Mr. Hughes is the true likeness.

Of Veli, M. de Vaudoncourt says, he " in many respects resembles his father. Like him he is covetous, ambitious, false, and distrustful. He is rapacious, and does not perform what he promises. He is often in want of money, but does not find people inclined to lend, as his brother does. He is a lover of magnificence and show; dress and furniture are important concerns with him; and his effeminate and dissolute way of life is very expensive. By his extravagance he has deeply involved himself in debt. Those who serve him are paid ill, or not at all." In some of the lighter parts of the censure bestowed on Veli, Mr. Hughes concurs; but his general character of him is more favourable. " He was," says he, " considered the most accomplished gentleman in the Turkish dominions; and though a strong bigot to the Mahometan faith, had a decided taste for the habits, arts, and luxuries of civilised Europe. Dissipated to excess, he was generous in his prodigality, though the indulgence of his inordinate passions often urged him on to acts of the most rapacious injustice. He had a fine person, set off by the most engaging manners, with much natural sagacity and good sense: nor was he devoid of courage, or uninfluenced by the love of military glory. In his political career he had devoted himself constantly to the interests of his lawful

---

* See pp. 65 and 156.

sovereign, and probably there did not exist a more attached and faithful subject of the Porte." His comparative humanity seems to be proved by the fact that, during his government of the Morea, the number of executions was much smaller than at any preceding period. His taste is shown by his having once turned aside, which no Turk ever did before, to visit the ruins of Athens. On that occasion, he pitched his tents beyond the walls, and requested that he might be considered as *enas Milordos* come to examine the curiosities of the place.

Having been frustrated in his purpose of drawing Ali to Schumla, the sultan, who hated him as one of those who caused the dethronement and death of Selim, and felt that the same arts might be employed against his own authority and life, is said to have given his sanction to a plan which could hardly have failed to prove the destruction of the satrap. It was arranged that a force from Corfu, aided by a large corps, under Marmont, from Dalmatia, should attack the pasha in the heart of his territory. The project was rendered abortive, in the first instance, by the troops being called off to stop the progress of the British in Spain; and, though the French would have subsequently made the attempt from Corfu alone, they were so closely watched by our squadron that it was impossible for them to accomplish their design.

As he could not yet overthrow Ali, the sultan took measures to diminish his power. Kurchid Pasha was again appointed Rumili-valisee, and was ordered to reside at Monastir, doubtless that he might be at hand to watch the proceedings of the vizier. By this step Cisaxian Macedonia was withdrawn from the domain of Ali. At the same time Veli was transferred from the pashalik of the Morea to that of Thessaly, which was taken from his father. The known loyalty of Veli offered a security for the allegiance of Thessaly, and it was hoped that his nomination to this government would excite the jealousy and anger of Ali, and alienate him from his son.

Thus curtailed on one side, Ali sought to indemnify himself on another. The first victim was Ibrahim Pasha, whom Ali suspected, or pretended to suspect, of having had a hand in the recent hostile manifestations against him. Ibrahim was closely besieged in Avlona, while, to prevent the introduction of supplies from the French, the port was blockaded by two English frigates. The beys of the place were also incited to revolt by the vizier; and the unfortunate pasha was, in consequence, under the necessity of flying in disguise, with a few of his followers, to the mountains of Liapuria. There, with his wife, he was betrayed to his enemy. Far from showing him the attentions due to his rank and relationship, Ali, after having imprisoned him for twelve months at Konitza, at length tore him from the arms of his wife, and threw him into a dungeon at Ioannina, where he languished for years, exposed to daily insult.

In the hope of checking their deadly foe, a league was now formed by the pasha of Delvino and the chiefs of Liapuria, Argyro Castro, and Gardiki. It was almost instantly dissolved, by the defeat of their forces, in a battle which took place near Delvino. Ali entered Delvino, and made prisoners two sons of Mustapha, who had fled to Gardiki. These he consigned to solitary confinement at Ioannina; two others escaped to Corfu, where they were soon after assassinated by one of his emissaries. The victory obtained by Ali produced the submission of many of the beys and agas of the surrounding country, and made him an object of terror and feigned respect to the pashas of Upper Albania. One act of his, ungrateful though it be, we may view with satisfaction. After having for a while flattered and caressed the beys of Avlona, who betrayed Ibrahim, he threw them into prison, and confiscated their property, to the amount of more than seven hundred thousand pounds.

Ali next turned his arms against the large city of Argyro Castro, which is situated in the valley of the Drino, between Tepelen and Ioannina. It is built on unequal rocky acclivities, intersected by deep chasms, and contains a population of about fifteen thousand souls. At the time when Ali marched against it, Argyro Castro was the principal dépôt for internal trade. From its position, and the bravery of its inhabitants, it had always been looked upon in Albania as impregnable. But, on this occasion, it did not sustain its ancient reputation. The citizens were intimidated by the novel instruments of warfare, battering cannon, howitzers, and rockets, which Ali employed against them; and were also apprehensive for the safety of numbers of their countrymen, travelling merchants, who had been seized by the vizier. They surrendered, therefore, before the besiegers had made any further progress than destroying some mills and aqueducts. As soon as he was put in possession of the place, Ali began the construction of a strong fortress, to contain subterranean magazines, barracks for five thousand troops, a seraglio, and a mosque.

There was now only one city to be subdued, and against that he had a long-hoarded store of vengeance to pour forth. This city was Gardiki, by some of the inhabitants of which his mother and sister had many years before been outraged in the most brutal manner. It was situated on a conical hill, encircled by fine mountain scenery, in one of the lateral vales which join the valley of the Drino, and its population was wholly Mahometan. It formed a sort of republic. A representative was sent to the council by each family, and out of the whole number, thirteen were chosen, and intrusted, for one year, with all the powers of government. In cases of capital condemnation, it was necessary that eight of them should concur in the sentence. The bearing of arms within the city walls was forbidden, and a murderer was punished with death, and with the forfeiture of all his property to the family of his victim.

Gardiki was rendered strong by its advantageous site, the construction of its houses, which were of stone, and loop-holed, and its citadel and other works. The citizens could not be ignorant of the deadly hatred which was borne to them by Ali; and their courage and animosity were still further stimulated by Mustapha of Delvino, and many of the Kimariot beys, who had taken refuge in the city. It is said, too, that they were encouraged to resistance by the sultan, who hoped that the failure of Ali in this attack would induce the malcontents in various parts of Albania to rise in arms against the man whom they abhorred. A protracted defence at least, if not a successful one, was therefore expected from the Gardikiots.

Aware of the difficulty of the task, Ali devoted to it a formidable army, under Omer Bey and Yusuf Araps, two of his most experienced officers No less than fifteen thousand men are said to have been employed on this occasion. The siege, nevertheless, proceeded but slowly; either from the stubborn opposition made by the citizens, or, as some have supposed, from the reluctance of the vizier's generals to storm the town, and put their brother Mussulmans to the sword. A month having elapsed, Ali, impatient of the delay, despatched Athanasi Vaia, with a large body of Greeks and Albanians, and ordered him to act promptly with all the other Greeks of the army. On his arrival, Vaia, without informing the Turkish generals of his design, proceeded to put his orders into execution. At the head of the Greeks, he first carried by assault a large farm, near the foot of the hill, which was occupied by the garrison as an out-post. He then led them against the town, and succeeded in making himself master of it. Accounts differ as to the mode by which he accomplished his purpose. It is affirmed by some that he stormed the city, and that it was given up to all the horrors attendant upon such an event; but M. Pouqueville, who was then at Ioannina, affirms that a favourable capitulation was granted, and he gives the terms of it. The balance of evidence seems to be on his side. Both statements may, however, be reconciled. It is not improbable that Vaia may have pushed his first advantage so far as to gain a portion of the works, or even of the city; and have thought it prudent to grant terms, when he found that the remainder could not be reduced without delay and loss.

By the treaty it was agreed, that Mustapha Pasha, Demir Dost, the governor of Gardiki, and nearly eighty beys and agas, "should proceed freely to Ioannina, where they should be received and treated with all the honour due to their rank, and that their property and families should be respected." When they reached Ioannina, the arch-deceiver Ali seemed to go even beyond the stipulations of the treaty in his reception of them. Each had his particular quarters assigned to him in the castle of the lake, and was permitted to retain his arms, accustomed guard, and domestics, the latter of whom were complimented by Ali for their fidelity. In the course of a few days, however, an attempt was made to assassinate them. It failed; but they were finally deprived of their arms, and were then sent prisoners to the monastery of Sotiras, under pretence that they had attempted to escape.

Ali now announced his intention of visiting Gardiki, for the purpose, as he said, of establishing order in that town, instituting a court of justice, and forming a police for the protection of the inhabitants. The 19th of March, 1812, was the day fixed upon for his departure. On that day the French consul was admitted to an audience. For the language of the vizier in this interview we seek in vain to find a rational motive. He was seated on the edge of his sofa, leaning upon a battle-axe, and seemingly absorbed in melancholy thought. Recovering from his fit of abstraction, he looked earnestly at M. Pouqueville, and made a sign for his ministers to withdraw. Then, taking the hand of the consul, and raising to heaven his eyes, which were suffused with tears, he exclaimed, "It is you, then, my son! Destiny is fulfilled; notwithstanding their late attempt to escape, my enemies have not been able to exhaust my patience: they are in my power, but I will not use it to destroy them. Believe me, my dear consul; forget your prejudices against me. I will not again ask you to esteem me; I will force you to do so, by following a system the reverse of that which I have hitherto pursued. My career is accomplished, and I will crown my labours by showing that, if I have been terrible and severe, I also know how to respect justice and humanity. Alas! my son, the past is out of my power; I have shed so much blood that its wave pursues me, and I dare not look behind." After a pause he continued—" I desired fortune, and she has been prodigal of her gifts; I wished for palaces, a court, magnificence, and supremacy, and I have obtained them all. Comparing my father's hut with this palace, adorned with gold, arms, and precious carpets, I ought to be supremely happy. My grandeur dazzles the vulgar; all these Albanians, prostrate at my feet, envy the fortunate Ali Tepeleni; but if you knew what all this pomp costs me, I should have your commiseration. I show myself naked to you; pity me. Relations, friends, I have sacrificed all to my ambition. I have stifled even the voice of nature. I am surrounded by those whose families I have destroyed. But enough of these mournful recollections! My enemies are in my power, and I will vanquish them by benefits. Gardiki shall become the flower of Albania, and Argyro Castro the retreat of my old age." After having emphatically reverted to his eager wish for Parga, he closed the conference by requesting that the consul would write to the French ambassador, to communicate what he had now heard, as his enemies would not fail to slander him at Constantinople.

With what view was this singular confession made by the vizier of Ioannina? Had remorse really touched his bosom, and inspired him with a resolution to tread no longer the path of blood? If it were so, the feeling was but transient. The seed fell upon stony ground, and the produce soon withered away. It is not improbable that, to the performance of the horrible deed which we are about to relate, his malignant passions were roused by a letter from his fiendish sister Shainitza, who was become more ferocious than ever, since the death of Aden Bey, her favourite son. "Neither the title of Vizier, nor the name of brother, will I allow thee, if thou dost not keep the oath sworn to our mother over her lifeless corpse. If thou art, indeed, Khamco's son, thou oughtest to destroy Gardiki, exterminate its inhabitants, and deliver up its females to me, to dispose of as I choose. It is only on mattresses stuffed with their hair that I will henceforth repose. Absolute master of the Gardikiots, forget not the outrages we suffered from them in the days of our humiliating captivity. The hour of vengeance is come; let them be swept from the earth."

On his way to Gardiki, the vizier visited his sister, who dwelt at Liboovo. Since the decease of her son, she had yielded herself up to sorrow, her palace had been hung with sombre drapery, and her attendants apparelled in mourning. After the arrival of Ali she discarded her grief, dressed her house and females in gay colours, and gave banquets, at which the laugh and the song again resounded. The change, the mirth, were ominous of woe to the inhabitants of Gardiki.

From Liboovo Ali proceeded to the fort of Schindriada, which crowns an abrupt eminence, in the valley of the Drino, at some distance from Gardiki. From thence he sent a herald, to proclaim a general amnesty to the Gardikiots, and to summon the whole male population, from the age of ten years, to meet him, that they might hear from his own lips " the decree which was to restore them to happiness."

Notwithstanding the honied words of the vizier, it was not without gloomy forebodings that the inhabitants obeyed his summons. Many a mournful farewell was taken, and, as they moved onward, many a moistened eye was turned to the homes which they had quitted. The khan of Valierè, situated at the entrance of their territory, was the place appointed for their meeting with Ali, and, on their arrival there, they were stationed in the walled court of the building. Thither Ali repaired, with three thousand of his troops. Having first ascertained, by riding round the khan, that there was no possibility of his victims escaping, he ordered each individual to be brought separately before him. He minutely inquired their age, parentage, and profession, and setting aside a few of them, he directed that they should be conveyed to a place of security. To the rest he spoke with a delusive kindness which was meant to render disappointment more poignant; some, whom he had formerly known, he reminded of past scenes, of battles, and of the sports of youth. He then remanded them, about seven hundred in number, into the court of the khan.

The signal for slaughter was given by Ali firing off a musket, and exclaiming "Kill!" But here he found that there was still a limit to his power. The Mahometan soldiers threw down their arms, and refused to dip their hands in the blood of their brethren. In spite of his threats, they persisted in their resolution. He then turned to the Mirdites, who are of the Latin church; but, though he offered liberal rewards, his proposal was met with murmurs of disgust. "We have never feared to face death," said their leader, " but we will not be degraded into assassins. Restore their arms to the Gardikiots; let them meet us in fair field, and, if they are willing to fight us, you shall soon see what we are able to perform in your service." Foaming with rage, and not wholly free from apprehension as to the consequences which might arise from this resistance to his authority, Ali was doubtful what course to pursue. He was extricated from the dilemma by the sanguinary Athanasi Vaia, who exclaimed, " Perish the enemies of my lord; I offer him my arm;" and then rushed at the head of his Greek battalions towards the walls of the khan which enclosed his victims.

The wretched Gardikiots no sooner saw the summit of the walls occupied by these murderers, than they prepared for their fate. The vizier lifted his battle-axe as a signal, and the massacre commenced by a general discharge of musketry. Long-continued shrieks of horror and agony immediately arose from all parts of the enclosure. Soldiers placed at the foot of the walls handed up loaded muskets to those above; so that an incessant fire was maintained, the report of which was mingled with the groans of the dying. Fathers and children, age and youth, fell in one indiscriminate carnage. Some, who were but slightly wounded, strove to scale the walls, and were despatched by the poniard. A few retreated into one of the apartments of the khan; but the Greeks set fire to it, and the fugitives perished in the flames. At length, after this butchery had continued about an hour and a half, the cries ceased, and all was silent. The bodies were then left unburied, to decay on the spot; the gateway of the enclosure was walled up; and over it was placed an inscription, which signifies, "Thus perish all the enemies of Ali's house." On the same day that this catastrophe took place, the beys, who were in prison at Ioannina, were conveyed to a convent in the island opposite Mitzikeli, where they were all strangled. Every Gardikiot that could be subsequently discovered was put to death, and his mangled body sent to swell the heap at the khan of Valierè.

The fate of the unhappy females, who had remained at Gardiki, was more terrible than that of their murdered relatives. After having been exposed to all that the licentiousness of a brutal soldiery could inflict, they were dragged before the still more brutal Shainitza. Unmoved by their prayers and tears, she ordered their veils to be torn away, their persons indecently exposed, and their hair cut off, and stuffed into the cushions of her sofa. Then, seating herself on the trophy of her vengeance, she issued the following sentence, which was immediately repeated by the public criers. "Woe be to whoever shall give food, raiment, or shelter, to the wives, daughters, and children of Gardiki, whom I condemn to wander through the forests, and, when destroyed by famine, to be devoured by wild beasts" The hapless beings, thus severed from society, were then driven forth, to stray among the rocks of Liboovo, exposed to the pangs of grief and hunger, and the inclemency of the season. Many fell a sacrifice, and all must have perished had not Ali mitigated their sentence—if, indeed, the change can be called a mitigation—by directing that they should be sold as slaves into distant regions.

The barbarous work was consummated by razing the city to the ground, and strictly prohibiting the spot from being ever again inhabited. Walls, houses, tombs, and mosques, were involved in one common ruin. A solitary minaret alone was left standing, as if meant to show that the place was once the abode of man. This scene of desolation was visited, about two years afterwards, by Mr. Hughes, who thus forcibly describes the feelings which it excited. "We entered into the mournful skeleton of Gardiki, a peopled city made a desert place, where no living being disturbed the solitude, but serpents, owls, and bats. A chilling kind of sensation, like the fascination of some deadly spell, benumbs the senses, and almost stops the respiration of him who treads, as it were, upon the prostrate corpse of a great city, just abandoned by the animating spirit. The feeling is very different from that which he experiences amidst the fine ruins of antiquity, whose aspect, mellowed down by time and unconnected with any terrible convulsion, inspires only pleasing melancholy, or animating reflections; but here the frightful contrast of a recent dreadful overthrow appals him; and while the deep silence is broken only by the breeze sighing in the ruins, and the funereal cypresses which here and there wave over them, he almost expects to meet a spectre at every step."

Returning to Ioannina, Ali pursued without remorse his career of blood. Scarcely was he seated in his capital before he sacrificed a new victim. Learning that the Porte either had reinstated, or was about to reinstate, Mustapha in the pashalik of Delvino, he resolved to put an effectual stop to the measure. Mustapha was therefore gradually starved to death in prison; one small piece of bread and a draught of water being all that was allowed him daily. There was yet another pasha in the vizier's hands, Ibrahim of Berat, whom he longed to destroy, but he was prevented from making an attempt by apprehension of the consequences. It seems to have been for the purpose of discovering how far he might venture, that he resorted to a curious stratagem. All at once, Ibrahim disappeared from his apartment; no tidings of him could be obtained by his daughters, and it was of course supposed that he had been secretly murdered. As Ali was silent on the subject, the death of Ibrahim was believed and lamented by all the inhabitants of Ioannina.

There was then residing at Ioannina a dervise, named Yusuf, who was an object of universal admiration for his many virtues and austerity of life. Ibrahim had been his intimate friend. As soon as he heard the rumour of the pasha's death, Yusuf hurried to the palace of the presumed murderer. Ali, who had a singular respect for the dervises, rose from his divan, advanced to meet Yusuf, and sought to place him by his side. But his venerable visitor indignantly rejected the offer, and addressed him in a strain of vehement reproach. Every crime of his now trembling auditor was dwelt upon, and their atrocity painted in the darkest colours. The dervise concluded with the following emphatic words:—" I cannot tread on a carpet here, I cannot look on anything, which is not wet with the tears of the wretched. The very sofa on which thou wishest me to sit is steeped in blood; it reeks with that of thy own brothers, whom thy mother put to death in their childhood. Those ataghans, which hang on thy walls, have been blunted on the skulls of the Suliots and Kimariots, whose errors our religion teaches us to deplore, as long as they submit to our authority. From this window I behold the tomb of Emina, that virtuous wife of whom thou wert the murderer. Beyond, I see the lake into which thou didst cast seventeen innocent matrons, and which daily, like the hell that waits to swallow thee, devours the victims of thy insatiable fury. Thy sister, that daughter of Belial, the encourager of thy crimes, has profaned our most sacred laws, by rending off their veils from the Mahometan females of Gardiki. She tore—thou shudderest!—She tore open the body of one of her women, that she might crush the innocent unborn, because its father was a Gardikiot.* Wretch! for once thou shalt hear the truth! In and out of the city, and in the midst of the mountains, every thing proclaims thy crimes; not a step canst thou stir without treading on the grave of some being, created in God's image, who accuses thee to Heaven of having shortened his days. Thou livest surrounded by pomp, and luxury, and flattering panders; and time, that marks every child of Adam with the ineffaceable seal of old age, has not yet taught thee that thou art mortal, and that an hour must come when—" "Stop, stop, my father!" exclaimed the vizier, his voice broken by sobs; "thou hast pronounced the name of Emina—overwhelm me not with the weight of thy curse!" The der-

* Shainitza is said to have committed this horrible act with a razor, and with her own hand.

vise made no reply, but, after shaking the dust from off his feet against the palace walls, he returned to his home.

Intelligence of the death of Ibrahim had, meanwhile, been transmitted to Napoleon's ambassador at Constantinople by M. Pouqueville, who, in common with all the French ministers and agents, was a bitter enemy of the vizier. The despatches are said to have been stopped and perused by Ali's agents, and then allowed to proceed. On receiving the news, the divan sent to Ioannina a capidgi bashi of the highest rank to investigate the circumstances. When the capidgi arrived at Ali's capital, the wily satrap counterfeited the utmost surprise, and instantly ordered two of his ministers to accompany the Turkish officer to Ibrahim. The astonished Turk found the pasha in one of the best apartments of the seraglio, surrounded by every comfort, and was desired by him to express his boundless gratitude to the sultan, his perfect satisfaction with the manner in which he was treated, and his wish that as he was now too old to govern, his pashalik might be allowed to remain under the wise administration of his dear and trust-worthy friend Ali Pasha. It is scarcely necessary to say, that Ibrahim was compelled to perform this part by a threat of torture. After this interview, the capidgi bashi was loaded with presents, splendidly entertained, closely watched, to prevent him from obtaining any further information, and, finally, escorted homeward by a select guard of honour, which never lost sight of him till they saw him enter the gates of the Turkish capital. The purpose of his temporary liberation being answered, the unfortunate Ibrahim was replunged into his solitary dungeon. At the same time, to punish M. Pouqueville for his interference, the vizier strictly interdicted all his subjects from entering the consul's dwelling.

While Ibrahim was languishing in his prison, the palace was ringing with the sounds of festivity, occasioned by the marriage of his grandchild, Ayesha, eldest daughter of Veli, to Moustai Pasha, the vizier of Scutari. It was in vain that Ayesha, and all his family, entreated him to suffer her to see Ibrahim, and receive his blessing; he was inexorable. The bride was escorted to Scutari by Yusuf, bey of Dibres, an old enemy of Ali, who prudently refused to trust himself within the walls of Ioannina. Yet his prudence was fruitless. He is said to have been shortly after destroyed by Ali, who sent him a firman sealed in a cylindrical case, which was filled with fulminating powder. A similar instrument of destruction, which was sent to Moustai, through the hands of Ayesha, was the cause of her death. She was wrongfully accused by her mother-in-law of being an accomplice in the crime, and was taken off by poison.

In the course of the year 1812, Ali is asserted by M. Pouqueville to have been ordered to go into exile to Tepelen, in consequence of the complaints made against him by the French ambassador at the Porte; to have resided for a while at Argyro Castro, and not to have returned to Ioannina till after the reverses sustained by Napoleon. The fact of the vizier's disgrace is, nevertheless, doubtful. It appears to be certain, however, that in the following year, danger impended over him. Demetrius Paleopoulo, who was residing at Constantinople, presented several memorials against him to the Divan, and the sultan is asserted to have once more determined upon his overthrow. But again he escaped; and for this good fortune he is believed to have been indebted to the friendly offices of the British government.

CHAPTER X.

Designs of Ali upon Parga—Description of Parga—Customs, Character, &c. of the Parghiotes—History of Parga—First Attempt of Ali to obtain possession of Parga—Shameful Conduct of Russia to the Parghiotes—Parga ceded to Napoleon by Russia—The Parghiotes make the French Garrison Prisoners, and put themselves under the protection of Great Britain—Speech of one of the Citizens—Rage of Ali on not obtaining the Place—His Cruelty to the Kimariots—His extortions on the Marriage of Sali—Gustavus Adolphus of Sweden visits him—Ibrahim Menzour Effendi—His Anecdotes of Ali—The Palace of Ali at Tepelen consumed—Ali renews his Attempts for the Cession of Parga—The British Cabinet consents to give up Parga—The Inhabitants resolve to quit their Country—Their Departure.

From nearly the farthest north of Albania to beyond the Gulf of Arta on the south, the whole of the country was now in the undisputed possession of the vizier Ali. All the tribes, which had long enjoyed a rude but highly-valued independence, had been successively reduced under his yoke or exterminated; all save one, which still preserved its ancient freedom, and which therefore he hated, and determined to enslave, whatever might be the pains and costs required to effect his purpose. Nor did he despair of success; for he had already, in more than one instance, experienced what might be accomplished by a system of persevering hostility. The solitary exception to the general state of subjugation was displayed by the small town and territory of Parga, opposite to the south extremity of Corfu, of which island, in consequence of its importance to it as a military out-post, Parga was called the eye and ear. Ali ultimately triumphed; and it is a painful reflection for an Englishman, that the vizier was mainly, or rather wholly, indebted for his triumph to the British government.

Old Parga, situated to the east of the modern town, was the primitive abode of the Parghiotes previously to the fourteenth century. At what period it was founded is unknown. But when the Turks overran the provinces of the eastern empire, inflicting upon them all the horrors of conquest, the priests of Parga, foreseeing that they would soon share the same fate, were desirous of inducing their countrymen to choose an asylum near the sea, calculated equally for defence, or for facilitating their retreat to some hospitable shore, in case of their being unable to resist attack. Ordinary considerations would have been found inadequate to prevail upon a whole people to abandon their paternal hearths: recourse was therefore had to supernatural interference. About the year 1400, a shepherd, who was in search of a sheep, discovered in a cave an image of the Panagia, or Blessed Virgin, which was transported with much pomp to Parga. But as, notwithstanding all the veneration manifested for it by the inhabitants, the image twice returned to its cavern, without the intervention of human means, this double miracle induced the people to follow it. They built a church over the cavern, and installed the image with great ceremony, and it was around this sacred palladium that the modern Parga arose. Thus Sinitzia and Agia were deserted for a promontory almost impregnable by nature.

Situated on a rock, about a mile in circumference, Parga is surrounded on three sides by the sea. The only entrance into this fortress is by an opening made in the angle of the rock which forms the peninsula. From the citadel on the summit of the rock, at the height of two hundred and fifty feet, there is a magnificent prospect. On one hand is the whole territory of Parga, and the mountains of Albania, by which it is bounded. Looking southward, the eye ranges, from east to west, over a part of the Ionian Sea; on the left is seen the isle of Santa Maura, and the promontory from whence Sappho terminated her woes: further on appear the mountains of Cephalonia; and on the right, at the distance of twelve miles, are the islets of Faxo and Anti Paxo.

"Few situations upon these shores," says Mr. Hughes, "rival that of Parga in beauty: a conical hill, covered with houses and surmounted by a fortress, juts out in the sea, and forms two excellent harbours, one on the east, and the other on the west; but the bay stretches out its long arms in two fine curves, of which that towards the Acherusian district is terminated by the promontory called Megali Pagagna, and the other towards Paxo and Corfu, winds round like a sickle towards the high precipices of Cheladi, which are crowned by a convent and a lighthouse. The whole territory of Parga may be taken in at one view; for it lies supine upon a theatre of hills, the highest of which rises to a peak in the very centre of the chain; the whole of these are covered with the finest olives in the world, intermingled with orange trees and cedrats, adorned with gardens or vineyards, and refreshed by rivulets and perennial fountains, where the Parghiot virgins were once seen, like the heroines of the Odyssey, carrying linen for ablution, or bearing upon their heads pitchers of the purest water for the use of the family." The principal supply of water was obtained from the beautiful fountain of San Trifone, about a mile distant from the city, and was carried upon the head, in vases of elegant shapes. The whole causeway was often covered with females, many of them exceedingly beautiful in feature and form, going and coming in this occupation, which they regarded as an amusement.

The territory annexed to Parga is surrounded on

the side of Thesprotia by the chain of Mount Penzovolos, or the Sparrow-hawk mountains. This semicircle resembling a theatre, of which Parga forms the proscenium, comprehends an extent of about fifteen miles, and extends in breadth about three miles from the sea to the Turkish frontier. The upper regions of the mountains present only an expanse of sterility: at their centre some few tufts of trees are seen; but at their base groves of orange, lemon, and cedrat trees, diffuse around their fragrant odours, and descend into a picturesque valley, where they become grouped with the olive trees, and form ever-verdant gardens and bowers, which reach to the suburbs of the town itself. Oaks, plane-trees, and cypresses, are also scattered over the land, and give a pleasing variety of shape and hue to the mass of foliage.

The balmy and exhilarating air breathed by the Parghiotes gave them a freshness and health which distinguished them from the Ionians; and the liberty which they enjoyed under every protecting power materially contributed to the development of their physical faculties and their ardent passions. The men were brave, temperate, and hospitable, rather above the middle size, and generally strong and robust. Their costume was that of the Greek islanders; it consisted of an embroidered jacket and large breeches of blue cloth, and a red scull-cap. They wore mustachios, and were usually armed with a musket, a pair of pistols, a poniard, and a sabre. The females, most of whom were handsome, were arrayed in a long plaited petticoat, and a cloth or silk jacket, embroidered or trimmed with gold. A double cord of red silk intertwined the hair, which was gracefully fastened up behind. In public, they covered the head with a coloured handkerchief. They were chaste, though they enjoyed the highest degree of social freedom.

Both sexes were of a gay disposition, and indulged in the dance upon all festive occasions.

"Among their usages," says Colonel de Bosset, "there is one which deserves particular mention. When a young man has paid his addresses to a female and the respective families have agreed on the preliminary arrangements for their union, the destined bride is introduced into the paternal home of her lover. Everything is done to render her abode agreeable, and on her part she takes the greatest pains to conciliate the good-will of the family to which she is about to belong. But the marriage is not immediately concluded, and it is only at the expiration of a year that the union of the betrothed is irrevocably ratified by the seal of religion. In the interval their mutual intimacy and confidence become strengthened, and they enjoy under the same roof, that liberty without which it would be difficult to know and appreciate each other. If, before the expiration of a year, one of the parties should allege well-founded reasons for breaking off the arrangements, a representation is made by the family of the complainant to the other family; who generally raise objections and difficulties; the affair is laid before the proto-papa, or chief of the clergy, who, by the aid of arbitrators, commonly taken from both families, decides definitively; audience is given to both parties and to their witnesses. Recourse is frequently had to matrons, and if, after due deliberation on the arguments adduced on either side, the physical or moral incompatibility on which the appeal is made, be clearly proved, the whole affair is placed *in statu quo*, and the young female is taken home to her parents. Separations of this kind are, however, rare, and are not allowed except on very strong grounds. If, at the end of the probationary year, the affianced persons suit each other, the nuptials then take place, and the union is consecrated in the church with all due solemnity."

The members of this little community were chiefly occupied in agriculture and navigation. A tolerably good wine, and fruits of different kinds, they exported to the neighbouring islands. Their tobacco, which was in much repute, was sent to the surrounding countries. Oil, oranges, citrons, and cedrats, were however the principal articles of their commerce: of these the first three were mostly purchased by the subjects of Ali. The cedrats, for the cultivation and excellence of which Parga was celebrated, were conveyed to Trieste, in small Parghiot vessels. This fruit is gathered green, before it becomes as large as a citron, and is packed with great care. They are consumed by the Jews, whose ritual requires them to be used in religious ceremonies at a certain season of the year. If the Parghiotes failed to sell them to advantage at Trieste, they carried them into Poland, where, in consequence of the Jews being numerous, a ready market was sure to be found. Some profit the Parghiotes derived from grinding corn for the Paxiotes; the island of Paxo having no streams to impel water-mills, and being subject to such long and frequent calms that windmills are of little use. Many of the natives of Parga were accustomed to migrate to Italy, where they established themselves as coffee-house keepers, or waiters in coffee-houses; and when they had acquired a sufficient sum, they returned to settle in their native country.

Such were the simple occupations of the Parghiotes. These unfortunate people have, however, been foully calumniated by hireling writers; by men as base as the destroyers whom they used their venal pens to defend. Going beyond those bandits, who always add murder to robbery, the betrayers of Parga and their advocates have laboured to stab to the heart the reputation of their victims. To their slanders upon the character of the Parghiotes it will suffice to oppose the evidence of an unexceptionable witness. " The Parghiotes," says Mr. Hughes, " were represented to us, by every one connected with them, as a very industrious, honest, and moral people; though many have since been interested in depreciating their good qualities; their attachment to liberty is well known by the determined opposition which they made for thirty years against the attacks of an inveterate enemy; and by the assistance which they always rendered to the Suliots or any other Christian people whose country lay under the fangs of an infidel despoiler. Their valour, which has never been questioned, has always shone forth in defence of their rights, never in aggression; for the Parghiotes had not, at the time of their expatriation, increased their territory by a single foot of ground since their ancestors first congregated together upon this hill altar of liberty. As for the crime of piracy, with which they have been charged, I believe that a person who should now assert it would be laughed at for his ignorance, since there never was a more industrious and commercial people, nor was ever an instance known of a Parghiote pirate on the coast of the Adriatic. Though they adhered strictly to the rites and ceremonies of the Greek church, they appeared to do so conscientiously, according to the faith in which they had been brought up; and it would perhaps have been better to have cleared their minds from error and superstition by rational argument and kind forbearance, than to have turned their religion into a reason for delivering up their country to the *Turks*." It may be as well to mention, that the opinion of Mr. Hughes was not founded upon mere hearsay, or the testimony of those who knew little of Parga; he himself visited the town, and among those who bore witness to the merits of the Parghiotes was their English governor, Sir Charles Gordon.

Shortly after their removal to the new town of Parga, the inhabitants sought the powerful protection of the Venetian republic. It was willingly granted, and a treaty of federation was signed between the parties, on the twenty-first of March, 1401. Venice engaged to maintain in the town a body of Italian or Sclavonian troops; and a Corfiote nobleman, with the title of governor, was to reside at Parga, as representative of Venice. But, on behalf of the Parghiotes, it was stipulated, that they should govern themselves freely and independently, according to the laws and customs of their ancestors; that they should not be liable to serve by sea or land, in the militia or galleys of Venice, nor to engage in any war but in defence of their own territory and the Venetian settlements in Albania; that they should pay no taxes, capitations, or export and import duties; and should be chargeable with only half the ordinary duties when trading to the ports of Venice. In August, 1447, this treaty was confirmed with the same solemnities which had been observed on its first being signed. The Parghiotes did not suffer it to be infringed with impunity; for, whenever a governor was guilty of attempting to violate it, they kept him under arrest, till they had obtained justice from the governor-general at Corfu.

Twice, in 1500 and in 1560, notwithstanding the support derived from the Venetians, Parga was burned by the Turks. In the first instance, the injury was transient; but, on the second occasion, the whole territory was laid waste, and the inhabitants were driven to take shelter among the wandering tribes of the neighbouring mountains. Some time elapsed before the scattered fugitives ventured back to their ancient possessions, and a still longer time passed by before they could resolve to raise their town from its ruins. "They then sent deputies to Venice to demand their assistance, and the renewal of their ancient alliance; requesting, among other things, that the senate would assist in fortifying their city, and would also lend them a sum of money to enable the poorer part of the citizens to rebuild their habitations. The senate was not only just but generous. It undertook the whole expense of erecting the fortifications; and, instead of a loan from its treasury, it sent, as a free gift, the requisite materials for the construction of their houses. When the particular points of the embassy were adjusted, a new charter, ratifying and confirming all the former treaties, was regularly signed on the fifth of February, 1571. It was afterwards repeatedly renewed; and was always religiously fulfilled, not only in its letter, but its spirit, till the final extinction of Venice by the ambition of France and Austria in 1797."

It has been seen, in a preceding chapter, that, after the fall of Prevesa, in 1798, Ali attempted to terrify the people of Parga into submission. In his first letter to them, upon that occasion, he summoned them to become subjects of the Porte. "Whatever political government you desire," said he, "I shall be disposed to give you; but if you will not do this, know that I am at war with you, and the sin be upon your heads." No answer having been returned to this letter, he addressed a second to them, in which, after reproaching them for their silence, he desired them "to drive out or kill the French," and informed them that he would despatch Hassan Effendi "to treat verbally with them on the whole affair."

The reply of the Parghiotes was worthy of men the

race of whom had for centuries been free. "The submission which you require of us cannot possibly be admitted, because your living examples lead us all to prefer the glorious death of liberty to a dishonourable and tyrannical bondage. You write to us to drive away or kill the French. Not only are we unable to do this, but even if we could we would not, because for four centuries our country has been proud of her good faith, which has often been defended with her blood. Can we now, then, sully her glory and respect? No, never! To threaten us unjustly is in your power: but threats are not worthy of great men. We, however, have never submitted to threats, but are habituated to glorious war in defence of our country. God is just: we are ready: we wait the hour to glorify the Giver of Victory. Health."

By the treaty of 1800, between Russia and Turkey, it was agreed that Butrinto, Prevesa, Vonitza, and Parga, should be ceded to the Porte; but should retain all their Venetian privileges, enjoy their laws, both civil and criminal, as before, and pay no taxes but such as had been anciently paid to Venice. No mosque was to be built within their territory, nor any Mussulman permitted to settle or hold land within it. The sole additional mark of sovereignty accorded to the sultan was the right of sending a bey or officer of rank from Constantinople as voiwode, and even this was modified by a stipulation, that the functions and place of residence of this officer should be determined altogether to the satisfaction of the republic of the Seven Islands.

From what has been stated in the previous part of this chapter it is obvious that Parga was not a subject of Venice, but a free state under its patronage. By what right, therefore, except the right of the strongest, Russia took upon herself to cede Parga to the Porte, it would be difficult to discover. Nor can a valid reason be assigned, for her turning a deaf ear to the many entreaties of the Parghiotes, to be incorporated with the republic of the Seven Islands. The nature of her policy on other occasions may justify us in suspecting that, in this instance, her motives were dishonest.

Favourable as the terms of the treaty apparently were, the Parghiotes were too much attached to their independence to consent to resign it. Besides, they could not but be aware, that there was no solid security for the due performance of them. The Porte itself might be willing to act up to the contract; but there was no reliance to be placed upon its viceroys; and it was not improbable that Ali would, by one means or other, possess himself of Parga. The Parghiotes, therefore, for some time refused to submit. At length, the dislike of yielding even a nominal obedience to the Porte was overcome by the dread of Ali, and they resolved to own the paramount authority of the sultan. By means of the ambassador of the Septinsular republic, who exerted his influence for them at Constantinople, a voiwode, or governor, was sent to them as a protection; and this was the only Turk who entered their walls. So little was their freedom of action interfered with by this officer, that they assisted the Suliots in their final contest, and gave an asylum to the remnant which escaped from the murderous grasp of Ali.

The shameful violation by Ali, of every clause of the treaty of 1800, when, in 1806, he obtained permission from the Porte to enter Prevesa, Vonitza, and Butrinto, sufficiently indicated to the Parghiotes what would be their fate if their deadly enemy once obtained a footing within their walls. They, therefore, sought protection from the Russian admiral, and he sent them a garrison, The treaty of Tilsit, however, as we have already stated, transferred Parga to Napoleon, and Ali, whose co-operation was useful to the French monarch, embraced this opportunity of claiming that the town should be given up to him, in compliance with the treaty of 1800. Napoleon was at first disposed to admit the claim. A farther examination taught him to reject it; and he replied, that, as Ali had violated every part of the treaty to which he referred, the whole stipulations of that treaty, as far as regarded the towns, must be held to be annulled, and that neither the vizier nor the Porte had now any claim to the military occupation of Parga.

The French standard continued to float on the walls of Parga till the commencement of 1814. It was, however, easy to foresee that, pressed on all sides as France then was, her few remaining territories in the Adriatic could not fail to be speedily wrested from her. The Parghiotes, therefore, thought it necessary to secure themselves a protector. England was the power to which they naturally looked for support, and they accordingly opened a negotiation with the British commanders in the Adriatic. As yet, however, nothing had been concluded upon. Ali soon obtained information of what was going forward, and in consequence hastened the preparations, which he had for some time been making, to attack Parga. He had in vain made alluring offers to M. Pouqueville and General Donzelot, to obtain the cession of the town, and he now, though Turkey was at peace with France, determined to obtain his object by force. Ali had reckoned upon taking the Parghiotes by surprise; but M. Pouqueville, at much hazard, succeeded in transmitting intelligence which put them upon their guard.

The Albanians, under Omer Bey Vrione and Hugo

Muharda, took the field about the middle of February, and, on the twenty-eighth, they carried by assault the frontier villages of Aja and Rapesa, where they put numbers of the inhabitants to death, and sold the rest into slavery. They then proceeded towards Parga. The advanced guard of the Parghiotes, being abandoned by the French garrison, was obliged to fall back. It took up a position at Labovitissa, not far from the town, and there it was joined by the whole disposable force of the Parghiotes, consisting of about eight hundred men, accompanied by even the women and children, who handed ammunition, and loaded the muskets of their husbands and parents. After a hard struggle, the troops of the vizier were compelled to retreat. Among the slain was one of his near relatives. He buried him on the frontier, within view of Parga, and created over him a mausoleum, on which he is said to have resolved to sacrifice the Parghiotes, whenever he could subdue them.

Foiled in his attempt to reduce Parga by arms, Ali had recourse to artifice. He requested a conference with Mr. Foresti, the British resident, and, with tears in his eyes, besought him to prevail upon the English to aid him in obtaining Parga, for which, he declared, he was willing to do homage to Great Britain. But Mr. Foresti, instead of complying with his wishes, arranged with General Campbell that, in the event of the town being evacuated by the French, it should be occupied by the British. Ali then adopted another scheme. Colonel Nicole, the commander of the French garrison, was one of the officers who were sent to Ioannina by Napoleon before the peace of Tilsit, where he became a favourite of the vizier. He was also by birth an Ottoman subject, a native of Asia Minor. After having fought under the standard of the celebrated Egyptian chief, Ali Bey, he had passed into the service of France. To this officer Ali now wrote, addressing him as an old friend and a brother, and promising him a splendid reward, the restitution of his paternal property in Asia, and his continuance for life in the command of Parga, if he would consent to surrender the fortress to the Turks.

This letter fell into the hands of the Parghiotes, and excited great alarm amongst them. Their doubts as to the trust-worthiness of the French governor had already been excited, and those doubts seemed to receive full confirmation from the language which was used by Ali. For them to contend successfully against treason within and force without, would, they feared, be impossible. In this emergency, they sent a message to Captain Garland, who had lately taken possession of the island of Paxo, requesting to be received under British protection. After some delay, a British officer was despatched to Paxo, by General Campbell, the governor of the Ionian Isles, to hold a conference with Captain Hoste of the Bacchante, Captain Black of the Havannah, and the Parghiote agents. The result was, that Parga should be taken under British protection, provided that, in the first place, the inhabitants required it by written documents, signed by their archontes or principal men ; and, secondly, that on the appearance of two English frigates, they should of their own accord strike the French flag, and hoist the British union. The deputies having agreed to these terms, a flag was procured, with which, having secreted about their persons, they returned to Parga.

As soon as the deputies landed, a meeting of the principal inhabitants was called to discuss the British proposals. One amongst them, an aged citizen, much revered for his patriotism and experience, but who had long ceased to take a very active part in public affairs, now came forward and made the following speech. It has been justly observed, that, in political wisdom and manly vigour, as well as in its general tone and manner, this harangue seems to bear a very striking resemblance to the business speeches which we meet with in Thucydides.

"Fellow citizens—The expulsion of the French appears to me to be so necessary, that I will not waste words in recommending it. But I exhort you well to consider, before you yield yourselves up to the English, that the king of England now has in his pay all the kings of Europe, obtaining money for this purpose from his merchants; so that in that country the merchants and the king are but as one; whence, should it become advantageous to the merchants to sell you, in order to conciliate Ali, and obtain certain commercial advantages in his harbours, the English will sell you to Ali. If, however, you still persist in surrendering yourself to England, beware how you confide in the promises of military men, whose trade, whatever may be their dignity, is but that of a servant; therefore, being taught only to obey, they seldom have wisdom to weigh their promises, and never have power to fulfil them as you do, because you are all free men. But go and present yourself before their king. If he mean to be master of this city, let him swear it upon the Gospel of Christ. Yet I would not entirely trust even him. For within these twenty years, Christian princes have openly turned their subjects and friends into merchandise, and have shown but little regard to the Gospel. But suppose you are once in the hand of England— you may be governed well, or you may be governed ill. But the *well* is uncertain, and if *ill*, you will have bereft yourselves of all remedy. The king of England has not that sword of justice in his hands, that he can, like Napoleon, Alexander, or the sultan, decapitate the misgoverning pashas of his distant provinces. On the contrary, his justice is feeble, because, being surrounded by contending parties, he is compelled to lean for support upon one party to-day, and to-morrow upon another ; and yet to pay regard to all ; while each party, in its turn, conceals as much as it can, defends, and often praises, the blunders of its partisans ; so that a governor may treat you as slaves, and yet be fearless of punishment. Nor would you, O men of Parga,—I say *you*, because I hope soon to lay me down in the peace of God, and be buried by your hands in this church,—nor would you be able to obtain redress. This our city is small and poor, and weak and ignorant ; whence then shall it have power, how find money ? and where the learned citizens, who, being sent to the king of England, might show him the truth ? However, this Parga still possesses those arms which have, for so many generations, prevented a single armed Mussulman from entering her walls. I say not this that you should be proud of the defeat which that butcher of the Christians lately sustained at your hands ; for that victory came from God,— God who will not cease to protect you as heretofore, and who can do so because he is just, and because he is almighty ; whilst the Russians and the French, just and unjust, powerful and weak, by turns, have, as the fruit of their protection, exposed you to inconceivable perils, and kept you for several years in perpetual anxiety. These English too are but men ; and may you not live to see them expelled from all countries which they have no longer money to pay, caged up in their island, and preying upon each other from want ? Why then recur to foreign aid ? Parga is sufficient to nourish and to defend you. Ali cannot take her by land : he cannot blockade her by sea, by

s

which your countrymen in the islands can always supply you with food, and which, in case of extremity, will always afford you an easy escape; though I, for my part, let the danger be ever so great, would never exhort you to go forth vagrants and beggars, with your wives and children, into a foreign land. Let us all die here at home; and when no way of safety remains for the city, set it on fire, that these infidels may triumph only over our ruined houses and mangled carcasses. However, this danger cannot last long: for as much as Ali is now old, and his head is always under the sword of the sultan, whose wrath, though it has so long slept, should it at length awake, no Turk will be able to escape. At all events, as long as you remain masters of your own city, so long will you be able to follow that line of conduct, which, under the mercy of God, circumstances may render fit. The infidels, indeed, may force you to give them battle, and reduce you to great extremity: yet you will slay many of them to appease the blessed souls of so many Christians slain by them. But, once garrisoned by strangers, you will be subject to the will of another; you will not be able to use good fortune should it ever befal you; and you will for ever lose the right of defending your country, and even of burying yourselves under its ruins near your dear forefathers."

Finding that his arguments could not move his countrymen from their resolve to place themselves under British protection, he advised them at least to be careful in enforcing the condition, which the British officers themselves had promised, namely, that Parga should follow the fate of the Ionian Islands. For himself, however, he declined to be a party to the agreement, and he entered a regular protest against it.

On the 17th of March, 1814, nine of the primates of Parga, in behalf of their fellow-citizens, signed the declaration which was required from them by the British officers. "At the moment when the frigates of his Britannic Majesty shall appear before our fortress," said they, " we will subject our country and territory to the protection of the invincible arms of Great Britain, and will plant on the walls of our fortress her glorious flag — it being the determination of our country to follow the fate of the Ionian Isles, as we have always been under the same jurisdiction."

No sooner, then, did the Bacchante frigate appear off Parga, than the British flag was unfurled by the Parghiotes. As it was only hoisted near the shore, the officers who brought the succour were not satisfied, and declared that unless the inhabitants displayed it from the citadel, they would sail on the following day, and leave the town to its fate. Nicole had already been summoned, and had replied, that if any attempt were made to dislodge him, he would fire the magazine, and thus destroy the place. The Parghiotes had, therefore, a perilous task to execute; but they were too brave to shrink, and they performed it with remarkable dexterity. Night was the time chosen for the enterprise. To obtain admission into the fortress they made use of a widow, Turcoianni by name, who dwelt in it, and was accustomed to return home at a late hour. Under her dress the British flag was concealed. As soon as the gate was opened, a signal was given, and a party of Parghiotes rushed upon and secured the sentinel. The first notice which the garrison received of this attack, was their feeling the bayonets of the assailants at their breasts. In a few minutes the inhabitants were in complete possession of the works, and the British flag was triumphantly floating on the summit of the citadel. The French troops were allowed to retire to Corfu; and, on the 22nd of March, Sir Charles Gordon landed with his detachment, and took possession of Parga in the name of his Majesty.

This event, which seemed to annihilate Ali's hopes of becoming master of Parga, excited at first his indignation, and he had the face to complain bitterly of English ingratitude. At length, he suppressed or concealed his feelings, and determined to leave no stone unturned to accomplish his purpose. "I will have Parga! I will have Parga!" exclaimed he, and he emphatically declared that, "if he could but erect a palace on that scanty rock, he should find consolation for whatever misfortunes might befall him." How he succeeded we shall soon see.

Compelled to suspend the work of destruction in one quarter, Ali indemnified himself by pursuing it the more vigorously in another. With the view of securing the power of his youngest son, whom he designed for his heir, he had resolved utterly to root out all hardy chiefs and independent tribes, whose struggles for liberty might be feared. The Kimariots, inhabitants of the ancient Acroceraunia, were the victims on the present occasion. As, however, they offered no resistance, Ali could find no pretence for their extermination; his only plan, therefore, was to order a general expatriation of their tribes. This unhappy people sent a deputation of elders, to entreat that they might not be torn from their native land. The petition was heard in full divan, at which he was present, and all but the inexorable vizier were moved by the pathetic eloquence of the deputies: he alone, stern and unmoved, pronounced the fatal negative; nor would he even allow them to remain till the spring. His troops marched into their mountains, and drove off, like so many cattle, men, women, and children, young and old, amidst all the inclemencies of a rigorous winter. Peaceful husbandmen driven from their paternal acres, mothers with children at their breasts, or on the point of bringing their wretched offspring into existence, young maidens, and children, forced from their domestic hearths, and venerable old men, borne down with years and infirmities, were all dragged along to be transported into the rice fields of the pestilential marshes of Acherusia. That no leaders might remain, to animate the people to resistance, eighty of the principal beys and agas of Thesprotia were sent, loaded with chains, to Algiers, to end their days in slavery. While these hapless beings were thus quitting the tombs of their fathers, part of the Christian population of Prevesa, a town which was the peculiar object of Ali's hate, and numerous colonists from the fertile Thessaly, were transplanted with equal violence to repeople the bleak and deserted mountains of Kimara.

This measure was succeeded by one which, though less cruel, was not less tyrannical. He converted the whole district of Zagori, consisting of forty villages, into a chifflick, as an inheritance for his son Sali Pasha. In vain did the chiefs remonstrate, in vain did they represent that they had been proprietors from time immemorial. The principles of justice were set at naught, and more than five thousand families were deprived of their lawful possessions, and attached to the soil as serfs.

The marriage of Sali afforded another opportunity of practising extortion. The citizens of Ioannina, and the country people of the neighbouring districts, were called upon for contributions, so that for some time the streets of the city were blocked up by beasts of burden carrying the nuptial gifts. Even the poorest villagers were not excused from presenting these offerings. The women came in troops, each bearing a little honey or a few faggots, and were escorted to the serai by the Albanian guards, who beat them with long sticks in order to make them sing.

In January, 1816, Ali received a visit from a dethroned monarch. In expectation of a firman from the Porte to visit Palestine, Gustavus Adolphus of Sweden landed at Prevesa, whence he proceeded to the court of Ali. The vizier received his guest with the respect which was due to his rank and misfortune, purchased from him some valuable jewels, and was presented with a sword which had belonged to Charles the Twelfth.

Some months before the visit of the deposed sovereign took place, two eminent public characters had quitted the dominions of Ali. After having endured the long martyrdom of his consulship at Ioannina, M. Pouqueville was removed to Patras, by the French government; and he gladly quitted a city which, of late years, the vizier had contrived, as far as regarded the consul, to convert not merely into a prison, but also into a solitude, no inhabitant daring to keep up an intercourse with a man who lay under the displeasure of Ali. Nearly at the same period, the functions ceased of Mr. G. Foresti, the English resident, who was remarkable for his talents, integrity, and firmness. Both these gentlemen, especially the latter, possessed considerable influence over Ali, and, when they were gone, he seems to have given himself up without restraint to the violence of his passions.

About this time an adventurer made his way to Ioannina, who has left in print many particulars respecting Ali. This individual, who took the appellation of Ibrahim Manzour Effendi, was born at Strasburg, of Jewish parents, and his real name was Cerfbere. After having, among other mutations, been a French republican officer of hussars and a royalist agent, he went to Constantinople, embraced Mahometanism, and obtained an appointment on the staff of the regular forces which the ill-fated sultan Selim was endeavouring to establish. The death of the sultan made Cerfbere once more a wanderer. He revisited and again fled from France, traversed Denmark, Sweden, and Russia, was for a while employed by the Westphalian minister for foreign affairs, then fought under the kaimakan of Bosnia against the Servians, and next engaged in the vizier Ali's service, as one of his principal artillery officers. In the satrap's army he remained for three years; but the bondage becoming unbearable, he effected his escape. He subsequently pursued his erratic course through various parts of Asia, Africa, and America. Poverty at length broke the spirit of this unfortunate roamer, famine stared him in the face, and, in 1826, he put an end to his existence at Paris, by blowing out his brains.

From the anecdotes recorded by Manzour, most of which are similar in tenour to those which the reader has perused, we shall select one, because it appears to prove that Ali could be cruel, not only from policy, or what he supposed to be policy, but for the sake of mere amusement. It was the custom, in the Ramazan season, to distribute, at the gate of one of the vizier's serais, small bags of paras, as an alms to the poorer women of Ioannina. The distribution was committed to some of the pages. For hours the miserable suitors, weakened by fasting, and often exposed to severe weather, were kept waiting at the gate for the arrival of the pages, who at length appeared, attended by Albanian guards, armed with long white sticks. Every kind of trick was then played to excite a quarrel among the females, and the result was a scuffle, in which the stronger threw down and trampled on the weaker, in order to reach the distributor of the money, while others maliciously tore off from the more modest their veils and even their clothes. A signal being given, the Albanians rushed in among the women, and dealt their blows around till the blood flowed from the heads of the sufferers, and death not unfrequently ensued. The sickening scene was generally closed by the pages carrying off a great part of the money as their own perquisite.

Unaware that this brutal exhibition was contrived for Ali's amusement, who sat at a latticed window to view it, Manzour, at supper, expressed disgust at what he had witnessed, and a hope that it would be prevented in future. When supper was over, and the attendants had withdrawn, Ali whispered these ominous words into the ear of his guest: "Ibrahim Effendi, you are as yet too young at my court to know exactly how to conduct yourself: in time you will become civilised; but as I love and cherish you as my own son, I will give you a bit of advice; and that is, not to meddle with affairs that don't concern you; or you will perhaps find that *the great serpent* can bite."

On one occasion, Ali condescended to give a reason for some acts of severity, upon which Ibrahim had ventured to animadvert. "You are not yet acquainted with the Greeks and Albanians," said the vizier: "when I hang up one of these wretches on a plane-tree, brother robs brother under the very branches: if I burn one of them alive, the son is ready to steal his father's ashes to make money of them. They are destined to be ruled by me, and no one but Ali is capable of restraining their evil propensities."

In 1818, a circumstance occurred, which to most persons would have been a heavy misfortune; but, by a kind of sinister alchemy, in which he was a proficient, Ali converted it into a source of wealth. Either by lightning, or by the carelessness of some of Sali's attendants, the new palace at Tepeleni was burned to the ground. It was some time before those about him would venture to communicate the calamitous tidings. As soon as he heard them he departed from Ioannina, and never paused till he reached his native place. On arriving, he had the satisfaction to find that the subterranean chambers where he kept his plate and valuables, and the garden-tower in which his treasure was deposited, had escaped the fury of the flames. "His first care," says Mr. Hughes, " was to issue proclamations throughout his dominions, stating that the vengeance of Heaven had fallen upon him, and that Ali had no longer a home in the place of his ancestors: he called therefore upon his loving subjects to assist him in his distress, and fixed a day on which he expected their attendance. At the time appointed, Tepeleni was crowded with deputies from various districts; with his old associates and friends; with his children, and relations of every degree. At the outer gate of the seraglio the vizier was seen seated upon a dirty mat, cross-legged and bare-headed, with a red Albanian cap in his hands to receive contributions. He had been cunning enough to send beforehand to several of his retainers, from whose poverty little could be expected, large sums of money; which they now brought and restored to him as if they had been voluntary presents from their own stores. When therefore any bey or primate offered a sum less than his expectations, he compared his niggardly avarice with the liberality of others, who must have deprived themselves even of the necessaries of life for his sake: refusing the present in the following terms: " What good will this do to Ali, a man afflicted by the divine vengeance? Take it back, murrie, take it back, and keep it for your own necessities." Such a hint was quite sufficient to double or treble the contribution ; and by these means he collected a sum of money which enabled him not only to rebuild the seraglio, but to add very considerably to the treasures in his garden " To crown the whole, he carried to Ioannina some of the females of his Tepeleni seraglio, and sold them to his familiars ; assigning as his reason that he was not rich enough to keep such a number of slaves.

While Ali was thus occupied he did not neglect his paramount object of making himself master of Parga. As in his eyes all means were good which were calculated to accomplish his purpose, he did not hesitate to descend to fraud. Among his sinister practices was the procuring a memorial, in the shape of a petition, praying the Porte to take Parga under its immediate jurisdiction. This document purported to be signed by fifty of the Parghiotes ; a few of the names he had obtained by bribery, the rest he had forged. This attempt was defeated by General Campbell. At the same time the vizier's agents were active at London, Corfu, and Constantinople. In the Ottoman capital, by dint of the persuasive eloquence of gold, they succeeded in procuring a demand from the Porte for the surrender of Parga. As soon as the lord high commissioner, Sir Thomas Maitland, arrived in the Ionian Islands, the vizier put in practice all his arts to win over the new dignitary. He invited his lordship, with his family and suite, gave them splendid entertainments, and, under the name of presents, pelisses, cashmere shawls, and gold snuff-boxes, some plain, some ornamented with brilliants, were distributed among the guests. "The vizier," says Lieutenant-colonel de Bosset, " calculated on the immediate cession of Parga, as the certain consequence of the good grace and readiness with which his offers were accepted ; and he was the more confirmed in his belief that the cession would be the price of them, as it appears that, contrary to the usual etiquette in such transactions, no presents were given in return. Accordingly, his disappointment was extreme, on finding himself outdone in the art of acquiring property, and for a long time he continued to vent his chagrin in acrimonious language on the subject." It was probably while he was in this state of irritation that, as we are told, he at times designated the English by the most opprobrious terms, and that a British officer was fired at and severely wounded by three of his Albanian soldiers, whom he continued to employ on the very spot where they had committed the crime.

For nearly three years, the Parghiotes continued prosperous and happy under the protection of Great Britain. Their commerce and agriculture made a rapid progress, and gratitude attached them strongly to a power whose sway was so beneficial. It was not till the year 1816 that fears and doubts as to their fate were excited, by no mention being made of them in the treaty of Paris, which consigned to Great Britain the superintendence of the Ionian Isles. Twice in the course of that year they sent memorials to Sir Thomas Maitland, entreating to know the determination of Great Britain as to their future political existence. To the last of these he verbally replied, that he had no instructions upon that head, but should any be sent him, he would communicate them to the primates.

At this moment the doom of Parga was already sealed. As a compensation for consenting to the arrangement respecting the Ionian Isles, the Porte had demanded the cession of Parga ; and, without any communication whatever on the subject being made to the Parghiotes, without the slightest attention being paid to their well-known feelings, they were turned over by the British government to the Ottoman sway, or, rather, to the tender-mercies of Ali Pasha. All that was done for them was to insert an article in the treaty, that such of them as did not choose to live under the Turkish dominion, might emigrate, and should be remunerated for the loss of their property. They were allowed the melancholy privilege of going into exile!

In the month of March, 1817, the secret of this iniquitous compact was first disclosed to its victims. As a preliminary to the disclosure, three hundred men, under Lieutenant-colonel de Bosset, were sent to reinforce the garrison. This step was not unnecessary; as well to guard against possible commotions, arising from the despair and indignation of the Parghiotes, as " to prevent any tricks from Ali Pasha," which was the reason assigned by Sir Thomas Maitland. The intelligence that such an event as the cession of their country was probable, filled them with consternation and despair, and the strongest explanations and assurances were necessary to restore their confidence. Fortunately, the lieutenant-colonel was an able and humane officer, and the sympathy which he manifested for the devoted people calmed their irritated feelings. Imagining that it might be economy which induced the British to give them up, they offered to defray by a contribution the expense of protecting them but they were told that this proposal could not be acceded to.

While the negotiation, relative to the sum to be paid for the property of the Parghiotes, was carrying on by the British and Ottoman commissioners, Ali was straining every nerve to gain possession of the place at an easier rate, and he repeatedly declared that " he was determined not to pay a single para to the inhabitants." To sow dissensions and purchase partisans among the Parghiotes, to excite animosity against the English as their betrayers, to poison their bread and water, to prevent their procuring supplies of provisions, to introduce secretly a number of his adherents, and to blow up the powder magazine in the citadel, were among his attempts and projects, and, to second them, he increased his force in the vicinity of the town. This state of things, and the uncertainty as to their fate, were highly detrimental to the welfare of the people. All stimulus to exertion being thus taken away, commerce and agriculture languished, employment for the humbler class was no longer to be obtained, and the scarcity of subsistence began to border upon famine. In this extremity the head of the church and the public functionaries generously renounced their emoluments, and the more opulent citizens raised a fund, for the purpose of purchasing grain at Corfu, and relieving the poor.

The reader has already seen, in the early part of this chapter, the extent of territory which was occupied by the Parghiotes. The population consisted of 4,000 souls. According to the admission of their enemies, the number of houses and cottages was 869; of olive trees, 80,447; of wild olives, 9,486; of orange and citron trees, 23,082; of other fruit trees, 13,012; of Valona oaks, 513; besides vineyards and cultivable lands. This estimate does not include the church and corporation estates, and the possessions of the local government, nor the lands not cultivated or built upon, for all which the Turkish commissioners obstinately and inequitably refused to allow of any compensation, though most of it was the private property of different families. The Parghiotes remonstrated against this injustice; but no attention was paid to their remonstrances. In fact, they were not suffered to take any part whatever in the proceedings by which their fields and dwellings were transferred to other owners.

The negotiation was protracted through a period of nearly two years. Ali seems to have studiously spun it out, in the hope, perhaps, that circumstances might arise to put Parga into his hands, without the necessity of his drawing his purse-strings—an operation which he mortally hated. The value at which the Parghiotes estimated all that their territory contained was £500,000; an estimate which can hardly be thought exorbitant, when we consider that of trees alone there were 127,000, three-fourths of which were among the finest olive trees in the world. As, however, this estimate was held to be wholly inadmissible, British agents on one side, and Turkish on the other, were appointed to make a new one. The former reduced the sum to £276,000; the latter, with an impudence which was almost ludicrous, to £56,756. At length the bargain was closed by the lord high commissioner consenting to receive the sum of £150,000, as an equivalent for all that was to be given up by the Parghiotes. It might have been supposed that the whole of this pittance would be paid to them; but, no! a deduction of nearly £8,000 was made to obtain the payment in Spanish dollars instead of debased Turkish coin; though the original calculation had been in dollars, and though justice required that the claimants should not be defrauded with base money. As if this were not enough, a fifth part of the sum was ordered to be withheld, till the expense of the commission, and of the freightage of the specie in a British frigate, should have been ascertained!

While this lingering treaty was on foot, strenuous attempts to dissuade the Parghiotes from emigrating were made by Hamed Bey, the Turkish commissioner, and by other agents of Ali; for, though nominally the Ottoman representative, Hamed was, in reality, one of the vizier's instruments. These attempts were fruitless. So detested were even the Turks of Hamed's retinue that, though they were desirous to win popularity by paying largely for everything, no shopkeeper would stay in his shop when one of them entered it, and it was only in obedience to an official order that they would sell anything to them. When the Parghiotes were called, one by one, before the commissioners, to say whether they would remain, they unanimously declared that, even were they to lose all they possessed, they would abandon their country, and would disinter and take with them the bones of their ancestors, that those sacred relics might not be profaned by the worst enemies of their race. "One of them, named Attanasia Clotzoni, who was deaf and dumb, having had explained to him the interrogatories as to the course he purposed to take, indignantly turned to the Turkish commissioner, and gave him to understand, by the most energetic and unequivocal gestures, that he would never remain under the dominion of the Pasha, who only sought to retain the people in order to cut their throats; then pointing to the British flag, which was floating on the citadel, he vehemently testified that violence alone could withdraw them from the protection which they now enjoyed."

The dreaded moment at last arrived when British protection was to extend no farther than to enable the Parghiotes to retreat in safety. On the 9th of April, 1819, it was notified to them, by a proclamation from Sir Thomas Maitland, that he had resolved to admit part of Ali's troops into the territory of Parga, and that such of the citizens as wished to emigrate should be furnished with the means of embarking. These tidings, and the simultaneous march of the Albanian army, excited a terrible ferment in the minds of the people, who with one voice declared, that if a single Turk entered their boundaries before they had quitted the city, they would put to death their wives and children, and defend themselves to the last extremity against any force, whether Turk or Christian.

The closing scene cannot be better described than in the animated language of Mr. Hughes. " The English commandant, perceiving by their preparations that this resolution was fixed, despatched information of it to the lord high commissioner, who instantly sent to *expostulate* with the Parghiotes. When the British officers arrived at Parga, the inhabitants were disinterring the bones of their ancestors from the churches and cemeteries, and burying them or burning them in secret places to prevent their profanation by the Turks. The primates, with the proto-papas at their head, assured the officers that the meditated sacrifice would be immediately executed unless they could stop the entrance of the Turks, who had already arrived near the frontier, and effectually protect their embarkation. This appeared to be no idle threat, and fortunately means were found which prevailed with the Albanian commandant to halt his forces: in the mean time the Glasgow frigate, which had been sent from Corfu, having arrived, the embarkation commenced; and then this brave people knelt down to kiss for the last time the land which gave them birth, and watered it with their tears: some of them carried away a handful of the soil, to be a solace in their misfortunes, an inheritance to their children, a memento of their wrongs, and a stimulus to the recovery of their country: others took for the same purpose a small portion of those sacred ashes, which had been once animated by the spirit of their forefathers, and many carried away the bones which they had not time to burn. When the bands of Ali Pasha reached the walls, all was solitude and silence. The city, as it has been observed, received its infidel garrison as Babylon or Palmyra salutes the Christian traveller in the desert —nothing breathed, nothing moved ; the houses were desolate, the nation was extinct, the bones of the dead were almost consumed to ashes, whilst the only sign that living creatures had been there was the smoke slowly ascending from the funereal piles."

CHAPTER XI.

Extent of Ali's Dominions—Population of them—Difficulty of ascertaining the Population—Estimate and Sources of Ali's Revenue—Modes of raising Money which were employed by Ali—His Conduct to Nicolo Bretto—Chiflicks—Exactions under the name of Restitutions—Threat used by Ali—Military Force of the Vizier—Vigilance of his Police and Spies—Composition of Ali's Divan—His State Officers—His Palaces— Mixture of Magnificence and Meanness in his Dwellings.

WE may now be considered as having arrived at the period when Ali had obtained the summit of his prosperity. Here, then, we will pause a while, from describing his actions, to give a view of the extent of his territory, and its population, his revenues, resources, and military establishments, and to collect into one group the various sketches, of his personal appearance and intellectual qualities, which have been drawn by intelligent travellers and residents at his court.

The dominions of Ali formed, in extent, no inconsiderable kingdom. They included all Epirus, a full half of Albania Proper, a large part of Thessaly, a portion of Macedonia, and the whole of Western

Greece, from beyond the Lake of Ochrida, on the north, to the Gulf of Lepanto on the south, and from Mount Pindus to the Adriatic.

The amount of the population over which his sway extended, it is impossible to state with any degree of certainty. The means of forming an estimate, which are usually abundant in civilised countries, can scarcely be said to exist in Turkey. Regular census there is none; and the few other statistical documents of a similar kind are calculated only to mislead. "The Ottoman government," observes M. de Vaudoncourt, "having imposed under the name of karatch, or capitation tax, a tribute on the Raias, or tributary persons not being Mussulmans, the estimate of this most numerous class of the Ottoman states, is usually established in the treasury registers of the empire, in conformity to the produce of this impost. No one, however, can fail easily to conceive what great obstacles are opposed to the exact distribution of the karatch. Two causes tending to a contrary result are opposed to each other, and concur to render the produce uncertain, arbitrary, and disproportioned to the exact amount of the population, which ought to serve as the basis. The first is the natural resistance of the Raias, who, through personal interest and national hatred, seek to lessen their number, in order to diminish the impost. The second is the spirit of rapacity so congenial to the Turkish agents, who endeavour to collect the karatch from the natives even when absent, and who frequently for several years continue the same names on the list of assessments. The excessive laziness of the Osmanlis prevents them from keeping exact check rolls in each canton, and setting down the changes from one year to the other; whence the exaction of the karatch always excites discussion between the collector, who insists on the increase of births, and the tributaries, who persist in a diminution on account of the deceased and absent.

" In general, these contentions end in an impost in mass, which the tributary subjects afterwards divide among themselves. Such a town usually paid the karatch for ten thousand souls, when, by a present made to the collector, it is now perhaps only rated at nine thousand, or, on the contrary, through an arbitrary act, it possibly may be assessed at twelve thousand. The latter is the case of almost all the cantons depending on Ali Pasha. It may with certainty be established, that every canton which he favours, or is in any way independent of his oppressions, is rated, in its returns, below its real population; whereas the contrary happens in those places where he governs in an absolute manner, or which he has it in view to punish.

" With regard to the Mussulman subjects, it is still more difficult to ascertain their exact number; because, being exempt from all domiciliary visits, the registers of the Cadis, that is when they have any, do not contain more than voluntary declarations or nominal returns; whence, as the Mussulmans have no karatch to pay, and their vanity leads them to exaggerate the number of the members of their families, particularly of their children, their population is thus liable to be overrated."

Under such circumstances, any statement of the numbers of a people can be nothing more than an approximation. M. Pouqueville calculates that a million and a half of souls were under the sway of Ali. Dr. Holland believes that this calculation is below the mark, but that an estimate which should exceed two millions would probably err as much in the other extreme. " The most populous portions of his territory," says Dr. Holland, "are unquestionably some of the districts in Albania to the north of Ioannina. In Thessaly, and the country southward to the gulf of Corinth, the population is less considerable; in the ancient Acarnania and Etolia, the country is very thinly peopled, and there are no towns of any importance." Supposing the dominions of Ali to have extended two hundred miles from north to south, and one hundred from east to west, (which supposition is not wide of the fact,) the lowest estimate gives seventy-five persons, and the highest one hundred, for each square mile.

The exact amount of the revenue which Ali drew from the country, is no less difficult to ascertain than the number of the contributors; for he followed no fixed rule in the repartition and collection of his imposts. It was certainly large. For him alone the harvests ripened, the flocks bore their fleecy loads, and the vine displayed its golden clusters. M. de Vaudoncourt considers his annual revenue to have been, on an average, between six and seven hundred thousand pounds. His tribute to the Turkish government, which he always regularly paid, is stated to have been eighty thousand pounds, and an equal sum was yearly expended in bribes and presents to the ministers of the Divan. His clear income was, therefore, little if at all short of half a million sterling. The revenues of his three sons, and their children, were said, in 1817, to be about six hundred thousand pounds. The hoards of treasures which he had amassed, and which were all in Venetian gold, must consequently have been immense. All the precious stones and pearls which he could hear of, in the countries under his sway, he appropriated to himself. He possessed vast collections of watches, valuable clocks, gold and silver vessels, and immense magazines of goods of every kind, all of which he kept in subterraneous vaults; into those vaults no one but himself was allowed to enter. The produce of his own private domains was of considerable magnitude; of sheep alone he had about fifty thousand.

To what may be called the regular branches of his revenue, among which may be reckoned a tax of ten per cent. on the produce of land, an arbitrary tax on towns and cities, an import and export duty of six per cent., a ten per cent. duty on property determined in a case of commercial or civil litigation, and the assumption of a right to the possessions of those who died without male heirs, must be added the resources which he derived from confiscations, exactions, arbitrary droits, fines, and commutations of penalties, all levied according to his own caprice. Even these were not sufficient to satiate his lust of accumulation. His rapacity extended to everything, and to gratify it no pretext was too frivolous or too mean. If a merchant arrived in his dominions with goods, he would send for him, examine his samples, affect fair dealing, and then purchase the articles at a price arbitrarily fixed by himself. The wares thus honestly bought were as honestly sold. A few specimens of his talents in this way may be amusing. Having purchased, at a very low rate, a cargo of damaged coffee, he sent for some coffee-dealers and Jews of Ioannina, asked the price of coffee, and was told that, including freight and duties, they could not sell it for less than four and a half piastres the pound. "Well," said he, "I have some excellent coffee which I will sell you for five piastres, by which you will avoid all trouble and risk."—"Please your highness," replied the unlucky dealers, "we have a great quantity at this time on hand, and it is quite a drug in the market."—"Get out, you horned rascals," exclaimed Ali, "you shall buy it for *six ;*" and, as it would have been somewhat dangerous to contend with a despot, for six piastres the damaged coffee was accordingly purchased. On a similar occasion, he sold several hundred dozen of worthless sword-blades, which he had obtained for a trifle, because, on account of the badness of their manufacturing, no one else would look at them.

One of the modes which Ali employed to fleece his subjects was to make presents to them. One morning, the mother of Mr. Hughes's host ran up to him, crying and crossing herself, and imploring him to interfere in her behalf with the Pasha. He was astonished to hear, that her affliction was caused by the Pasha having just sent her a present of ten kiloes of wheat; but his astonishment was soon removed by the by-standers, who informed him that this onerous present must be acknowledged by her sending twice the market price of it, and that the messenger was then in the house waiting for the money. "In like manner," says Mr. Hughes, "he bought a large assortment of watches made to sell, as well as snuff-boxes, rings and toys, from a travelling Geneva merchant. He then sent for the archbishop of Ioannina—'Here is a watch for you, very beautiful, and very excellent: I expect that to-morrow you will make me a present of sixty sequins.' The two Greek primates next received each a gratuitous snuff-box, and almost every Greek possessed of wealth and reputation in the place was gratified by his sovereign's gracious condescension and a present, with which, after receiving it in silence, he touched his forehead and lips, in token of respect, and departed."

When one of his rich vassals died, Ali was on the alert to grasp at least a part of the deceased's property, and he did not hesitate to resort to the most unblushing fraud and forgery to accomplish his purpose. Neither justice to the heir, nor respect to the memory of the dead, was allowed to stand in his way. Ali had long treated as his bosom friend, and had rarely passed a day without desiring the society of, a wealthy and benevolent merchant of Ioannina, of the name of Anastasio Argyri Bretto. Anastasio, however, had been buried but a few days before the Pasha called Nicolo, the son of the deceased, into his presence, ostensibly to condole with him on the loss which they had both sustained. "At the conclusion of the conference," says Mr. Hughes, " he took occasion to introduce the subject of his father's will, expressing his entire satisfaction that his old friend had remembered him in it, since he understood that he had bequeathed him all his fine lands, gardens, and orange groves, in the vicinity of Arta, a legacy which he had indeed always promised him during his life-time. Poor Nicolo was struck with consternation, being deprived at one blow of the best part of his inheritance: he just ventured to observe, that he had not remarked any such item in his father's testament, although he certainly had bequeathed to his Highness a diamond ring of great value. At these words the vizier's countenance changed suddenly from that serenity in which he had studiously clothed it; and he declared vehemently that a son who thus violated the respect due to so excellent a father, in neglecting to fulfil his last promises, was not fit to live. Nicolo began now to tremble for his head, a possession upon which he set a still greater value than his land; he was therefore glad to appease the tyrant's wrath by a speedy compromise, and humbly besought him to accept both of the Arta estates and the ring, since the intention of his father was perfectly clear, although, most unaccountably, no document respecting it had been discovered.

One great engine of oppression, which Ali used for the purpose of swelling his landed possessions, and of course his coffers, was the system of 'chiflicks. In Albania all the villages are either free villas or chiflicks; the former of which we may consider as leasehold or copyhold holdings, the latter as tenancy at will. Each free villa is divided into portions, according to the number of proprietors; of the produce a tenth part is due to the sultan, for the maintenance of the spahis, a kind of yeomanry cavalry, but liable to foreign service, either in person or by deputy. The portions of indigent owners were bought by Ali, and those proprietors who were not poor enough to be tempted to sell this birthright for a mess of pottage, he soon contrived to make so, or to drive to such despair that they were glad to buy quiet at the expense of surrendering their property. His first step, in this case, was to double the impost which was payable to the Sultan. To govern the village, and receive the taxes, he then appointed a balouk bashee, with a party of soldiers who were paid by the unfortunate inhabitants: the latter were also loaded with the expenses of lodging and boarding all civil and military officers, soldiers upon the march, and travellers, whether natives or foreigners, who were furnished with a bouyourdee; nor was any transfer of land allowed to be made without the vizier's permission, which, as may well be imagined, was not easily obtained. If all this was not sufficient, Albanian troops were sent in succession through the district, to live at free quarters on the inhabitants of the villas. The result of this night-mare pressure generally was, that the impoverished proprietors were driven to throw up their free holdings, and to become chiflick holders, or, strictly speaking, serfs of the worst kind; having to pay not only the Sultan's tenth, but also two parts out of three out of the produce of the soil, reserving to themselves for their subsistence only the scanty remainder, and being subject to removal whenever, and to what quarter soever, their tyrant pleased.

Another item of his revenue was that which, not always unjustly perhaps, he called Restitutions. It was a levy upon those who had ever had the management of money for him. He seems to have thought, with Hamlet, " such officers do the king best service in the end: he keeps them, like an ape, in the corner of his jaw; first mouthed, to be last swallowed: when he needs what you have gleaned, it is but squeezing you, and, sponge, you shall be dry again." Being in want of a hundred bags, (about four thousand pounds), his son Mouctar applied to Ali's Jew steward, to advance it. The Jew, however, whose avarice overcame his prudence, protested that he had no money, and therefore could not comply with the request. Mouctar was irritated by the refusal, which he probably knew to be founded on an untruth, and he complained to his father. Ali immediately sent for the Jew, and, after having reproached him for not confiding in his master's son, he added, " Hark ye! you have now been twenty years in my service, and, according to a very moderate calculation, you must have robbed me yearly of five bags; you shall therefore instantly pay me a hundred bags." He wound up this pithy speech by his accustomed ominous warning, which no one dared to disregard, " Do what I command, or the black serpent shall eat your eyes out." The black snake was too formidable to be encountered, and the disconcerted Jew was obliged to submit quietly to the loss and disgrace of giving, or, as his employer deemed it, refunding the hundred bags.

No mode of raising money was disdained by Ali.

To pay his tradesmen, he is even said to have often drawn bills at sight upon persons who owed him nothing; and these drafts, such was the dread which he inspired, were always duly honoured.

Ali was his own treasurer and financial minister. He had, indeed, a nominal treasurer, to issue money for the current expenses of the state, and this place was filled, in 1807, by one of his nephews. This officer, however, was nothing more than a paymaster, who was compelled to specify minutely all the disbursements from one chest of money before he was intrusted with the keys of another. The Jewish steward, who has just been mentioned, collected the revenue of the private domains, and paid them into the hands of his master. No written accounts were kept by the pasha; he trusted entirely to his tenacious memory, seldom if ever made a mistake, and certainly never to his own disadvantage.

The magnitude of his revenue enabled Ali to call into the field a powerful military force. The efficiency of that force was, however, somewhat diminished by the circumstance of his army being composed of different elements, which made it incapable of forming one consistent whole, regularly organised and disciplined. First in his confidence, and constituting as it were the nucleus of his army, was a body of from six to seven thousand men, raised by a kind of conscription, from among the vassals on his own domains. The governors of the provinces dependent on him were obliged, on the first requisition, to furnish him with such contingents as he thought proper to demand. The vassals were paid by Ali himself; the contingent troops by the provinces which supplied them. To complete his ranks he enlisted mercenaries from all quarters, particularly from among the followers of his mountaineer beys, who carried on the trade of chiefs of banditti, and hired themselves out, first to one pasha and then to another. His military peace establishment did not exceed twelve or fifteen thousand men employed to garrison his forts, and to secure the quiet and obedience of the country. In war, however, he could put treble that number in motion. In 1807, he had in arms not less than forty thousand men, of whom ten thousand were in the Morea with his son Veli, eight thousand in Lepanto, under Mouctar, ten thousand headed by his brother Yussuf Bey, and four thousand at Prevesa, commanded by his selictar, or sword-bearer.

The pay of his troops varied, according to the intrinsic value of the man. Experience, courage, and the number of campaigns which the individual had served, formed the data by which his worth was appreciated. Some had fifteen piastres monthly; others not more than eight or nine: the average may be taken at ten piastres per month. Out of this the soldier had to provide himself with arms and clothing; ammunition, and a ration, consisting of two pounds of maize or buckwheat flour and some vegetables, were supplied by the pasha. The campaign of 1807, which lasted ten months, cost Ali four millions of piastres for pay, and two millions for provisions, about half a million sterling, besides the military stores which were contributed by France.

Of cannon, generally ill-mounted and worse served, he had, as early as 1807, about two hundred pieces, in the strong places of Epirus and Albania. The number in the fortresses of the other governments is not known; but to this part of his artillery still less attention was paid than to the other. He had a few field-pieces, which he received from the French government. At the outset they were, however, of no use to him. "The Turkish artillerymen," says general de Vaudoncourt, "both lazy and ignorant, are not susceptible of being taught; invincible prejudices, a deep-rooted obstinacy in favour of their own ancient customs, together with an insurmountable aversion for everything that is labour or study, prevent the possibility of making anything of them." Neither the strenuous efforts of the French officers to discipline them, nor even the fear of bringing down upon themselves the vengeance of their rigid master, could produce the desired effect upon these untractable animals. "The prejudices of the Turks, which do not allow them to use instruments made out of hogs' bristles for cleaning their pieces; their foolish dread of seeing the ammunition chest blow up, which, indeed, their want of care and dexterity renders extremely possible; their great laziness, which prevents them from pointing their piece unless in a sitting posture, and which converts the traces and all the other apparatus into objects of terror; all these united motives compelled Ali to give up the use of his field-pieces."

At Bonila, where Ali had likewise a military school, he established a cannon foundry, which was under the direction of an Italian, not devoid of talent, who had formerly held a similar situation in Tuscany. The situation of the director was by no means a sinecure, in any sense of the word: for he was tormented by the rapacity and avarice of the pasha, who plundered him of his tools, and refused the necessary quantity of materials. The pasha had heard that a twenty-four pounder weighed only 5,900 pounds, and he had the folly to require that a cannon of that calibre should be delivered to him complete on his furnishing an equal weight of metal. The loss of metal in melting, casting, and boring, he either did not or would not understand. His establishment at Bonila was much improved by a French officer of artillery, who was sent to him in 1807, and who taught the workmen to cast mortars which were equal to any in Europe. Towards the end of Ali's career, his artillery was much improved, and increased in number, and he had skilful cannoneers.

Of powder-mills Ali had several; the principal one was at Jarovina, in the sanjiak of Ioannina. The produce was of a very inferior kind. Large quantities of powder and ball were also purchased from the Venetians. There was a circumstance which rendered it impossible for him to make his armies be followed by regular supplies of ready-prepared cartridges. Each Albanian soldier chooses a musket as his whim prompts him, and, as the calibres vary widely, from balls of five to those of eight drachms, he is obliged to form the cartridges himself, or to purchase them. Ali had no manufactories of muskets in his dominions; his fire-arms were procured from Upper Albania, or from Italy. Sword blades were imported from Upper Albania and Bosnia.

His fortifications were contemptible. His country abounded with positions and towns which might have been rendered impregnable; but the talent of turning them to account was wanting. The plans of the French engineers were neglected, and labours which required the science of a Vauban, a Coehorn, or a Cormontaigne, were committed to two men, rivals in obstinacy and ignorance, his selictar and an Albanian named Peter. The fort of Prevesa, on which Ali prided himself, was a pitiful indefensible redoubt, his castle of Litharitza could have stopped only a Turkish army, and Argyro Castro, on which he spent immense sums, was commanded by a neighbouring eminence.

To secure obedience and tranquillity in his states, Ali organised a vigilant and numerous police. "This police," says M. de Vaudoncourt, "is not only severely and watchfully busied about the public safety; for Ali Pasha does not even spare the klephtes, his ancient companions; but it enters into the interior of houses, superintends the conduct of the inhabitants, and its officers render in to Ali an exact account of the actions, conversations, and projects of all; in a word, of everything that can interest or convey information to him. The police follows up the Greeks in all their relations at Constantinople, and discovers every step they are taking; so that Ali Pasha, apprised of everything they wish to effect, has sufficient time to frustrate their views. All the letters which leave his dominions are read by him or his agents before they are delivered to the courier who is to convey them. He pays no more regard to the despatches of the official agents residing at his court, and he opens them all, in the hope of finding out one which is not written in cipher. He does not respect foreign couriers, nor even those of his sovereign; and on the first complaint he throws off the blame from his own shoulders by causing some poor wretch to be hanged whom he had taken out of his prisons, or carried away from the country for some grudge or other. In 1807 he caused three couriers to be assassinated, of whom two were French, and he was extremely displeased in having only found letters in cipher on them. His agents scattered in various parts, and the correspondence of the Greeks who are in his service, make him acquainted with the principal events passing in Europe, as well as the situation of the great powers. His own notions, and the intelligence thus obtained, serve him as a thermometer for his political conduct, and make him decide on what connexions he is to form with foreign states, for he is always anxious to have a point of support out of Turkey.

The political information which his spies procured for him was of the most accurate kind, and was transmitted with astonishing promptitude. All the resolutions of the Turkish Divan are said to have reached him within a very few days of their having been taken. The same was the case with respect to other quarters; so that Ioannina often became the channel through which Constantinople and the Ionian Isles were informed of events which had occurred in central Europe. At the same time, Ali took especial care that his enemies should have little or no knowledge of his movements. He not only opened all letters, but he took effectual means to prevent his subjects from making oral communications. Without a license from him, no man was permitted to leave his dominions, for however short a time, the frontiers and passes were guarded with the utmost diligence, and, to strengthen still further the iron circle which was thus drawn round Albania, the property of every fugitive was confiscated, and his relatives were thrown into prison, to be answerable for his return.

Yet, repugnant as all this is to our feelings, it must be owned that the Albanians had less cause of complaint than any of their Greek neighbours. The power that tyrannised over them would tolerate no subordinate oppressors; and they could not but gain something by "flying from petty tyrants to the throne." Ali might extort from them their substance, but when he withheld his hands they were at rest, for they were not exposed to be squeezed by a swarm of underlings. The peace of the country was also effectually preserved by the vigorous exertions of the police; and, as Ali was no respecter of persons, the disturbers of public tranquillity were impartially punished, no matter to what class or religion they might belong.

The divan of Ali consisted of three secretaries of state, one of whom carried on the correspondence with the Porte; four under secretaries, all Greeks, whose business it was to correspond with the various beys, agas, and governors, in the Albanian provinces; two dragomans, or interpreters, both of whom were Greeks; four physicians, who also acted as secretaries and interpreters; and several individuals, holding no office, but analogous to English privy-councillors, whose fidelity he had tried, the principal of whom were Mezzo Bonno, Dervish Hassan, Agha Mordari, and his favourite general, Athanasi Vaià, who possessed his entire confidence, was intrusted with all his secrets, and had access to him even in the hours of his most perfect retirement.

"This council is, however," says M. de Vaudoncourt, "only constituted for the sake of form, and not one of its members dares to express an opinion contrary to his. He therein proposes subjects for deliberation, discusses them, receives the approbation of the persons present, and then decides. He is himself his own minister in all the branches of adminstration, and his secretaries write down the orders dictated by him, which he addresses to his various subordinate officers. His prodigious memory enables him to enter into the most minute details; and though, according to the custom of the Turks, he keeps records of nothing, nothing nevertheless escapes him; and no measure clashes with the orders previously given, unless through the effect of a change of system introduced by him in his administration, which very rarely happens. His indefatigable activity makes him find time for everything, and no affair whatever experiences the smallest delay. He requires the same activity from every one who surrounds and serves him, and in this particular he is even so extremely strict, that he carries things through which scarcely appear credible. His constant custom is to ordain what is impossible, in order to obtain all that human nature is capable of performing. As it is well known that he never pardons a non-compliance with his orders, and that he never admits of an excuse, dread makes his servants perform miracles."

The state officers of Ali were numerous, and in many instances as trivial or useless as those which swell the court kalendars of Europe. At the head of them were the Selictar Aga, or sword-bearer; the Bairactar Aga, or standard-bearer; the Devichtar Aga, who carried the ink-stand; and the Mouchourdar Aga, or signet-bearer. The police guards were superintended by the Capi-Baloukbashe, who had a lodging in the palace. The Ibroghor Aga was chief groom of the stables; the Capsilar Aga master of the ceremonies; the Caftan Aga threw the pelisse over such as were so honoured by the Vizier; and the Rachtivan Aga had the care of the silver-bridles and housings for the stud. Four Shatir Agas, each bearing a sort of halbert by the side of the vizier's horse, attended him in processions; two Bouchurdan Agas perfumed him when he went to the mosque; the Shamdan Aga preceded the wax candles into the apartment; the Sofrageebashi set out the table; the Ibriktar Aga poured the water from the golden pitcher over Ali's hands; the Macramageebashi held the towels; the Peskir Aga threw the silken shawls round him and his guests; the Cafigee bashi superintended the coffee; and the Tutungee bashi the pipes. About twenty Chasushevas, and as many Kaivasis, carried silver-knobbed sticks before him in procession, and were the porters or keepers of his door: one of the latter was always sent to act as executioner, whenever a great man was condemned by Ali. The Mechterbashi, or chief of the band, and the Tatar Aga, who was at the head of one hundred Tatars, were among the high officers. The general expenses were superintended by a house-steward, called Vechilhargi, who had under him a crowd of subordinate persons.

Of palaces and country residences Ali possessed a great number. Some of them he derived from his second wife, a wealthy widow, whom he married for her riches, and whom he soon shut up in his harem, where she died in obscurity. Others were wrested from persons whom he had either put to death, or compelled to seek for safety in flight. Several were erected by himself. He was not only his own architect, but also directed the furnishing and decorating of the apartments, and he prided himself upon his skill. But his works were a strange and ludicrous mixture of splendour and meanness; and bad taste was displayed even when the most costly materials were employed. Splendid saloons, where gold, velvet, and embroidery, were lavished, even upon the floor, were approached by dark and narrow passages. Gobelin tapestry, hung on poles, sometimes supplied the place of doors; and gold embroidery, half a yard wide, to which rich fringes were attached, was joined to cloth not worth five shillings a yard. If the audience chambers were resplendent with gilding, arms brilliantly inlaid, and sofas covered with the delicate brocades of Lyons, they were also filled with furniture of every description, heaped together without the least taste or discrimination—the produce of his extortions either at home or abroad. Thus, wooden benches were to be seen near a table of the rarest marble, and a gorgeous bronze clock from the manufactures of France would stand contemptuously by the side of its humble Dutch companion. It was the same in the arrangement of the buildings. Close to the highly-embellished saloon of audience might be seen a confused range of irregular apartments, chiefly serving as magazines for the motley collection of articles which he had obtained by confiscation and pillage. These repositories rather resembled the warehouses of a broker than the magazines of a prince. In 1807, when he wanted some cannon to be cast, he delivered out of these storehouses, several thousand pounds weight of copper in the shape of kitchen utensils. Whenever he received a stranger, or took him into his service, he himself looked out the pots, pans, kettles, and other things which he intended for the use of the new-comer. His own personal appearance presented the same antithesis as his edifices. Thus, at one moment he was to be seen engaged in this unprincely occupation, or seated among his workmen, discussing important affairs amidst the din of hammers, and, at the next, clad in the most precious stuffs, wearing a cuirass glittering with diamonds, his head covered with a richly embroidered cap, his fingers sparkling with jewels of immense value, and his hand displaying a snuff-box covered with brilliants, or a costly string of large oriental pearls.

CHAPTER XII.

Character and Anecdotes of Ali Pasha—Character of Ali drawn by two French Agents—Character of M. de Vaudoncourt—Extraordinary Memory of Ali—His Manner of administering Justice—Character of M. Pouqueville—Dread excited by Ali's Visits—Abjectness of some of the Greeks—Terrors occasionally felt by Ali—His Tolerance—His affection for his favourite Wife Vasiliki.

THE character of Ali Pasha has been drawn, sometimes only in outline, sometimes in a more finished manner, by various persons. No Turkish governor, with the exception of Mehemet Ali, has ever attracted from Europeans so much attention as was given to the ruler of Albania;—for Passwan Oglou and Djezzar of Acre were objects of but temporary curiosity. His continued success, his long possession of power, and the political weight which he derived from his local situation and the circumstances of the times, all contributed to turn the public gaze upon this extraordinary individual. His court was in consequence visited by the diplomatic agents of different nations, anxious to secure his alliance, and by travellers, mostly English, who wished to explore his romantic and little-known territory, witness the barbaric splendour which he displayed, and form a correct estimate of his talents and his crimes.

From the portraits of Ali, delineated by the most intelligent of those diplomatists and travellers, we shall select those in which the likeness is most strongly marked. As, in tracing the same portrait, one painter may succeed best in one part of the countenance, and another painter in another part, and, from seeing all their works, we may form a more correct idea of the individual than from seeing a single picture of him; so, from the several sketches of Ali Pasha which we shall lay before him, the reader will be enabled to body forth to the mind's eye a complete image of the despot ruler of Albania. He will observe that, with respect to the principal features, the artists are in unison, and that each has added some traits and shades of expression which have been unnoticed by others, by the union of all which the resemblance is made perfect.

The first attempt at this kind of portraiture appears to be that which was made by two French officers, who were sent to Albania, by Napoleon, for the purpose of obtaining political and military information, relative to that country and its master. "Ali," say they, " is from fifty to fifty-five years old, but does not exhibit any traces of a premature old age. His manly and open face is marked with decided features, which strongly express the passions which agitate him. Having the most perfect command over his physiognomy, his glance is seductive, and his well-practised smile indicates a sentiment the very reverse of that by which he is affected; but when inflicting punishment he is unable to control his anger, which manifests itself by a terrible convulsion of his features, indicative of the violence of his character. He is brave to an extreme : his arms and breast are covered with honourable scars. Steady in his plans, if ever he finds himself compelled by circumstances to deviate from the line he has traced out, he returns to it again and again, and never loses sight of his object until it be attained. Extremely attentive to the convulsions which agitate, and the disasters which shake, the Turkish empire, he with the utmost dexterity avails himself of the weakness of the government, to extend his frontiers, and to occupy advanced posts. Strong in the self-devotion of his creatures, and in the powerful friends whom he subsidises even in the Divan, the Porte itself, aware of his resources, finds it expedient to conciliate his friendship. While aiming at actual independence, he never fails in the payment of tribute, certain that with money the favour of the Ottoman is always secure. He is fond of repeating that he is the modern Pyrrhus (Bourrhous, as he pronounces it). In fact, if the generosity and elevation of character, so prominent in Pyrrhus, be wanting, Ali at least possesses all his activity, restlessness, discernment, and rapid *coup-d'œil* both in the cabinet and in the field; but his policy has far greater stability. Ali is never lulled into a false security. Superior in knowledge and experience to the other pashas, he is continually awake to what is passing in Europe: the newspapers are translated to him; and it is rarely that a foreigner passes through his dominions without being introduced to Ali, who never fails to glean from him some information: the various political events which affect the amicable relations of sovereigns are also the frequent subjects of deep reflection and acute investigation. The whole of his military establishment is in a very high state of improvement.

"In the acquirement of friends, or the destruction of enemies, Ali unites the arts of political craft to the other powerful means already in his possession. Far from annoying the agas, by repressing their extortions, he permits them to continue their peculations with impunity*. Hence, therefore, it is that the greater part entertain for him all the devotion of fanaticism."

As the two officers had many objects to investigate, and comparatively but a small time for the performance of the task, that report is of necessity incomplete. An opportunity for more close and deliberate observation was possessed by Colonel de Vaudoncourt, an intelligent and well-informed French officer, who was, for a considerable period, in the service of the Albanian ruler. "The basis of the character of Ali Pasha," says M. de Vaudoncourt, "is falsehood and ambition. These two propensities, of which the last is a devouring passion, and the first a habit and a want, have mutually served each other as an aliment and support. In him they have called forth and nourished all the

---

* This assertion is certainly erroneous. Ali did not suffer any tyrants and exactors but himself. At least, if he ever did suffer them, it must have been in the early part of his reign, before he was thoroughly fixed in his seat.

vices which can inspire horror into those who may become his victims, or fear among his most confidential satellites. The want of money, under which he laboured from the very commencement of his career, and was so long an obstacle to his elevation, the certitude which by experience he acquired that with this powerful stimulus venal souls are always found and impelled to favour every species of crime, caused him early to contract the habits of avarice and rapacity. It is impossible to carry these two vices to a higher pitch than they are found in him. His rapacity extends to every thing, and resorts to all kinds of pretexts. To give is a word foreign to his vocabulary, and a feeling estranged from his bosom. He only seeks to purchase when he is compelled to draw gold from his coffers. Not a reward is bestowed that is not intended to seduce him who receives it, and to bring in to the giver a fruit doubly equivalent to the amount of the recompense. Sometimes, nay even frequently, he despoils the venal agent who has served him, and then smiles within himself at the idea of having punished a traitor.

"His insatiable ambition has also rendered him jealous and vindictive, and these two other vices have acquired in his soul all the violence of which so ardent a character as his could render them susceptible. Nothing that approaches him is exempt from the suspicions by which his restless jealousy is unceasingly agitated. His nephews, his children, even the persons most devoted to him, those who are generally supposed to enjoy the plenitude of his confidence, are to him more or less objects of fear and distrust. The protestations of their fidelity have no credit in the eyes of a man who calls good faith a weakness in mankind, and a defect among sovereigns. The fidelity of past services is no secure pledge for the future in the breast of one who changes his conduct and connexions as often as his own interests require. Even the ties of blood are not, in his mind, a sufficient guarantee; and if any thing can give credit to the charge alleged against him of being the assassin of his brother and mother, undoubtedly it is the apprehensions under which he lives with regard to his own children, and the certitude with which he affirms that, after his death, the youngest of his sons will become the victim of the ambition of the two eldest, and that the latter will mutually seek to destroy each other.

"He knows only one means of securing the fidelity of those he employs; that is, to obtain hostages from them. Even his own children are not exempt from this precaution. When they departed to take upon themselves their respective governments, he retained their families under his own eye, and did not even conceal from them the motive of this preventive caution. The only one of his relations in whom he appears to have confidence is his natural brother, Yussuf Bey, born of a black slave in his father's harem. But the mildness of Yussuf's character, totally devoid of ambition, his admiration of Ali, and absolute devotion to him, and, above all, his quality of natural instead of legitimate son, which divests him of all pretensions and deprives him of all personal credit, have appeared to Ali sufficient motives not to fear him. Nevertheless, he holds him in an absolute dependence, keeps him at a distance from all civil and political affairs, and employs him only at the head of his troops, where his courage and good sense render him useful.

"The vengeance of Ali Pasha is implacable, and knows no limits either in manner or place. The only modification of which it is susceptible is that it is more cruel the longer it is delayed, or where his anger is more violent. His power, his credit, his address, as well as his dissimulation, render its effects almost infallible and inevitable. His hatred increases with delay, and his memory, always present and always faithful, never suffers him to forget any offence, true or supposed, which he has to avenge, whatever be the interval that separates the date of the act from the existing moment. A short period before my arrival at Ioannina, Ali Pasha, in causing a body of troops to defile before him at Bonila, recognised and singled out, at a distance of more than three hundred paces, an Albanian soldier in the ranks, who he pretended had offended him twenty years before. This unfortunate man had been arrested at the time, and plunged into a dungeon, but by some lucky occurrence had effected his escape. After wandering about in several provinces of Greece, he at length enlisted among the troops of a bey who entered into the service of Ali Pasha. The inexorable Ali put him to death. Another example of the astonishing memory of this extraordinary man took place in my presence at Prevesa. An individual belonging to Liapis had been arrested and brought before Ali, who always filled the office of judge in the places where he chanced to be present. The Pasha himself cited all the traits of brigandage of which this man had been guilty, stating the dates and the names of the persons who had been victims, and did not condemn him till after the culprit had avowed each one of the facts. The periods which Ali recalled in his interrogatory embraced a space of fifteen years.

"His dissimulation is impenetrable to one who knows him not by his actions, or who does not judge him in conformity to the only basis of his interest and ambition. It is not only blended in his words and protestations, but is also to be found in his demeanour and habits. He is an extremely handsome man, and possessed of a physiognomy which he knows how to render engaging when he conceives it necessary, but which is nevertheless habitually soft and smiling. Extremely attentive in his behaviour, his address and manners are elegant. He is choice in his dress, and his garments are even sumptuous. He affects a dazzling luxury in the ornaments and furniture of his palaces, and an Asiatic softness in his habits. He is continually occupied about buildings, furniture, and decorations; yet this is only affectation, and the occupation which he thereby gives to those who surround him withdraws them from a serious attention to his actions and designs.

" His address is prepossessing, and even endearing: his countenance wears the impression of frankness and honesty, and particularly of a profound wheedler, who could not be suspected if his features had not something of a studied sameness. Indeed, in his countenance the expression of any one of the passions which agitate him within is never to be read; jealousy, fear, hatred, and vengeance, are there confounded under the form of a cloudless satisfaction, and under the soft expression of an irreproachable conscience. Moderate, and even obliging in his expressions; dextrous in the manner of representing objects; clear and methodical in the classification of his ideas; gifted by nature with a sure logic and persuasive eloquence, in which he knows how to disguise his sophisms; it is difficult not to be convinced or borne away by him when he enters into a conversation for the purpose of furthering some object or view. To resist him, it is necessary to be possessed of a perfect knowledge of his character, and always to hold the picture before one's eyes; and still his dissimulation is so disguised and so profound, that one almost feels a reproach for being on one's guard, and acting with a salutary distrust.

" This dissimulation, uniform, and so constantly

sustained, and which has been of such great assistance in all his political operations, can nevertheless be upheld only with the greatest precaution, and by an unceasing attention to hide the springs he employs in order to arrive at the accomplishment of his designs. These precautions, which he has never laid aside, furnish however a fresh proof of the egotism and cruelty of his character. When he has been unable to succeed by his ordinary means, which are to excite dissensions, to render discords implacable, or cause crimes to be committed by those very persons he has singled out for his victims—in a word, to excite all the passions which can give rise to disorders, in order to avail himself of them either as mediator or avenger —he then resolves to proceed towards his object by the most direct road. The violence of his passions, and his impatience to enjoy, do not allow him to wait when he believes he is possessed of the means of striking his blow. It is in his character never to delay to the next day what at the present moment he thinks he can effect, unless insurmountable obstacles compel him to display as much patience as he naturally evinces impetuosity. When, therefore, he is under the necessity of employing an agent for one of those operations which he neither can nor wishes to avow, the care of externally keeping up appearances dictates to him the barbarous precaution of afterwards ridding himself of his instrument. Thus does a bloody and impenetrable veil cover to the eyes of the generality of his subjects the plots and crimes of their master.

" At the side of these capital vices in the character of Ali Pasha are found some of the qualities which constitute great sovereigns. A profound knowledge of the human heart, which makes his choice good of those who are to be employed near him, enables him correctly to decipher their respective talents, and to assign to them the offices most suited to their abilities. In affairs he possesses a perspicuity which exhibits to him their tendency even at first sight, and prevents him from being deceived in the means he ought to employ to cause them to redound to his advantage. He knows how to wait for or produce opportunities favourable to his political views, and he improves them with astonishing rapidity. He is courageous, and his valour, by which he distinguished himself in the first years of his political career, is far from being extinguished. He possesses that calm courage which knows how to measure danger, and discover the means of escaping or resisting it in a deliberate manner. This courage has served to sustain himself with so much tranquillity, as well as to ward off the dangers by which another would have been overcome. In order to be secure in the midst of his subjects, all of whom fear, and nearly all hate him, he takes no visible precautions of defence; since by a feigned security he has made to himself one that is real. He generally goes out accompanied only by one or two pages, one of his confidants, and a couple of soldiers; and such is the dread inspired by his personal courage, and the persuasion that a conspiracy could never succeed, that few attempts have been made against his life. A fortunate chance has uniformly saved him, and even this same chance has contributed to his future security.

" The government of Ali Pasha may be considered under two aspects, viz. under that of the oppression he has exercised, as well as the cruelties he has committed against all persons powerful through their strength, riches, or influence, whether it was to augment his fortune or to rid himself of dangerous rivals; and hence may it justly be called both cruel and tyrannical.

With regard to the security the people enjoy, the religious toleration accorded to the Greeks much more in his dominions than in the rest of the Ottoman empire, and the privileges he grants to these same Greeks by employing them indistinctly about his person, or in subaltern commands, his government is moderate and equitable. This apparent contradiction is not, however, such in point of fact; it is the immediate consequence of the situation in which he is placed, and of the system which his political views have caused him to adopt. The provinces which now constitute his dominions have never formed a whole, uniform and concentrated round the authority of one. His project is to bring them to this form; but since he considers himself as the true centre of action, and his will as the only guide by which his subjects ought to act, he has been under the necessity of removing everything that could be detrimental to this union; and, by opposing resistance to everything that could clash with his main object, he has sought to create a connecting link between a variety of parts. Such at least is the solution he himself gives to his past as well as present conduct; that, however, which might explain in a satisfactory manner the inequalities and extravagances of his administrative government can only be found in his own character.

" A despot through the natural consequences of his boundless ambition, he has no other rule for his government than his present will, and that is guided by the interest of the moment. The weak inspire him with neither fears nor jealousy; and it is by temporising with them, and even by protecting them, that he seeks to acquire the reputation of justice and equity. The rich and powerful appear to him as objects of danger, and in exercising towards them a despotic justice he at the same time satisfies his ambition and

his rapacity. The following anecdotes will convey an idea of the manner in which he administers justice:—
The chief of the small town of Metzovo was an unjust and griping man, who availed himself of every opportunity that occurred in order to commit vexations, and enrich himself out of their produce. For a considerable time past the inhabitants of this town had presented, or caused to be presented, to Ali Pasha, petitions against their chief, without having been able to obtain his removal. In one of the circuits which Ali from time to time performs in his dominions, he at length passed through Metzovo. The inhabitants in crowds went out to meet him, and prostrated themselves at his feet, crying out *amman*, or mercy. He caused the subject of this prayer to be explained to him; and when he was told they demanded that their chief should be punished with death, he assembled the priests, and exhorted them to engage the inhabitants not to suffer the blood of one of their fellow-creatures to fall upon them. Seeing, however, that the people insisted, he ordered the execution of the delinquent, telling the inhabitants 'that on them was his blood to fall;' and, in order to complete this hypocritical farce, he said to those who surrounded him, that he was happy in not being the author of the death of an individual, since he had been compelled to yield to the wishes of the people. He however took care to confiscate the property of the deceased to his own personal advantage.

"Some years afterwards, having learned that the chiefs of one of the cantons of Zagoria, under the pretext of levying by his orders an extraordinary contribution of one hundred and fifty thousand piastres, had extorted considerable sums from various individuals, he caused them to be brought to his presence, and condemned them to restore the money they had taken;

compelling them, however, to lodge the one hundred and fifty thousand piastres in his own treasury, thanking them also in an ironical manner for the care which they had taken to furnish him with money. They remained in prison till the entire sum had been paid, and they were still there when I arrived at Ioannina. Pretexts of justice also induced him to rid himself of his nephew, the same Mahmoud respecting whom he had entered into correspondence with prince Potemkin. Being informed that, following the example of his uncle, he had placed himself at the head of a band of klephtes, and that his party had been increased by several lucky expeditions, he had the address to draw him into his palace at Litharitza, alone and without arms, where he himself killed him with a pistol ball*.

"His affectation of protecting the Greeks has the same foundation, and this protection is, in fact, only apparent. It is to his interest to temporise with them; he stands in need of their talents in order to exercise several branches of the administration which he cannot confide to Albanians too ignorant, and does not wish to place in the hands of the Turks, whom he mistrusts and hates. Hence does he employ and grant to them exterior marks of his confidence. It is to his interest to uphold them to a certain degree, in order to be able, in the provinces which are Albanian, to oppose them to the Osmanlis when he thinks the time is

---

* In this instance, Ali appears to be calumniated. Mr. Hughes, an unexceptionable witness, distinctly negatives the charge. "I once," says he, "spent an hour in that very apartment with Ali's chief physician waiting for an audience; and this gentleman, in whose arms the young bey expired, gave me the particulars of his death, which was the consequence of a fever: he informed me that the vizier was so fond of the youth that he could scarcely be induced to quit his bed-side, and so inconsolable at his loss, that he had never entered into the room from that time."

come to separate himself entirely from the Ottoman empire. Nevertheless, he fears them, because he knows that at the bottom they hate him. He is not ignorant that the Greeks would not lend themselves to the execution of his plans, unless to avail themselves of his aid, and thus paralyse the efforts of the Porte, and that whilst they at this moment flatter him with the title of King of Greece, their intention would not be to suffer him to enjoy it as soon as they had reconquered their own liberty. On his part he only seeks to make use of them as instruments to attain his own ends, and by no means has in view to raise these people to command over his Albanians. Nevertheless, always constant in the practice of dissimulation, he is surrounded by Greeks, affects to speak their language equally well with the Albanian, and even not to know the Turkish language well. He enters into the details of their instruction, and sometimes causes the children of his Greek domestics to repeat their catechism before him, and has granted them the foundation of a university at Ioannina. He draws up the greatest part of his public acts in Greek, as well as of his own private correspondence, and has no hesitation to make use of the date of the Christian era. I am myself possessed of several autographical letters of Ali Pasha written in this manner. He, however, takes the greatest care to prevent the Greeks from becoming too powerful: he excludes them from the most important posts, and particularly the military commands, and is also extremely solicitous to keep them at a distance from his children, and to prevent them from gaining any ascendancy over their minds."

M. Pouqueville comes next among the delineators of Ali. He had ample opportunities of studying his subject; but a prejudice, which dated from his first interview with the vizier, and continued to increase has obviously induced him to distort the lineaments, and to colour them in the darkest hues. " Ali," says he, " had attained his sixty-second year, when I was accredited to his court as consul-general; and, at these years, he displayed marks of premature old age, arising from the violence of his passions, of which ambition was the prime mover. Under the mask of a simulated mildness, I soon detected the suspicion and uneasiness which are usual among men of high dignity in the East. Never treating those about him with cordial frankness; always acting a part, or standing on his guard, because he constantly thought himself watched or threatened by those who approached him; sweet confidence was always banished, even from his familiar conversation. Fawning to those whom he wished to deceive, proud to those who were under him, his abrupt transition from arrogance to obliging manners, by giving something ambiguous to his physiognomy, prevented the existence of that calmness which is customary with the impassible and wily Mahometans. Like them, however, if he is sometimes liberal, it is with selfish views; and when he receives presents, it is without any gratitude, because he is convinced that they are offered from an interested design. A cunning scrutiniser, his questions are insidious, his answers prompt and always double-tongued, though probable. Fertile in pretexts, he constantly disguises his true motive, even when he has no purpose to answer by concealing it. Hence the perjuries, the caresses, the poison hiden under the seeming charm of his speeches, and even the tears which he can shed at pleasure to forward his schemes.

" It is from the centre of his mountains, from the recesses of his den, the arsenal of crime, that this new Cacus directs his intrigues, and sows discord in distant parts. A fever of activity consumes him. He mixes business with pleasure; he gives the plan of a castle at the same time with an order for burning a village. While he hears a firman read, he examines his steward's report of his expenses. He signs a sentence of death, and a marriage contract; and whatever may be his occupations, they are all connected with the calculations of his avidity. In his method, present interest prevails over the more momentous interests of the future. In the midst of an important enterprise, he stops to attend to trifling details; and he sketches a thousand affairs without completing anything great or stable, because, as he can do what he pleases with impunity, he has a right to reverse his resolutions. Attentive to the least breath of popular rumour, he is always catching at news, true or false, which he receives without discrimination. He maintains spies in the capital; he bribes creatures in the divan; and he pensions even the chiefs of the eunuchs, that he may participate in the cabals of the seraglio. He has emissaries among his neighbours, hired cut-throats, perpetually ready to strike; and his territory is watched by a swarm of informers and assassins.

"'In the presence of sovereigns,' says a modern author, 'every thing assumes a deceptious appearance. The roads are strewed with flowers; the towns and hamlets are decorated, and the people put on their holiday clothes.' In Turkey, on the contrary, the mere announcement of a visit from a pasha excites fear and trembling. In vain was Ali preceded by bouyourdees of paternal love, in which he assured the people of the districts through which he was to pass that he held them near his heart, and that they should soon have the felicity to kiss the dust of his golden boots. The news of such a favour only raises cries for mercy. The inhabitants of the canton, which is threatened with a visit from 'the good master,' meet together, subscribe, and send a deputation to ransom themselves from an excess of honour of which they confess that they are unworthy. 'Can such poor folks as we are deserve to be looked at by your highness?' they exclaim. If avarice find their reasons irresistible, the visit is postponed, or the route is changed. But if the storm cannot be averted, the necessary measures are taken. The boys, girls, and infants, which can be stolen, are sent away to some secluded spot; all valuables are removed, as on the approach of an enemy; and the priests, and a few men in rags, remain to do the honours of their villages. Instead of acclamations, such as wait on good princes, nothing is heard but the muttered sounds of 'Fly, the vizier will devour thee;' and when the suppliants are admitted to the honour of kissing his feet, their hearts are chilled by deadly fear.

" I have never followed any road previously travelled by Ali Pasha, without seeing some newly filled-up grave, or some wretches hanging on the trees. His footsteps are stained with blood, and it is on these occasions that, to display the extent of his power, he orders executions equally terrible and unexpected. Like Tiberius, his motto is 'Let them hate, so they fear.'

"If the journeys of the vizier are a calamity for the country which he governs, his administration is a rust which eats into its substance; for tyranny strikes at the very roots of the social tree. Every day of his mischievous life he is up before the dawn, and reads the despatches, petitions, and numerous denunciations, which are addressed to him by a people whom his influence has demoralised. Then, closeting himself with his secretaries, he invents fiscal operations, and would consider himself as losing a day of his life if he were to pass it without committing some extortion. He overloads with taxes, statute labours, and requisitions, the villages which he wishes to compel to sell themselves as chifflicks, that he may unite them to his private domain. When he pays his troops it is with clipped money, and his treasurer has always a stock of counterfeit coin. At the period of collecting the revenue he takes care to publish a tariff, fixing at less than its real value the money in which it is exclusively to be paid. When he sends his tribute to Constantinople, he calls on the merchants to furnish him with a certain number of golden sequins, in exchange for a like sum in other coin; and when they cannot procure the specie which he requires, he draws it from his own treasury, employs Jews to sell it to them, and thus makes a double profit. In short, descending to the slightest details of avidity, he levies contributions on his stewards, contractors, secretaries, keepers of his palace, magistrates, and jailers, and even wrests from the executioners the spoils of their victims.

"The archbishops and bishops, objects of his perpetual watchfulness, are exposed to periodical disfavour, from which they can redeem themselves, only by paying considerable sums. The monasteries and churches are ruinously taxed. The codja-bashis, or Greek primates, are raised, are overthrown, and see the fruits of their rapine sink into the gulf which swallows up even the hopes of the future. No one can call his property his own; each trembles for his life, and for the fate of his children, which is entirely at the mercy of the vizier; for, by a special refinement of despotism, he alone has the right of match-making among the opulent classes of society. For money, he will give the hand of a rich heiress to an informer sullied with crimes, whom he wishes to reward; and, with an unexampled excess of barbarity, he compels the most virtuous citizens to form immoral and monstrous connexions.

"By a custom peculiar to Turkey, the satrap has constituted himself the universal heir of his vassals. In virtue of this, he seizes the property of those who have no male children, and makes no allowance to the daughters, whom he reserves to dispose of in marriage as he pleases. It is a natural consequence of this violation of principles, that, whenever a person dies without direct heirs, the brothers and collateral relations are excluded from the succession. Widows, who have no male offspring, are driven from their husbands' houses without a dowry, without the restitution of the portion which they brought, or of their apparel; and may think themselves fortunate when they are not tortured, or dragged to prison, under the pretext of their having concealed bills of exchange, jewels, or other valuables. Friends, relations, brothers even, apprehensive of compromising their own safety, dread to give an asylum to these forlorn widows, whom I have seen reduced to sleep in churches, and to beg alms, after having held an honourable rank in society.

"Terror shuts all hearts against pity; but—will it be credited? tyranny has its dastardly fawners. Opulent Greeks, who know that their property will go to the satrap, economise, submit to privations, refuse to secure anything secretly to their relations, and hoard up their riches, consoled by the idea that it will be said, after their decease, that they left a noble inheritance to him who was their oppressor. Some, fully conscious of their situation, not satisfied with merely securing their capitals, guard long beforehand against all the chances of life, and even anticipate the celebration of their funeral rites*. Others, though residing in a foreign country, and out of his grasp, remember him in their wills, that they may protect their families from his resentment. Others, again, driven to despair, seek to steal their property from him by spending their days in conviviality, and often outlive their fortunes.

"Public immorality, which springs from the want of virtue in the head of the government, causes encouraged vice to render him daily new homage. Accordingly, independent of the criminal brood of informers and hired cut-throats, we see all the malignant passions direct towards the seraglio the steps of those whom they inspire. The gate of the cruel monarch is never closed against them. He who cannot obtain the payment of a bill of exchange, makes Ali a present of it, that he may ruin his debtor; a brother, who contests with his brother a portion of the paternal inheritance, makes his claim over to the tyrant, that he may render him hostile to the man whom he wishes to destroy. On one side, nothing is to be seen but disturbances and weeping families; on the other, nothing is heard but protestations of zeal, service, and attachment. Some give proofs by denouncing all that ought to be dearest to them: children, by accusing their parents; wives, by disclosing the riches of the family; and—shall I say it? more than one priest by —but let me stop—religion has performed too many miracles before the face of tyrants, not to be respected

---

* This fact happened at Ioannina in 1807. A Greek, a rich bachelor, whose property after his decease was to go to the vizier, knowing that his obsequies would be performed at the expense of public charity, caused them to be celebrated during his life-time. The ceremony took place at the metropolitan church, the archbishop officiated in person, the burial service was chanted, and this provident man had, as he said, 'the consolation of assisting at his own funeral.'

even in the failings of its ministers. But who can excuse the prostitution of the infamous adorers of tyrannical power? In what terms can I describe the enthusiasm of a dervise, who, at the wedding of the vizier's third son, threw himself from the top of Ali's palace, exclaiming that he 'invoked upon his own head all the misfortunes which might threaten the youthful bridegroom * ?' How can we sufficiently brand the stupid devotedness of a Greek, who laid himself down in a rut, to prevent Ali from being jolted in his carriage! These facts, this prostitution of man, created in the image of God, are the work of tyranny, which is never so terrible in the excess of its fury as by its debasing and brutalising influence.

"The formidable vizier must be approached with full hands; it is necessary to fee his door-keepers, of whose presents he takes a share; he must have a gift to grant the signal favour of kissing his feet. A piece of cloth, a live sheep, some fruit, will raise the curtain of his gilded halls. The bread of the unfortunate, the widow's mite, all flow to the seraglio; and nothing is ever thrown into circulation again by this devouring vortex.

"A landed proprietor, a usufructuary, a farmer-general of the imperial domains, a custom-house officer, an extortioner, a monopoliser, Ali Pasha holds in his hands every branch of commerce and jobbing. To enumerate his various exactions would be impossible. Sometimes they are imposed by his absolute will; in other instances he issues circulars, in which

---

* The Orientals are persuaded that in the life of every man there are *unlucky hours*, which will bring misfortune upon his person or his undertakings. Accordingly, if, in building a house, a mason or a tiler is killed, they say 'he has met with the misfortune which threatened him.' 'May the evil which hangs over you happen to me,' is the usual compliment paid on approaching a person of consequence.

he calls on 'those who love him' to assist him in his need: and it may easily be imagined that he finds every one eager to serve him. Under the name of *taim*, a sort of tax in kind, he seizes upon whatever suits him in the public markets. At other times, pretending to be visited by conscientious feelings, he affects to pity the distress of the merchants. He calls them together, and says, 'the times are bad; I know that you are not well off, and I mean to help you, by the loan of some money.' He then assigns to each individual a certain sum, the interest of which he fixes at twenty or thirty per cent. 'Turn this to account, my children,' exclaims he, 'you shall repay me when you can.' The exorbitant rate of usury becomes thus a new burthen, but that the victim may not seem to be rich, and to avoid utter ruin, he submits to this extortion, though with a heavy heart.

" With similar hypocrisy he rewards the persons in his service, by authorising them to demand presents, which cannot be refused, or by sending them to live at free cost, and collect arbitrary demands in the towns. Without drawing his purse-strings, he meets all his expenses. Accordingly, the carriage of all articles for his consumption, the palaces which he builds, the fortresses which he constructs, are all executed by *angari* (compulsory labour), a very ancient word in the East, and which seems to belong to the very essence of its government*.

" If he triumph in crime, it is only by dint of silencing reflection; and the words which are attributed to him, 'I have gone so far, that I cannot go back,' are an indirect homage paid to virtue. Tears fill his eyes when he is wounded in his affections. Hurt by de-

---

* According to Herodotus the term *angari* derives its origin from the ancient Persian language, whence it passed to the Hebrew and Greek.

served reproach, I have seen his countenance change, when he was told that 'he had lost all claim to belief even when he spoke the truth.' His mental pangs are sometimes betrayed by the complaints which he utters, of never having found any but accomplices in his crimes, or cowardly executors of his mandates. It is during illness, especially, that his mind is racked by the most dreadful terrors. He sees the hand of an avenging God raised over his head. He accuses himself, he grieves, he utters deep groans, he conjures his physicians, whom he calls his brothers, to save him, and promises that they shall be loaded with rewards. He sets prisoners at liberty, he implores the prayers of the dervises, and he has even recourse to those of Christians. But scarcely is he a little recovered before his fears are allayed, and he charges his doctors with incapacity, that he may not be obliged to recompense their services. Equally irreligions, he consigns again to their fetters the poor wretches whom he had released; and thinks that a trifle of money is quite enough to give for the prayers which have been put up for the restoration of his health.

"The diseases of the satrap, like his sleep, give, nevertheless, notwithstanding the scandal of his impiety, this advantage, that, while they last, the people and the unfortunate enjoy an interval of quiet. But, besides these special cases, a crisis takes place at certain periods in the constitution of Ali*. As subter-

---

* It was in one of these crises, in the month of April, 1818, that Ali shut into the cage of his tiger an Albanian, who had robbed him of thirty thousand piastres, though the culprit had confessed his fault, and restored the money, with the exception of about twenty pence. The animal, less ferocious than the vizier, having refused to devour the man, though everything was done to irritate him, was banished to Bonila; and the man was taken from the cage and cut to pieces by the executioner. At the same period of his

raneous convulsions are preceded by certain sinister signs, so the change which is about to take place in him may be perceived by the gloomy cast of his ideas. He retires then into his innermost apartment, and woe be to whoever dares to talk to him upon business. The period at which 'the lion's fever' occurs is usually at the last quarter of the lunations, upon the approach of the rainy season, or when the unhealthy sirocco has blown for several days. The people then expect disastrous events; his wives, his children, his agents, cannot approach him without trembling. Every one inquires whether the vizier has slept, whether he sighs, and all watch for the moment when his melancholy is redoubled, as they know that the paroxysm is about to terminate. Then he summons his divines, questions them, describes his dreams; and in proportion as their responses are satisfactory, he recovers his calmness. Such interpretations as tend to excuse the abuse of his power he receives with eagerness. He is transported with those which promise him a protracted life; for death shows him nothing in the future that is not terrific.

"Ali now abruptly resumes the noisy course of his occupations and pleasures. The palace echoes with the songs of gypsies and mountebanks; the tombs are closed; the executions have ceased; and he reappears upon the scene with festivals. Careless of selection and etiquette, he descends from the pinnacle of greatness to the lowest ranks of society. He invites himself to dine at the archbishop's, whom he keeps stand-

---

blood-fever, Ali ordered to be thrown into a cauldron of boiling oil a Greek, who had stolen some property belonging to the inhabitants of Arta who had died of the plague. Lastly, about the same time, he ordered one of his pages to be shot from the mouth of a cannon, his clothes having previously been dipped in spirits of wine, that he might have the pleasure of burning him while he put him to death; and at all these executions he was present.

ing during the dinner; to the beys, who serve him upon their knees; and to the houses of the Greek primates, whom he calls his slaves. He does not despise the banquet of the Jews, of his boot-maker, of his tailor, or of any other artisan, because this sort of entertainment is always followed by presents*. He presides at all the weddings of his servants and officers, to whom he gives as a marriage portion a part of the spoils which he derives from his innumerable inheritances †. But neither this honour, nor the feasts which are given to him, prevent him from next day loading his hosts with chains, should his whim or his interest require it.

"The vizier's audiences are not less singular than his diversions and his private habits. The court-yards of his palace are filled with thousands of petitioners imploring an interview. Some fix their petitions on long reeds, to attract his notice; others pass whole days prostrate under his windows, in a suppliant attitude, braving the inclemency of the weather; the majority of them pass years without obtaining a look from the tyrant, and many die of want and misery before they can obtain access to his presence.

"So far, everything is explicable by the nature of despotism, of which rapacity is the natural conse-

---

* The customary presents, on such occasions, are a pair of drawers and as many shirts : these two articles are indispensable. But if his Highness should chance to carry his courtesy so far as to be shaved in his host's house, which is a special distinction, a present must then be made to him of silver water-jugs, and a complete coffee service; not forgetting to give a present to the barber, who is an important personage at a satrap's court, and even at the sultan's.

† The warehouse, where Ali Pasha keeps the moveables which he has acquired from the successions claimed by him, is at one of his country-houses. I have frequently found him sitting amidst a pile of old clothes, rusty arms, kettles, and pans, superintending with the minutest attention the cataloguing of the most trifling objects.

quence. But how, without knowing him, could we account for the policy of Ali Pasha towards his vassals? Mahometans or Christians, equally slaves, he seems to grant protection peculiarly to those whom his religion reprobates. This kind of partiality has its origin in fiscal and political considerations. The raya who labours, enriches him, while his ignoble nature hinders him from rising above his present condition; while the Turk, on the contrary, incapable of producing, but belonging to the conquering caste, may be elevated to the rank of Pasha. Under this point of view, a Christian, when a sentence is to be passed, is more mildly treated by the vizier, who always, the crimes being equal, hangs a Mahometan in preference. To this may, perhaps, also be traced the protection granted to public instruction in favour of the Christians, even in the interior of the seraglio, where I have seen, in the same room, a priest explaining the catechism to young Greeks, and a codja interpreting the Koran to Turkish children. Is this tolerance, or indifference? the fact is so, and that is all I know about it.

" As a consequence of this system, the vizier allows his wives an entire freedom in matters of religion; and the beloved wife of his heart, Reine Vasiliki, is a model of the tenderest piety. Such is the singularity of her fate, that she has passed from the situation of a mere peasant girl * to that of the sovereign of Epirus, without abjuring those baptismal laws which she received at her birth. In vain, in the moments of his fondest affection, the satrap has entreated the new

---

* Vasiliki, born at the village of Plichivitza, in Chaonia, is one of those prodigies of fortune, many instances of which have occurred in absolute governments. Her father was prosecuted by Ali, in 1800, for coining. Having seized all her family, his notice was attracted by Reine, then a child. She was brought up in the harem, and he at length married her.

Esther to embrace Mahometanism, that he might raise her above all the females of his harem. 'Were I to renounce my God,' said she, 'were I to abjure that Virgin who protected my infancy, what trust could you place in the attachment of a woman capable of sacrificing an invaluable good for perishable honours?' Far from irritating Ali, this generous resolution only increased his love for her. He permitted, he even desired, that Reine should have in the palace an oratory adorned with images, where she might daily offer up incense to the God whose unsearchable will allowed her to be the companion of the vizier, that she might plead to him for the unfortunate. In conformity, however, with etiquette, to which even the most powerful must submit, the empty title of Cadina, or Lady of the Harem, was left to a Turkish female, while the Christian in reality rules here, by her graces, her mildness, and the happy ascendancy of her disposition."

CHAPTER XIII.

Characters and Anecdotes of Ali Pasha continued—Visit of Lord Byron and Mr. Hobhouse to the Court of Ali—Lord Byron's Poetical Description of Ali and his Court—His interview with the Vizier—Interviews of Mr. Hobhouse with Ali—Mr. Hobhouse's Estimate of Ali's Character—Interviews of Dr. Holland with the Vizier—Description of Ali's Conversation, Manners, &c.—His Belief in Alchemy and the universal Panacea—Extent of his political Knowledge—His general Character—Interview of Mr. Richards with Ali—Character of Ali by an Albanian—Mr. Hughes's Description of the Person and Character of Ali—Ali's Government beneficial, on the whole, to the Albanians—Self-command of Ali.

THE moral and physical portraitures of Ali, which were contemplated in the preceding chapter, are, as the reader will have observed, all sketched by natives of France. Those which the present chapter contains, are, with one exception, the productions of Englishmen. It will be remarked that, on the whole, the latter are somewhat more favourable to Ali than the former. This may, perhaps, be accounted for by our countrymen having resided but a comparatively short time in Albania, and having been treated with more than common kindness and respect by the politic Ali, who was anxious to conciliate the British government by his conduct towards its subjects. On the other hand, though we may suspect that spleen and prejudice, generated by the preference which he gave to their rivals, may have darkened the traits in the French likenesses of the pasha, we should remember, that the fact though probable is not certain, and that the long stay of M. de Vaudoncourt and M. Pouqueville at the court of Ioannina gave them opportunities of minutely studying their subject, which did not fall to the lot of our English tourists.

Among the earliest British travellers who, since the commencement of this century, have visited the Albanian territory, and given the result of their observations to the public, are the late highly-gifted Lord Byron and his friend Mr. Hobhouse. The existence of Ali may almost, indeed, be said to have been first made known to the people of England by their writings. Albania itself was, in fact, a country respecting which our information was, at that period, so scanty, and withal so imperfect, as to be of no value whatever. The remark of Gibbon long continned to be true, that we knew less of Albania than of the wilds of North America.

Lord Byron, in that part of Childe Harold which relates to Ali, does not dwell on the qualities or appearance of the pasha; a few bold touches are all that he bestows upon them. But his picture of the court of the satrap, its barbaric pomp, and its strangely diversified inmates, is drawn with a truth and power which may well excuse its introduction into this volume.

> " The sun had sunk behind vast Tomerit,
> And Laos wide and fierce came roaring by ;
> The shades of wonted night were gathering yet,
> When, down the steep banks winding warily,
> Childe Harold saw, like meteors in the sky,
> The glittering minarets of Tepelen,
> Whose walls o'erlook the stream; and drawing nigh,
> He heard the busy hum of warrior men
> Swelling the breeze that sigh'd along the lengthening glen.

> " He pass'd the sacred harem's silent tower,
> And underneath the wide o'erarching gate
> Survey'd the dwelling of this chief of power,
> Where all around proclaim'd his high estate.
> Amidst no common pomp the despot sate,
> While busy preparation shook the court,
> Slaves, eunuchs, soldiers, guests, and santons wait;
> Within, a palace, and without, a fort:
> Here men of every clime appear to make resort.

> " Richly caparison'd, a ready row
> Of armed horse, and many a warlike store,
> Circled the wide-extended court below.
> Above, strange groups adorn'd the corridor;
> And ofttimes through the area's echoing door
> Some high-capp'd Tartar spurr'd his steed away :
> The Turk, the Greek, the Albanian, and the Moor,
> Here mingled in their many-hued array,
> While the deep war-drum's sound announced the close of day.

" The wild Albanian kirtled to his knee,
   With shawl-girt head and ornamented gun,
   And gold-embroider'd garments, fair to see;
   The crimson-scarfed men of Macedon;
   The Delhi with his cap of terror on,
   And crooked glaive; the lively supple Greek;
   And swarthy Nubia's mutilated son;
   The bearded Turk that rarely deigns to speak,
Master of all around, too potent to be meek,

" Are mixed conspicuous: some recline in groups,
   Scanning the motley scene that varies round;
   There some great Moslem to devotion stoops,
   And some that smoke, and some that play, are found:
   Here the Albanian proudly treads the ground;
   Half-whispering there the Greek is heard to prate;
   Hark! from the mosque the nightly solemn sound,
   The Muezzin's call, doth shake the minaret,
' There is no God but God!—to prayer—lo! God is great!'

" Just at this season Ramazani's fast
   Through the long day its penance did maintain;
   But when the lingering twilight hour was past,
   Revel and feast assumed the rule again.
   Now all was bustle, and the menial train
   Prepared and spread the plenteous board within;
   The vacant gallery now seem'd made in vain,
   But from the chambers came the mingling din,
As page and slave anon were passing out and in.

" Here woman's voice is never heard: apart,
   And scarce permitted, guarded, veil'd, to move,
   She yields to one her person and her heart,
   Tamed to her cage, nor feels a wish to rove.
   For, not unhappy in her master's love,

>   And joyful in a mother's gentlest cares,
>   Blest cares! all other feelings far above!
>   Herself more sweetly rears the babe she bears,
> Who never quits the breast, no meaner passion shares.
>
>   " In marble-paved pavilion, where a spring
>   Of living water from the centre rose,
>   Whose bubbling did a genial freshness fling,
>   And soft voluptuous couches breathed repose,
>   ALI reclined, a man of war and woes;
>   Yet in his lineaments ye cannot trace,
>   While Gentleness her milder radiance throws
>   Along that aged venerable face,
> The deeds that lurk beneath, and stain him with disgrace.
>
>   " It is not that yon hoary lengthening beard
>   Ill suits the passions which belong to youth,
>   Love conquers age—so Hafiz hath averr'd,
>   So sings the Teian, and he sings in sooth.
>   But crimes that scorn the tender voice of ruth,
>   Beseeming all men ill, but most the man
>   In years, have mark'd him with a tiger's tooth,
>   Blood follows blood, and, through their mortal span,
> In bloodier acts conclude those who with blood began."

In a letter to his mother, Lord Byron briefly notices his first visit to the Albanian satrap. " He received me standing, a wonderful compliment from a Mussulman, and made me sit down on his right hand. His first question was, why, at so early an age, I left my country?—(the Turks have no idea of travelling for amusement.) He then said, the English minister, Captain Leake, had told him I was of a great family, and desired his respects to my mother; which I now, in the name of Ali Pasha, present to you. He said he was certain I was a man of birth, because I had small ears, curling hair, and little white hands, and expressed himself pleased with my appearance and garb. He told me to consider him as a father while I was in Turkey, and said he looked on me as his son. Indeed, he treated me like a child, sending me almonds, and sugared sherbet, fruit and sweetmeats, twenty times a day. He begged me to visit him often, and at night, when he was at leisure. I then, after coffee and pipes, retired for the first time. I saw him thrice afterwards. It is singular, that the Turks, who have no hereditary dignities, and few great families, except the sultan's, pay so much respect to birth: for I found my pedigree more regarded than my title *."

At the interviews, mentioned by Lord Byron, Mr. Hobhouse was present, and he has given a fuller account of them than his noble friend has done. " About noon, on the 12th of October (1809), an officer of the palace with a white wand announced to us that we were to attend the vizier; and accordingly we left our apartment, accompanied by our dragoman, and by the secretary, who put on his worst cloak to attend his master, that he might not appear too rich, and a fit subject for extortion.

" The officer preceded us along the gallery, now crowded with soldiers, to the other wing of the building, and leading us over some rubbish where a room had fallen in, and through some shabby apartments,

---

* Ali did not forget his noble visiter. He stated his recollections of him to Dr. Holland, and sent a letter to his lordship, through the medium of that gentleman. " Yesterday," says Byron, " I had a letter from Ali Pasha! brought by Dr. Holland, who is just returned from Albania. It is in Latin, and begins ' Excellentissime, *nec non* Carissime,' and ends about a gun he wants made for him;—it is signed ' ALI VIZIR.' "

he ushered us into the chamber in which was Ali himself. He was standing when we came in; which was meant as a compliment, for a Turk of cousequence never rises to receive any one but his superior, and if he wishes to be condescending, contrives to be found standing. As we advanced towards him, he seated himself, and desired us to sit down near him. He was in a large room, very handsomely furnished, and having a marble cistern and fountain in the middle, ornamented with painted tiles, of the kind which we call Dutch tile.

" The vizier was a short man, about five feet five inches in height, and very fat, though not particularly corpulent. He had a very pleasing face, fair and round, with blue quick eyes, not at all settled into a Turkish gravity. His beard was long and white, and such a one as any other Turk would have been proud of; though he, who was more taken up with his guests than himself, did not continue looking at it, nor smelling and stroking it, as is usually the custom of his countrymen to fill up the pauses of conversation. He was not very magnificently dressed, except that his high turban, composed of many small rolls, seemed of fine gold muslin, and his ataghan, or long dagger, was studded with brilliants.

" He was mightily civil; and said he considered us as his children. He showed us a mountain howitzer, which was lying in his apartment, and took the opportunity of telling us that he had several large cannon. He turned round two or three times to look through an English telescope, and at last handed it to us, that we might look upon a party of Turks on horseback riding along the banks of the river towards Tepeleni. He then said, That man whom you see on the road is the chief minister of my enemy, Ibrahim Pasha, and he is now coming over to me, having deserted his master to take the stronger side. He addressed this with a smile to the secretary, desiring him to interpret it to us.

"We took pipes, coffee, and sweetmeats, with him, but he did not seem so particular about these things as other Turks whom we have seen. He was in great good-humour, and several times laughed aloud; which is very uncommon in a man of consequence: I never saw another instance of it in Turkey. Instead of having his room crowded with the officers of his court, which is very much the custom of the pashas and other great men, he was quite unattended, except by four or five young persons very magnificently dressed in the Albanian habit, and having their hair flowing halfway down their backs: these brought in the refreshments, and continued supplying us with pipes, which, though perhaps not half emptied, were changed three times, as is the custom when particular honours are intended for a guest.

"There are no common topics of discourse between a Turkish vizier and a traveller, which can discover the abilities of either party, especially as these conversations are always in the form of question and answer. However, a Frank may think his Turk above the common run, if his host does not put any very foolish interrogatories to him, and Ali did not ask any questions that betrayed his ignorance. His liveliness and ease gave us very favourable impressions of his natural capacity.

"In the evening of the next day we paid the vizier another visit, in an apartment more elegantly furnished than the one with the fountain. Whilst we were with him, a messenger came in from Berat, the place which Ali's army (of about five thousand men) was then besieging. We were not acquainted with the contents of a letter, which was read aloud, until a long gun, looking like a duck gun, was brought into the room; and then upon one of us asking the secretary if there were many wild-fowl in the neighbourhood, he answered, yes; but that for the gun, it was going to the siege of Berat, there being a want of ordnance in the vizier's army. It was impossible not to smile at this war in miniature.

"During this interview, Ali congratulated us upon the news which had arrived a fortnight before, of the surrender of Zante, Cefalonia, Ithaca, and Cerigo, to the British squadron : he said, he was happy to have the British for his neighbours; that he was sure they would not serve him as the Russians and French had done, in protecting his runaway robbers; that he had always been a friend to our nation, even during our war with Turkey, and had been instrumental in bringing about the peace.

"He asked us, what had made us travel in Albania? We told him, the desire of seeing so great a man as himself. 'Ay,' returned he, 'did you ever hear of me in England?' We, of course, assured him, that he was a very common subject of conversation in our country; and he seemed by no means inaccessible to the flattery.

"He showed us some pistols and a sabre; and then took down a gun that was hanging over his head in a bag, and told us it was a present from the king of the French. It was a short rifle, with the stock inlaid with silver, and studded with diamonds and brilliants, and looked like a handsome present; but the secretary informed us, that when the gun came from Napoleon, it had only a common stock, and that all the ornaments had been added by his highness, to make it look more like a royal gift.

"Before we took our leave, the vizier informed us, that there were in the neighbourhood of Tepeleni some remains of antiquity—a palæo-castro, as all pieces of wall, or carved stones, are called in Albania and Greece, and said that he would order some horses for us to ride to it the next morning.

" According to his advice, we went on Sunday to see these ruins, which are very trifling, being only a few bits of wall, as it appeared to me, not ancient, on a hill about five miles to the north-west of Tepeleni.

" In the evening of the same day, we paid his highness our last visit. He then asked us which way we intended to go; and we told him it was our wish to get from Ioannina into the Morea. He appeared to be acquainted with every road, and all the stages, and the state of the country most minutely. He said, that we could not go by the common road through Triccala, as that part of the country was infested by large bands of robbers; but that we might go through Carnia, crossing the gulf of Arta at Salora, or going to the head of the gulf; and that, as that country was also suspicious, he would give us orders to his several military posts, to take as many guards as might be necessary. In case, however, we should not like to go through Carnia, he furnished us with an order to his governor at Prevesa, to send us in an armed galliot to Patras. He also gave us a letter to his son Veli, pasha of the Morea, and wished to know if he could do any thing to serve us.

" We only asked permission to take our Albanian Vasilly to attend us whilst in Turkey, which he readily granted, and asked where the man was. On being informed that he was at the chamber-door, he sent for him, and accordingly Vasilly entered; and, though with every proper respect, still was not embarrassed, but, with his hand on his left breast, answered the vizier's questions in a firm and fluent manner. Ali called him by his name, and asked him, why, being at the door, he had not come in to see him? 'for you know, Vasilly,' added he, 'I should have been glad to have seen you.' He then told him that he was to attend us, and to see that we wanted nothing, and talked a good deal to him about the different stages of our route, summing all up by telling him in a jocose way, that if any accident happened to us, he would cut off his head; and that we were to write, mentioning how he had behaved. Shortly after this, and having agreed to give his highness some relation of our travels by letter, we withdrew, and took our last leave of this singular man."

After stating the difficulties which the pasha had had to encounter in putting down the predatory bands, and the severities which he exercised, Mr. Hobhouse adds, "It is by such vigorous measures that the vizier has rendered many parts of Albania, and the contiguous country, perfectly accessible, which were before annually overrun by robbers, and consequently by opening the country to merchants, and securing their persons and goods, he has not only increased his own revenues, but bettered the condition of his subjects. He has built bridges over the rivers, raised causeways across the marshes, laid out frequent roads, adorned the country and the towns with new buildings, and by many regulations has acted the part of a great and good prince, without perhaps a single other motive than that of his own aggrandisement."

"All the Albanians, even those who have not yet submitted to his power, speak with exultation and pride of their countryman, and by a comparison with him, they constantly depreciate the merits of others. We frequently heard them say, when talking of some other pasha, 'He is not such a one as Ali—he has not such a head.'"

"Of the natural disposition of Ali we had no opportunity of forming a judgment, except by hearsay; and it would be hardly fair to believe all the stories of the Greeks, who would represent him as the most barbarous monster that ever disgraced humanity. Certainly no one but a man of a ferocious and sanguinary disposition would have been able or willing to tame the people whom he has brought into subjection; not only beheading, but impaling and roasting, might be necessary to inspire that terror of his name, which has of itself, in many instances, given peace and security to his dominions; for large bands of robbers have submitted voluntarily, and been enrolled amongst his soldiers. Executions are now but seldom seen in Ioannina; but during the Suliot wars, twenty and thirty prisoners were sometimes beheaded at one time in the streets of that city. Such cruelty shocks our humane feelings; but '*voilà comme on juge de tout quand on n'est pas sorti de son pays.*' It is not fair to appreciate the merits of any man without a reference to the character and customs of the people amongst whom he is born and educated. In Turkey the life of a man is held exceedingly cheap, more so than any one, who has not been in the country, would believe; and murders, which would fill all Christendom with horror, excite no sentiment of surprise, or apparent disgust, either at Constantinople or in the provinces; so that what might, at first sight, appear a singular depravity in an individual, would, in the end, be found nothing but a conformity with general practice and habits. We may, therefore, transfer our abhorrence of Ali to the Turkish nation, or rather to their manners."

Three years after the departure of Lord Byron and Mr. Hobhouse from Albania, that country was visited by Dr. Holland; a man excellently qualified for the task of observation. He had also the advantage of living for some time at the court of Ali, and of obtaining, as medical adviser, a considerable portion of his confidence.

"The morning of the 1st of November," says Dr. Holland, "was made interesting to us, by our introduction to this extraordinary man. At ten o'clock, Colovo again called, to say that the vizier was prepared to give us an audience; and shortly afterwards, two white horses, of beautiful figure, and superbly caparisoned in the Turkish manner, were brought to us from the seraglio; conducted by two Albanese soldiers, likewise richly attired and armed. Mounting these horses. and a Turkish officer of the palace preceding us, with an ornamented staff in his hand, we proceeded slowly, and with much state, through the city to the great seraglio.

"Passing through the almost savage pomp of this outer area of the seraglio, we entered an inner court, and dismounted at the foot of a dark stone staircase. On the first landing-place stood one of the vizier's carriages; an old and awkward vehicle, of German manufacture, and such as might have been supposed to have travelled a dozen times from Hamburg to Trieste. At the top of the staircase, we entered into a wide gallery or hall, the windows of which command a noble view of the lake of Ioannina and the mountains of Pindus; the walls are painted, and numerous doors conduct from it to different parts of the palace. This hall, like the area below, was filled with a multitude of people; and the living scene became yet more various and interesting as we proceeded. We now saw, besides Turkish, Albanese, and Moorish soldiers, the Turkish officers and ministers of the vizier; Greek and Jewish secretaries, Greek merchants, Tartar couriers, the pages and black slaves of the seraglio; petitioners seeking to obtain audience, and numerous other figures, which give to the court and palace of Ali Pasha a character all its own.

"A curtain was thrown aside, and we entered the apartment of Ali Pasha. He was sitting in the Turkish manner, with his legs crossed under him, on a couch immediately beyond the fire, somewhat more elevated than the rest, and richer in its decorations. On his head he wore a high round cap, the colour of the deepest mazarine blue, and bordered with gold lace. His exterior robe was of yellow cloth, likewise richly embroidered, two inner garments of various colours, and flowing down loosely from the neck to the feet, confined only about the waist by an embroidered belt, in which were fixed a pistol and dagger, of beautiful and delicate workmanship. The hilts of these arms were covered with diamonds and pearls, and emeralds of great size and beauty were set in the heads of each. On his fingers the vizier wore many large diamond rings; and the mouth-piece of his long and flexible pipe was equally decorated with various kinds of jewellery.

"Yet more than his dress, however, the countenance of Ali Pasha at this time engaged our earnest observation. It is difficult to describe features, either in their detail or general effect, so as to convey any distinct impression to the mind of the reader. Were I to attempt a description of those of Ali, I should speak of his face as large and full; the forehead remarkably broad and open, and traced by many deep furrows; the eye penetrating, yet not expressive of ferocity; the nose handsome and well-formed; the lower part of the mouth and face concealed, except when speaking, by his mustachios and the long beard which flows over his breast. His complexion is somewhat lighter than that usual among the Turks; and his general appearance does not indicate more than his actual age, of sixty or sixty-one years, except perhaps that his beard is whiter than is customary at this time of life. The neck is short and thick, the figure corpulent and unwieldy; his stature I had afterwards the means of ascertaining to be about five feet nine inches. The general character and expression of the countenance are unquestionably fine, and the forehead especially is a striking and majestic feature. Much of the talent of the man may be inferred from his exterior; the moral qualities, however, may not equally be determined in this way; and to the casual observation of the stranger, I can conceive, from my own experience, that nothing may appear but what is open, placid, and alluring. Opportunities were afterwards afforded me of looking beneath the exterior of expression. It is the fire of a stove burning fiercely under a smooth and polished surface.

" He inquired how long it was since we had left England? where we had travelled in the interval? when we had arrived in Albania? whether we were pleased with what we had yet seen of this country? how we liked the appearance of Ioannina? whether we had experienced any obstruction in reaching this city? Soon after the conversation commenced, a pipe was brought to each of us by the attendants, the mouth-piece of amber, set round with small diamonds, and shortly afterwards coffee of the finest quality was handed to us in china cups, within golden ones. The vizier himself drank coffee, and smoked at intervals, during the progress of the conversation.

" The inquiries he made respecting our journey to Ioannina gave us the opportunity of complimenting him on the excellent police of his dominions, and the attention he has given to the state of the roads. I mentioned to him generally, Lord Byron's poetical description of Albania, the interest it had excited in England, and Mr. Hobhouse's intended publication of his travels in the same country. He seemed pleased with these circumstances, and stated his recollection of Lord Byron. He then spoke of the present state of Europe, inquired what was our latest intelligence of the advance of the French armies in Russia, and what was the progress of affairs in Spain. On the former point, it was evident that the information we gave was not new to him, though he did not expressly say this; his manner, however, evinced the strong interest he felt in the subject, and he seemed as if he were seeking indirectly to obtain our opinions upon it.

"The next subject of conversation was prefaced by his asking us, whether we had seen at Santa Maura one of his armed corvettes, which had been seized and carried thither by an English frigate. In bringing forward the subject during our interview with him, the vizier spoke with animation, or even a slight warmth of manner. He complained of the injustice done to him in the capture of his vessel, denied the right of capture in this particular case, and alleged his various good offices towards our government, as well as to individuals of the English nation, as what ought to have secured him against such acts of hostility. We answered, that as mere travellers we could not venture to give a reply that might be deemed official, but that we doubted not, from our knowledge of the dispositions of the English government, that when the affair was properly explained, its final arrangement would be both just and satisfactory to his highness. This of course meant little, and the vizier doubtless understood it as such. He added only a few words, and then, with a loud laugh, expressed his desire of changing the subject.*

"Before audience concluded, he mentioned his having been informed that I was a physician, and

---

* The corvette in question was eventually given up to Ali Pasha, less from any doubts of the legality of the prize, than from the nature of our political relations with him at that time.

asked whether I had studied medicine in England? Replying to this in the affirmative, he expressed a wish to consult me on his own complaints before we should quit Ioannina, a proposition to which I bowed assent, though not without apprehensions of difficulty in prescribing for the case of such a patient. He dismissed us very graciously, after we had been with him about half an hour.

"The manner of the vizier in this interview was courteous and polite, without any want of the dignity which befits his situation. There is not, either in his countenance or speech, that formal and unyielding apathy, which is the characteristic of the Turks as a people; but more vivacity, humour, and change of expression. His laugh is very peculiar, and its deep tone, approaching to a growl, might almost startle an ear unaccustomed to it.

"A day or two afterwards he again sent for us to the seraglio, and some general conversation having taken place, he asked several questions, which evidently had relation to his health, and formed a sort of exercise of his judgment upon me.

"After this preamble, he entered upon a narrative of his complaints, which, though I could only distantly follow it in his own language, yet was evidently marked by good precision and force in the manner of relation. He continued speaking for about fifteen minutes, and afforded me during this time a fine occasion of marking the feature of his countenance and manner. The narrative was translated to me with little abridgment, and much seeming accuracy, by the dragoman Colovo. In its substance, I may remark generally, that there was a good deal of credulity and prejudice displayed on some points; on others, more soundness of judgment than is common to the Turks as a nation. For various reasons, I do not feel myself at liberty to give the particulars of this narrative, nor would they afford anything new to the medical reader. It may suffice to say, that at this time he was suffering under no acute disorder; that his symptoms were chiefly of a chronic nature, depending mostly upon his age, partly upon circumstances in his former life, with other symptoms which I learnt more from my own observation than his report, which required the use of preventive means, to obviate eventual danger.

"In these interviews, however, which were very frequent during the last week of our stay at Ioannina, the conversation was not confined to medical matters alone, but went into other topics of a more familiar kind. Situated as I now was with him, I could feel perfectly at ease in this intercourse, which every circumstance contributed to render highly interesting. He usually sent for me to the seraglio in the afternoon or evening; sometimes alone, or occasionally with my friend, when he had nothing to say about his complaints. At whatever time it was, the approaches to the seraglio were always crowded with the singular groups already described. The vizier was rarely to be found in the same room on two successive days; and, during my present stay at Ioannina, I was with him in eight different apartments. His dress was not greatly varied; and only on one occasion I saw him with a turban instead of the blue cap, which he wore at the time of our first interview. His attitude was also very uniform, according to the Turkish habit. I seldom saw him rise from his couch, though he once did so, while explaining to me the decline of his bodily powers, striding firmly at the same time across the chamber, as if to show that still much of energy was left. His manner of reception was always polite and dignified. There was evidently more form intended when many persons were present, and his manner became more easy and familiar when we were alone.

"The most frequent topics introduced by the vizier in conversation were those relating to general politics; and in these it was evident that he was more interested than in any other. The conversation was usually carried on by question and reply; and his inquiries, though often showing the characteristic ignorance of the Turks in matters of common knowledge, yet often also were pertinent and well conceived, and made up by acuteness what they wanted of instruction. Some of these questions, which I noted down, may serve as specimens of their usual style. We were talking about England. He inquired the population of the country; and whether I thought it as populous as those parts of Albania I had seen. The answer to this question led him to describe briefly the northern parts of Albania, as being much better inhabited than those to the south of Ioannina. He then pursued the former subject; asked what was the size and population of London; and expressed surprise when informed of its magnitude. He inquired the number of our ships of war; the comparison of their size with the frigates he had seen on his coast; and where they were all employed.

"He inquired the distance of America from England and France; its extent; and to whom it belonged. He asked respecting its population and the longevity of its inhabitants, and dwelt especially on the latter point, to which I observed him always to attach a peculiar interest. He remarked, that he had heard that the Indians and Chinese live to a great age, and asked whether I knew this to be the case, or was acquainted with any particular means they used for the purpose. Seeing him inclined to follow this topic, I stated the remarkable instances of longevity in our own countrymen, Parr and Jenkins; at which he expressed surprise, and much desired to know if there were any means in nature by which this end might be obtained. It was evident that in this question he had reference to himself; and I took the opportunity of enforcing upon him some of the medical advice I had before given. He gave assent to what I said; but at the same time pursued the question, whether there were not some more direct means of procuring long life. I mentioned to him generally the attempts that had been made some centuries ago, to discover the Elixir Vitæ; and stated that this was a project which now had been abandoned by all men of reflection. Alluding accidentally, at the same time, to the search after the philosopher's stone, he eagerly followed the subject, and wished to know whether there were not some secret methods of discovering gold, which gave their possessor the power of procuring any amount of this metal. There was a strong and significant interest in his manner of asking this question, which greatly struck me; and it was accompanied by a look toward myself, seeming to search into the truth of my reply. I answered, of course, that there were no means of making gold and silver; that these metals were obtained only from the earth; and that the advantage of philosophy was in being able to employ the best means of raising them from mines, and purifying them for use. I doubt whether he was satisfied with this reply, or did not still believe in further mysteries of the alchemic art. The desire of gold and longevity are natural to a despot; and especially to one who, like Ali Pasha, has been ever pursuing a scheme of ambitious progress.

"Our conversation had often a reference to the politics of the day, on which I found him well and accurately informed. It was at this time that Bonaparte was pursuing his memorable campaign in Russia; in all the events of which Ali Pasha felt a lively interest, naturally arising out of his relation to the two great powers concerned. It was obviously for his advantage, that they should mutually wear out their strength, without either of them obtaining the preponderance. While at peace, they checked each other as to Turkey; when at war, if either were eminently successful, there was eventual danger to him. The vicinity of the French in the Illyrian provinces would speedily give effect to any designs they might adopt in that quarter, either from views of general ambition, or from motives of personal hostility to himself, which he might be well aware that he had created by his conduct at Prevesa, his recent connexion with the English, and by other circumstances of less notoriety. Of the power of Russia, and the ultimate danger to the Turkish empire from this source, he was well informed; and he, as well as his sons, had felt and known the weight of the Russian armies pressing upon the Danube. He understood, too, that all foreign attempts at the restoration of Greece, whether with selfish or honourable motives, must of necessity imply a previous attack upon his power : and I believe he was fully sensible of his incapacity of resisting permanently the efforts of a regular European army. At various times I have heard him converse, more or less directly, on these topics; and in general there was an air of sound judgment in his remarks, which implied as well sagacity as freedom from the prejudices of his nation.

" I happened to be with him at the seraglio, on the evening of the day when he received information of the French having entered Moscow. He was evidently in low spirits, and discomposed by the intelligence. I spoke to him of the perseverance and resources of Russia, and of the evils that might arise to the French army from the burning of Moscow, and the approach of winter. He was not satisfied by these arguments, but alluded in reply to the pacific temper of Alexander, to the mistakes which had been committed in the last Polish campaign, to the treaty of Tilsit, and, above all, to the character of Bonaparte, which he justly characterised ' as one that the world had never before seen.'

"The assiduity with which he applies himself to all his business is very great. He rises commonly before six, and his officers and secretaries are expected to be with him at this hour. There are no pauses in business during the day, except at twelve o'clock, when he takes his dinner, sleeping afterwards for an hour; and again at eight in the evening, which is his hour of supper. I have found him as late as nine o'clock, with three secretaries on the ground before him, listening to the most minute details of that branch of expenditure which relates to the post-houses; each article of which accounts he separately approved. His hours of pleasure are also in part subservient to the furtherance of business. I have seen him in the gardens of his pavilion surrounded by petitioners, and giving judgment on cases which were brought before him. Even when retiring to the harem he still preserves his public capacity; and in the petty discords of three hundred women secluded from the world, it is not wonderful that his occupation and authority as a judge should still be required.

"In his habits at table, Ali Pasha is temperate, though by no means so strict a Mussulman as to refuse himself wine. He almost always eats alone, according to the custom of Turks of high rank, and at the hours already mentioned. His dinner usually consists of twelve or sixteen covers, which are separately placed on a tray before him. The dishes are chiefly those of Turkish cookery; in addition to which a whole lamb, provided by his shepherds, is served up at his table every day in the year. His appetite is not at all fastidious, and I have been told that his cooks, in providing for him, take liberties which, under a luxurious despot, would infallibly cost them their heads.

"The adherence of Ali Pasha to the tenets of the Mahomedan religion is by no means rigid, and probably depending more upon a sense of interest than upon any zeal or affection for those tenets. He has few of the prejudices of a Mussulman; and in regarding those around him, his consideration obviously is, not the religion of the man, but whether he can be of service to any of his views. I have seen a Christian, a Turkish, and a Jewish secretary, sitting on the ground before him at the same moment,—an instance of the principle which is carried throughout every branch of his government. In Albania especially, the Christian and Mussulman populations are virtually on the same footing as to political liberty; all indeed slaves, but the former not oppressed, as elsewhere in Turkey, by those subordinate agencies of tyranny, which render more grating the chain that binds them. It may fairly be said, that under this government all religions find an ample toleration. I have even known instances where Ali Pasha has directed Greek churches to be built for the use of the peasants, as is the case in one or two villages on the plain of Arta.

"Truth compels the addition of other features of less pleasing kind; and to the general picture of eastern despotism must be annexed some traits peculiar to the man. The most striking of these are, a habit of perpetual artifice, shown in every circumstance of his life; and a degree of vindictive feeling, producing acts of the most unqualified ferocity. The most legitimate form his cunning assumes is on political matters, where, according to frequent usage, it might perhaps have the name of sagacity and adroitness. He is eminently skilled in all the arts of intrigue, and his agents or spies are to be found everywhere in the Turkish empire, doing the work of their master with a degree of zeal which testifies at once his own talent in their selection, and the commanding influence of his powers over the minds of all that surround him. His political information, derived from these sources, and from the ample use of bribery, is of the best kind; and it may, I believe, be affirmed as a fact, that not a single event of importance can occur at Constantinople, even in the most secret recesses of the divan, which is not known within eight days at the seraglio of Ioannina."

The character of Ali, as a ruler, is thus ably summed up by Dr. Holland. "Speaking generally of his administration, it may be said to be one of absolute individual despotism, supported by a union of powerful personal qualities in the individual. Quick thought, singular acuteness of observation, a conjunction of vigour and firmness in action, and much personal resolution, are connected with an uncommon faculty of artifice, an implacable spirit of revenge, and the utter disregard of every principle interfering with that active movement of ambition, which is the mainspring and master-feeling of his mind. The effect of these remarkable qualities has been exhibited in the progress he has made to his present state of elevation. Their influence is strikingly apparent in the entire subjection of so many warlike tribes, in the perfect tranquillity of his dominions, in the despotic exercise of his government; and, above all, in the mysterious awe with which even his name and mandate are regarded by every class of his subjects. It is pleasant to be able to allege, as one proof of his superior understanding, a degree of freedom from national and religious prejudices rarely to be found among Turkish rulers. He has studiously adopted into his territory several of the improvements of more cultivated nations; he has destroyed the numerous bands of robbers who infested the peaceful inhabitants of the country; by his direction roads have been made, bridges constructed, and agricultural improvements attempted. This laudable spirit has added respect to the terror inspired by his government; and even those who, out of the immediate reach of his power, can venture to express hatred of his tyranny, are obliged to allow that Albania is more happy and prosperous under this single and stern dominion, than when divided among numerous chieftains, and harassed by incessant wars. From this opinion, no deference to the principles of despotism can be inferred. The experience of history has proved, that a single tyrant is less injurious to the happiness of a people, than tyranny divided among several; and the vizier of Albania has himself become a despot, only by the annihilation of the many despots who preyed on that heretofore distracted and divided country."

The next delineation which we shall give of Ali Pasha, is from the pen of Mr. Richards, a British merchant, residing at Malta, who visited Albania with several ships, for the purpose of purchasing cows and oxen for the supply of the Maltese. It is only a sketch, but it gives some characteristic touches of the individual whom it represents. " At the appointed hour of eight in the morning," says he, " I waited upon the vizier's prime minister, signor Colovo, and remained with him about half an hour before I could be introduced. It would have shocked the delicate nerves of an English under-secretary of state to have seen Ali's first secretary sitting in a miserable room, upon a low coarse sofa, surrounded with papers, the due arrangement of which entirely depended upon himself. Here was no elegant escritoire with its convenient pigeon-holes, no luxurious fauteuil, no massive silver standish, no obsequious amanuensis, to relieve the onus of state correspondence. All the papers were in confusion, not a table was to be seen; and signor Colovo, resting his paper on his left hand or on his knees, and dipping his pen into a small ink-bottle attached to his girdle, thus penned his despatches. We had some difficulty in gaining admittance within the gates of the seraglio, an order having been issued that no one should enter; but, after waiting a short time, we were called up-stairs into a large ante-room, elegantly fitted up: through this we passed into another much handsomer; here we rested about an hour: this room is well painted in the Italian style; about fifty different kinds of muskets, swords, and pistols, decorated the walls; some common, others handsomely set in gold and silver. In this chamber were twenty or thirty trunks filled with state-papers: a large window, forming entirely one side of the room, commands a beautiful view of the town and the surrounding country. Every room that we passed through was crowded with soldiers, officers, servants, &c. While we were waiting, twenty-six porters came out of the audience chamber, carrying fifty-six thousand dollars. The vizier's youngest son, and also his nephew, a boy about eight years of age, had audience before us. At length it was our turn, and we were ushered in. I walked up to the vizier, who was seated on a sofa at the further end of a large room, kissed his hand, and paid the usual compliments. His chamber was beautifully painted, with abundance of gilding; an

English carpet covered the floor, and round the room were sofas and cushions of red velvet embroidered with flowers of gold. The vizier sat upon a beautiful large silk-embroidered cushion. He was more plainly dressed than when I saw him at Prevesa. On his head he wore a quilted purple velvet cap, with a narrow gold lace border; a brilliant diamond ring, about the size of a large button, glittered on his right hand; he had on silk stockings; and his pelisse, as usual with Turks of consequence, was made of silk stuff, lined with costly fur. On a small sofa near the fireplace, lay pistols, swords, inkstands, snuff-boxes, &c. &c., all richly ornamented with precious stones. Different sorts of arms, superbly mounted, hung round the room. The treasure in it must have been immense; but, as I am informed, nothing in comparison to what Ali possesses in other chambers.

" I was received very graciously; fortunately the vizier was in good humour. Having complained, that, through the roguery of his agents, the contract I had made with him when at Prevesa had not been executed to my satisfaction, he expressed his sorrow, assuring me at the same time of his good wishes towards all the English. After a little further conversation, he ordered signor Colovo to write an order, empowering me to take such part of the articles contracted for as I pleased, and when I chose. While the order was being made out, I had much familiar conversation with his highness, who asked me many questions about Malta, England, &c. &c. He also pressed me very much to return to Prevesa, and to remain there as his merchant. I asked him for a bouyourdie or passport through his country, and he immediately had one prepared in my presence; he moreover ordered one of his officers to accompany me wherever I chose, to procure me whatever I wanted, and to announce me as a person employed upon his special service. Having once more kissed his hand, I took my leave.

"I should suppose Ali to be from sixty to sixty-five years of age: he certainly possesses quick intellects, and an excellent memory. Although very fat, he is active on horseback; he gives but a few hours' notice before going a journey, and usually sets off in the night. Where the roads are good, he generally travels in a carriage. He sleeps but little; and is employed nearly the whole of the day in the management of his affairs. He is very close in money matters: eager to receive, but very remiss in his payments.

"He is very strict in the administration of justice, not making the least distinction between Greek, Turk, or Jew. Ali is everywhere absolute; his will is law. Instances of Ali's cruelty are too numerous to admit of any doubt that it arises from a natural depravity of heart. The peculiar character of his subjects should, however, be taken into consideration. Under a mild government it would be scarcely possible to live amongst them: fear is the only principle by which they can be acted upon."

Mr. Richards is not the only one who has urged the sinister character of the Albanians as a palliation of Ali's conduct. An Albanian philosopher, who had frequented the society of the literary contemporaries of Voltaire, expresses himself, upon this subject, in the following terms. "I was born at Premiti, and am an undeniable proof that a wise and prudent man can be happy everywhere. I have seen Versailles and the king of France: I have witnessed the most refined civilisation: I have resided among the most polished nation in the world; and yet I sighed to revisit my native land. For fifteen years I have served Ali

Pasha as his interpreter, without experiencing at his hands either ingratitude or great favour. His government, which to you may perhaps appear severe, is the best calculated for the subjects which he commands: his extortions and his cruelties are suited to the ferocious character of the Albanians: a nation of robbers must have a tyrant for their ruler. My language may, perhaps, astonish you; but only ten years ago you would have been assassinated, or sold as a slave, by the very people who now surround you, and from whom you receive the attentions of hospitality."

This series of personal and moral likenesses of Ali we shall close by the portrait which Mr. Hughes has drawn of him. That accomplished and intellectual traveller had abundant opportunities for observation, and he has finished the picture in an elaborate and masterly style. The impression which the vizier made upon him at first sight, he thus describes. "As we approached the audience chamber I felt my heart palpitate at the thought of entering into the presence of a being who had long held so dire a sway over the destinies of his fellow mortals, and whose steps in his dark career were marked indelibly by the stain of blood! At the entrance of his apartment stood several Albanian guards, one of whom opened the door, and we marched into the room, saluting the vizier as we entered, who sat upon a lion's skin at the angle of the divan, handsomely but not superbly dressed; a band of gold lace which bound the scarlet cap upon his head, a broad belt of the same material which passed round his waist, and the pommel of his handjar glittering with diamonds, alone denoted the man of exalted rank: a houka stood near him which he is rather fond of exhibiting, as the use of it shows a considerable strength of lungs. As soon as we were seated upon the divan he returned our salutation by placing his right hand upon his breast with a gentle inclination of his head, and expressed his satisfaction at seeing us in his capital.

"At a first introduction it could not be expected that we should acquire much insight into the character of the pasha: my own attention was directed chiefly to the contemplation of his countenance; and this is in general no index of his mind. Here it is very difficult to find any traces of that bloodthirsty disposition, that ferocious appetite for revenge, that restless and inordinate ambition, that inexplicable cunning, which has marked his eventful career: the mien of his face on the contrary has an air of mildness in it, his front is open, his venerable white beard descending over his breast gives him a kind of patriarchal appearance, whilst the silvery tones of his voice, and the familiar simplicity with which he addresses his attendants, strongly aid the deception. He appears as he is described by the animated bard*. Still, after very attentive consideration, I thought I could perceive certain indications of cruelty and perfidy beneath his grey eyebrows, with marks of deep craftiness and policy in the lineaments of his forehead; there was something sarcastic in his smile, and even terrible in his laugh. His address was engaging, his figure very corpulent, although it is said to have been graceful in his youth; as his stature is rather below the middle size, and his waist long in proportion, he appears to greatest advantage as we now saw him seated on the divan, or on horseback."

The result of Mr. Hughes's inquiries and remarks is thus summed up. We may, perhaps, without injustice, surmise that his intimate acquaintance with M. Pouqueville operated to give his mind a bias

---

* In the quotation in page 321, from Lord Byron's Childe Harolde.

against Ali; but, still, it cannot be doubted, that, in all the main points, the delineation is nearly correct.

"The great basis of Ali's character is extreme selfishness, and he possesses many qualities, positive and negative, natural and acquired, which are well adapted to promote this ruling passion. He has few feelings in common with the rest of men: he regards all human beings as objects calculated to advance his own views and interests, whilst his very successes have resulted as much from a deficiency in human sympathies and moral virtues, as from his talents and courage. No pity, no remorse, ever turned him aside from the object of his pursuit: with him faith and justice are but terms invented to dupe the ignorant or unsuspecting; and the most favourite art with which he is acquainted is that of deceiving all mankind.

"Deprived of the advantages of early education, his study has been the human heart, and with the intricacies of that complicated labyrinth he is well acquainted: the native vigour of his genius readily supplies expedients for the suggestions of his ambition, and his moral courage always rises in proportion to the exigences that require it. He has a quick perception of circumstances, and very rarely allows the opportunities of action to escape him: he possesses decision, and that decision is followed by the most indefatigable perseverance: he feels his ground before he commences operations, but never neglects to go where fortune seems to point: he is gifted with the talent of discovering amongst his followers the fittest instruments to be employed and the most faithful guardians to be entrusted; nor does he allow the etiquette of oriental dignity to prevent his communication with society and intercept the knowledge thence to be acquired. He has dexterity enough to dazzle the multitude, and strength of mind to discard many national prejudices which might oppose his advancement. He attaches his troops to his interest not more by a ready participation in their hardships, difficulties, and dangers, than by the easy familiarity with which he engages their confidence or flatters their vanity, and by the ability with which he associates their military enthusiasm with his success and identifies their glory with his own. He is a great master of political intrigue, and so versed in the arts of simulation and dissimulation, that he has not only deceived his own government, but every other which has attempted to turn him to its advantage: each in turn has discovered its plans betrayed and itself deserted, as soon as a more powerful ally or a more beneficial cause attracted his regards. 'Divide and conquer' is his favourite motto: he has no remorse in setting father against son, and son against father, brother against brother, and friend against friend: in every town or district which attracts his cupidity, dissensions are studiously promoted, jealousy and distrust increased, and intestine wars excited to disunite the inhabitants and desolate the country: he then procures for himself an invitation as an ally or arbitrator, when he contrives to eject both the innocent and guilty, and remains master of the contested territory. His perfidy is more than Punic: he will make a treaty and violate it in the same hour: he will allure his adversaries into his power by the kindest words and fairest promises, and then destroy them without compunction. His desire of vengeance is deeply seated, knows no limits, and increases by delay; neither does he possess the least portion of that magnanimity of soul which can requite valour and generosity in a foe. In discourse he is equally skilful at discovering the sentiments of others, and veiling his own amidst impenetrable obscurity. As his actions seldom correspond with his promises, so his looks rarely indicate his thoughts; he can throw into his manners and his countenance the appearance of frank honesty and an affectation of gentleness, whilst rage and fury fester in his heart: he frequently seems most gay, when he is inwardly torn by chagrin, and most courteous when he meditates the darkest deeds. Yet Ali is not wantonly savage, nor does he require, like a Djezzar Pasha, to be lulled to rest with the cries of innocent and agonised victims; but let his own safety or even his interest be endangered or threatened, and no principles of religion, no ties of friendship, no dues of gratitude, will restrain him in his sanguinary career.

" As Ali gazes at power with an eagle's eye, so he clings to wealth with the appetite of a vulture. His avarice is so excessive that one might almost think his desire of dominion proceeded from the wish of gratifying this insatiable cupidity. In procuring wealth he has recourse not only to a legal revenue, but to the meanest artifices and the most shameful extortion. He has not political knowledge enough to see that the encouragement of commerce and agriculture, with equitable laws and financial arrangements, would, by an increase of capital, and extension of credit, augment his revenue and support his government; but he prefers to fill his treasury by forced avanias and grievous exactions, annihilating industry and stifling all the bounties of nature in their birth. A vast deposit is always kept unemployed, and used as the necessities of the times may require; when this is satisfied, the expenditure is replaced by additional contributions.

" To no art does he owe more of his success than to that of bribery, and his gold has often penetrated into those places which were proof against his arms; neither does his inordinate avarice repress, but rather promotes this system, for he scarcely ever fails to recover the bribes sooner or later with interest, whilst the life or liberty of the traitor is sacrificed to his skilful hypocrisy; yet with the power of assuming the most winning manners, and clothing his stern countenance in complacent smiles, he contrives to draw fresh victims into his fatal snares, directs their villany to his own advantage, and persuading each deluded votary that his fortune will be more prosperous than that of others, overwhelms at last both adversaries and adherents in a common ruin. He once gave a man a bouyourdee to kill another who was obnoxious to him the bloody deed was perpetrated, but the assassin found in the pocket of his victim a similar bouyourdee for his own destruction. He carried it to the vizier, and expressed some signs of astonishment; when Ali, laughing, replied, 'Hey, murrie, if I had not given him this, he would never have put himself in your way, and you would have had no chance of effecting your purpose.' In fact, the tyrant wished to get rid of both or either of them.

"Let us now contemplate the portrait in a light which will perhaps show us some of its features in a more agreeable point of view. Though we cannot give our unqualified admiration to any man, however brilliant may have been his career, whose actions have been directed solely by self-interest and discoloured by the most glaring vices, and though it is easy for a despotic tyrant to benefit one part of the community by oppressing another, or excite the admiration of future generations, by adding to the miseries of the present race, still we ought to estimate the character of a person with a reference to the habits of his country, the system of his education, and the principles of his religion, keeping in view also the example which others, placed in similar situations, exhibit for his imitation.

" Bearing in mind these considerations, I should pronounce the people of Albania comparatively happy, whether reference be made to their own state before the consolidation of Ali's power, or to that which still exists in other parts of the Turkish empire. In one case the contiguity of many small, fierce, independent tribes, engendered constant and implacable discord. If blood was shed even by accident, vengeance, uncontrolled by law, and entrusted to individual discretion, swallowed up all other passions, and rendered society a scene of terror and suspicion. So lawless were the natives of these wild mountains that every defile and rock was rife with muskets aimed against the unwary traveller or the unprotected merchant; if he escaped with life, his property was plundered and his person sold into slavery; to such an extent did brigandage prevail that agriculture was neglected, commerce languished, the very arts of civilisation began to disappear, and the whole land to present one unvaried scene of poverty and wretchedness. In the other case, I mean that which regards the general state of the Ottoman empire, it is sufficient to allude only to that horrid theocratic principle which makes power depend solely upon faith, and converts every Mahometan zealot into a remorseless tyrant. On the contrary, in Albania, though all are subject to one mighty despot, no petty tyrants are permitted to exist, and protection is given equally to the Turk, the Greek, and the Albanian, against the aggressions of each other. Religious toleration is freely granted, and the regularity of monarchical power has in some measure succeeded to the factions of aristocracies and republics. There exists at present a security in these dominions which we should seek in vain where the baneful influence of the crescent elsewhere extends: a police is organised, robbers are extirpated, roads and canals are made or repaired, rivers are rendered navigable, so that the merchant can now traverse the Albanian districts with safety, and the traveller with convenience; agriculture, in spite of all obstacles, improves, commerce increases, and the whole nation advances, perhaps unconsciously, towards higher destinies and greater happiness.

" With regard to the domestic habits of Ali Pasha, his attention to business, and the distribution of his time, are amongst the most extraordinary. So jealous is he of power, that he rarely calls upon the services of his ministers, but transacts all affairs of government himself. He rises very early in the morning, and takes a cup of coffee with his pipe: he then gives audience to his various officers, receives petitions, and decides causes, pronounces judgment, settles the concerns of his army, navy, and revenue, till noon; he then dines upon very frugal fare, a few plain dishes, and a moderate portion of wine. After dinner he sleeps for an hour or two, and then smokes his houka whilst he is occupied in similar occupations till six or seven o'clock at night, or even much later: he afterwards takes his supper and retires to his harem. In the expeditions which he frequently makes through various parts of his dominions, he will sometimes partake of the frugal fare of a cottager, and sleep beneath his humble roof. No one knows beforehand where he intends to transact the business of the day: sometimes he fixes upon the serai of Litaritza, sometimes that of the castrou, and often he retires to the gardens of the kiosk, or to some one of the numerous tenements which he possesses both within and without the city. Wherever he may be, a large quantity of Albanian troops are generally seen scattered about, in their white capotes, waiting for his exit. This extraordinary attention to business is productive of vast inconvenience to his subjects, for in spite of all his quickness in decision, and the impossibility of appeal, a vast accumulation necessarily takes place, especially during his frequent absence from the capital.

"He is not at all strict, and is thought by no means sincere, in the article of religion. He visits a mosque but once in the year, at the festival of the Ramazan, when he goes in grand procession. His mind, strong as are its natural faculties, being untutored in philosophy or science, and unaided by religious truths, clings to the marvellous and bends beneath the power of superstition: hence it is that he is greatly alarmed at thunder and earthquakes, at which times probably remorse finds an opportunity of applying her vindictive lash.

'Hi sunt qui trepidant et ad omnia fulgura pallent.'

"He believes in charms, and thinks that chemical combinations of matter might be discovered, which would cure all diseases, and procure life to an indefinite extent; this makes him often the dupe of cunning and designing men.

"Though strongly addicted to sensual lusts, and proud of the success which formerly attended his amours, he pretends to take great concern in the morals of his people, and perhaps no town exists where public prostitution is so severely punished as at Ioannina. In his exterior deportment he discovers little of that ostentation which often sits so awkwardly upon persons who have risen to very exalted stations. Ali on the contrary is affable and condescending as well to strangers as to his own subjects. His firmness of mind and command over himself are well illustrated in the following anecdote.—In the year 1813, as he was inspecting some repairs in the great serai of the castrou, a large block of stone fell from a scaffold upon his shoulder, and laid him prostrate on the ground. Every one present thought he was killed, and a general alarm was spread: but Ali, though seriously hurt, ordered a horse to be equipped instantly, upon which he mounted and rode round the city, with a single Albanian attendant, without discovering the least mark of pain, though he had received a wound which confined him several weeks to his bed. After his recovery he told M. Pouqueville that he acted thus to assure his people of his safety, and to deprive his enemies of the pleasure of thinking he was likely to die. The consul replied, that every man had his enemies, but he could not think those of his highness went so far as to desire his death*. 'What?' said Ali; 'there is not a minute of the day in which they do not offer up prayers to Heaven for my destruction: how can it be otherwise? for forty years I have been doing everything bad to everybody: in this period I have caused thirty thousand persons to be hung and put to death in various ways; and they know that if I live longer I shall do more: would you have them not hate me then? their hatred, however, will not affect my health;'—and upon this he burst into his usual sardonic laugh."

---

* I had this anecdote, not from M. Pouqueville, but from another person who was present at the conference.

CHAPTER XIV.

Flattery lavished on Ali— His Forebodings—Ambition and Revenge two of his predominant Passions—Story of Ismael Pasho Bey—Incestuous Intercourse of Ali with his Daughter-in-law—Pasho persecuted by the Vizier—Stratagem of Pasho—Letter of his Wife to him — Pasho takes refuge at Constantinople — Is received into the Service of the Sultan—Decline of Ali's Influence in the Divan—Ali sends Assassins against Pasho—The Sultan deposes Ali—Situation of Ali—His avarice prejudicial to him—Is deficient in military Skill—Measures adopted by him to resist the Sultan's Army—He appeals to the Greeks—Ismael Pasho appointed to the Pashalik of Ioannina—Ali promises his Subjects a Constitution—Failure of Moustai—Impolitic Measure of Suleyman—First Movements of the Turkish Armies—Barbarities of Pehlevan Baba—Ismael Pasho commences his Operations—Progress of the Turks—Treachery of Ali's Generals—The Turkish Armies approach Ioannina.

From youth to manhood, from manhood to declining age, we have traced the progress of the vizier Ali; we now approach the catastrophe of his " strange eventful history." At the period when we resume our narrative he had apparently reached the summit of prosperity—he had beaten down his enemies and rivals under his feet, accomplished his plans, extended his dominions, consolidated his power, increased his riches, and obtained high dignities for his children and grandchildren; his court was visited by noble and learned foreigners, curious to study the character of a man so extraordinary; and even the rulers of nations did not hesitate to consider him almost in the light of an independent sovereign. The great, however stained with crimes, will always find flatterers; and we, therefore, need not wonder that Ali was covered with adulation by some of the base and mischievous tribe. At Vienna his praise was sung by a venal or an ignorant poet. In Italy, a herald tasked his skill to invent for him a coat of arms. This goodly specimen of blazonry, alluding to the title of Aslan, or the Lion, consisted of a lion, in a field gules, embracing three lion's whelps. It was not inappropriate; but might have been improved by introducing the gibbet, the impaling-stake, and the bow-string. A third fawner, a Macedonian, by the name of Michael Stephen Partzoulla, sounded "the very base string" of sycophancy. He published a Greek and French Grammar; and in his dedication of it to Ali, not content with bestowing on him the epithets of "most high, most puissant, and most merciful," he added, "The earth, most illustrious prince, is full of the glory of thy name; no one is ignorant of the bright and dazzling fame of thy noble virtues." If, indeed, this were meant for irony, it was poignant. Ali was probably best pleased with the labour of the herald; for his taste seems to have leaned towards marks of distinction. He had a splendid star fabricated, chiefly from the jewels sold to him by the deposed king of Sweden, and this he called his order. It was worn on his outer vest, in imitation of that which he had seen on the coat of Sir Thomas Maitland, the lord high commissioner.

But, amidst all his triumphs and enjoyments, the repose of Ali was far enough from being undisturbed. In spite of his seared conscience, remorse would sometimes wring his heart. Dark forebodings of misfortune would also arise and throw a gloom over the gayest scenes. In one of his pensive moods, while, reclining on a rich sofa, he listened to the warbling of the birds in his garden, he expressed to the French consul the pleasure he derived from their songs, and then added, " Among the women of my harem I have a peasant girl who sings, and so admirable are her strains, that I never hear them without being carried back to the days of my youth; I think myself transported again to my own Japygian mountains! My life was a tranquil one then! What a holiday it was for me when I and my companions feasted upon some goat which had been stolen from the shepherds of Mount Argenik!—and when I went to the weddings of my friends, there was no player upon the lyre within a hundred leagues round that could come up to me; I could challenge the best at dancing or a trial of strength; but those times will never return, and now, when life is drawing to a close, I can see nothing but domestic broils, storms to contend with, and—who knows? I shall, perhaps, not have the happiness of dying on the mat of my forefathers. I keep it still, to remind me that I was born poor, that I have known sufferings." Here, abruptly raising himself on his seat, he exclaimed, " And if it must be so, I will prove that I can defy even the extremity of wretchedness!"

There were likewise moments when Ali was not insensible to the perils which environ a lofty station. He more than once said that, in aspiring to be viziers, his children would be the cause of his destruction; and when speaking of his own power, he often repeated this maxim, " A vizier is a man covered with honours, seated upon a barrel of gunpowder, which may be blown up by a single spark."

" Yet,—so inconsistent is human nature,—his craving for additional power continued insatiable. Having brought under his sway all the centre and south of Albania, besides other territories, he was eager to extend his dominions in the north, and he began to prepare for seizing upon the pashalik of Scutari, where he kept in pay a faction ready to aid his designs. He saw, too, with infinite mortification, the post of Rumilivalisee conferred upon another, whose presence at Monastir was peculiarly disgustful to him, because he suspected, and perhaps rightly, that the new officer was meant to be a check and a spy upon him. Ali was also tormented by his unsatisfied longings for vengeance. Inflexible in his hatred, he was enraged that he could not venture to put to death his prisoner Ibrahim Pasha; a deed from which he was withheld solely by a conviction that it would cause his son Mouctar to be removed from the government of Berat. Nor was he much less dissatisfied that the Parghiotes had escaped the chastisement which he had intended to give them, for their stubborn resistance to his projects, and their dislike of his person.

This love of revenge was the vice which at last, in conjunction with his avarice, caused the downfall of Ali. The instrument of his ruin was a man whom he had devoted to destruction, but who had been fortunate enough to elude the repeated attempts of the vizier's emissaries. Ismael Pasho Bey, the personage in question, was a relative of Ali, and had fought under his standard upon various occasions. He fell, however, under the displeasure of the vizier, who, in 1807, that he might have a better opportunity of seizing upon Pasho's property, sent him to the Morea with Veli, as the new Pasha's selictar. Pasho was not ignorant of Ali's purpose in thus sending him to a distance. "He gets me out of the way, the villain!" exclaimed he; "he gets me out of the way; but I will punish him for it, whatever may happen; and I shall die satisfied, if I can deprive such a monster of his head, even at the expense of my own."

In pursuance of his resolution, Pasho, under the mask of regard for his master's interests, prompted Veli to adopt such measures as could not fail to render the son of Ali hateful to the people of Peloponnesus. But this did not suffice to satisfy his vindictive feelings. He was in possession of a horrible secret, the divulging of which would inflict a deadly wound upon both father and son, and he resolved to take vengeance by disclosing it. Ali had been guilty of an incestuous intercourse with Zobeide, the wife of Veli. Having previously administered to her a soporific potion, he stole to her bed, and consummated his crime. The unfortunate wife of Veli remained ignorant of the fact till she became pregnant, when her suspicions were excited by the dark hints of her female attendants, whom Ali had threatened with death if they disclosed his infamous conduct. In her despair she sent to desire an interview with the author of her misery. When he entered the harem, she embraced his knees, and conjured him to declare that her surmises were unfounded. His only reply was an avowal of his criminality. With much difficulty he put a stop to her tears and lamentations, and prevailed on her to promise silence respecting the atrocious deed; a deed which he soon after rendered more atrocious, by the murder of the unborn babe. Nor did Ali stop here. To remove all witnesses of his guilt, he ordered the women who were privy to it to be thrown into the lake by his black mutes. But he did not succeed in suppressing all evidence. By some means Ismael obtained a knowledge of the fact, and he communicated it to Veli, who was almost goaded to madness by the tidings. As might be expected, Ali indignautly protested that the imputation was a foul calumny; and Veli either credited, or affected to credit his father's protestations. At the same time the vizier sent six assassins to despatch the divulger of the secret; but Ismael was lucky enough to escape from their poniards, and have the satisfaction of seeing five of them hanged. Thinking it, however, no longer safe to remain with Veli, he quitted his service, and proceeded to Negropont.

Incessantly tracked by the murderous emissaries of the vizier, Pasho led a life of wandering and hardship. Flying from Negropont, he visited various cities of Egypt and Asia Minor, often having no other shelter than the porticoes of the mosques, and sometimes lying with beggars among the warm ashes from the public baths. At Alexandria he would have been entrapped had not his prudence saved him. Some Albanian mariners requested him to come on board their vessel, for the purpose of giving his advice as to the disposal of some goods, which they said they had just brought into the harbour. Pasho cautiously sent a person to look at the vessel, and this messenger informed him that, far from being laden, she was evidently ready to sail at a moment's warning. Convinced of the real character of the pretended sailors, Pasho declined their invitation; and, finding they were discovered, they instantly departed.

He next sought refuge in the court of Muhamet Ali, nazir of Drama, one of the most magnificent nobles of Thrace, and had the good fortune to acquire his favour and protection. In the course of a few months, Ali again traced him, and procured from the Porte a firman against him, the execution of which he intrusted to a capidgi-bashi. Pasho was on a hunting party with the nazir when the capidgi arrived. Not knowing the person of the proscribed fugitive, the messenger inquired of him, where he could find the nazir, as he had business of importance to communicate. The wits of Pasho were sharpened by the constant necessity of warding off danger, and he promptly replied, " I am the nazir; what is your business?" He was answered, that the speaker had brought a firman, obtained at the request of Ali Pasha of Ioannina. " Ah! my dear friend Ali Tepelini, how can I serve him?"—" By executing the firman, which enjoins you to cut off the head of a worthless fellow, one Pasho Bey, who contrived some time ago to get into your service."—" It shall be done; but I warn you that he is a very difficult man to catch; he is brave, violent, and much liked by my servants, so that we must act warily to get him into the snare. I expect him here every moment. It is of consequence that he should not see you, and that my folks should not suspect who you are. 'Tis only two leagues from hence to Drama; go and wait for me there; I shall be with you in the evening, and you may look upon your business as done."

Ismael did not think it prudent to rely upon the friendship of the nazir, who might perhaps find reasons for sacrificing him. As soon, therefore, as the capidgi had galloped off towards Drama, he made the best of his way in an opposite direction. He travelled all night through by-roads, bought the dress of a Bulgarian monk, and, after having traversed upper Macedonia, he stopped at a convent of Servian monks, represented himself as a brother just returned from the Holy Land, and was hospitably received.

Enraged at having missed his prey, Ali accused Muhamet before the Divan of having favoured Pasho's escape. The charge was easily refuted, and, as the innocence of Pasho became manifest in the inquiry, the vizier could not obtain another firman against him. It was then that Athanasia Vaia, who had discovered Pasho's retreat, begged for the honour of being allowed to immolate him. The request was granted, and, to cover his design, Ali affected to be highly exasperated against Vaia, and, to the astonishment of all Ioannina, drove him from the palace, swearing that had he not been his foster-brother he would have hanged him. Simulating the profoundest grief, Vaia applied to every person of influence to intercede with the vizier, but the only favour which could be obtained for him was a passport with permission to retire to Macedonia.

Displaying every outward sign of despair, Vaia set out for the place of his exile, and on reaching Vodena, he assumed, for the purpose, as he said, of greater security, the dress of a monk. On his road he met with a brother of the Servian convent, related to him his pretended misfortunes, and entreated that he might be received into the monastery as a lay brother. His request was made known to the superior of the convent, who granted it, and lost no time in informing Pasho that a new companion was about to arrive. By the description Pasho recognised Athanasia Vaia, and, guessing the object of his mission, he communicated his suspicions to the prior, who consented not to admit the assassin till Pasho was far on the road to Constantinople. It was there, in the capital of the empire, that Ismael resolved to defy and combat his powerful enemy. For his favourable reception in the Turkish metropolis, he is said to have been indebted to a letter of recommendation from the Pasha of Egypt.

The wife and children of Ismael having been detained as hostages at Ioannina, the dread of exposing them to the fury of Ali had hitherto withheld him from open hostility against the vizier. That impediment was now removed. His wife, having refused to be divorced, was dragged from her house and consigned to poverty. Pressed by want, disease, and sorrow, she addressed the following melancholy lines to the husband, whom she believed that she should see no more. "Your children are in chains," said she, "and your wife, banished to a hut, is reduced to spin for her bread. The Christian nuns support her out of the alms-money, when the infirmities which are weighing her down will not allow her to provide for her wants. Her bed, which once was covered with cloth of gold, now consists of a straw mat and a wretched horsecloth. She sends you the last ornament she possesses—her hair. Think no more of me but to avenge your family and your wife. AYESHA."

On his arrival at Constantinople, Pasho, in order to induce the vizier to imagine that he had renounced all connection with politics, affected to be wholly devoted to the practice of religious observances, and was a constant frequenter of dervises and ulemas. The stratagem so far succeeded that Ali relaxed in the pursuit. It is probable, also, that he thought it impolitic to venture on attacking Ismael almost in the presence of the sultan. The fugitive, meanwhile, was silently but actively labouring to undermine his foe. His personal advantages contributed much to his success. He was of lofty stature, possessed a fine countenance and a dignified deportment, and conversed with ease in all the various languages of the Turkish empire.

Among those with whom Pasho formed an intimacy was the Etolian chief Paleopoulo, who had for some years been living in the Ottoman capital, under the protection of France, but was now about to form an establishment in Russian Bessarabia. Paleopoulo communicated to him the memorial against Ali, which, as we have seen in a preceding chapter, he had formerly presented to the government. Pasho was of opinion, that it ought to be again brought forward; and the two friends in consequence proceeded to strengthen it by additional arguments and facts, among which, as most likely to make an impression, they did not fail to place in a prominent point of view the enormous revenues and treasures of Ali and his family. To remove the fear that the vizier's military resources might render an attack upon him abortive, Pasho pledged his head that, in spite of the troops and fortresses of the satrap, he would lead twenty thousand men to the walls of Ioannina without firing a single shot.

The time, however, was not yet come for the overthrow of Ali. His bribes, and the hope of extracting more from him, had still an effect upon some of the Turkish ministers. Pasho's zeal was applauded, but the consideration of his scheme was put off from time to time, and at last was abandoned. Discouraged by the delay, Paleopoulo was on the point of setting off for Bessarabia when death brought his projects to a close. Just before he died, he conjured Pasho to persevere, prophetically assuring him that ere long the house of Ali would fall beneath his blows. "In dying I only regret," said he, "that I cannot be with you on Mount Dryscos; Ali Pasha would again recognise Paleopoulo by the report of the long gun*."

Ismael Pasho resolved to follow the advice of his friend, but he changed his battery. Instead of presenting memorials and plans of reform, he confined himself to secretly sapping the influence of Ali, by becoming the champion of all who had to complain of the vizier and his sons. He drew up their petitions, and got them presented to the ministers of the Porte. His exertions and misfortunes at length became known to the sultan, who granted an audience to him, and after listening to his story, appointed him one of his capidgi-bashis, or chamberlains.

The wrath excited in Ali by the news of Pasho's promotion was not unmingled with apprehension. He seems to have had a foreboding that evil would result to him from this unexpected event. To all who approached him he inveighed against his old enemy, whom he believed to be occupied in thwarting all his schemes,

---

* Paleopoulo's gun, which was of an enormous calibre, was as celebrated among the Albanians as the sword of Roland was among the knights of old.

and he often exclaimed, " O that Heaven would but restore to me my youthful days, I would poniard him even in the Divan itself!" Yet, while he was thus prescient of evil, Ali unwisely neglected the most effectual means of averting it. Instead of scattering his treasures liberally to purchase impunity, his insane avarice prompted him to withhold the customary bribes. By this impolitic step he raised up enemies, among the most formidable of whom was Kaleb Effendi, the chief favourite of sultan Mahmoud.

It was probably through the influence of Kaleb and Pasho that another enemy of Ali's family obtained a seat in the Divan. This was Abde Effendi, of Larissa, one of the richest beys in Thessaly, who had been obliged to fly from the tyranny of Veli Pasha. Since Thessaly had been under the government of Veli its sufferings had been extreme. To support his own inordinate prodigality, and satisfy the cravings of his father, he had quintupled the taxes, and resorted to every form of extortion; till, at length, the province was in danger of being depopulated, multitudes of Greeks having emigrated to Odessa, while the principal Turkish families took refuge in Constantinople. Now that complaints could be heard, innumerable voices were raised against him, and the offender was in consequence punished by his removal to the obscure post of Lepanto. A prudent desire to deprive the vizier of the resources of a rich province may also have contributed to produce the deposition of Veli.

This was the first blow struck at Ali, and he felt all the force of it. Passion is a dangerous counsellor, and, unfortunately for the vizier, he listened only to its dictates. Not doubting that Ismael Pasho was the author of the disgrace which had been inflicted on him, he resolved, at all hazards, to destroy this hated foe. Two Albanians were easily found who were willing to execute whatever he might command; these men he despatched to Constantinople to assassinate Ismael Pasho. On arriving at the capital they proceeded to Ismael's residence, and desired to speak with him. The moment he appeared at the window they discharged their pistols, but he was only slightly wounded. The assassins immediately betook themselves to flight. They were, however, pursued by a well-mounted detachment; and, after a chase of sixty miles, one of them was taken. He refused to make any disclosure, but when the torture was applied, he confessed that he and his companion had been hired by the vizier to murder Pasho Bey. He was then hanged in front of the imperial seraglio.

This daring act at least precipitated, if it did not cause, the ruin of Ali. Such a flagrant offence it was impossible for the government to overlook, without exposing itself to contempt, and its members to danger. It has been supposed, that the sultan was moved to proscribe the pasha of Ioannina solely by a wish to become master of the treasures which Ali had accumulated. That a necessitous sovereign might be glad to recruit his exhausted treasury is nowise improbable; but there was undoubtedly another motive which had superior weight with Mahmoud. He had, at an early period of his reign, resolved to reduce within narrower bounds the dominion of those great vassals who, while they wasted the resources of the state, and alienated its subjects, left to the Porte scarcely the shadow of authority in its distant provinces. Ali would certainly have been earlier attacked, had not two reasons operated against such a measure. At one time the magnitude of his power was found to be useful in checking enemies: at another, it opposed an insuperable obstacle to the designs which, as we have seen, the Porte meditated against him; and, latterly, the sultan deemed it unwise to engage in a contest for an object which in a short time he would obtain without a struggle. In the course of nature, the aged vizier must soon pass from the scene, and Albania would then quietly fall into the possession of its sovereign. But, after this last outrage of the satrap, a collision was unavoidable.

Knowing the desperate character of Ali, the Porte was convinced that he would not submit without a struggle, and it prudently began its operations by displacing, in favour of trusty persons, the governors of a great number of military posts, especially those which commanded the passes on the Albanian frontier. These posts had hitherto been filled by the creatures of the vizier. His agents at Constantinople were also arrested, and the property in their hands belonging to him was confiscated. A sentence of *fermanli*, solemnly ratified by the fetva of the mufti, was then denounced against him, by which he was put to the ban of the empire, in case of his failing to appear, within forty days, at "the golden threshold of the gate of felicity," to answer to a charge of treason.

Ali was at this moment revelling in delights at Parga, where he had built a magnificent seraglio; his harem occupying the spot where a church dedicated to the Virgin had formerly stood. He was roused from his luxurious indolence by the tidings of the sentence which had been fulminated against him; but he had been so much accustomed to elude peril that his fears were not fully excited by that which now hung over him. He hoped that gold and intrigues would bear him safely through. Every day he despatched to the Ottoman capital protestations of fidelity, supplications, and splendid presents. All were unavailing; no one would espouse his cause; for the sultan had declared that whoever should dare to speak to him in favour of Ali should lose his head. A courier at last arrived from Constantinople, with intelligence that the vizier had nothing to hope. As a last resource, he is said to have applied to the lord high commissioner of the Ionian Islands, to become a mediator for him, or to give him succour, and to have received for answer that an asylum was all that could be granted. He was compelled, therefore, to prepare for war.

Unequal as the contest may seem between the monarch of an extensive empire and one of his viceroys, it was less so than it seemed. The disjointed condition of the Turkish government, the dilapidated state of its resources, the defective discipline of its armies, and the jarring interests and mutual jealousies of the pashas, the discontent which existed among a portion of the Mussulmans, and the ferment which had long been working in the minds of the Greeks, and was soon to explode with irrepressible violence, all combined to defalcate heavily from the sultan's means of asserting his authority against his rebellious subjects. Within the last quarter of a century, the Servians and Passwan Oglou had both shown how difficult it was for the Porte to put down revolt. Yet, in neither of those cases had the revolters possessed as many advantages as the pasha of Ioannina. Ali was master of five-and-twenty fortresses, an army of at least as many thousand men, four hundred pieces of heavy cannon, chiefly brass, fifty field-pieces, sixty-two mortars, a considerable number of Congreve rockets, and an abundant supply of ammunition. He had also plenty of excellent artillerymen; an essential force, in which the Turkish army was woefully deficient. It was in his power to rally round his banner the whole of the Greeks, the principal leaders of whom had repeatedly offered him the crown of Greece, if he would change his religion, and call the people to arms; and, assuredly, no religious scruples stood in the way of his accepting their offer, for the vizier had no religion at all. The country which he had to defend is calculated beyond almost all others for successful defensive warfare: it is intersected in all directions by chains of lofty and precipitous mountains, which are full of almost impenetrable defiles and commanding positions. An officer of talent and experience, who has visited the country, Colonel Charles Napier,* has justly remarked, that, " as to the natural strength of the ground, that occupied by the celebrated lines round Lisbon is not to be compared to the passes over Mount Pindus. One hundred soldiers might have arrested the mob that was dignified with the appellation of the Turkish army." To crown the whole, he had in his hands the great main-spring for putting in motion all the apparatus of war; he had a treasury full to overflowing with the accumulations arising from half a century of rapine.

To open his hoards, and scatter them abroad with an unsparing hand, was a measure which sound policy would have dictated to Ali. He was engaged in an enterprise in which there was no medium between triumph and ruin. It behoved him, therefore, to bring into the field every man he could muster, and, as he was not one of those characters who are followed from personal affection, his ranks could be swelled by the influence of money alone. Yet such was his avarice, that it overcame even the instinct of self-preservation. An offer was now made to him, which, had he embraced it, might have turned the scale

---

* In his excellent work, " The Colonies," a work which contains much important information, displays sound sense and an acute intellect, and is more amusing than many productions which are written for comic effect, Colonel Napier has given a brief but masterly estimate of the military character of Ali.

decisively in his favour. Two regiments of Albanian infantry, and a regiment of cavalry, chiefly composed of Germans, were about to be discharged from the Neapolitan service. They were in the highest order, and, in appearance, fully equal to any English troops. Here was a force not inconsiderable in itself, especially when warring against undisciplined bands, and which might have been made the nucleus of a regular army. Ali could have obtained it, with its arms and appointments, ready for service, at a small expense. It was proposed to him, by an English officer, to send the vizier's flotilla to Brundisi, where these regiments were assembled, land them at Avlona, clear the pashalik of Berat from the enemy, and then either join Ali at Ioannina or act on the communications of the Turkish army. Had this plan been adopted, it would have been impossible for the invaders to advance to Ioannina without their line of operations being broken in upon, and their retreat cut off, or at the least rendered circuitous and dangerous. Ali at first seemed disposed to adopt the plan, but the reluctance to part with his gold induced him to hesitate, chicane, and delay, and when the pressure of danger ultimately drove him to consent to the terms, it was too late, there being no longer a possibility of bringing over the succours, the Turkish fleet having arrived off the coast of Albania.

His ignorance of the first principles of military science, and his inordinate vanity, were no less conspicuous and prejudicial than his avarice. It was proposed to him to fortify the passes of Pindus, establish in each a strong detachment with artillery, construct telegraphs to communicate with Ioannina, and keep the bulk of his forces collected in a central position, so as to be ready to march towards whichever pass might be attacked. Nothing of this was done.

The English officer, who had been employed in negociating for the three regiments, offered to render Ioannina so strong that it might set the Turks at defiance, and also desired that he might have five hundred workmen, to fortify a piece of ground, which commanded the roads that enter the city from the north and west. Ali pretended to accede to the request for the workmen, and then secretly set them to work upon the spot pointed out, where they threw up a ludicrous sort of breastwork, of loose stones, of which the vizier was exceedingly proud. Disgusted with this folly, the English officer departed. In the same spirit, Ali thwarted all the plans of his engineer Caretto, and ordered the construction of lines, according to his own idea, which had not even the merit which Robinson Crusoe was willing to allow to the great wall of China, that of being " excellent to keep off the Tartars." Such being the state of his knowledge, it is not surprising that he should have rejected a plan of campaign by which he was boldly advised to forestall the enemy, by assuming the offensive, and thus holding him at a distance. By this plan the security of Upper Albania was to be committed to a strong garrison at Berat, Ali was to remain at Ioannina, with a sufficient number of troops to allow of his succouring any point on the coast from Avlona to Prevesa, and the remainder of his army was to be divided into three parts, of which one was to occupy a camp near Caraveria, another the valley of Tempe, and the third the passes of Thermopylæ: in case of being forced from their positions, the first of these divisions was to fall back upon Epirus by the defile of Milias, the second by that of Krio Nero, and the third by the valley of the upper Sperchius. By this arrangement the whole of Thessaly would have been retained, Epirus covered on the side of Macedonia, a safe opportunity of rising in arms afforded to the Greeks, and time gained for organising completely the defence of Albania, even supposing that it had ultimately become necessary to abandon Thessaly. In war, to gain time is, in many cases, to gain the victory.

The vizier, however, though he failed to adopt the measures most likely to be decisive, was by no means inactive. In order at once to swell his numbers and to have some check upon his Mahometan followers, many of whom might, perhaps, shrink from bearing arms against the sultan, his first step was to recal to existence the bands of Armatoles and klephtes, against whom he had so long been waging an exterminatory war. The tempting bait of booty and liberal pay, which he held out to their leaders, instantly produced the desired effect, and they flocked round him from all quarters. Odysseus, the elder and younger, Tachos, Stournaris, Hyscos, Varnakiotes, Zongos, and a crowd of other chiefs, all celebrated in the wild songs of the country, came forward to lend their aid. It must not be supposed that these men were actuated by any attachment to Ali; their motives were the hope of plunder, hatred of the Ottomans, and a wish to be ready to bear a part in the revolution for which the Greeks were now silently preparing. These chiefs Ali directed to commence without delay their operations in the mountains of the neighbouring provinces. The Armatoles were not dilatory in taking the posts assigned to them, and they went to work with such vigour that, under ordinary circumstances, the Porte would probably have consented to an amicable arrangement with the vizier. The couriers were robbed of their despatches, the caravans were intercepted, the taxes ceased to be paid, and from all sides a cry arose that no one but Ali was capable of putting a stop to the system of rapine. But the sultan would listen to no representations in favour of the doomed vizier.

Assembling the principal personages of Albania, not excluding even those whom he believed to be unfriendly to him, Ali called on them to stand by him, as much for their own sakes as his. He warned them that his ruin would be the forerunner of theirs. "You will," said he, "no longer be those Albanians who have hitherto been so formidable and respected. You will be lorded over and humbled by the cowardly Asiatics. I confess that to many of you I have given cause of complaint; I know that some of you are justly offended by the injuries which I have done to yourselves or your relations. But the honour of Albania and the interest of our country are paramount to private enmities; and, when all are in danger, the remembrance of past wrongs is a feeling unworthy of a generous mind. I now look upon you all as my children, the same as Mouctar and Veli. My treasures are open to you. I only ask you to do honour to the name which you bear."

An appeal to the Greeks of Epirus was the next step which was taken by Ali. The measure was probably suggested to him by some of the persons who, at this moment, were occupied in planning the deliverance of Greece from the Turkish yoke. However this may be, he convoked, about the middle of May, an assembly, which he called a grand divan, and which appears to have been chiefly composed of the most eminent individuals among the Albanian Greeks. He addressed to them a long and artful speech, in which he pointed out the religious tolerance he had displayed and the favours he had granted to them; glossed over the injuries which he had inflicted, attributing them wholly to " inflexible necessity" and the "perfidious and cruel orders of the Porte;" declared his readiness to repair those wrongs; flattered the courage of the Greeks; and held out to them the animating prospect of speedily raising up Greece, and driving beyond the Bosphorus the hostile race of the Osmanlis. This speech was loudly applauded by a part of the assembly; by another part it was heard with very different feelings, and the chief of the Mirdites did not hesitate to avow, in the name of his followers, that their swords should never be drawn against their sovereign the sultan. On the following day, the vizier issued a proclamation, calling upon the various Christian tribes to furnish specified contingents of troops, remitting their usual tribute, and exhorting them to rely upon him as their firm friend.

These bold proceedings were objected to by Mouctar and Veli, who endeavoured to persuade their father to make terms with the Porte; but their remonstrances were fruitless, for he was convinced that his ruin was sworn. Disinclined as they were to engage in the contest, it would perhaps have been prudent in Ali not to entrust them with commands. He, however, acted otherwise. Mouctar was appointed to head the forces at Berat, seconded by his brother Sali, to whom was committed the defence of Premiti and the defiles of Cleissoura, while Mahmoud, a son of Mouctar, was stationed at Tepelen. At the other extremity of the vizier's dominions, the government of Prevesa was entrusted to Veli, Parga to Veli's eldest son Mehemet, and Suli to Hussein, a son of Mouctar. The main army, consisting of fifteen thousand men, was confided to Omer Bey Vriones, next to whom in rank were Mantho, the vizier's secretary, and Alexis Noutza. It was destined to guard the passes through the mountains of Pindus. In aid of his own military resources, Ali likewise exerted himself to excite an insurrectionary spirit among the Montenegrins, Servians, Walachians, and other discontented subjects of the Turkish monarch.

The Porte, in the meanwhile, though far enough from displaying a proper degree of activity, was not wholly idle. A fleet was ordered to be fitted out, to convey troops to the coast of Albania. All the chiefs of Rumelia were directed to be ready to march, at a moment's notice, with the Spahis and Timariots of their governments. Similar directions were given to the Rumili-valisee, and to Moustai Pasha, the vizier of Scutari; and Pehlevan Baba, pasha of Rudschuk, and Muhamed Drama Ali, the nazir of Thrace, who was become the father-in-law of Pasho, were charged with the task of collecting the contingents of the valley of the Balkan and Transaxian Macedonia. And, finally, it was decreed that Ismael Pasho, with the title of pasha of Ioannina and Delvino, by right of *arpalik*, or conquest, should be placed at the head of the expedition against Black Ali. So confident of success was the new general, that he did not hesitate to repeat his pledge, that he would penetrate to Ioannina without burning a single match. This boast must have been prompted either by gross folly, or by his knowing that bribery or disaffection had already removed all impediments to his progress.

The slowness with which the Turks proceeded in their preparations was an encouraging circumstance for Ali. Month after month elapsed without his enemies advancing towards his frontiers. His internal situation also appeared to be highly satisfactory. At the least intimation of his wishes, his court was thronged with archbishops, bishops, beys, cadis, and other men of eminence; the multitude seemed to be enthusiastic in his favour; and he received protestations of fidelity, loud in proportion to their insincerity, from all quarters. " But all was false and hollow." Thus deceived, he never quitted his palace but amidst public acclamations. It was now become a part of his policy to show himself familiarly to the people. He was seen at all hours, and in all places where his presence was necessary; at one time on horseback, at another in a litter, and not seldom seated on a bastion, conversing with the workmen or with the soldiers, whom he daily inspected, and who emulated each other in exertions to gain his approbation So great was his ardour, that his physical strength seemed to triumph over the weight of years. While he was thus buoyed up, and thus occupied, he is said to have declared, that " henceforth he would not treat with the grand seignior till the Albanian army was encamped at Daoud Pasha," in the vicinity of Constantinople.

Not only did Ali endeavour to excite the zeal, emulation, and courage of his adherents by conversa tion and harangues, but he also judged it expedient to accommodate himself to the general spirit of the age, and to the views of political intriguers who had repaired to his court. He therefore announced his intention of giving a constitutional charter to the Albanians. Some in earnest, some in mockery, the Greeks exclaimed, " A charter for ever! yes, give us a charter!" " Will a charter increase and secure our pay?" inquired the Albanians. The Turks were indignant at hearing of such a thing. " A charter!" said they. " Have we not the Koran? Does the infidel want to change the sacred laws of our forefathers!" Ali promised everything that was required of him; and his agent Colovo, accompanied by Constantine Monovarda, a rich merchant of Ioannina, was despatched to Corfu, to collect the elements of a political code for the semi-barbarous Albanians.

But, though he doubtless expected some benefit from the farce of granting a charter, Ali was too shrewd to play it in that hope alone. He had other objects of consequence for his envoys to accomplish. They were instructed to purchase ammunition, and to deposit in a place of safety a part of their master's treasures; and they had also to perform the still more important duty of sending emissaries and money to Montenegro, Servia, Bosnia, the Morea, and other disturbed quarters, and to procure to be drawn up and printed an address to the Greeks, calling upon them, in the name of religion and their country, to shake off the yoke of their infidel tyrants. Having fulfilled their mission they returned to the mainland, where they were immediately seized by the revolted Tzamides, who delivered them up to the Turkish admiral. Some copies of the address to the Greeks being found on Colovo, he was put to the torture; his companion, Monovarda, was fortunate enough to be only imprisoned, and he subsequently escaped.

The result of the first movements of some of the pashas whom the Porte had called into the field was not favourable. The campaign was opened by Moustai, vizier of Scutari, who was joined by a considerable body of Mirdites. Durazzo opened its gates to him, he speedily recovered the district of Musakia, and he was in expectation of being received into Berat and Avlona, when he was suddenly recalled to the defence of his pashalik, by an irruption of the Montenegrins, brought about by the instigation of Ali.

Suleyman Pasha, who had succeeded Veli in the government of Thessaly, was singularly unlucky in his attempt to bring down mischief on the deposed vizier. Though he confined himself to a paper war, his conduct was more injurious to the Porte than the loss of several battles would have been. To the Greek ecclesiastics, primates, and persons in authority, and generally to the people, in Thessaly, he addressed a proclamation of extraordinary violence, calling upon them to take up arms, and " exterminate the impious race of Arnauts, who had adopted the sacrilegious cause of Ali Tepelen." His appeal to them, widely diffused, was promptly attended to, but not for the purpose which he designed, and the insurrection which he thus excited ultimately added much to the embarrassment of the Turkish Government. It is said, that, in taking this step, he was an unconscious instrument of his Greek secretary, Anagnostis, who was connected with the planners of the Greek revolution, and issued the proclamation only in his own language, of which his employer was ignorant. His imprudence, or misfortune, roused the suspicion of the Porte; he was removed from his pashalik, and soon after lost his head. Muhamed Drama Ali was appointed in his stead.

At length the disorderly armies of the Porte began to move in earnest. Their march was a scorpion scourge to the countries through which they passed. The inhabitants were hourly subjected to outrages and insults of the worst kind, both in word and action; extortion, plunder, murder, and violation, were seen on all sides. Among the worst of the Turkish generals, where all were bad in no common degree, was Pehlevan Baba, who had been nominated to the pashalik of Lepanto. His men distinguished themselves equally by their brutality and their spirit of wanton destruction. In their progress towards the gulf of Lepanto, where they were to act against Veli

Pasha, their object seemed to be not merely to pillage the land but to render it uninhabitable. The stock of butter and oil was consumed to keep up the fires by which they roasted their stolen cattle, the bee-hives were burned when stripped of their honey, the hay and straw, beyond what was required for the horses, was consumed, and the wine-vessels were staved that their contents might run to waste. Had it been the purpose of the Turkish commanders to provoke a general insurrection, they could not have adopted a more effective plan. Had Ali been popular, and endowed with talents of a higher order than he possessed, the Turks would soon have reaped the deadly harvest which they had sown. Even as it was, no long time elapsed before they felt the cousequences of their infamous conduct.

By the forward movements of the Turks some ground had already being gained from Ali. On the side of Thessaly, Muhamet Drama succeeded in putting down the Armatoles, and securing the country as far as the defile of Krio-Nero, driving back within the frontier of Epirus all the advanced posts of Ali. In the south, Pehlevan Baba had compelled Veli to abandon Lepanto, and retire to Prevesa. Ali was so doubtful of the fidelity of his Turkish subjects in this quarter, that he disarmed many of them at Prevesa and Arta, and required hostages from others.

Having at last arrived at Larissa, with an army of twenty thousand men, in which there were no less than six viziers and ten pashas of two tails, Ismael Pasho prepared to enter upon the struggle for his newly-granted pashalik. He ordered the Rumilivalisee to move upon Berat through the defiles of the Candavian mountains. By this movement, and the defection of part of the province, Mouctar was placed under the necessity of retreating from Berat, and shutting himself up in the fortress of Argyro Castro. On the other side, Pehlevan Baba was directed to recommence his operations. He obeyed, and met with no resistance; Missolonghi, Anatolico, and Vonitza were occupied by him, and thus all the territory between the gulfs of Patras and Arta was in his hands. He completed his task by forming the blockade of Prevesa to the landward, while the Ottoman squadron closed it in on the seaboard. As soon as the troops of the sultan appeared, the Mussulmans of Prevesa began to manifest an inclination to revolt, in consequence of which Veli, after having burned his father's magnificent seraglio, withdrew into the citadel.

The Turkish squadron had already displayed much activity. It had seized the forts of Port Panormo, Santi Quaranti, and various batteries on the coast, and seconded a rising of the friends of the deceased Mustapha, by which the castle of Delvino, the fortified monastery of St. Basil, and other posts, were wrested from Ali. It now, in conjunction with the land forces, proceeded to invest Parga. Mehemet, the son of Veli, was desirous to defend the place vigorously, but his garrison became mutinous, and, when only a few broadsides had been fired, he was compelled to surrender at discretion. He was, however, received in the most flattering manner by the Turkish admiral. On hearing of the fall of Parga, the expatriated Suliots flocked homewards from the Ionian Islands, and other parts, and, headed by Noto and Marco Botzari, joined the standard of Ismael Pasho, who engaged to reinstate them in their native mountains.

Though the success of the enemy had deprived Ali of a considerable portion of territory, he had as yet no reason to feel seriously alarmed. As long as he retained, unbroken, his central position, any advantage gained over him to the north or south of Ioannina would lead to nothing decisive, and might rapidly be lost. With respect to the forces under Pehlevan Baba, it seems certain, that had Ismael been routed, they would have been in imminent danger of becoming prisoners. The troops of Ali occupied all the passes which led from Macedonia and Thessaly, through the mountain chain of Pindus. The main body, under Omer Bey Vriones, was posted between the sources of the Voiussa and the Aspropotamos, and he was supported by the divisions of Mantho and Alexis Noutza. A single defeat would probably have dissolved the Ottoman army. But the invaders relied less upon their own valour than upon the treason of the chiefs who were opposed to them. After having worsted a detachment of Ali's troops at Krio-Nero, Ismael Pasho, instead of attempting to penetrate by the pass of Zygos, turned suddenly aside to the defile of Anovlachia, which was treacherously laid open to him by Stournaris, one of the captains of the Armatoles. Still, he might have been stopped at the pass of Cotari had not Mantho with his whole division gone over to the Turks. The example set by Mantho was followed by Omer Bey Vriones, and by Alexis Noutza, and thus, at one blow, Ali was left without an army. The bands of Ismael, and of the deserters from Ali then encampted together on Mount Dryscos, not far from the southern end of the lake of Ioannina, where a junction was speedily formed with them by the hordes of Pehlevan Baba, who, on his march, had made himself master of Arta, and marked his course by the burning of villages and the slaughter of their inhabitants. There was now nothing to impede their progress to Ioannina, at the distance of only three miles from which was stationed the advanced guard of the sanguinary Pehlevan, eager to revel in the spoils of a rich and populous city.

CHAPTER XV.

Apprehensions of Ali—He destroys Ioannina—His Resources—The Turkish Army arrives—Stratagem of Ali—The Sons of Ali surrender—Daring conduct of Shainitza—The Turks routed in a Sally—Ali conceals his Treasures—State of his Mind—Impolicy of Ismael Pasho—Ali gains over the Suliots—Victories obtained by the Suliots—Ismael is removed from the Command of the Army—Ismael defeats Ali—Kurschid Pasha takes the Command of the besieging Army—Ali opens a Correspondence with him—Ali's Proposals—They are rejected—The Greek Revolution breaks out—The Turks foiled in an Assault—Death of Shainitza—Fruitless Negociations—Intrigues of Kurschid—Success of them—Ali surrenders—Death of Ali, and of his Family.

THE defection of his army, and the near approach of his enemies, is said to have staggered the courage of Ali. In this emergency, he applied to the lord high commissioner of the Ionian Islands, to learn whether, in case he could effect his escape from the coast, he would be protected in his passage over the channel of Corfu. He was also desirous of procuring an escort to the place of embarkation. The reply was not encouraging. He was told, that no open aid could be given to one who was proclaimed a rebel by the Porte; that, consequently no escort could be granted; but that if he could manage to pass midway over the channel, he would then be within the British limits, and entitled to protection. This disheartening refusal was, however, finally softened by a secret message, which informed him that, for a certain period, some English gun-boats would be lying at Butrinto, upon which he might seize and cross the strait in safety. Of this underhand assistance Ali did not avail himself. Either he was reluctant to abandon his treasures, or he believed that an attempt to fly would induce those around him to become his betrayers, or his courage revived ; for he resolved to stand to the last.

The works which Ali had caused to be thrown up to secure Ioannina were as yet unfinished, and had they been completed, would have been useless, in consequence of their ridiculously faulty construction. That his capital might not be made use of to cover the approaches of the Turkish army, he resolved to destroy it. In this he again betrayed his want of military skill. "He might," says Colonel Napier, "have loop-holed the houses of the town, which are built of thick mud walls, well suited to make a desperate defence; he might have prepared barricades in the street, and so forth; but nothing was done." Had he adopted this plan, there can be no doubt that he might very considerably have lengthened his resistance. Not only would the besiegers have found it a difficult and tedious task to dislodge the besieged, but they would have been weakened by being compelled to extend greatly their line of circumvallation. The advantage which these circumstances would have given him was thrown away by the vizier.

As soon as the approach of the Turkish army, and the intended destruction of the city, became known, the inhabitants hastened to preserve their families, and as much of their property as possible, from the grasp of the invaders and the soldiers of Ali, both of whom were equally to be feared. The lake was instantly swarming with boats containing the wives and children of the fugitives; coasting the shore of the lake which was yet free from the enemy, they directed their course towards the Zagori. Before, however, the people could entirely quit the place a scene of tenfold confusion and violence began. The Albanians were let loose by Ali to plunder the devoted city. Temples, public buildings, private dwellings, immediately became the prey of a wild and lawless soldiery. Treasures, sanctuaries, and altars, were alike exposed to their unbridled fury; the privacy of the harem and public baths was invaded; and all the horrors of brutal violence were inflicted on the unfortunate victims. The cathedral, in which the Greeks, and even the Turks, had deposited their most valuable effects, was one of the first objects of pillage. Even the tombs of the archbishops were broken open in search of spoil, and the churches were stained with the blood of the robbers themselves, as they furiously contended against each other for the sacred vessels, which were of silver. On all sides groans, cries, threats, and imprecations, were heard. These sounds were soon overpowered by others of a more deafening kind. The work of pillage being completed, a heavy fire was opened upon the city from all the artillery of the forts. Seated on one of the bastions, Ali himself directed the cannonade, and pointed out the spots which the fiery storm had not yet reached. An incessant shower of bombs, howitzer shells, grenades, fireballs, and Congreve rockets, spread destruction on all sides, and, in the course of two hours, mosques, bazaars, public baths, edifices, and private dwellings, were all involved in one vast conflagration.

Escaping from the flames, the fugitives, a terrified and mournful crowd,—weeping females bearing their children, old men and women tottering onward, and the strong carrying their mutilated or half-burned relatives,—had not proceeded far before they fell in with the advanced parties of the Turkish army. Far from protecting the unhappy beings who had fled from fire and slaughter, the Rumeliot hordes fell upon the defenceless throng, wrested from them the remnant of their property, and tore their children from their arms. Dispersing on all sides, the exiles endeavoured to find an asylum in the mountains; but there they were met by an equally savage foe; they were stopped in the passes by the needy and rapacious mountaineers, who completed the spoliation.

The extremity of distress frequently rouses the weaker sex to uncommon exertions of physical and moral energy. So it was in this case. Women carrying their children at the breast traversed the steep chain of the Pindus to seek a shelter in Thesprotia; others performed in a single day the journey of fourteen leagues between Ioannina and Arta. But great was the number of those whose strength was unequal to contend with the miseries that beset them. Many, seized with the pangs of premature labour, expired in the forests. Young females, after having, that they might escape violation, disfigured themselves by frightful wounds, took shelter in caverns, where they perished with hunger. The paths and passes were strewed with the wounded, the dying, and the dead, and traces of the ruin of Ioannina were visible throughout the whole extent of Albania.

It is impossible to avoid feeling a "stern delight" on knowing that some of those who had been instrumental in producing all this misery were promptly punished for their crimes. Many of the Arnaut troops, who had plundered Ali's capital, were, like the soldier in Horace, more disposed at present to enjoy their booty than to run into danger. "Let us return to our homes" was their cry. But the majority of them never reached their native villages; they met a more formidable peril than that which they left behind. Lured by the riches which these deserters had gained, the peasants laid ambuscades for them, and were eagerly seconded by the wandering fugitives from Ioannina; stimulated by love of gold and revenge, this warfare was so hotly carried on, that, as far as the frontiers of Central Albania, nothing was for some time to be seen but Arnaut soldiers, mutilated, slaughtered, or hanged on the trees which were planted along the high-roads.

Ali, meanwhile, though confined within the limits of his fortifications, did not yield to despair. His three fortresses, of Litharitza, the lake, and the island, strong as regarded defence against Turks, were mounted with two hundred and fifty pieces of cannon, and abundantly supplied for a siege of some years, with provisions and ammunition, besides Congreve rockets; the engineer department was directed by Carretto, a skilful Neapolitan officer. Their garrisons consisted of eight thousand of the vizier's trustiest Arnauts, and of many adventurers, men of talents and resolution, all of whom knew that they must suffer the doom of rebels if the enemy prevailed. Ali was also master of the navigation of the lake, by means of a considerable flotilla, which enabled him to make descents, cut off the Turkish parties, and intercept their convoys. Besides, the Turkish heavy artillery had been stupidly left behind at Constantinople; and, as the rains regularly set in, on the table land of Ioannina, towards the end of October, there was reason to hope that a long time must elapse before it could be conveyed over the rugged chain of Pindus, and brought into action. It seemed probable, too, that, in the course of the autumn, snbsistence would become scarce in the hostile camp, and the Ottoman troops must be distributed into wide cantonments, where they would be open to attack; a circumstance which, aided by the gold of Ali, and the jealousies of the pashas, was likely to produce discontent and desertion.

The troops of Pehlevan Baba having effected a junction with the army of Pasho, the latter led his whole force to Ioannina, the ruins of which were still smoking when he made his entrance through the gate of Perilepti. On the twentieth of August, 1820, he set up his three horse-tails, the emblem of his dignity, and was proclaimed Pasha of Ioannina, amidst the shouts of the Turks, who exclaimed " Long live the victorious Ismael Pasha!—long live the glorious Sultan Mahmoud!" The cadi then read the sentence of deposition and excommunication against Ali, and a marabout, or priest, threw a stone towards the fortress of the " *black*" recreant, who was now for ever separated from the band of true believers. From his castle walls Ali witnessed this ceremony, to which the garrison replied by hootings and a heavy fire from all their guns and mortars, while the flotilla, dressed out in all its flags, steered to the shore, and joined in the cannonade. The sight of the troops, on whom he had relied, now serving against him in the enemy's camp, is said, however, to have thrown a temporary gloom over the mind of the besieged Pasha.

Ismael Pasho had scarcely sat down in sight of the fortresses before a stratagem was played off against him by Ali. Among the troops of the garrison was a band of Armatoles, led by the celebrated Odysseus, who subsequently bore so conspicuous a part in the struggles of the Greeks for freedom. Odysseus had retarded as long as he could the junction of Pehlevan Baba with Pasho, and had fallen back on Ioannina only a few days previous to the destruction of that city. Used to desultory warfare, his men now became tired of being confined in one spot, and displayed an inclination to desert. This circumstance was made known to Ali by their commander. Far from being angered by it, the wily vizier resolved to turn it to advantage. He converted it into a means of getting rid of all the lukewarm and disaffected, and throwing additional embarrassments in the way of Ismael Pasho. He therefore directed Odysseus to ascertain how many of the garrison were desirous to be gone. The number, including the restless Armatoles, was found to be fifteen hundred. These men were selected by the vizier, for the purpose, as he pretended, of making a sally, and, after their arrears had been fully paid to them, the gates of the castle were thrown open. Scarcely had they come in sight of the Turkish headquarters when Odysseus, who had been, by order of Ali, in correspondence with the Ottoman general, hoisted a white flag, and saluted Ismael with the title of Gazi, or victorious. The deserters were immediately received with loud acclamations, complimented on their loyalty, and had a spot assigned them for their bivouac. Ali having thus succeeded in his first object, soon contrived to render the new-comers suspected by the Ottomans, who were naturally jealous of the Albanians. Every day the latter were subjected to fresh insults and humiliations, and, as subsistence began to grow scarce in the camp, they were also looked upon as an incumbrance. At this moment, Odysseus suddenly withdrew to Ithaca, and his flight brought down increased suspicion upon them. At length, disgusted and ill treated beyond endurance by the Turks, they dispersed themselves through the neighbouring mountains, and thenceforth annoyed, by incessant attacks and depredations, the forces of Ismael Pasho.

September passed away, and nothing was done by the Ottoman army, which was still unprovided with the means of commencing the siege. Provisions, too, as Ali had expected, began to be scarce in the hostile camp. Of troops, indeed, there was no scarcity; for, hoping to share in the spoils of the deposed vizier, nearly thirty pashas had led their hordes to join Ismael, plundering and wasting the country as they moved along, and leaving behind them a deeply-rooted hatred in the hearts of the sufferers. Among the worst of these undisciplined marauders were the troops of the Rumili-valisee. Even the government of Ali began to be regretted by the people, and his emissaries found no difficulty in obtaining information and carrying on their intrigues. In the camp of Ismael there was not only want, but disaffection, and almost sedition. Murmurs were heard against the general; the pashas accused him of loving power and affecting sovereignty; the soldiers believed him to be guilty of filling his coffers by selling their provisions; and by all an opportunity was eagerly sought of rendering him an object of suspicion to the divan.

Well knowing the insecure tenure by which a Turkish officer held his head, Ismael felt it necessary to do something to protect his own, and, as he was not yet in a condition to succeed by the sword, he wielded the weapon of intrigue. As the sons of Ali were known to have engaged reluctantly in the contest, he was not without hopes that he might work on them to abandon the cause of their father. Veli, who was his friend, had always been attached to the Ottoman government, and might also be now influenced by his son Mehemet being a prisoner, and Mouctar might, on more than one account, be expected to cherish resentment against his unpitying parent. His calculation was not erroneous. He began by opening a communication with Veli Pasha, who was still blockaded in Prevesa by the Suliots and the Turkish squadron. In his letter he inclosed a strong temptation—a firman of the Sultan, appointing Veli to the pashalik of St. John of Acre, in Syria, on condition of his instant surrender. Backed as it was by his original principles, the unanimous advice of his counsellors, and the prayers of his son Selim, who on his knees conjured him to save the life of Mehemet, this lure prevailed over filial duty in the mind of Veli, and he gave up Prevesa to the Turkish commander. He was received with the semblance of the utmost respect by the Capitan Pasha, his son was restored to him, he was amused with a round of banquets and entertainments, and, finally, a vessel was granted to convey him to the bay of Gomenitza, where he could at the same time obtain medical assistance from Corfu and open a correspondence with Mouctar Pasha. The example and the exhortations of Veli, and a firman, by which he was appointed Pasha of Kutaya, in Asia Minor, were not lost upon Mouctar. He, too, deserted his father's side, resigning the strong fortress of Argyro-Castro without having fired a shot, and inducing his youngest brother, Sali, to give up Premiti. Sali, who had also been promised a sandjiacat in Anatolia, joined his brother, and they set out, under an escort, to Constantinople. On his way, Mouctar wrote to his son Mahmoud, who was then at Tepelen, directing him to deliver up that place to the officers of the sultan. The gallant boy—for he was no more than a boy—shrank indignantly from the treachery which was suggested to him. He assembled the garrison, and thus addressed them: " My father, my uncles, my cousins, and all those whom my grandfather honoured with his confidence, have betrayed it—can you wish Mahmoud Bey to do the same!" At these words his hearers unanimously exclaimed, that they would all perish sooner than be false to their master's grandson.

The distressing tidings of the defection of his children were received by Ali Pasha with wonderful equanimity. " I have long been aware," said he, " that they were unworthy of their parentage." He then himself made known to the garrison what had happened, telling them, likewise, that " henceforth he had no longer any other children and heirs than the brave defenders of his cause." At a later period, when, to grieve or intimidate him, a report was spread that his sons were put to death, he displayed the same stoical firmness. "They betrayed their father," said he coldly; "let us think no more of them!"

A spirit no less indomitable was manifested by the monstrous Shainitza, his sister. Believing that the time was come when they might safely take vengeance on her, a troop of Argyro-Castrites and Gardikiotes bent their course to her palace. At the threshold they were met by Shainitza, pistols in her girdle, a carbine in her hand, and followed by two fierce Molossian dogs. "Stop, madmen!" she exclaimed; "neither my life, nor the riches which you wish to tear from me, will ever be in your power. Enter within these bounds; penetrate, if you dare, to my seraglio! But, if one of you ventures to stir a step without my leave, this palace, and the very ground on which you tread, are ready to swallow you up. The vaults of this asylum of my widowhood are filled with ten thousand pounds of powder. I grant you, however, a pardon, which you are far from deserving. Withdraw, and if a single mouth has the audacity to reply, we will all die instantly. Take those bags of gold, which I have the kindness to give, to indemnify you for the losses you have lately sustained from my brother's enemies. Never again disturb my quiet; for I have other instruments of destruction at command besides gunpowder. I care nothing for life; think well of it, for your mountains may once more, by my orders, become the grave of your wives and children." She then pointed to fifty purses, which were lying at the door. Her terrified hearers gathered them up, and hastily departed. The dark threat by which she closed her speech, and which she is accused of having executed, is said to have alluded to articles of clothing, impregnated with the contagion of the plague, which she distributed among a band of gipsies, and by that means spread infection and death through a wide extent of country.

The success which had attended his negotiations with Veli and Mouctar, and the prospect of speedily coming into possession of Ali's treasures, restored the tottering credit of Ismael Pasha. By the arrival of his battering-train, he was also enabled to commence active operations. The trenches were opened, and a cannonade and bombardment were begun against the fortress. Before, however, the Turkish artillery, never well served, had made the slightest impression on the works, the Turks loudly demanded to be led to the assault. To this they appear to have been incited by the Bulgarian chief, Pehlevan Baba, who dazzled them with the idea of enriching themselves by the plunder of Ali's treasures. It is difficult to decide whether his conduct arose from treason, or from ignorance: the former is the most probable. Ismael succeeded in convincing his soldiers that it would be madness to comply with their wish; but Pehlevan persisted in representing the prudence of the general as cowardice, and, to revenge himself on him, he allowed his barbarous followers to plunder the country, laboured to spread insubordination in the army, and is said even to have entered into a correspondence with Ali. There seems to be reason for believing that he was already in the interest of the deposed vizier, and it is not unlikely that, in suggesting an immediate assault, his intention was to expose the Turkish forces to inevitable and perhaps fatal defeat. At all events, Ismael determined to punish him; but, as it would have been dangerous to do it openly, he resorted to poison. The treasure of the deceased pasha, amounting to between sixty and seventy thousand pounds, was immediately forwarded to Constantinople, where it contributed to silence for a while the murmurs which were caused by the slow progress of the Ottoman general.

Having thus got rid of a troublesome coadjutor, Ismael began to try what might be done in furtherance of his plans by sowing discord between Ali and the troops in garrison. At the outset, he succeeded to a certain extent. A part of the soldiers in the fortresses consisted of Albanians who had formerly lived under the sway of the pasha of Berat. By means of his emissaries, he adroitly persuaded these men that it was disgraceful to them to allow their old master to languish in a dungeon; and to silence their murmurs, Ali consented to liberate Ibrahim and his son from close confinement, on condition that they should not quit the fortress. Emboldened by having carried this point, they next clamoured for an increase of pay. This, too, they obtained, their pay being raised to about four pounds a month. " I never haggle," said he, " with my family; my adopted children shed their blood for me, and gold is nothing in comparison with the services which they render." Yet, so strong was the power of avarice over him, that, notwithstanding the danger which might arise from irritating his partisans, he endeavoured to draw back with one hand what he had been compelled to bestow with the other. In Turkey the soldiers provide for their own subsistence out of their pay. Availing himself of this circumstance, Ali secretly ordered his chief commissary to enhance the price of the commodities with which he furnished them. This fraud was soon discovered, and the spleen of the soldiery was vented in songs, in which their master figured under the title of " Ali the huckster." Fearful that their anger might be pushed to a more dangerons extent, Ali abandoned his system of extortion.

Though the concessions of Ali had been made with apparent good-will, it would betray gross ignorance of human nature were we to suppose that their being extorted from him did not deeply wound the pride of a man who had been accustomed to indulge, without opposition, in all the wildest caprices of tyranny. He did feel the insult, and was not slow in avenging it. From the reports of his spies, as well as from personal observation, he knew all who had been the most forward in the recent mutinous proceedings, and he determined that they should form the forlorn hope of a sally against the enemy. He managed so artfully, that he contrived to have them pointed out for the service by their comrades, as the fittest men to lead the way, and, by fixing high the price of heads, and of spiked or captured cannon, he so excited their thirst of gain, that they were clamorous to be led into the field.

At the appointed time the sally took place. Heated by perfidious praises of their valour, and by the hope of reward, the devoted van of the Albanians rushed upon the redoubts and batteries of the Turks. Their bravery was not exerted in vain, though it was no less fatal to themselves than to their enemies. In spite of the destructive fire which was poured upon them, they opened a way for the reserve, and all the positions of the besiegers were speedily carried by the troops of Ali. The whole Turkish army fled in utter dismay, and never paused till it reached Dgelova, more than a league from Ioannina, where the routed Ismael at last rallied them, and established his head-quarters.

After having stationed his troops in the deserted camp of the enemy, Ali returned to the fortress. In planning this sally, it had not been his only object to disencumber himself of the mutinous part of the garrison, or to give a check to the Turkish general. He was desirous to secrete his treasures beyond the reach of mutinous soldiers and of the sultan himself. Accordingly as soon as he came back to the fortress he began the removal, and it was perseveringly and silently continued for many nights. Having placed in the powder-magazine a sufficient sum to provide for his defence, he ordered the remainder of his hoards to be enclosed in strong coffers, and sunk in various parts of the lake. On this service a number of gipsies were employed; and that his secret might never be disclosed, he is said to have added to his crimes, by the horrible barbarity of putting his miserable agents to death. When all was completed, he recalled his troops into the forts.

Weighed down as he was by years, and surrounded by perils, the spirit of Ali, nevertheless, remained unbroken. It bent, indeed, for a short time, under the pressure; as though to prove that he was not wholly devoid of human feelings, not a mere incarnation of evil. His flesh wasted away, his fingers became like those of a skeleton, and his sunken eyes gleamed with a sort of lurid light. He seldom slept, and when he did slumber it was on the floor of a casemate, near the powder-magazine, with his head resting on the knees of Athanasi Vaia, while watch was kept at the door by Ibrahim Saratch, a renegade Jew. But he soon threw off the gloom which oppressed him; his brow became serene, his nights were no longer disturbed by fears and visions, and he appeared once more full of activity and hope. As soon as the morning dawned, he was seen at the door of the casemate, giving audience, and cheering such of his followers as seemed to be downhearted. Some he desired to remember, that " only perseverance and courage could save them now;" others, who complained of their losses, he reminded of his own destroyed palaces and confiscated property; and to all he promised boundless rewards whenever the victory was won. Pointing to the surrounding mountains, the summits of which began to be covered with snow, "That cord," said he, "will be fatal to our foes." At times he would joke with his soldiers, as to the anathema which had been hurled against him. "They call me Black Ali," exclaimed he; "they ought rather to call me Ali the Pearl; for where shall one of my age be found equal to me in the Turkish empire? The cowards! they shall regret me ere long, and shall learn, by the legacy of woes I will leave them, what the *old lion* and his brave soldiers were capable of had they been rightly estimated. They make war upon me for my riches, but shall only have them steeped in gore. I will rouse against them all the passions of hatred and revenge. Yet a few months, and I will shake the empire, and those who attack me shall tremble in the very heart of Constantinople. Infamous city! before he dies, Ali shall see thy palaces in ashes, and the injuries he has suffered shall be washed out in the blood of thy grasping ministers."

Though there was little probability that the sanguine expectations of Ali would be fully realised, there were circumstances which would have justified him in hoping that, as Passwan Oglou had formerly done, he should be able to make it necessary for the sultan to renew his lease of power. If those who were intrusted with the mission of destroying him had entered into a conspiracy to frustrate that mission, and to raise up allies for him, they could scarcely have acted otherwise than they did act. To say nothing of their enormous ignorance, the leaders of the besieging army were divided in opinion, jealous of each other, and disliked or despised their general, and their conduct towards the people was admirably calculated to provoke revolt. The Greeks were subjected to the grossest insult and violence, their property was wrested from them, and in several instances, their churches were burned, and the sacred emblems of religion profaned. The Parghiotes having refused to comply with the invitation of Ismael, to return to their native place, he was so iritated that he convoked a grand divan, in which it was resolved that the military service of the Armatoles, who were acting with the Turks, should no longer be accepted, that they should be dismissed to their homes without pay or compensation for any losses, and that, instead of them, there should be furnished a certain number of beasts of burthen and of peasants to labour in the trenches. It was haughtily added, that, thenceforth, the sultan would not recognise in Hellas anything but agas, or lords, and rayas taskable and taxable at his discretion, and that a list of infidels paying karatch must be sent in, as a preliminary to an increase of the tax.

The siege, meanwhile, was conducted with the least possible skill. The bombs of the Turks, though numerous, were so badly directed that they produced but a trifling effect, and not seldom they were empty. The cannon-balls, too, were often of too small a calibre to make any impression on the massy works of the fortress, while, on the contrary, those which were fired by the besieged, dismounted the Turkish artillery, and demolished large portions of the redoubts and batteries. All was of a piece in the camp. Discipline there was none. As soon as the snow began to make its appearance on the heights, parties of the Thessalian and Macedonian troops, without asking leave, daily departed to their homes, and the Thesprotians absented themselves for weeks, and returned when they pleased. For this, however, some excuse may be found in the scanty supply of provisions and fuel which Ismael could obtain. Ali, who was exactly informed of the situation of the Turkish army, insultingly sent coffee and sugar to its commander as a present from "a master who was attentive to the wants of a servant," scoffed at Ismael's plans of attack. and offered to relieve the distress of the Turks, by selling them provisions from his own magazines. To complete the mortification of the new pasha of Ioannina, he received a severe reprimand from the sultan for the slowness of his proceedings.

By an act which was as contrary to good faith as to sound policy, Ismael raised up new and formidable enemies. We have seen that, as soon as there appeared a hope of the downfall of Ali, the expatriated Suliots returned and offered their swords to the Turkish general, on condition of being reinstated in their native mountains. After having performed good service at the siege of Prevesa, they had joined the Turkish army before Ioannina, and they now claimed the performance of the promise which had been made to them. To be allowed to recover Suli at their own risk, and to hold it on the same terms as formerly, was all that they asked. Ismael, however, was not inclined to comply. He first endeavoured to elude giving them a definitive answer, and next endeavoured to prevail upon them to accept other districts. But the Suliots were not to be satisfied with anything short of being restored to their ancestral hills. Very soon, they became objects of suspicion and hatred to the Turks, who accused them of being in league with the bands of Odysseus; and Ismael, in consequence, ordered them to encamp at some distance from his army.

Ali was speedily apprised of this event, and lost not

a moment in turning it to account. To open a correspondence with the Suliots, he is said to have resorted to a singular contrivance. Perceiving that the shells which were thrown into their camp from the fortress did not explode, the Suliots were induced to examine them. Instead of a fusee, they found a roll of paper in a wooden cylinder, on the outside of which was written "open carefully." A letter was enclosed in the cylinder, desiring that a person might be sent to confer with Ali, and informing them that six thousand sequins would be found in the shells which had fallen into their camp. In consequence of this overture, a monk was despatched to have an interview with the vizier. In the hands of this envoy, whom he received with the utmost kindness, Ali placed a paper which was well calculated to rouse the wrath of the Suliots. It was a letter, which he had intercepted, from Haleb Effendi to Ismael Pasho, communicating a plan for a general massacre of the Christians, which was to be carried into execution in the ensuing spring. The Suliots were particularly mentioned as victims. Ali seems to have delayed making use of this document till an insult was offered to them by the Turks; he probably thought that, as long as Ismael Pasho treated them with kindness, they would give no credence to any charge which was urged against him by an enemy. To win over his ancient foes to his side, Ali offered to restore their territory, with the exception of the post of Kako Suli, and to pay them a year's pay in advance. With these propositions, the letter of Haleb Effendi, and presents for the chiefs, the envoy was dismissed by the vizier.

Previously to their entering into a negotiation with Ali, the Suliots determined once more to claim justice from Ismael. In fact, Ali had recommended that they should do so; he, perhaps, feeling convinced that there was no chance of their obtaining it, and that a refusal would add to their irritation. If such were his reasoning, it was justified by the result. Ismael not only refused to comply with their demand, but also insulted them in the grossest language, and threatened them with punishment. This was too much to be borne, and they accordingly determined to treat with Ali. Nothi Botzari and two other chiefs were commissioned to settle the terms of the compact. It was agreed, that Ali should advance five hundred thousand piastres, and supply them with a large quantity of ammunition, that he should retain the tower of Kiaffa, and that each party should give hostages for the due performance of the treaty. The hostage given by the vizier was Hussein Pasha, his grandson, the son of Mouctar. Ali advised that the Suliots should accomplish their retreat during the night; but, with an honourable pride which was worthy of his race, Botzari declared that he would quit the imperial camp in the face of day. The grandson of Ali having arrived at the camp, the Suliots broke up at dawn of day, fired a salvo of musketry, and uttered their war-cries as a defiance to the Turks, broke through one of Ismael's advanced posts, and then slowly pursued their march towards the mountains of Suli. Though he had recently been reinforced by fifteen thousand men, Ismael did not deem it prudent to follow the retiring Greeks.

Ignorant of the changes which had taken place since their departure from their country, the Suliots were astonished to see a formidable fortress in place of the former small tower of Kiaffa. As, however, they were put in possession of all the other posts, and had in their hands the grandson of Ali, they felt no fear of treachery on the part of the vizier. They also took the precaution of fortifying all the defiles, so that the commander of the fortress was, in fact, blockaded.

Their next step was to endeavour to obtain the co-operation of the Christians of Thesprotia; and in this they succeeded so well, that Nothi Botzari, who was elected polemarch, soon found the nine hundred warriors, with which he had quitted Ioannina, increased to the number of three thousand five hundred.

Plunging from one folly into another, Ismael Pasho, irritated by the defection of the Suliots, issued an order that the Armatoles should give up their arms within a limited time. He and his council had previously decided that, as soon as the disarming was effected, a massacre of the disarmed should take place. Of this fact those who were intended to be sacrificed were informed, by Anagnostis, who was now in Ismael's service, and who, as we have seen in the last chapter, was connected with the planners of the Greek revolution. The Armatoles and their leaders immediately provided for their safety by flight, and were ever after implacable enemies of the Turks.

Ismael had soon reason to repent of having alienated the Suliots. Their central position, on the flank of the line by which his convoys must pass from Arta to Ioannina, gave them a facility of attack, of which they were not backward in availing themselves. Being in want of ammunition, and also of money, Ismael had despatched a detachment of five hundred men, under the selictar of Drama-Ali, to escort a convoy of a hundred and thirty mules from Arta. To seize on this convoy, and also to occupy the fortified khan of the Five Wells, Nothi Botzari intrusted his nephew Marco with a division of troops. On the arrival of the Turks at the pass of Kumchadez, where Marco was lying in ambush, the Suliots sallied forth, and, after a short contest, entirely defeated them. Marco sent off his rich prize to the mountains, and then turned towards the Five Wells, where he found that the khan had been abandoned by the terrified enemy, who had left behind sufficient military stores for a two months' defence. To mark their contempt of the Turks, the Suliots put up to sale the prisoners whom they had taken at Kumchadez. Two mollahs, two beys, and a cadi, were among the captives; the mollahs were sold to a gipsy for an ass, the beys for some tobacco, and as nobody would bid for the cadi he was set at liberty.

Enraged at these checks, and anxious to clear the road to Arta, Ismael put in motion a division of five thousand men, under the Rumili-valisee and Baltadgi Pasha, to dislodge the Suliots from the khan of the Five Wells. Of this movement the Suliots were informed by Ali, and they prepared to give their enemies a warm reception. At earliest dawn the Turks furiously attacked the khan; some trying with hatchets to break open the doors, while others strove to scale the walls. To encourage them, a troop of dervises incessantly yelled out "Victory or martyrdom," and threw dust into the air, which was supposed to have the virtue of blinding the infidels. Notwithstanding the slaughter which was made among the assailants, a few of them succeeded in reaching the summit of the wall; but at this moment three parties of Suliots, whom Marco Botzari had stationed in ambush among the rocks, rushed out upon the Ottomans. Thus taken by surprise, the Turks lost courage, and were scattered in all directions, with great slaughter. Not one of them would have escaped had Marco had a force sufficient to occupy the pass of Thyriaki.

None of the Albanian troops had borne a part in this expedition, and they were not sparing of their jeers and sarcasms upon the beaten and dejected Turks. The mortified Ismael had still another vexation to endure on this unlucky day. In the evening a courier arrived from Constantinople to inform him that the sultan had removed him from the command of the army, and given it to Kurschid, the vizier of the Morea, who had distinguished himself in reducing the Servians to obedience. Ismael was, however, allowed to retain the pashalik of Ioannina and Delvino.

Fortune, which had hitherto frowned on Ismael, at length gave him an opportunity of closing with some reputation his career as general in chief. Ali had formed a plan of attack upon the imperial camp, the success of which he hoped would give a fatal blow to the besieging army. While he himself sallied with all his troops from the fortress, and joined the disaffected Albanian and Christian leaders with whom he had opened a correspondence, the Suliots were to occupy, in ambush, a position, from which at the critical moment they were to rush on the Turks, complete their overthrow, and intercept their retreat. The letter, containing Ali's instructions to the Suliots, fell into the hands of Ismael; and, in conjunction with Drama-Ali and Omer Vriones, the latter of whom had been appointed pasha of Berat, he took measures to make the projected sally destructive to Black Ali himself.

On the 26th of January, 1821, the appointed day, a heavy cannonade was opened from the fortresses, and the troops of Ali were seen rapidly advancing against the Turkish batteries. Such was the impetuosity of the assailants that the batteries were carried, and the Turks who manned them were either slain or compelled to fly towards the intrenched camp. The signals of Ali had been answered, he believed that he saw the Suliots at their assigned post, and he pressed forward in full confidence of victory. But he was soon convinced of his error, by receiving, at half musket-shot distance, a volley from the concealed troops of Omer Vriones, whom he had mistaken for the Suliots. A part of his army was thus placed between two fires. In the hope of restoring the combat, Ali displayed the most undaunted valour; he returned repeatedly to the charge, exposed his person more than the meanest soldier, and was at last with difficulty persuaded and almost forced by his officers to retire from the field. In this encounter five hundred of his men were slain. Of the division which had been hemmed in by the movement of Omer Vriones, a part succeeded in gaining the fortresses, and about six hundred broke through their opponents, and reached the mountains of Suli.

Ali was not disheartened by this disaster. His fortresses were yet but slightly injured; through the medium of Alexis Noutza, his former betrayer, who had now again come over to the vizier's interest, he had obtained promises of support from the Albanian chiefs, whom the insolence and menaces of the Turks had disgusted; he had successfully intrigued in the Morea, Servia, Walachia, and other quarters; and he had bound the Suliots firmly to him, by promising that they should be put into possession of the fortress of Kiaffa. "Serve me till the month of March," said he to the Suliots, "and the sultan will have so much upon his hands, that we shall be able to dictate the law to him."

The Porte, meanwhile, was pressing Kurschid to hasten his march to Albania. It also directed him to calm, no matter at what expense, the spirit of discontent which was prevalent in that province. Ali, too, wrote to him, as soon as he heard of his being appointed generalissimo. Kurschid had never declared violently against him, and Ali, therefore, hoped that he might be induced to become his intercessor. Disclaiming all idea of resisting the authority of the sultan, for whom he professed the utmost veneration, he threw all the blame of his revolt upon the divan, which had enconraged the iniquitous falsehoods of his servant Pasho Bey; and he artfully endeavoured to interest on his side the feelings and the pride of Kurschid, by recalling to his recollection the insults which he had himself experienced from the base and greedy ministers of the Porte. Pasho and his late proceedings he painted in the darkest colours; he solicited Kurschid to stand his friend with the sultan; and he declared his willingness to submit to any pecuniary sacrifice, so that an amnesty might be granted to him. To this overture the new generalissimo verbally replied, that Ali " would always find him a friend ready to listen to him, and to intercede in his behalf with the sultan."

While, however, Ali was thus soliciting a reconciliation, he did not desist from his efforts to embarrass his enemy. He recommenced his sallies, and his emissaries and partisans were active in stirring up revolt in many and widely distant quarters. Ismael again found himself encircled by difficulties; his convoys were intercepted, and his foragers were cut off even within sight of the imperial camp. He endeavoured to rid himself of the hostility of the Suliots, and was so far successful as to obtain an armistice for a month, on payment of three hundred purses, (about £5000,) which they claimed as due to them for arrears of pay while they were in the sultan's service. But they were aware that he meditated perfidy against them, and they had no intention to expose themselves to destruction by laying down their arms.

At the head of twenty-four thousand men, Kurschid arrived in the camp before Ioannina, on the second of March. He knew that symptoms of insurrection had already appeared in the Morea, and that danger was to be apprehended in other parts of Greece, and he seems to have seriously wished to put an end to the contest with Ali, even at the expense of some concession. Ali appeared to be animated by the same feelings. As soon as Kurschid reached the camp, Ali saluted him with twenty-one pieces of cannon, and sent him a complimentary letter. Kurschid directed the salute to be returned, forbade the epithet of kara, or black, to be applied to Ali, spoke of him as vizier, and declared that he himself was to come to Epirus as a peace-maker. On the following morning he despatched one of his principal officers to confer with him. By this officer, Kurschid sent a letter, which he had intercepted, from prince Alexander Hypsilantis to the Greek leaders in Epirus, advising them to make use of the vizier of Ioannina merely as an instrument to forward their designs, and in the hope of becoming masters of his immense riches, with which they might secure the triumph of freedom in Greece. The envoy of Kurschid was instructed to dwell upon this decisive proof that Ali must expect nothing from the Christians, and to assure him, that the general would gladly receive any proposals likely to lead to a prompt accommodation, and that it would give him far more pleasure to end the struggle in this manner, than to acquire the certain glory of reducing, with the formidable forces under his command, a valiant prince whom he had always looked upon as one of the firmest supports of the Ottoman empire.

The seeming earnestness of Kurschid to bring about a peace induced Ali to imagine that the Porte felt its weakness, and dreaded the continuance of his hostility. Misled by this idea, he assumed a haughty tone, and demanded terms which a sovereign could hardly be expected to grant, after having sustained more than one defeat. He did, indeed, submit to express sorrow that he had incurred the displeasure of the sultan, to sue for pardon, and to offer to pay on the spot the arrears of his tribute and the expenses of the war ; but he insisted, in return, that Pasho Bey, his servant, should lose his head, that a complete amnesty should be granted to all his partisans, and that, during his life, he should retain the pashalik of Ioannina, the coast of Epirus, and Acarnania with its dependencies, without being obliged to receive the annual investiture, and subject only to the customary dues and homage which belonged to the sultan. "If," said he, "these conditions are not accepted, without any modification, I am prepared to defend myself to the last extremity." Kurschid replied, "that his powers did not extend so far, that he would transmit the proposals to Constantinople, and that there should be a suspension of arms till an answer was returned."

The Porte was not slow in answering. Far from conceding any part of Ali's demands, it imperiously summoned him " to repair within twenty-four hours to the tent of Kurschid Pasha, who pledged himself that he should be honourably conducted to Constantinople, where he would be admitted to justify himself before the dazzling majesty of the glorious sultan." Convinced that he had no mercy to expect, Ali immediately recommenced hostilities, by opening a heavy cannonade on the Turkish army.

Either ignorant of the storm which was about to burst upon it, or stupidly regardless of the danger, the Porte seemed anxious to increase the number of its foes. In a manner the most offensive, it abruptly put an end to the armistice which existed with the Suliots. In reply to their claims, the high-spirited mountaineers were informed, that the Turkish monarch would pardon them, and grant them the favour of being ; like the islanders of the Archipelago, the sultan's rayas, under the superintendence of the captain pasha, and that if, within four days, they did not send twenty hostages as security for their submission, hostilities should be renewed. This offer was spurned by the Suliots; and Ali seized the opportunity of binding them to his cause, by delivering up to them the fortress of Kiaffa, with all the stores and ammunition which it contained.

At length, in the month of March, 1821, the explosion took place, which was destined to shake the throne of the sultan, and rend from him a portion of his empire. The flame of insurrection broke out in Moldavia and the Morea, and, though it was soon extinguished in the first of those provinces, it rapidly spread through almost every part of southern Greece. This event, to which Ali had long anxiously looked forward, and which he had largely contributed to produce, relieved him in some degree from the pressure of the Turkish army. Compelled to send out considerable detachments on all sides, Kurschid could but languidly carry on the siege. In three months the only success of which he could boast consisted in obtaining possession of the island in the lake, which, with the magazines, was betrayed to him by its commander. The Greek inhabitants lent their aid to facilitate the enterprise, and the Turks rewarded them by murder, pillage, violation, and the pollution of the monasteries and churches.

Having at length effected a breach in the castle of Litharitza, Kurschid, on the eighth of June, gave the signal for an assault. The Turks advanced bravely towards the ramparts; but they were met with equal bravery. Though he was suffering under an attack of gout, Ali was carried in a litter to the scene of action, and headed a sally of the garrison. The besiegers were finally driven back to their lines, with the loss of three hundred slain. When the combat was over, the victor sent a message to Kurschid. " The bear of Pindus," said he, " is still alive. You may send for your dead to bury them. I restore them to you without ransom, and I will always do so when you attack me like a man of courage." In his reply, the Turkish general made known to the vizier the recent decease of Shainitza, who died of apoplexy; and this news so deeply affected Ali, that not even his victory, nor the congratulations of his partisans, could elevate his dejected spirits.

Whether Ali was provoked by some act of the besiegers we know not, but it is certain that he did not long continue to manifest that chivalrous feeling which dictated his message to Kurschid. His next proceeding seemed rather to be prompted by the malignant shade of Shainitza. In Mahometan countries, a tacit truce between contending parties has almost uniformly existed during the fast of Ramazan and the succeeding festival of Bairam, which are the Mussulman Lent and Easter. Ali conformed to the custom during the fast, because it afforded an opportunity for his troops to mingle with the besiegers, and gain information; but there his forbearance ended. While, unsuspicious of danger, the principal officers of Kurschid were solemnising, in the mosque of Lootcha, the arrival of the Bairam, Ali ordered thirty cannons, mortars, and howitzers, to be directed against the mosque. The deadly fire was kept up till the sacred building was a pile of smoking ruins, under which lay the mutilated bodies of sixty officers and two hundred soldiers. "Ali Pasha is not dead!" was his triumphant exclamation, when the smoke cleared away, and allowed him to feast his eyes on the havoc which he had made.

If Ali had any other motive for this deed than revenge or the love of slaughter, it was probably a desire to propitiate the Greeks, by showing to what extremity he could proceed against their enemies.

This stroke of policy, however, if such it were, failed to accomplish its purpose. It did not win over the Christians to a solid alliance with him; and it could not fail to alienate many of his Mussulman supporters. In truth, after the commencement of the Greek revolution, circumstances were daily occurring, which tended to deprive him of his Mahometan friends. Two of his principal Albanian officers, Tahir Abas and Ago Vessiaris, were converted about this period into concealed enemies, by what they observed on their way to Missolonghi, whither they were sent by Ali, to confer with a meeting of the Greek chiefs. They found all along their route that the mosques had been demolished, and the Mussulmans exterminated, and that the Greeks meant Ali to be only a tool in their hands; and they returned to Ioannina fully resolved to undeceive their fellow-countrymen, and make their peace with the Porte.

A part of Ali's magazines in the castrou, or castle of the lake, having been destroyed by the shells of the besiegers, Kurschid, who, pressed on all sides, was anxious for a peace with the vizier, believed that his obstinate antagonist might now be prevailed on to negociate; and he, therefore, despatched to him an officer, who was the son-in-law of Veli Pasha. "Think well upon it, vizier," said the envoy, "the Christians bear on their banners the emblem of the cross; you are nothing but an instrument in their hands, beware that you do not become the victim of their policy." The terms which Kurschid offered were, a complete amnesty for the past misdeeds of Ali, on condition of his giving up the fortresses, paying the cost of the war, and retiring to Asia Minor to live there in privacy; but the clemency of the sultan was the only guarantee which was offered to secure these concessions. Abating no jot of his former pretensions, Ali insisted that, as a preliminary, and for the sake of example, his perfidious servant Pasho Bey should be hanged, after the performance of which act of justice, and on condition that the Ottoman army should withdraw from Epirus, and the government of the province be committed to him for life, he would engage to pay a stipulated sum for the expenses of the contest, and to suppress at his own charge the insurrection throughout the whole of the territory between the straits of Thermopylæ and the gulf of Arta. As it was impossible for the parties to agree where such a wide discordance existed, the negociation was broken off at the end of three weeks. Ali had actively employed that time in re filling his magazines, and in exciting a formidable insurrection among the tribes of central Albania.

Three more months passed by without Kurschid having made any apparent progress. But, though his arms were impotent, his gold and his arts were victorious. Already murmuring at the length of the siege, and the want of punctuality in paying them, the Albanians who garrisoned the fortress of Litharitza were well disposed to listen to the voice of a tempter, especially when the tempter seconded his speech by a bribe. Kurschid practised on them so effectually that, towards the end of October, they opened to him the gates of the fortress, and, to the number of several hundreds, enrolled themselves under his banner. By this desertion Ali was confined within the limits of the castron, and his force was reduced to six hundred men.

Though none of the Greeks felt the slightest kind ness for Ali, policy forbade them from suffering him to be crushed. By his fall, not only would the army before Ioannina be let loose upon them, but, master of the treasures of the vizier, Kurschid would be enabled to bring innumerable mercenaries into the field. It was therefore determined that the Suliots, in conjunction with the insurgents of Central Albania and other bands, should make a decisive effort to compel Kurschid to raise the siege, or, failing in that, to throw reinforcements into the fortress. But their plan was rendered abortive by Ali himself. His conduct seems to have been prompted partly by avarice —for he now clung to his riches with more tenacity than ever—and partly by his suspicion and hatred of his Christian allies. "Old serpents are always old serpents," said he to his officers; "I fear the Suliots and their friendship." He, however, replied to them in flattering terms. He declined their offer, on the ground of his having the means of defending himself for years; and he told them that the best service which they could do for him was to continue the siege of Arta, and to take alive his enemy Pasho Bey, of whom he spoke with an envenomed bitterness. To do that would, he said, be to cut up the evil by the roots, and, if they achieved it, he would richly reward them. The allies, in consequence, struggled hard to gain possession of Arta; but, although they effected a lodgment in a part of the town, they were ultimately compelled to retire. One consolation Ali, nevertheless, received; his hated adversary Pasho was deposed and sent into exile; Ali did not survive long enough to learn that the head of Pasho was exposed on a pike before the gate of the sultan's palace.

The long career of Ali was now hastening towards its close. Kurschid, who had already profited so much by well-directed intrigue, continued to make a skilful use of the same formidable weapon. In this he was powerfully aided by the fears which the Greek insurrection excited in the minds of the

Mahometans. If Ali succeeded in triumphing by means of the Christians, it was obvious that the Mussulmans could expect little favour from a race over which they had tyrannised for ages. The journey of Tahir Abas and his companion to Missolonghi had given to those envoys ocular proof of the evils which must ensue from the ascendancy of their Christian enemies, and, as we have seen, they had determined to abandon the vizier rather than contribute to make the Greeks their masters. This feeling Kurschid laboured, and with much effect, to spread among the Albanian leaders who were attached to Ali. The first result of his exertions was that he obtained their neutrality; more they were not willing to give, for they still cherished a wish to save " the old lion" of Ioannina, whose character, congenial with their own, was an object of their admiration. To win their active support, Kurschid did not scruple to make use of falsehood. He protested to them, that the life of Ali would be safe; and he even went so far as to show them firmans, in which it was declared that, if the vizier would submit, he should be conveyed with his treasures, household, and harem, into Asia Minor, there to end his days in peace. This was backed by showing to the agas the letters of Mouctar and Veli, in which they gave testimony to the kindness with which they were treated. These assurances, and an advance of eight months' pay, prevailed with the Albanian leaders, and they joined the Turkish army.

Ali, meanwhile, with a singular infatuation which seems akin to insanity, was doing his best to disgust his few remaining followers. Clinging to his gold, he evaded paying his scanty garrison, because he imagined that they were too deeply implicated in his treason to venture upon deserting him. He was mistaken; as soon as it was known that the Albanian chiefs were in the Ottoman camp, some of their countrymen nightly escaped from the fortress. A heavier blow was speedily given to him. For his protracted defence he had been mainly indebted to the skill of Caretto, a Neapolitan engineer officer, who had hitherto served him with undeviating fidelity and zeal. Wearied at length by the caprices and the meanness of the vizier, Caretto now abandoned him: though he was strictly watched, he contrived to fasten a rope to a cannon and descend into the moat; the rope being too short, he broke his arm by the fall, but he reached the camp of Kurschid, and was favourably received. Discouraged by this event, and by an epidemic disorder which raged among them, and disgusted by the avarice of the vizier, the soldiers broke out into mutiny, and threw open the gates of the fortress to the besieging army.

With only a handful of faithful soldiers Ali retired to a sort of citadel, to which he had given the name of his Refuge. It was a stone tower, well provided with cannon, beneath which was an extensive natural cavern, containing his valuables and riches, and his stores of ammunition and provisions. Two thousand barrels of powder were piled in this gloomy vault, at the entrance of which, with a lighted match in his hand, stood a fanatical partisan of Ali, who was willing to sacrifice himself by exploding the mine, the moment that the signal was given by his master.

A negociation was soon entered into between Kurschid and Ali. The latter, though he was resolved to perish with his enemies if terms were refused, seemed not unwilling to submit on certain conditions; the former, who knew the desperate spirit of the vizier, was desirous to prevent the loss of the treasures which were contained in the tower, as well as to avert the danger which threatened his forces from a tremendous explosion. Kurschid played his part so well, that he at length prevailed on Ali to leave his citadel, and take up his quarters on the island in the lake. It has been asserted by the Turkish government, that Ali consented to remove, without having made any stipulation for his safety. This, however, is too improbable to be credited. Ali was too fond of revenge to throw away the chance of involving his foes in his own destruction, It is more likely that, as M. Pouqueville affirms, the vizier was led to take this step by his receiving, in the first instance, a paper, with the signatures of sixty of Kurschid's principal officers, promising to intercede with the sultan, and, subsequently, an assurance from Kurschid himself, that the monarch intended to pardon.

The closing scene of Ali's long and eventful life is thus described by one of the Turkish ministers. "Ali Pasha asked time at first to reflect upon the decision which he should make; at last, after several conversations with the selictar, he consented to leave the citadel, and he retired into the island with all his little troop, with the exception of one of his trusty friends, with whom he agreed on a signal which would instruct him whether he was to set fire to the powder, or give up all that was intrusted to his care to the officers of Kurschid Pasha.

" The selictar received Ali Pasha in the island, at the head of an equal number of men with that which accompanied the vizier. They paid him all the honour due to his rank; and, after having been treated for several days by Kurschid Pasha with the greatest respect, Ali had confidence enough to order the surrender of all that he had left in the citadel. They immediately made haste to transport the powder into a place of safety.

"Directly afterwards, Ali-Pasha requested that one of his officers, who commanded a small party of a hundred men in the neighbourhood of Ioannina, might be permitted to join him in the island. Kurschid Pasha consented to this, but sent at the same time a detachment composed of an equal number of men, to keep Ali's troops in awe.

"Different pashas of inferior rank had been several times to visit Ali. On the 13th day of the moon Djemaziul Awwel (the 5th of February, 1822) Mohammed Pasha, governor of the Morea, offered to procure for Ali every possible comfort, naming particularly provisions. Ali replied to this offer, that he desired nothing more than a supply of meat; he added, however, that he had still another wish, though his unwillingness to offend the scruples of religion forbade him to give utterance to it. Being pressed to name it, he owned that it was wine which he wished for, and Mohammed Pasha promised that he should receive it. The conversation continued for some time in the most friendly manner, till, at last, Mohammed Pasha rose to take leave. Being of the same rank, they rose at the same moment from the sofa, according to the usual ceremony, and before leaving the room, Mohammed Pasha bowed profoundly. Ali returned the compliment, but at the instant of his inclination, Mohammed executed the will of his sovereign, and put him to death by plunging a poniard into his left breast. He immediately quitted the apartment and announced that Ali had ceased to exist. Some men of Mohammed's suite then entered, and divided the head from the body. The former having been shown to the sultan's troops and to those who had embraced the rebel's part, a strife followed in which several men were killed. But the minds of the people were soon calmed, and all discord was appeased by shouts of "Long live Sultan Mahmoud and his vizier Kurschid Pasha *."

The body of the vizier was buried in the tomb of his wife Emina, with all the honours due to his rank; the head was enclosed in a silver box, and sent to Constantinople, where, placed in a dish, it was exposed to the popular gaze, before the gate of the Seraglio. Appended to it was the yaphta, or statement of the crimes which had brought down on its owner the penalty of death.

The vengeance of the sultan was not satiated by the destruction of Ali; it required the sacrifice of all the vizier's family. Of the progeny of Ali only one was spared. It was Ismael, the second son of Veli, who had been sent from Ioannina to Constantinople by Kurschid. At the Ottoman capital he had gained friends by his talents and amiable character, and at their intercession, the monarch, though reluctantly, exempted him from the doom which was decreed against his family. Orders for the execution of Mouctar, Veli, and Seli, and their children, were despatched into Asia Minor. After having witnessed the execution of his brother Sali, and his sons Mehemet and Selim, Veli, already half dead with terror, submitted to his fate. Mouctar displayed a spirit more congenial with that of his sire. When the firman of death was presented to him, he killed with a pistol-shot the capidgi-bashi who brought it, and exclaimed, "Rash wretch! an Arnaut does not die like an eunuch! I am the son of Tepeleni! To arms, comrades, they intend to murder us!" Aided by his attendants, he made a great slaughter of the assailants,

---

* The story of Ali's death is somewhat differently related by M. Pouqueville. He affirms, that, on finding he was betrayed, the vizier defended himself with the utmost courage, and that he and his attendants killed and wounded several of the Turkish assassins.

and held them at bay till they were joined by a reinforcement with artillery. At length, covered with wounds, he set fire to his powder, and perished in the explosion.

"To what base uses we may return!" exclaims Hamlet. "Why may not imagination trace the noble dust of Alexander till he find it stopping a bung-hole?" The head of Ali—of the man who for more than a third of a century had ruled an extensive dominion, had been in correspondence with sovereigns, and had shaken the throne of his master—that head narrowly escaped the indignity of being made a show for money, to gratify the idle curiosity of a gaping crowd in a distant land. A merchant of Constantinople imagined that it would be an excellent speculation to purchase the head, and send it to London for exhibition; and it would have become an object for the wonderment of rustics and mechanics, at fairs and merry meetings, had it not been rescued by Solyman, a dervise, who had been one of the vizier's confidential agents. He outbid the speculating merchant, and having also obtained the heads of Ali's three sons and grandson, he deposited them in a sepulchre near the gate of Selyvria, and raised over them five tombstones of white marble, bearing sculptured turbans, and the titles of the deceased.

THE END.

WORKS

PUBLISHED BY

THOMAS TEGG AND SON, 73, CHEAPSIDE.

I.
TEGG'S CHRONOLOGY, CORRECTED TO 1835.

In One Volume, duodecimo, closely printed in Double Columns, Price 6s. in cloth boards,

A DICTIONARY OF CHRONOLOGY; or, HISTORIAN'S COMPANION; being an Authentic Register of Events, from the Earliest Period to the Present Time. The Fourth Edition, considerably enlarged, edited by THOMAS TEGG.

II.
DR. ADAM CLARKE'S MISCELLANEOUS WORKS.

This Day is published, printed in duodecimo, embellished with a fine Portrait. Price 6s. in cloth boards.

THE MISCELLANEOUS WORKS OF DR. ADAM CLARKE, Volume 3, containing the First Volume of his Translation of Sturm's Reflections on the Works of God.—(Sturm will be completed in Two Volumes.)

** A volume of this popular Work will be published Monthly until the whole is completed, which may probably extend to Twelve Volumes.

III.
WRIGHT'S GREEK AND ENGLISH LEXICON.

In One Volume, uniform with Dymock's and Meadows's Dictionaries Price 7s. in canvass boards. or 7s. 6d. bound and lettered,

A GREEK AND ENGLISH LEXICON, on a plan entirely new; in Four Parts, viz. Greek-English, difficult inflections, English-Greek, and proper Names, containing the interpretation of all the words which occur in Greek classic authors, the Septuagint, and New Testament; with the quantity of all the doubtful vowels, as far as it can be ascertained from the Poets: and an Introduction, comprising an explanation of the more important terminations. By M. WRIGHT.

IV.
DOMESTIC LIFE IN ENGLAND.

In One Volume, duodecimo, embellished with 33 Woodcuts, Price 5s. boards.

DOMESTIC LIFE IN ENGLAND, from the Earliest Period to the Present Time, with Notices of Origins, Inventions, and Modern Improvements, in the social Arts.

"No money is better spent than what is laid out for domestic satisfaction."—*Johnson.*

WORKS PUBLISHED BY THOMAS TEGG & SON, 73, CHEAPSIDE.

V.
MEADOWS' NUGENT'S DICTIONARY.

In One Vol. 18mo., the Sixth Edition, Price 7s. in cloth boards, or bound, 7s. 6d.,

MEADOWS' NEW FRENCH and ENGLISH PRONOUNCING DICTIONARY, on the basis of Nugent's, with many new words in general use, in two Parts: French and English—English and French; exhibiting the Pronunciation of the French in pure English sounds, the Parts of Speech, Gender of French Nouns, regular and irregular Conjugation of Verbs, and Accent of English Words. To which is prefixed, Principles of French Pronunciation, and an Abrigded Grammar.

By F. C. MEADOWS, M. A., of the University of Paris.

VI.
NOVUM TESTAMENTUM GRÆCE.

Most beautifully printed with pearl type, in one small pocket volume, Price 5s. bound in cloth,

Η ΚΑΙΝΗ ΔΙΑΘΗΚΗ.
NOVUM TESTAMENTUM.

VII.
HAREWOOD'S DICTIONARY OF SPORTS.

In One handsome Volume, duodecimo, printed by Whittingham, and embellished with 152 Engravings, Price 7s. 6d. in extra boards,

A DICTIONARY OF SPORTS; or, Companion to the Field, the Forest, and the River side; containing explanations of every term applicable to racing, shooting, hunting, fishing, hawking, archery, &c., with Essays upon all national amusements. By HARRY HAREWOOD, of Springfield in the county of York, Esq.

VIII.
CARPENTER'S BIBLICAL COMPANION.

In imperial octavo, Price 18s.; quarto, Price 27s.,

THE BIBLICAL COMPANION; or, Introduction to the Reading and Study of the Holy Scriptures; comprising a comprehensive Digest of the Principles and Details of Biblical Criticism, Interpretation, Theology, History, Natural Science, &c., adapted for popular use. By WILLIAM CARPENTER, Author of "Lectures on Biblical Criticism," &c.

"We should not regard it as the great object of attention, simply to hear another interpret what the Bible contains, but rather this, *to ascertain how we may be able ourselves to discover its contents.*"—PROFESSOR PLANCKE.

University of California
SOUTHERN REGIONAL LIBRARY FACILITY
305 De Neve Drive - Parking Lot 17 • Box 951
LOS ANGELES, CALIFORNIA 90095-1388
Return this material to the library from which it was b

UCLA YRL
ILL-NYP
DUE: JAN 0 3 200

UCLA ACCESS SERV
Interlibrary Loan
11630 University Research Library
Box 951575
Angeles, CA 90095-1575

Made in the USA
Middletown, DE
10 January 2017